PAST AND PRESENT
IN HUNTER GATHERER STUDIES

PAST AND PRESENT
IN HUNTER GATHERER STUDIES

Edited by
Carmel Schrire
Department of Human Ecology
Cook College
Rutgers University
New Brunswick, New Jersey

1984

ACADEMIC PRESS, INC.

(Harcourt Brace Jovanovich, Publishers)
Orlando   San Diego   New York   London
Toronto   Montreal   Sydney   Tokyo

ACADEMIC PRESS, INC.
Orlando, Florida 32887

United Kingdom Edition published by
ACADEMIC PRESS, INC. (LONDON) LTD.
24/28 Oval Road, London NW1 7DX

Library of Congress Cataloging in Publication Data

Main entry under title:

Past and present in hunter gatherer studies.

    Includes index.
    1. Hunting, Primitive--Congresses. 2. Agriculture,
Primitive--Congresses. I. Schrire, Carmel.
GN407.3.P37 1984   306'.3   84-11191
ISBN 0-12-629180-2 (alk. paper)

PRINTED IN THE UNITED STATES OF AMERICA

84 85 86 87   9 8 7 6 5 4 3 2 1

For
Toddy and Sylvia Schrire,
who raised me on ethnography
and have nurtured me on it ever since

Contents

10

To Find Ourselves: Art and Social Geography of Prehistoric Hunter Gatherers   253

MARGARET W. CONKEY

Contributors

Numbers in parentheses indicate the pages on which the authors' contributions begin.

MARGARET W. CONKEY (253), Department of Anthropology, State University of New York, Binghamton, New York 13901

JAMES R. DENBOW (175), National Museum and Art Gallery, Independence Avenue, Gaborone, Botswana

ROBERT J. GORDON (195), Department of Anthropology, University of Vermont, Burlington, Vermont 05405

P. BION GRIFFIN (95), Department of Anthropology, University of Hawaii at Manoa, Honolulu, Hawaii 96822

CARL L. HOFFMAN (123), Department of Anthropology, University Museum, University of Pennsylvania, Philadelphia, Pennsylvania 19104

RHYS JONES (27), Department of Prehistory, Research School of Pacific Studies, Institute of Advanced Studies, Australian National University, Canberra ACT 2600, Australia

J. DAVID LEWIS-WILLIAMS (225), Department of Archaeology, University of the Witwatersrand, Johannesburg 2001, South Africa

JOHN E. PARKINGTON (151), Department of Archaeology, University of Cape Town, Rondebosch, Cape 7700, South Africa

CARMEL SCHRIRE (1, 67), Department of Human Ecology, Cook College, Rutgers University, New Brunswick, New Jersey 08903

Foreword

The Third International Conference on Hunting and Gathering Societies met at the Reimers Foundation in Bad Homburg in June, 1983. The topic was the sociology of land use and the sessions were organized to provide both historical and current perspectives on data from a broad range of hunter and gatherer societies. Two interwoven themes emerged as the conference progressed. First, a group of papers taking a historical and archaeological approach focused on the importance of understanding the history of the interactions that hunters and gatherers have had with other peoples in order to understand both their past behavior and their current ways of life. A second group of papers dealt with the current problems faced by hunters and gatherers living within large nation states. This volume contains a selection of papers dealing with the first theme.

These papers challenge the view that isolation has allowed contemporary hunters and gatherers to maintain their past lifeways and hold that, since hunter gatherers can be shown to have had contact with farmers for a long time, they cannot be considered "true" hunters and gatherers. These essays look both for continuity in hunting and gathering societies through time and for the effects of changing degrees of contact with surrounding farmers, herders, traders, and settlers. What is striking about the findings of this archaeological and historical research is the nature and implications of the contact that hunters and gatherers have had with other peoples throughout their more recent history. This in turn raises the question of the continuity and integrity that they have maintained in their own societies despite outside influences. For instance, despite the apparent long-term and intimate interactions between hunters and herdsman in southern Africa, as found by Denbow and Gordon, there appears to be some ideological continuity from the past until the present, as illustrated by the evidence of the eland dance presented by Lewis-Williams. Such ideological continuity may result from continued efforts to maintain rituals that are central to San culture. Additional evidence for continuity in the Kalahari San life-style may be sought in their sophisticated hunting and gathering techniques, such as their arrow poison technology, in their sophisticated knowledge of the uses of plants, and in their complex social networks, which create strong dependencies between groups of San separated by vast distances. Such sophisticated hunting and gathering technology and social networks have not been found among groups like the Tasaday, who, according to current knowledge, seem to have split off from agricultural groups less than 1000 years ago.

The evidence in this volume indicates that some current hunter gatherers continued to maintain traditional lifeways in the face of change, while adapting to neighboring herders, farmers, and traders. An interesting example of relationships that hunter gatherers have developed with surrounding farmers comes from the rain forests of central Africa and Southeast Asia, where, on occasion, some hunters seem to live in symbiosis with agriculturists. This raises many interesting questions concerning the nature of past interactions and the social mechanisms that might allow hunter gatherers to maintain their own life-styles apart from but complementary to that of others. In understanding what changes and what remains through time we will certainly gain some insight into what is essential in the hunting and gathering way of life and into what differences exist between hunters and gatherers in a world of hunters and those in a world of agriculturalists and industrialists.

I. EIBL-EIBESFELDT
POLLY WIESSNER
*Forschungsstelle für Humanethologie
am Max-Planck-Institut für Verhaltensphysiologie
8131 Seewiesen, Federal Republic of Germany*

Preface

Most studies of contemporary hunter gatherers depict them as the product of a long and timeless past. While no one holds that they are living fossils, their present existence is often explained in terms of extreme isolation. They are assumed to have existed far beyond the reach of farmers, slavers, colonial settlers, and traders, and so, are thought to retain in their present existence, aspects of a distant past that illuminates the evolutionary history of all people.

These essays challenge the isolationist view by analyzing forces that operate in the lives of living hunter gatherers to make them what they are today. It focuses on their prehistory and on changes in the environment in which they operated through time. It analyzes historical evidence to see the degree to which the wider world impinged on these people and drew them into the networks of international trade. Finally, it advocates that the present hunter gatherers should be seen in a broader and deeper context, not as relics of the past or exemplars of humanity stripped of the details of pastoral and urban life, but rather as part of the wider world to which they have always belonged.

All of the essays interweave archaeology, history, and ethnography to relate past and present. The question of relationships between living and prehistoric hunter gatherers is explored to assess the degree to which continuity through time may be asserted. This is a far cry from the stolid dogma of Victorian ethnology that presumed living hunter gatherers to be lineal descendants and living representatives of prehistoric man. It represents a step in a new direction, away from the strong evolutionary perspective of most classic modern texts, in that it makes an effort to assess the degree to which shifts in forager identity were made in response to demands of local farmers, herders, and traders.

Where continuity of behavior and belief is concerned, Lewis-Williams uses a mixture of historical and modern ethnography, as well as archaeological evidence, to argue that images found on prehistoric objects suggest a "pan-San" ideological continuity that goes back 20,000 years and stretches from

Tanzania to the tip of Africa. Conkey outlines the way in which European rock art may be analyzed to reveal the social geography of its makers, arguing for the need to view this problem as intently through archaeological data as through the generalized models of modern hunter gatherer life. Jones and Schrire discuss continuity in a context of marked environmental changes in Tasmania and Australia. Jones describes the exciting new finds of ice age man in the impenetrable forests of southwestern Tasmania. He suggests that closer parallels exist between ice age people in both hemispheres than between living Tasmanians and their presumed prehistoric equivalents. Schrire handles a shorter time frame, revoking a former belief in the stability of Holocene north Australia by arguing that the extensive wetland foraging grounds of modern Aborigines only came into existence there in the past 1000 years.

The Southeast Asian chapters opt for a considerable fluidity in the relations of hunters and horticulturists. Griffin describes the flexible nature of the Agta of northeastern Luzon, holding that the intensity of occupation depends on the plant food base. He sees the Agta as opportunists who take advantage of whatever production strategy suits them best at a given time and outlines the variable environmental factors that influence such decisions. Hoffman is concerned with a more specific problem: the nature of Borneo's Punan. He interprets their use of the primary forest as a direct response to the long-term demands of Chinese traders for forest products. While recognizing the interplay of farming and foraging, he argues that Chinese trade allowed the Punan to specialize in forest-based activities.

Four chapters dealing with the southern African hunter gatherers address, among other things, the question of whether these people shifted their cultural identities through time. Lewis-Williams argues for ideological continuity, in which is subsumed a degree of stability, in the forager mode of production. Parkington interweaves evidence from his excavations in the southwestern Cape with historical data to argue, likewise, for a strong economic and social identity of protohistoric hunter gatherers. Taking a rather different stance, Denbow presents empirical data about pastoralism in the Kalahari and sees its antiquity as suggestive of long-term, intimate interactions between hunters and herdsmen. Finally, in what is probably the most startling study in this collection, Gordon spells out what it was like to be a Bushman in the Kalahari over the past 100 years. Gone is the timeless world of Marshall and Lee, replaced by the violent and black-humored evidence of trade manifestos and law records that comment pointedly on some of the experiences that shaped the people we modern ethnographers call Kalahari hunter gatherers.

This volume originated at the Third International Conference on Hunter–Gatherers, held at Bad Homburg, Federal Republic of Germany, June 13–16, 1983. The original proposal, written by I. Eibl-Eibesfeldt and Polly Wiessner, organized the conference around the theme of sociology and land use among hunter gatherers. Various people were invited to organize specific sessions within this framework—Edwin Wilmsen on the sociology of land tenure, Bion Griffin on Southeast Asian foragers, and I on the archaeological and ethnohistoric aspects of land use.

The importance of the past in determining the nature of present hunter gatherers became clearer as the conference progressed, and participants in different sessions were plainly concerned with this issue. As a result, we agreed that six papers could form the core of a book, namely those by Conkey, Denbow, Griffin, Parkington, Jones, and Schrire. After the meeting, I began to assess the essays for this book, and three other authors who had not attended the conference were also invited to contribute.

The authors, both those who participated in the conference at Bad Homburg and those who did not, acknowledge the support and generosity of the Werner Reimers Stiftung, the Fritz Thyssen Stiftung, the Max-Planck-Institut für Verhaltensphysiologie, and the Maison des Sciences de l'Homme in sponsoring the meeting on which this volume is based. We are especially grateful to Professor Eibl-Eibesfeldt, without whom the meeting could not have occurred, for the skill and effectiveness with which he organized the funding and the sessions themselves. He was ably assisted by Polly Wiessner and Edwin Wilmsen, whose advice and encouragement are gratefully acknowledged.

My editing was done at considerable speed, to complete the book in less than nine months. During this time I traveled widely, using typewriters and telephones in Cape Town, Tucson, London, and Boston. The editors at Academic Press showed nothing but good humor in all our long-distance exchanges, and I am grateful for their constant encouragement. Finally, my thanks to the Department of Human Ecology, Rutgers University, for support services.

1

Wild Surmises on Savage Thoughts*

CARMEL SCHRIRE

There exists today in hunter gatherer studies a marked gap between observed facts of the existence of contemporary groups and inferences drawn about prehistoric people. It is as though contemporary hunter gatherers have been catapulted from a timeless and stable past into a turbulent, labile present, with ancient adaptations crammed into a dissonant framework. Scholars imagine themselves as standing on the interface of past and present, watching former hunters teetering on the cusp as they hurtle into modernity with no previous experience of change and no lessons gained from the past. Starting with Darwin's wonderment at the savages of Tierra del Fuego (1958:176ff.), through Lee's (1979:438) and Silberbauer's (1981:497–498) encounters with the Bushmen, to Nance's widely publicized penetration of the Tasaday (1976), we hear repeated cries of joy as the observer, regardless of history, proclaims his or her delight in being one of the first to see the untrammeled hunter gatherer preparing to face, for the first time, the discontents of civilization.

This ahistorical rather than antihistorical approach to anthropology is often traced to Radcliffe-Brown's famous condemnation of conjectural history, in which he stated that research aimed at the preliterate past was a matter of speculation that could not possibly serve to explain or to broaden our grasp of contemporary practices (1956:3). It goes without saying that he missed the potential of modern archaeological research in tracing the past, and it is particularly instructive to see how findings in Australia have since belied his

---

*The use of terms such as *savage* and *Indian* in this essay reflect historic usage and in no way reflect my judgments or beliefs.

opinions. Whereas Radcliffe-Brown so strongly disparaged the efforts of distributional studies as indicators of past patterns, work of men such as D. S. Davidson (1937) formed the foundations on which the antiquity of certain modern practices, such as food prohibitions (Jones 1978) and burial customs (Hiatt 1969), are based. Gellner, criticizing the synchronic nature of both the functionalist and structuralist positions, claimed that Radcliffe-Brown's functionalism was every bit as conjectural in establishing linkages as historical data: "if the past has no effects, what has? Is not the past the *only* thing that could have effects? . . . Only present forces can operate at present . . . [but] . . . the past may be and often is a necessary source of evidence about what forces are operating at present" (Gellner 1958:194).

Arguing the power of ethnohistory in anthropology today, Helms (1978) regards modern studies as floundering about in a state similar to that which characterized natural science before the Darwin–Wallace synthesis burst on the scene in 1858. For her, a historical perspective would integrate discordant aspects of anthropology and put an end to the snapshot approach, in which societies are portrayed as frozen tableaux, each locked forever in its instant of capture.

The purpose of this book is to explore the interface between past and present in hunter gatherer societies, to see how archaeology and protohistoric inferences may articulate with historical records to provide a better understanding of current situations. It represents a big step away from the well-entrenched evolutionary perspective on hunter gatherers, which rests on the tacit assumption that they have no history to speak of at all. Modern foragers tend still to be viewed in most of the current anthropological literature as sequestered beings whose very existence is due to the fact that they live beyond the reach of the trade routes of foreign powers. They are depicted as quintessential isolates, whose world was merely glimpsed in passing by explorers, and who remained remote until anthropologists penetrated their lives.

It is easy to sum up the essence of an approach and yet to miss the richness of detail encased within its bounds. The evolutionary approach to hunters and gatherers has directed a great deal of effort to defining their behavior within a specific framework, yet it has maintained a high level of enthusiasm by advocating, explicitly or subliminally as the case may be, that our roots lie in the forager societies. In order, therefore, to provide a realistic perspective for efforts at elucidating the present in terms of the past, we need to review the historical roots of hunter gatherer studies, showing their strong commitment to the notion of these people as representatives of their own past as well as that of humanity in general.

This evolutionary perspective on hunter gatherer studies can be traced through two interconnected threads to the beginning of the sixteenth century. First there is the vulgar preoccupation with exotic humans, where pathological specimens and ethnological curiosities competed under the orchestration of showmen for the attention and pennies of the crowd. Second, there is the slow and inexorable development of scientific thought about the nature and origin of man, where a variety of different fields contributed their findings to culminate in the watershed of Darwin's *Origin of Species* in 1859.

The earliest exhibition of hunter gatherers, other than those that might have taken place in antiquity, was that of three Eskimos in Bristol, England, in 1501 (Altick 1978:45). They were followed by a slew of African and American indigenes brought to England by seafarers, partly to show them to the world but partly also to impress on them the power and glory of the kingdom to which they would be expected to pledge their allegiance. By the eighteenth century, the British public had expressed a marked preference for exotic nobility, such as the "princes" of Tahiti or Indonesia, though regular savages could still draw an audience, as in the case of Captain George Cartwright's Eskimos, who, being visually striking, if rather fetid, in their seal skins, attracted large crowds on Westminster Bridge in 1772 (Altick 1978:47–48).

The attraction of these foragers was part of a wider range of exhibits that included freaks and congenital monsters. Vast gentlemen, bearded ladies, conjoined (later to be called Siamese) twins, boneless children, and limbless adults were all popular at these public viewings. Against such competition, the charms of a shy Bushman or furred Inuit pales, and we must therefore ask more pointedly why the crowds came to gape at such people? Altick's answer is that they fed the rising philosophical interest in human origins:

> The ordinary Londoner staring at a dark-skinned tribesman in a Charing Cross tavern had no notion that he was participating in what modern historians of ideas were to call the study of primitivism, nor would he have cared. The cultivated Londoner had a somewhat clearer idea: the exhibit was a Noble Savage, an exotic type of hero, the concept of whom had been imported from France after the Restoration and who was now appearing as an Aztec or a Peruvian, in the plays of Davenant, Howard, and Dryden and the romances of Aphra Behn. (Altick 1978:45–46)

This same Noble Savage would later be romanticized by Rousseau and invested with lofty moral overtones to provide a striking contrast to the corruption of Western society. For now, however, the nobility of the early eighteenth-century savage was as much a social as a moral issue, which is why, though people flocked to see all varieties presented, they preferred the savage nobility of Polynesia to the more vulgar, sweating hunters of the Arctic seas.

The nineteenth century heralded a more scientific approach to the world's hunter gatherers. The combined interest in what would be called *ethnology* in the 1840s and a mission to explore and claim far reaches of the world in the name of the Crown meant that showmen were fired with eagerness to retrieve examples of their potential subjects who might be viewed and classified according to the tenets of scientific racism. The most notorious of all such specimens was the Hottentot Venus, one Sartje or Saartjie Baartman (Pinney 1968:31), formerly of the Cape Colony, whose large steatopygous backside propelled her thence in 1809 first to an exhibition hall in Piccadilly, then to a baptismal font in Manchester, and finally to Cuvier's famous table in Paris. Here, the "magician of the charnel house" examined her while she was alive and then dissected her after her death in 1815. Today her skeleton stands in the Musee de l'Homme, gazing up at her renowned *tablier* or genitalia, which float wistfully in a jar above Broca's similarly bottled, but now leaking, brain (Altick 1978:268–272; Gould 1982).

By the mid–nineteenth century, ethnology was incorporated into the British Association for the Advancement of Science under the heading "Zoology and Botany," yet the climate of thought that placed the Anglo-Saxon at the pinnacle of achievement precluded a dispassionate view of exotic peoples. The procession of exhibits continued; included among these were several sets of Bushmen whose presentation as a tableaux in 1847 was designed to boost the local self-esteem by providing a living example of wild and vile existence. So horrified was Charles Dickens at the spectacle of these creatures, that he lost all social conscience, and proclaimed:

> My position is, that if we have anything to learn from the Noble Savage, it is what to avoid. His virtues are a fable; his happiness is a delusion; his nobility, nonsense. (Dickens *Household Words* 7:168. 1853. Quoted in Altick 1978:283)

Exactly where then did the inventor of Little Nell, Tiny Tim, and Little Dorritt stand on wider social issues? Witness Dickens' opinion of the social and moral position of the tiny Bushmen, as offered to the readers of the *Times:*

> I have never seen that group sleeping, smoking, and expectorating round their brazier, but I have sincerely desired that something might happen to the charcoal smouldering therein, which would cause the immediate suffocation of the whole of the noble strangers. (Dickens 5.19. 1847. Quoted in Altick 1978:281)

These gaudy displays may be seen today as representative of the eighteenth-century European vision of their own past (Figure 1.1). They reflect, in part, a dominant paradigm of the eighteenth century, namely the Great Chain of Being, which, together with the doctrine of Progressionism held that all life was created in a single instant, with each form set indelibly from that point on in its relation to the next and with man at the pinnacle of all creation. Since it was clear that men and apes were close together in the grand scheme of things and that all men were patently not equal, different types of men could be used to fill the gap between civilized men and apes. Travelers were at pains to allot a rung on the ladder to the curious people they encountered (e.g., Labillardière 1800:vi–vii; Smith 1960:111). Inevitably each group of hunter gatherers was likened to the great apes living closest to them, so that

FIGURE 1.1   Kalahari Bushmen making fire at the Van Riebeeck Tercentenary Festival, Cape Town, 1952. They are regarded with proprietal interest by three white officials, who in turn come under the quizzical scrutiny of a "colored" or mestizo workman. If the Bushmen were intended to reflect the past and the officials the present, then the unintentionally included third party represents the mingling of these two elements for the duration of contact in southern Africa. (Photograph by courtesy of *Cape Argus.*)

the ethnographically infamous Hottentot (including those whom we now call Bushmen) was likened to the African ape and Asian forest dwellers to the orangutan, while Australian Aborigines, living well beyond the pongid realms, were simply seen as moral brutes with a highly developed instinct for finding food (Eiseley 1961:253–264; see also Lubbock 1869:539).

The broader social and philosophical aspects of these beliefs seem gentler inasmuch as the hunters are concerned. People such as the Tasmanians, Australians, and Fuegians came to epitomize the celebrated "hard primitives" of Rousseau's second Discourse (1775). Tough, wiry, and resilient, they were thought to be living in that happiest of states, *la societe naissante,* located midway between the amorality of apes and the rigors of civilization (Lovejoy and Boas 1965:240–242). But such enlightened philosophy could not tone down the horrors of field observation, and Darwin's youthful rendition of the people of Tierra del Fuego as being just short of beasts, brutal to infants and the aged, and existing in a "lower state of improvement than in any other part of the world" still echoes down the years (1958:198). Yet, at the heart of

Darwin's words there lies a germ of compassion. On the icy beach where Darwin parted with the young Fuegian, Jemmy Button—whom Captain Fitzroy had captured some years before in order to exhibit him in England—the lad lit a huge signal fire, illuminating our ignorance as only Eiseley can express:

> It is perhaps too much to expect of one man in an intellectually confused period that he should have solved both sides of the human mystery, or have distinguished clearly between the biological and the cultural. On that day in his youth, however, in a great surge of human feeling, he stood very close to doing so. The fire from the dark headland stings the eyes a little even now, and Jemmy Button's wistful forgotten face is an eternal reproach to those who persist in projecting upon the bodies of living men the shadow of an unknown vanished ape. (Eiseley 1961:265)

However close Darwin may have come to recognizing the common humanity of hunter gatherers and Britons, he assiduously avoided discussing the position of humans in his evolutionary schemes until the dust of the *Origin of Species* (1859) had settled sufficiently for him to publish his *Descent of Man* (1871). By then, the first Neanderthal had been recognized and named (in 1856), and Christy and Lartet were well known for their excavations in the limestone valleys of the Dordogne and Vézère (Daniel 1967:78–85). Archaeologists were faced with the overwhelming evidence of the antiquity of man as spelled out in the repeated association of innumerable hand axes and bones of large, extinct animals (Daniel 1967). The interpretation of these remains relied on finding parallels elsewhere, and in the same way as fossil elephants of the Somme could be understood in relation to living pachyderms in India, ancient hunters could be compared with living ones (Sollas 1911). "In fact," concluded Lubbock, "the Van Diemaner and South American are to the antiquary what the opossum and the sloth are to the geologist" (1869:416).

It was one thing for a mid-Victorian scholar to recognize the antecedents of elephants and quite another to grasp the nature of the antecedents of man. Lubbock realized that some information about the behavior and ecology of prehistoric elephants could be gleaned from studying living ones, but the absence of recognized hominid fossils together with a strong residual belief in the position of man at the pinnacle of existence combined to make it impossible for him to generalize his argument from elephants to man. He held that nothing in his world—that is, in Europe—could illuminate Stone Age human behavior because known historical events there left an enormous gap between past and present. Only in a situation in which there was no past, in which time could safely be presumed to have stood still, could one find anything comparable with early man in Europe. Just such a place was Australia, Tasmania, or wherever hunter gatherer populations still roamed (Lubbock 1869:416–417).

The discovery of the first presapient fossil, *Pithecanthropus erectus,* in Java in 1891, should have clarified the position of living hunter gatherers, but it did not. Parts of the scientific community were unprepared for its appearance and continued to label this and other fossil forms as aberrant, atavistic, and even more apish than some living men. Confusion piled on confusion, as in the case of the strange large brains of Mousterian and Upper Paleolithic people. These skulls were puzzling because neither they nor any of their living large-brained representatives in Australia, Tasmania, or Africa seem to have achieved the cultural heights commensurate with such vast intellects. William Sollas, at least, recognized that he was caught in a bind here, and neatly deduced some form of reverse evolution. Big brains were an ancient characteristic that gave way eventually to the smaller, more efficient ones of civilized men (Eiseley 1961:277–279, 284).

If Sollas' theories about brains attracted few lasting followers, the same cannot be said of his views about hunter gatherers, which spread widely and still exist, in some subtle forms, today. Where the United States was concerned, the notion of indigenous people having a changeless past prevailed until the 1930s. Trigger traces the concept of the ahistorical Indian back to the Puritan dogma that justified the seizure of Indian land by whites on the grounds that the indigenous people had simply lived there but had never really earned the land by developing or changing it in any way (Trigger 1981:5). Willey and Sabloff (1974:86–87) attribute the popularity around the turn of the century of the concept of the unchanging Indian in a featureless past to Boas' teachings, to ignorance of stratigraphic analysis, and to a realization that the American past was exceedingly shallow as opposed to that of Europe. Meltzer challenges these ideas in a spirited and elegant paper (1983) in which he exonerates Boas, whose teachings were not sufficiently popular to have dominated ideas at that time. Likewise, American scientists were sufficiently conversant with stratigraphic details to maintain a prolonged debate about the geological evidence for the antiquity of man in the United States. Citing Trigger (1980), Meltzer points to a far more insidious element in the origins of American archaeology, namely the deep-rooted belief in the permanent fixture of the Indian on the lowest rung of the ladder to civilization. It was this conviction, together with the relatively recent human occupation of America, that produced the notion of the unchanging, stable past. The effect on official research was inevitable: "By condensing the past into a mirror image of the ethnographic present, BAE [Bureau of American Ethnology] archaeology became absorbed within ethnology and forfeited its claim to time" (Meltzer, 1983:40). This is not the place to try and assess the major contributions of workers like Boas, Kroeber, White, and Steward to our understanding of hunter gatherer behavior, though it may be instructive to observe a certain selectivity in their recognition of the hunter gatherer past and their application of this knowledge to particular problems. For example,

Steward paid due attention to the Ute past when assessing their current predicament for administrative purposes (Steward 1974) but tended to ignore both prehistoric and protohistoric changes as well as those emanating from European contact in his classic theoretical paper on band societies (Steward 1936). Here he insisted that all groups under discussion had a purely hunting and gathering economy (1936:331), betraying a surprisingly uncritical acceptance of his sources. True, one cited authority uses these exact words to describe the Bushmen (Schapera 1930:3), but Schapera goes right on to identify them as people who have suffered most from European contact (1930:5). Likewise Ling Roth's (1899) compendium of Tasmanians written twenty years after the death of the supposed last survivor had surely to be treated as the sine qua non of reconstructionist anthropology. One might argue that Steward was simply blocking out the extraneous noise of historical facts so as to produce some elegant generalizations, but in reading that the horse-owning Tehuelche of Patagonia must formerly have been organized like the foraging Fuegians (1936:337) I perceive an uncomfortable echo of Lubbock.

The echo is partly dispelled by Steward himself. Thirty years after this landmark paper, he addressed the famous symposium on *Man the Hunter* in Chicago in 1966 (Lee and DeVore 1968; Steward 1968) and pointed to possible sources of confusion about the identity of the patrilineal band. One such source relates directly to the interplay of past and present in that Steward observes that food resources such as game have fluctuated widely through time (Steward 1968:332). But when it actually came down to the hard question of relating the ethnography of living foragers with prehistoric ones, he remained convinced that elements of traditional existence could be separated from their modern context: "The starting point is to compare the special purpose encampment of a primary band with a prehistoric site where the same factors can be inferred . . . where the ethnographic and archeological sites are reasonably permanent, factor determination of the pre-conditions of such sites is possible" (Steward, 1968:334). What then was the general consensus of archaeologists at this famous symposium? Though some of the ideas offered there read quaintly, even ironically today, it is instructive to summarize them here in order to create a baseline from which later views may be assessed.

A dominant feature was the rejection of ideas expressed by Sollas, Lubbock, and the like: Living people are not fossils. Discussions of the relation of living foragers to prehistoric ones were laced with repeated insistences that living people are not equivalents of extinct ones. Freeman's short summary (1968) was particularly vehement on this score, examining as it did the proposition that "the most serious failings in present models for interpreting archaeological evidence are directly related to the fact that they incorporate numer-

ous analogies with other groups" (Freeman 1968:262). He advocated meticulous attention to the message of the archaeological data, staying as far as
possible from seductive residues of living foragers, because "The idea that
prehistorians must interpret their evidence solely in terms of inferences
derived from social and cultural anthropology is as fallacious as the idea that
interpretations of the behavior of modern groups must be derived from
prehistory" (Freeman 1968:267).

Isaac was considerably less vehement, suggesting that the range of social
and economic activities of modern foragers could provide a useful guide to
the past (Isaac 1968:253). He agreed with Binford's stand, reiterated in a
paper at the same conference (Binford 1968:269), that archaeological deduc-
tions must stand on their own merit as verifiable hypotheses, but then went
on to ignore all these reservations in a brief review of the evidence from
Olorgesaillie. He interpreted this Middle Pleistocene African locality as a
butchery site (see also Clark 1968:277), showing specialized hunting of ba-
boons and even the massacre of an entire baboon troop such as that witnessed by Woodburn among the living Hadza of northern Tanganika (Isaac
1968:259–260).

Isaac's weakness for ethnographic information about living hunters (pace
Binford 1983:41–43, 61–62) is unusual in this generally cautious and judicious scholar (see Isaac and Crader 1981 for a particularly measured assessment of dietary inferences that may be drawn from Pleistocene deposits).
More surprising is Freeman's susceptibility to an uncritical use of modern
parallels in interpreting archaeological material in his repeated reconstruction of the famous Spanish sites of Torralba and Ambrona as camps of Middle
Pleistocene hunters who drove elephants into swamps with fire and butchered them in complicated ways (Freeman 1981:114–124). Today, critics suggest that the elephant bones never received the scrutiny they deserved and
that they show unquestionable signs of having been abraded by water and
washed into position. Instead of reflecting the rise of the ancestral big game
hunter (Pfeiffer 1972:151–170), they probably mirror the rise of the local
rivers and streams that carried these bone "pebbles" to their present locale
(Binford 1983:16–17; Shipman and Rose 1983).

While most prehistorians at the conference were concerned with the distant past, dealing with modern hunter gatherers in a very generalized way,
one notable exception raised the possibility that the relatively recent history
of certain groups may have radically altered their traditional organization to
produce the misleadingly "ancient" patterns found today. Deetz singled out
the Australian, the Gê, and the California foragers as the only ones to avoid
the perturbations of historic interaction before the sixteenth century, in contrast to the Bushmen whose interaction with the wider African scene went
back many millennia (Deetz cited in Lee and DeVore 1968:283). As it turns

out, he was probably wrong about the Australians in that Aborigines living on the northern coast experienced Asian contact for many centuries, if not millennia, before that time (see MacKnight 1976: Schrire 1972, this volume), but the comment is exceedingly important because it was one of the rare recognitions that considerable modifications might have preceded the first written accounts of hunter gatherer life.

These provocative issues were largely ignored in subsequent field studies of living hunter gatherers, the most famous of which was directed at the San or Bushmen of the Kalahari. Lee (1979), their chief proponent, saw the *Man the Hunter* symposium (Lee and DeVore 1968) as serving the interests of students of human evolution (Lee 1976:11–12). At the risk of flogging what is, in fact, a very live horse (Schrire 1980), I should like to trace the impact of the strong evolutionary view that has colored so much of that work.

Lee originally chose to work in the Kalahari because he wanted to find suitable living analogs of early man. Given the long ancestry of man in Africa, he prefered the Kalahari to regions such as the Australian central desert (Lee 1976:10). As far as the past was concerned, he hoped to find patterns that would help interpret prehistoric living floors (Lee 1976:14), a hope that sounds rather anachronistic here in view of findings that many so-called living floors represent the debris of nonhuman carnivores (Binford 1981; Brain 1981). Lee was not an archaeologist, nor did he ever pretend to be one. He relied on his expert, John Yellen, whose views, as it turned out, were particularly ambiguous on this score.

Yellen's major statement about the ethnoarchaeology of the San (1977) is, by and large, a detailed and painstaking record of the residues of their camps. He makes a number of generalizations about inferring behavior but specifically denies the long-term implications of his study:

> data are scant, and the question of climatic successions remains an intriguing and largely unanswered one. . . . I feel fairly sure that the northern Kalahari *has experienced numerous and very pronounced climatic changes* that will prove extremely difficult to disentangle by geological means. (Yellen 1977:34, emphasis mine)

It comes as a surprise therefore to find him saying quite the opposite in a roughly contemporary piece:

> In western Ngamiland it is possible to use ethnographic data . . . to compare . . . distributions of present-day dry season !Kung camps with their Late Stone Age counterparts. The conclusion drawn from striking similarities is that these prehistoric hunters and gathers (sic) patterned certain of their responses to the environment in the same way as their modern counterparts. . . . *Given that environmental conditions during the late Stone Age prevail today,* and that present !Kung are probably descended from these prehistoric ancestors, the analogies drawn are probably valid. (Yellen 1976:50, emphasis mine)

It is always tempting to try and attribute such discrepancies to the long time that might have elapsed between writing the papers and seeing them in print. However this hardly applies here since no detailed evidence of Kalahari sequences showing stability through time appeared in the interval under discussion. Binford's trenchant critique of Yellen's approach in terms of its logic and power to negate his propositions (1978:357–360) is likewise inapplicable here other than to note that in the general discussion that followed he challenged an implicit but fundamental premise of Yellen's study, that the residual patterns of modern San are the same as those of their protohistoric counterparts (Binford 1979:592).

Paradoxically, the evolutionary perspective on the San has stressed the impact of the present on the past while neatly ignoring the effect of past experiences and interactions on present populations. Lee was always at pains to emphasize the geographic isolation of the !Kung region both today (1979:19) and in the past (Solway and Lee 1981). Silberbauer took the complex historical interactions of the /Gwi seriously in his earlier work (1965) but failed to integrate it into his later, more comprehensive one (Silberbauer 1981; see Wilmsen 1983 for an analysis of this position). Guenther (1976) actually used archival sources to document sociocultural change among farm Bushmen. He seems considerably less committed than other authors to the notion of long-term isolation of these people, yet he subconsciously propounds an image of traditional existence in the face of some rather ambiguous historical data. Specifically, a number of cited early nineteenth-century sources reported the existence of large, predatory Bushmen groups led by autocratic captains. Instead of analyzing the implications of these observations, Guenther labels them "nontraditional" and dismisses them because they seem to reflect the effects of acculturation on an idealized small-scale society (Guenther, 1976: 130, footnote 13; Lee and DeVore, 1976:397). Since everyone concerned realized that innumerable archival sources existed in libraries in places such as Cape Town, Gaborone, Windhoek and London (see Gordon, this volume) we have to conclude that the exclusion of a trained ethnohistorian from the research design of Kalahari work might point to a deep-seated commitment to maintain the timeless and stable image of the San past.

Moving from the particulars of one large study to more general synthesis, it is instructive to realize the degree to which the past is ignored in defining the patterns of modern existence. Foremost among these is the application of evolutionary ecological theory by the authors in Winterhalder and Smith's volume (1981), whose commitment to the use of optimization models leaves no room for exploring the degree to which such features may have operated in the past or the way in which present concerns affect hunter gatherer behavior. Winterhalder considers, for instance, that optimization arose among the Cree in response to food shortages in the past (1981:67) but musters no evidence to test this proposition (see Durham 1981:229). Likewise, the analysis of the central desert Aborigines foraging optimally from the back of the ethnographer's vehicle (O'Connell and Hawkes 1981) dismisses the possibility that recent profound changes in their lives may have determined if not produced the patterns observed today. The overriding theoretical imperative of the book has been criticized harshly as being misconceived (Martin 1983), but for our present purposes, its lack of temporal perspective reduces the foragers' behavior under review to mechanistic and dehumanized roles.

Hayden's (1981) review of subsistence patterns describes how food is distributed in the ecosystem and then hunted, gathered, butchered, shared, cooked, stored, and eaten among innumerable foraging groups. It is a largely synchronic picture, but since it appears in a volume concerned with the diet of all primates, whether living or extinct, Hayden is occasionally obliged to discuss the long-term implications of his findings. He assumes that features such as a readiness to shift camp frequently or to share food, which appear to be advantageous to contemporary foragers, conferred "adaptive advantages" on Pleistocene and Holocene ones too (Hayden 1981:375, 387). Likewise, prehistoric foragers probably walked as far from their home bases as do modern ones (Hayden 1981:283) and might well have been after the fat in big game to satisfy the same biological needs they presumably share with their modern representatives (1981:397).

These are fairly innocuous assumptions, even if one is a little reluctant to draw the parallels so close to each other. It is only when one moves away from prehistoric times into the historic realities of hunter gatherer existence that the analogies become strained. Hayden acknowledges very briefly (1981:353) the difference between the ideal environments occupied by historic groups as opposed to the putatively "marginal" territories of present-day ones; he admits to the recent introduction of certain techniques such as boiling food (Hayden 1981:384) and even concedes that foragers such as the Aboriginal people of the western desert of Australia have since reduced their densities on the land by moving into European stations (1981:364). But his overall perspective remains strongly ahistorical, avoiding the issues of whether the foragers' landscape changed over time, of the impact of introduced species into the ecosystem in historic times, and of the continuity between the numerous groups listed in scholarly journals or travelers accounts and prehistoric occupants of the same regions.

Consider, for instance, the ease with which the ceremonial behavior and communal hunting practices of western desert Aborigines are integrated into a general pattern despite the fact that they stopped living off their land some decades back when they moved into white stations. Likewise, selected Eskimo data is seen to typify all Arctic groups despite the argument that some extant groups only assumed their ethnographic identity a few hundred years ago (Burch 1978). The impact of guns on the diet of certain groups is ignored, not only among armed hunters, but also among those whose land once rang with the crack of their rifles but now lies depleted, partly through their own predation (Solway and Lee 1981; see also Gordon, this volume). Finally there is the big bugaboo of Western food. It is one thing to ignore former foragers who eat very little wild foods, but it is quite another to ignore the physiological impact of addictive substances like sugar, tobacco, and alcohol on the demands and needs of ethnographically observed groups. One of the most cited studies of Aboriginal diet, made in Arnhem Land in 1948 (McCarthy and McArthur 1960:147), is quite explicit on this point since the authors entreated their subjects from the outset of the work to ignore their craving for mission foods. Hayden's essay ends up by presenting a smorgasbord of diets among historically known groups, the relation of which to prehistoric practices remains obscure.

Attempts to categorize hunter gatherers inevitably raise the question of their past. One such effort is an original look at current groups by Woodburn (1980), who classifies groups according to their economic systems based either on immediate returns, where surpluses are unacceptable, or on delayed returns, where capital is accumulated to allow for future planning. Unlike farmers who only have delayed return systems, hunter gatherers have both types: People such as the !Kung, the Mbuti, the Hadza, and the Batek Negritos travel light, seldom store food, and enjoy immediate returns, whereas the Cree, some Inuit, and the Plains Indians are more like farmers. The inclusion of Australian Aborigines in his latter, delayed-return system, group is predicated on their widespread capacity to control the labor and reproductive potential of females: Succinctly, Woodburn sees Australians as "farmers in disguise who are concerned with farming (and farming out) their women" (1980:108–109).

Woodburn's division of economic systems stresses the power of ideology over whatever limits may be perceived in the environment or technology of particular people (Barnard 1983:205). To Barnard this "bold and radical" new scheme helps to close the gap between hunter gatherers and ourselves by drawing the boundary between us closer to their end of the scale (1983:206). I would argue, however, that where Woodburn uses this scheme to reconstruct the past (1980:113), it evokes nineteenth-century views of hunter gatherers as timeless and unchanging people whose history has little if any bearing on their present situation. True, Woodburn makes a stab at the possibility that the contact situation might have produced some of the immediate-return systems found today (1980:112), but he uses the assumed technological stability of hunter gatherers to conclude somewhat diffidently, "In principle I can see no reason why modern hunters should be substantially unrepresentative of those in the past" (1980:113).

A more recent and scholarly review summarizes significant issues in the ecology and social organization of contemporary hunter gatherers (Barnard 1983). It is succinct and comprehensive, and though the author sees it as a critical rather than an encyclopedic effort, it is certainly nowhere near as penetrating as Martin's look at optimal foraging (1983). In all the fields that Barnard lists, he stresses the synchronic outlook rather than the potential implications of asking how historical sources and archaeology affect current interpretations of contemporary people. Only at the end, when he embarks on the question raised by Arcand at the Second International Conference on Hunting and Gathering Societies in 1980 as to whether the term "hunter gatherer" is a meaningful one at all, does he explore the economic changes in certain groups over time, conceding that "Social change and acculturation are very complex problems, as hunter-gatherer specialists are only beginning to realise" (Barnard 1983:209).

The absence of a diachronic perspective in these general syntheses leads us into a consideration of case studies that do employ this view. Literature on Arctic and sub-Arctic peoples differs markedly from some of that on Bushmen and Aborigines in its meticulous attention to ethnohistoric sources (see for example Asch 1980; Bishop and Kretch 1980; Leacock 1980; Yerbury 1980 for a well-integrated discussion of the use of ethnohistory in sub-Arctic ethnography). Slobodkin (1980:52) attributes the popularity of ethnohistory in the American northeast to the extensive documentation found there, specifically the Jesuit Relations and reports of traders and missionaries who lived with local people. I think it likely that another reason may lie in the relatively short time range with which these scholars are concerned. The entire Arctic occupation lasted no more than 10,000 years (Old Crow notwithstanding). This is a mere fraction of the time that people have lived in Africa, Europe, and Asia and only one fifth of the time since man first crossed the sea to occupy Australia. Documentation of Arctic existence covers about 5% of the total time of man's existence there—a vast extent compared with other areas under discussion—making its prehistory perhaps more intelligible or accessible to literate scholars.

Although he does not deal here with hunter gatherers, Trigger's magisterial account of the Huron to 1660 (Trigger 1976) provides a striking example of how judicious use of ethnohistory can add a new dimension to our grasp of preliterate people. In his particular study, prehistoric data reveal that native commerce and political alliances preceded the fur trade by many centuries, establishing a pattern that would be elaborated later with the historic expansion of the Huron confederacy (Trigger 1976:175–176). The changing nature of prehistoric interactions belies the notion of Indians existing in a stable and unchanging world before Western incursions shook them into their present-day adaptations; instead, the historical developments form part of a trajectory that is firmly rooted in far older tradition (Trigger 1976:841). Trigger's attention to detail is particularly impressive, not only because he spots discrepancies between stereotypes and realities, but also because he integrates the history of the Huron into the wider framework of Western perceptions of the primitive, in which elements of European identity are mixed, almost randomly, with those of various so-called savages to produce a standard, but flawed, picture of the composite savage.

This is particularly obvious in early paintings and lithographs, as for example in a depiction of Huron farming where cornhills conform to a local account but the people and their tools are copied from sightings made in Florida (Trigger 1976:35). Likewise, naked Indians and palm trees at the battle of Lake Champlain ring false (Trigger 1976:253), as does the European ornament atop an otherwise authentic suit of Huron armour (1976:71). Such discrepancies are brilliantly integrated into the wider field of European values in Bernard Smith's analysis of Pacific exploration (1960), but it is instructive to realize how persistently scholars still accept at face value the messages of historical drawings. A particularly painful, if amusing, example is to be found in analyses of Burchell's famous triptych, "View of a Bushman Kraal" (Burchell 1824:Plate 4). My interpretation (Schrire 1980:22–23) holds that this is a stereotypic view of Bushmen deliberately created to obscure and deny the fact that Bushmen sometimes herded sheep and cattle and that the distinctions between them and so-called Khoi may be more of our, than of their own, making. The subtleties of my argument clearly missed their mark, for Andrew Smith uses this very picture to illustrate a typical Khoi kraal on the front page of a recent edition of *World Archaeology* devoted to a study of pastoralism (Smith 1983)!

Rainey's (1971) retrospective of archaeological research in northwest Alaska since 1939 challenges Toynbee's (1934:4–7) proposition that the Eskimos represent a people who exemplify par excellence how to get frozen into an unchanging cultural tradition through environmental constraints. He shows how 10,000 years of Arctic occupation reveal changing environmental conditions and cultural expressions but notes that most anthropologists argue for continuity of the present Eskimo tradition over the past 4000 years (1971:31). This would include the rather dissonant Ipiutak culture, whose latest manifestation occurs as a large summer encampment near Point Hope on the Bering Strait. Here people seem to have concentrated on walrus hunting between A.D. 0 and 500, but their artifacts indicate a high degree of interaction with the wider world that belies a strictly local developmental tradition. Specifically, there are links to be seen between stone tools and ivory carvings in Siberia and the Urals. Walrus ivory and lines made from walrus hide were highly prized in Asia, and interchanges across the Bering Strait suggest that this village of Arctic hunters was part of a wider network that actually stimulated local predation beyond immediate needs. To fully appreciate, therefore, the nature of present-day Eskimos, one would be advised to think about earlier interactions as possible influences of present practices.

I have deliberately left until last, what I think is the finest multidisciplinary exploration of the identity of a contemporary hunter gatherer group. Burch's paper on the Caribou Eskimos weds archaeology, history, and linguistics with meteorological information to argue for the very recent existence of that cultural and ecological composit we call the Caribou Eskimos. They are a historic Inuit-speaking group living along and inland from the western shores of Hudson Bay. They were named and defined by the Fifth Thule Expedition of 1921–1924 (Birket-Smith 1929) and served to epitomize how hunters living in the harshest of worlds maintain an age-old balance with nature through the judicious practice of female infanticide (Birdsell 1975:372–375; Birket-Smith 1929:I-65ff.). Burch shows that the area currently occupied by these people was periodically abandoned due to depletion of game during the "little ice age" (1978:21–23) and that there is a marked discontinuity between occupation by the Thule people and the Caribou Eskimo. Ancestral Caribou people seem to have settled on the shore of Hudson Bay a mere 200–300 years ago, acquiring their distinctive characteristics only toward the second half of the nineteenth century (Burch 1978:28). This was well after European influences were first felt in the region and only 70 years before the Thule Expedition came through.

The historical reappraisal of the Caribou Eskimos suggests that it is high time to amend the notion of them as "impoverished models of the kind of life that must have been possible around the edges of the last glacier to advance into Europe" (Birdsell 1975:373). Yet Burch does more than simply reveal the shallow past of these people. His paper is replete with critical acumen directed at historical sources. Consider for instance, his analysis of the famous but anomalous account of a large village of "Iskemays" at the mouth of the Churchill River in 1717. It was recorded by one James Knight, an elderly factor of the Hudson's Bay Company, who spoke of hundreds of people living in a large town and building great boats (Burch 1978:9). Burch tries to understand why Knight would falsify his report and ends up by observing that Knight was old and probably intent on making a reputation for himself as a significant force against a worthy and numerous foe. Once this is realized, the rest of the historical accounts fall into neat and acceptable focus (Burch 1978:9–11).

It is far easier to try to understand the reasoning of an early, literate traveler than that of an early Arctic hunter; nevertheless this is just what Riches tries to do, using a humanistic approach that relies "partly on citing factors which plausibly were part of an actors' knowledge" (Riches 1982:2). He investigages the practice of female infanticide from the Eskimo man's perception of environmental pressures and agrees with Freeman (1971) that it was a response to perceived shortages of food and energy costs and a means of avoiding having to betroth a surplus female to a nonkin male (Riches 1982:60–61, 223). He then produces what he calls a diachronic perspective by suggesting that Eskimos perceived similar pressures during the "little ice age" and early contact period (Riches 1974:359–360) and responded then, as now, with female infanticide. This kind of projection back in time should not be confused with substantial historical analysis. Had Riches explored the minds of his sources rather than those of hypothetical indigenes, he would have discovered two crucial aspects of Arctic infanticide: first, that the prime source, Rasmussen, could never add and consequently published erroneous figures (Schrire and Steiger 1974:166, 180), and second, that a systematic misaging of females in many Arctic sources produces an impression of systematic female infanticide the plausibility of which can be investigated and even refuted using simulation models (Schrire and Steiger 1974).

The ethnohistory of the San, the Australian Aborigines, the Fuegians, and other such people still await their Burchs. True, there has been considerable effort to use ethnographic records, but the deeper meaning of the accounts as reflected in the personality and aspirations of the authors, has not as yet been fully realized. In South Africa, for example, the diary of the first governor of the Cape, Jan van Riebeeck (Thom 1952, 1954, 1958) is a treasure house of information about daily interaction with indigenous people; yet van Riebeeck's apparently slavish acceptance of Dutch East India Company policy repeatedly rings false, especially with regard to his assertions that the Dutch stood aloof from hostilities and competition among local groups. Likewise, the monumental diary of George Augustus Robinson, that Hollinshed of the twilight of traditional Tasmanian life (Plomley 1966), has repeatedly been mined for its factual data but seldom subjected to deep, critical analysis. Jones tests Robinson's observations of Tasmanian diet against prehistoric evidence (1978) and his account of seasonal movements against the presumed itinerary of tribal groups (Jones 1974). Lourandos (1980) wonders if Robinson's later observations in Australia lacked the commitment to detail of those he made in Tasmania, Wilson (1978:172–174) ponders his altruism, and Ellis is concerned at the prospect of his adultery (1976:38–39). Interesting and diverting though all these concerns may be, someone has yet to integrate Robinson's character with the picture of Tasmanian existence he presents.

My concluding remarks make three rather simple points. The first advocates greater understanding of archaeological principles and inferences, the second asks what all our current data on foragers really reflects, and the last point calls for the integration of current studies into a wider international perspective.

The question of why archaeological findings assume such a peripheral role in modern hunter gatherer studies takes us back to the original design of four fields of American anthropology: archaeology, cultural anthropology, physical anthropology and linguistics. Concerns about the past were subsumed in archaeology, and until the development of ethnohistory as a legitimate field, there was a strong tendency to leave the question of prehistoric foragers to the archaeologist. Whatever the aspirations of teachers of the four fields, as it turns out most social anthropologists, who study social behavior and interactions, do not fully appreciate the epistemological basis of prehistory. It may be that the techniques of archaeology are beyond the interest and grasp of cultural anthropologists, and certainly in my twenty or so years of professional anthropology, I have rarely met a nonarchaeologist who was well conversant with the logic of archaeology and with the levels of inference encoded in so much of its data. The Bushman past, as it appears in countless versions of the life and times of the Kalahari San, takes no account whatever of the well-known archaeological difficulties involved in asserting cultural continuity for a linguistic group over thousands of years. The past remains an introductory aside in the lives of contemporary foragers in much the same way as *environment* and *ecology* were crammed into the prefatory statements in the 1940s and 1950s before the heyday of socioecological concerns.

We turn now to the uncomfortable question of what most of the ethnographies of hunter gatherers with which we deal today really reflect? There can be no doubt that, one way or another, all describe societies coping with the impact of incursions by foreign forces into their territories. Anthropologists have used these studies to postulate commonalities among groups in their search for those features that are residual or intrinsic to the hunter gatherer mode. The big question that arises is, are the common features of hunter gatherer groups, be they structural elements such as bilateral kinship systems or behavioral ones such as a tendency to share food, a product of interaction with us? Are the features we single out and study held in common, not so much because humanity shared the hunter gatherer life-style for 99% of its time on earth, but because the hunters and gatherers of today, in searching for the compromises that would allow them to go on doing mainly that, have reached some subliminal consensus in finding similar solutions to similar problems?

Finally there is the matter of removing studies of current hunter gatherers from the temporal confines of their local archaeological sequences, and moving them into the wider field of international affairs. Today we recognize that contemporary foragers are being integrated into the nation-states within which they have been encapsulated for some time, but a fresh perspective on their history generally reveals that they have been a part of a wider system for a considerably longer time. The impact of this articulation has been extensively explored with regard to the North American fur trade, and the Kalahari fur trade has also become a focus of such research (Solway and Lee 1981; Wilmsen 1983). In concluding this essay I now describe the interactions in one particular example in order to pull the many rather esoteric references discussed here into a central focus.

The example concerns the efforts of a few rough Dutch seamen to turn over a small profit by harvesting seal skins in the mid–seventeenth century on a tiny island about 60 km northwest of the very tip of Africa. Dassen Island, small by any standards, is about 4.4 km at its maximum and lies about 8 km off the coast. It is a favorite summer basking spot for seals, who clamber up at that time with their pups in tow. When the Dutch established their station at Cape Town in 1652, they came upon the French, who had already harvested some 39,000 skins there in one season (Thom 1952:175ff.). After due discussion about skinning techniques, methods of train oil extraction, and foreign markets, the Dutch ousted the French and went on to harvest thousands of skins per month for the four summer months each year (Thom 1952:269, 301). Archaeological findings suggest that local mainland foragers normally killed seals in winter (Parkington 1976:133) so that a summer harvest, which concentrated on the "prettier" skins of young seals, must have diminished the available supplies. Historical sources admit to a drop in Dassen Island numbers within 3 years of commercial operations there, concluding that the animals had become "shy" (Thom 1954:27). The impact on coastal foragers has yet to be archaeologically tested, though we can predict that it, together with the inexorable expansion of Dutch influence inland, helped diminish the viability of both hunters and herders in the region. In 1657, however, the Dutch efforts faltered following a directive from the Council of Seventeen in Holland to desist. Skins were poorly treated, they smelled bad, and the train oil produced could not compete in Europe with that of the Greenland operations (Roux 1975:91ff.). The Dutch turned from international to local markets and killed seals for meat and oil instead, maintaining supplies until the early nineteenth century (Roux 1975).

This esoteric story draws together the affairs of indigenous hunters from the remotest tips of northern and southern land masses through the mediation of great mercantile networks. No Greenlander could imagine his seals giving those of the Cape Bushman a break in outside predation, yet, in the same way as mistaken notions of human evolution brought representatives of these very same two peoples together in a London salon, international economic affairs combined their concerns in a wider framework.

Similar links are discernable elsewhere. The pianos of Leipzig rang to the tune of ivory hunted by Kalahari San until there were no more elephants left on the pans (see Gordon, this volume). Chinese beliefs in male potency affected the fortunes of Aborigines on the north Australian coast, where trepang was harvested (see MacKnight 1976: Schrire this volume), as well as the lives of hunters in East Africa, who shipped out whole rhinoceros horns through middlemen at Mombasa for centuries. Asian demand for rhinoceros horn maintained hunters in Borneo's forests, their taste for tortoiseshell affected the Australian Aborigines (J. Urry, personal communication, 1980), and their need for forest products may indeed be the raison d'être of some of the hunters of Kalimantan (Hoffman, this volume).

It is only by realizing these processes at work in our field, by spelling them out in research designs and hammering out their meanings in analyses, that we can break out of the confines imposed by hunter gatherer studies over the past centuries. A broader perspective will help release hunter gatherers from the frozen tableaux of our thoughts and integrate them into the wider world of which they have always been a part.

Acknowledgments

This chapter was written for Lew Binford, in partial fulfillment of my promise to describe for him the exhibition of wild Bushmen that I watched at the Van Riebeeck Tercentenary celebrations in Cape Town in 1952. I am grateful to Robert Gordon for providing material on the Kalahari, to George Morren for critical comments, to Arthur Joyce for useful American references, and to E. S. "Tiger" Burch for introducing me to the details of Caribou Eskimo life. Finally, Ward Goodenough and Bill Davenport kept me from the library at the University of Pennsylvania one full day, providing endless hours of information about the articulation of hunter gatherers in a wider world.

References

Altick, Richard D.
  1978   *The shows of London.* Belknap Press of Harvard University Press, Cambridge and London.
Asch, Michael I.
  1980   Steps toward the analysis of Athapaskan social organization. *Arctic Anthropology* XVII(2):46–51.
Barnard, Alan
  1983   Contemporary hunter–gatherers: current theoretical issues in ecology and social organisation. *Annual Review of Anthropology* 12:193–214.
Binford, Lewis R.
  1968   Methodological considerations of the archaeological use of ethnographic data. In *Man the hunter,* edited by Richard B. Lee and Irven DeVore, pp. 268–273. Aldine, Chicago.
  1978   Dimensional analysis of behavior and site structure: learning from an Eskimo hunting stand. *American Antiquity* 43:330–361.

1979 Comments on confusion. *American Antiquity* 44:591–593.

1981 *Bones: ancient men and modern myths.* Academic Press, New York.

1983 *In pursuit of the past: decoding the archaeological record.* Thames and Hudson, New York.

Birdsell, Joseph B.

1975 *Human evolution. An introduction to the new physical anthropology.* (second ed.). Rand McNally College Publishing Company, Chicago.

Birket-Smith, Kaj

1929 *The Caribou Eskimos: material and social life and their cultural position.* Report of the Fifth Thule Expedition 1921–1924. 5, 1–2. Nordisk Forlag, Copenhagen.

Bishop, Charles A., and Shepard Krech, III

1980 Matriorganization: the basis of Aboriginal subarctic social organization. *Arctic Anthropology* XVII(2):34–45.

Brain, C. K.

1981 *The hunters or the hunted? an introduction to African cave taphonomy.* University of Chicago Press, Chicago.

Burch, Ernest, S. Jr.

1978 Caribou Eskimo origins: an old problem reconsidered. *Arctic Anthropology* XV(1):1–35.

Burchell, William J.

1824 *Travels in the interior of Southern Africa* II. Longman, Hurst, Rees, Orme and Brown, London.

Clark, John Desmond

1968 Studies of hunter–gatherers as an aid to the interpretation of prehistoric societies. In *Man the hunter,* edited by Richard B. Lee and Irven DeVore, pp. 276–280. Aldine, Chicago.

Daniel, Glyn

1967 *The origins and growth of archaeology.* Penguin Books, Harmondsworth.

Darwin, Charles Robert

1859 *On the origin of species by means of national selection, or, the preservation of favoured races in the struggle for life.* J. Murray, London.

1871 *The descent of man, and selection in relation to sex* (2 vols) John Murray, London.

1958 *The voyage of the Beagle.* Bantam Books, New York. (Original work published 1839.)

Davidson, Daniel Sutherland

1937 The relationship of Tasmanian and Australian cultures. *Philadelphia Anthropological Society: Twenty-fifth Anniversary Studies* I:47–62.

Durham, William H.

1981 Overview: optimal foraging analysis in human ecology. In *Hunter–gatherer foraging strategies: ethnographic and archaeological analyses,* edited by Bruce Winterhalder and Eric Alden Smith, pp. 218–231. University of Chicago Press, Chicago.

Eiseley, Loren

1961 *Darwin's century: evolution and the men who discovered it.* Doubleday, New York.

Ellis, Vivienne Rae

1976 *Trucanini, queen or traitor?* Australian Institute of Aboriginal Studies, Canberra.

Freeman, Leslie G. Jr.

1968 A theoretical framework for interpreting archaeological materials. In *Man the hunter,* edited by Richard B. Lee and Irven DeVore, pp. 262–267. Aldine, Chicago.

1981 The fat of the land: notes on paleolithic diet in Iberia. In *Omniverous primates: gathering and hunting in human evolution,* edited by Robert S. O. Harding and Geza Teleki, pp. 104–165. Columbia University Press, New York.

Freeman, Milton M. R.
   1971   A social and ecological analysis of systematic female infanticide among the Netsilik
            Eskimo. *American Anthropologist* 73:1011–1018.
Gellner, Ernest
   1958   Time and theory in social anthropology. *Mind* LXVII:182–202.
Gould, Stephen J.
   1982   The Hottentot Venus. *Natural History* 10:22–27.
Guenther, Mathias G.
   1976   From hunters to squatters: social and cultural change among the farm San of Ghanzi,
            Botswana. In *Kalahari hunter–gatherers: studies of the !Kung San and their neigh-
            bours,* edited by Richard B. Lee and Irven DeVore, pp. 120–133. Harvard University
            Press, Cambridge and London.
Hayden, Brian
   1981   Subsistence and ecological adaptations of modern hunter/gatherers. In *Omniverous
            primates: gathering and hunting in human evolution,* edited by Robert S. O. Hard-
            ing and Geza Teleki, pp. 344–421. Columbia University Press, New York.
Helms, Mary W.
   1978   Time, history and the future of anthropology: observations on some unresolved
            issues. *Ethnohistory* 25:1–14.
Hiatt, Betty (Meehan)
   1969   Cremation in Aboriginal Australia. *Mankind* 7:104–119.
Isaac, Glynn L.
   1968   Traces of Pleistocene hunters: an East African example. In *Man the hunter,* edited by
            Richard B. Lee and Irven DeVore, pp. 253–261. Aldine, Chicago.
Isaac, Glynn L., and Diana Crader
   1981   To what extent were early hominids carniverous? An archaeological perspective. In
            Omniverous primates: gathering and hunting in human evolution, edited by Robert
            S. O. Harding and Geza Teleki, pp. 37–103. Columbia University Press, New York.
Jones, Rhys
   1978   Why did the Tasmanians stop eating fish? *In Explorations in ethnoarchaeology,*
            edited by Richard A. Gould, pp. 11–48. University of New Mexico Press, Albuquer-
            que.
   1974   Tasmanian tribes, appendix to *Aboriginal tribes of Australia,* by Norman B. Tindale,
            pp. 319–354. University of California Press, Berkeley and Los Angeles.
Labillardière, Jacques Julian de
   1800   *An account of a voyage in search of La Pérouse* (translated from the French). John
            Stockdale, London.
Leacock, Eleanor
   1980   A reappraisal of Aboriginal Athapaskan social organization: Comments. *Arctic An-
            thropology* XVII(2):60–63.
Lee, Richard B.
   1976   Introduction. In *Kalahari hunter–gatherers: studies of the !Kung San and their neigh-
            bours,* edited by Richard B. Lee and Irven DeVore, pp. 3–24. Harvard University
            Press, Cambridge and London.
   1979   *The !Kung San: men women and work in a foraging society.* Cambridge University
            Press, Cambridge.
Lee, Richard B., and Irven DeVore (editors)
   1968   *Man the hunter.* Aldine, Chicago.
   1976   *Kalahari hunter–gatherers: studies of the !Kung San and their neighbours.* Harvard
            University Press, Cambridge and London.

Ling Roth, Henry
   1899   *The Aborigines of Tasmania.* F. King and Sons, Halifax England.
Lourandos, Harry
   1980   Change or stability?: hydraulics, hunter–gatherers and population in temperate Aus-
          tralia. *World Archaeology* 11:245–266.
Lovejoy, Arthur O., and George Boas
   1965   *Primitivism and related ideas in antiquity.* Octagon Books, New York.
Lubbock, Sir John
   1869   *Pre-historic times as illustrated by ancient remains and the manners and customs of
          modern savages.* (second ed.) Williams and Norgate, London and Edinburgh.
McCarthy, Frederick D., and Margaret McArthur
   1960   The food quest and the time factor in Aboriginal economic life. In *Anthropology and
          nutrition: records of the American–Australian scientific expedition to Arnhem Land,
          1948* (Vol. 2), edited by Charles Percy Mountford, pp. 145–194. Melbourne Univer-
          sity Press, Melbourne.
MacKnight, Campbell C.
   1976   *The voyage to Marege: Macassan trepangers in northern Australia.* Melbourne Uni-
          versity Press, Melbourne.
Martin, John F.
   1983   Optimal foraging theory: a review of some models and their applications. *American
          Anthropologist* 85:612–629.
Meltzer, David J.
   1983   The antiquity of man and the development of American archaeology. In *Advances in
          archaeological method and theory* (Vol. 6), edited by Michael B. Schiffer, pp. 1–51.
          Academic Press, New York.
Nance, John
   1976   *The gentle Tasaday: a stone age people in the Philippine rain forest.* Victor Gollancz,
          London.
O'Connell, James F., and Kristen Hawkes
   1981   Alyawara plant use and optimal foraging theory. In *Hunter–gatherer foraging strat-
          egies: ethnographic and archeological analysis,* edited by Bruce Winterhalder and
          Eric Alden Smith, pp. 99–125. University of Chicago Press, Chicago.
Parkington, John E.
   1976   Coastal settlement between the mouths of the Berg and the Olifants Rivers, Cape
          Province. *South African Archaeological Bulletin* 31:127–140.
Pfeiffer, John E.
   1972   *The emergence of man.* Harper and Row, New York.
Pinney, Roy
   1968   *Vanishing tribes.* Thomas Y. Crowell, New York.
Plomley, Norman James Brian (editor)
   1966   *Friendly mission: the Tasmanian journals and papers of G. A. Robinson 1829–1834.*
          Tasmanian Historical Research Association, Hobart.
Radcliffe-Brown, Alfred Reginald
   1956   *Structure and function in primitive society.* Cohen and West, London.
Rainey, Froelich
   1971   The Ipiutak culture: excavations at Point Hope, Alaska. *Addison-Wesley Modular
          Publications* 8:1–32.
Riches, David
   1974   The Netsilik Eskimo: a special case of selective female infanticide. *Ethnology*
          XIII(4):351–361.

1982   *Northern nomadic hunter–gatherers: a humanistic approach.* Academic Press, New York.

Rousseau, Jean Jacques
1775   *Discours sur L'origine et des fondemens de L'inegalité parmi les hommes.* M. M. Rey, Amsterdam.

Roux, A. P.
1975   *Die geskiedenis van Saldanhabaai, St. Helenabaai en Dasseneiland 1652–1806.* Unpublished M.A. dissertation, Department of History, University of Stellenbosch.

Schapera, Isaac
1930   *The Khoisan peoples of South Africa: Bushmen and Hottentots.* George Routledge and Sons, London.

Schrire, Carmel
1972   Ethno-archaeological models and subsistence behaviour in Arnhem Land. In *Models in archaeology,* edited by David L. Clarke, pp. 653–670. Methuen, London.
1980   An enquiry into the evolutionary status and apparent identity of San hunter–gatherers. *Human Ecology* 8(1):9–32.

Schrire, Carmel, and William Lee Steiger
1974   A matter of life and death: an investigation into the practice of female infanticide in the Arctic. *Man* (n.s.) 9:161–184.

Shipman, Pat, and Jennie Rose
1983   Evidence of butchery and hominid activities at Torralba and Ambrona: an evaluation using microscopic techniques. *Journal of Archaeological Science* 10(5):465–474.

Silberbauer, George B.
1965   *Report to the Government of Bechuanaland on the Bushman survey.* Bechuanaland Government, Gaborone.
1981   *Hunter and habitat in the central Kalahari Desert.* Cambridge University Press, Cambridge.

Slobodkin, Richard
1980   Some recent developments in subarctic culture history and ethnohistory. *Arctic Anthropology* XVII(2):52–59.

Smith, Andrew B.
1983   Prehistoric pastoralism in the southwestern Cape, South Africa. *World Archaeology* 15(1):79–89.

Smith, Bernard
1960   *European vision and the South Pacific 1768–1850: a study in the history of art and ideas.* Oxford University Press, Oxford.

Sollas, William Johnson
1911   *Ancient hunters and their modern representatives.* Macmillan, London.

Solway, Jacqueline S., and Richard B. Lee
1981   *The Kalahari fur trade: San articulation with the world system.* Paper presented at the American Anthropological Association meeting, Los Angeles.

Steward, Julian Haynes
1936   The economic and social basis of primitive bands. In *Essays in anthropology presented to A. L. Kroeber,* edited by Robert H. Lowie, pp. 331–350. University of California Press, Berkeley.
1968   Causal factors and processes in the evolution of pre-farming societies. In *Man the hunter,* edited by Richard B. Lee and Irven DeVore, pp. 321–334. Aldine, Chicago.
1974   *Aboriginal and historic groups of the Ute Indians of Utah: an analysis* (with suppl.) Paper presented before the Indians Claims Commission of the U.S. Department of Justice. 1953. Garland, New York and London.

Thom, Hendrik Bernardus (editor)
  1952   *Journal of Jan van Riebeeck* (Vol. I). Balkema, Capetown, Amsterdam.
  1954   *Journal of Jan van Riebeeck* (Vol. II). Balkema, Capetown, Amsterdam.
  1958   *Journal of Jan van Riebeeck* (Vol. III). Balkema, Capetown, Amsterdam.
Toynbee, Arnold J.
  1934   *A study of history* (Vol. III). Oxford University Press, London.
Trigger, Bruce G.
  1976   *The children of Aataentsic: a history of the Huron people to 1660* (2 vols.). McGill-Queen's University Press, Montreal and London.
  1980   Archaeology and the image of the American Indian. *American Antiquity* 45:662–676.
  1981   Archaeology and the ethnographic present. *Anthropologica* 23(1):3–17.
Willey, Gordon R., and Jeremy A. Sabloff
  1974   *A history of American archaeology.* Thames and Hudson, London.
Wilmsen, Edwin N.
  1983   The ecology of illusion: anthropological foraging in the Kalahari. *Reviews in Anthropology* 10(1):9–20.
Wilson, Edward Osborne
  1978   *On human nature.* Harvard University Press, Cambridge.
Winterhalder, Bruce
  1981   Foraging strategies in the boreal forest: an analysis of Cree hunting and gathering. In *Hunter–gatherer foraging strategies: ethnographic and archaeological analysis,* edited by Bruce Winterhalder and Eric Alden Smith, pp. 66–98. University of Chicago Press, Chicago.
Winterhalder, Bruce, and Eric Alden Smith (editors)
  1981   *Hunter–gatherer foraging strategies: ethnographic and archeological analyses.* University of Chicago Press, Chicago.
Woodburn, James
  1980   Hunters and gatherers today and reconstructions of the past. In *Soviet and Western anthropology,* edited by Ernest Gellner, pp. 95–117. Columbia University Press, New York.
Yellen, John E.
  1976   Settlement patterns of the !Kung: an archaeological perspective. In *Kalahari hunter–gatherers: studies of the !Kung San and their neighbours,* edited by Richard B. Lee and Irven DeVore, pp. 47–72. Harvard University Press, Cambridge and London.
  1977   *Archaeological approaches to the present: models for reconstructing the past.* Academic Press, New York.
Yerbury, J. Colin
  1980   Protohistoric Canadian Athapaskan populations: an ethnohistorical reconstruction. *Arctic Anthropology* XVII(2):17–33.

2

Hunters and History: A Case Study from Western Tasmania

RHYS JONES

Introduction

The concept of hunters as representing a static stage of human society by remaining unchanged in a changing world has a long history. Indeed, it is deeply embedded in the very beginning of prehistoric archaeology as an intellectual discipline.

In the middle of the nineteenth century when it was finally demonstrated that human existence extended back in time on a scale measurable by geological means (Lyell 1863), there was an urgent need to try to understand the nature of the technology, economic life, and even social organization and beliefs of the people who had left behind the broken pieces of pots or flakes of stone in the superimposed layers of earth that archaeologists were only just beginning to find ways to organize into coherent chronological sequences. At the very birth of prehistoric archaeology there was a welding of cultural analogies drawn from contemporary ethnography with the stratigraphic methods of geology.

In Europe in the Middle Ages, artifacts from the past or strange physical anomalies such as glacial erratics were referred to the actions of historically known peoples such as the Romans or ancient Britons dimly perceived through the pages of Tacitus or Pliny or they were seen as the work of supernatural forces of a Merlin or some giant—perhaps a folk memory from a pre-Christian cosmology. Even stone tools were scarcely recognized as such, but were described as "elf stones," the tips of lightning bolts. The discovery of the New World greatly extended the scope for the explanation of the past through analogies derived from observed peoples. Here in the forests of what later became New England or on the cays of Florida and the Outer Antilles were peoples who were almost naked, did not use pottery or metals, and acquired their food not by agriculture but by hunting game or gathering berries and tubers. The customs of some of these peoples, such as the cannibalism practiced by the Caribs and the apparent lack of social organization or government more complex than that of family or band-sized groups, evoked in the minds of late Renaissance scholars, steeped as they were in the classical tradition, Lucretius' early image of the first men: *"Sed nemora, atque cavos monteis sylvasque colebant"* ("But in scrubs, also mountain caves and forests they lived" 1695:Vol. 5, p. 953).

It was partly from the pages of Richard Hakluyt's voyages that Shakespeare's Caliban, "on whose nature, nuture can never stick," had stepped. Very quickly such images were used as a model for the societies that may have lived in distant times in Europe too. Thus John Aubrey, the antiquarian who with Edward Lhuyd and William Stukeley laid the basis for British field archaeology in the seventeenth century, wrote a short essay between 1656 and 1670 entitled "The Olden Time" in which he tried to imagine "what kind of countrie this was in the time of ancient Britons"—the land "a shady dismal wood" of oak trees and the inhabitants speaking Welsh, only "two or three degrees, I suppose less savage than the Americans" (Aubrey 1949; Daniel 1967:37–38). During the eighteenth century the comparison between peoples with simple technology living in the newly discovered worlds and ancient peoples representing earlier stages in the development of more complex societies, such as Europe, became more formal. On the simple technological level, Lhuyd in 1699 argued that stone tools found in Scotland were "just the same chip'd flints the natives of New England head their arrows with at this day" (Gunther 1945:425). More comprehensive was an important strand of French thought, exemplified perhaps in Rousseau's famous *Discourse on the Origin of Inequality among Men* (1754), that whole sets of cultural behavior, including the nature of government, morals, and religious concepts, observable for example in some contemporary Native American societies corresponded to previous phases in the development of more complex ones, a device that Voltaire in a neat reversal used when he criticized his own society through the eyes of an imagined Huron ethnographer. This model of social evolution was thus firmly established in European thought almost a century before Darwin; and in a feedback situation, it was to affect deeply how European navigators and naturalists would perceive the peoples of Oceania and the Pacific, constituting in some ways an "action replay" of the discovery of the Americas (e.g., Burridge 1973; Mulvaney 1971; Smith 1960).

It was however the Darwinian revolution that was to give direct diachronic

substance to this idea. Archaeologists by the 1840s had established by stratigraphic excavations and analyses of museum collections that a chronological
sequence could be built on technological grounds. The most recent peoples
utilized iron tools, those somewhat older used bronze, before that stone
(Thomsen 1848). Later the Stone Age became divided into two phases based
on the presence of pottery (New Stone Age) and the absence of it (Old Stone
Age; Lubbock 1865). It was in the caves and gravel pits of France, Belgium,
and southern Britain that this Old Stone Age (Paleolithic phase) was established to be so ancient that some Stone Age men were contemporary with
now extinct suites of animals and their tools covered by deposits that could
only have been formed under radically different climatic conditions to those
of the present (Frere 1800). Lyell in his *Geological Evidence of the Antiquity
of Man* (1863) produced a coherent and sustained argument that the people
who had made and discarded these stone tools had gained their food exclusively from the products of the chase, and by 1865 in Lubbock's *Prehistoric Times* the Old Stone Age was clearly identified with hunters and
gatherers, the New Stone Age or Neolithic with subsistence agriculture and
pastoralism, and the final metal ages with the beginnings of urban societies.
In a parallel development too complex to detail here, social theorists such as
Tylor (1865) and Morgan (1877) were also classifying ethnographically observed societies into different groups, such as savagery, barbarism, and civilization, based on a number of social criteria, and these were posited to have
had an evolutionary relation to each other, the simplest being the most
ancient and the most complex emerging last.

Thus by the middle to the end of the nineteenth century both cultural
anthropology and prehistoric archaeology shared a major theory that, simply
put, posited human society had evolved from very ancient beginnings, certainly to be measured in terms of at least hundreds of thousands of years, and
these first people lived in a state of savagery, used stone tools, and were
exclusively hunters and gatherers for their food. Later came the stage of
barbarism, of which agriculture and pottery were characteristic. Finally, civilization was associated with the roots of modern societies, that is, increasing
urbanization, metal technology, and social inequality engendered by craft
specialization, priestly cults, and military castes. Such changes had not everywhere in the world proceeded at the same rate, so that there existed societies
in remote places that still exhibited the technology, subsistence mode, and
social organization that in other parts had long since been superseded by
more complex forms. Social evolution was also but part of a general process
of physical evolution, at least in the long span of the stone ages, it being
posited that these changes had partly been brought about by the evolving
physical and intellectual capacity of man.

Australian and Tasmanian Aborigines as Exemplars of Stone Age Man

In the gradual formulation of the theory discussed in the preceding section, ethnographic evidence from Australia, including Tasmania, became increasingly important. Thomas Huxley, making the first professional anatomical inspection of the original Neanderthal skull cap and another Paleolithic skull from Engis Cave, chose to compare them with a series of skulls from southern and western Australia held in the Hunterian Museum. He wanted to look at the range of variation in a single modern race, the Aborigines in his opinion being "probably as pure and homogenous in blood, customs, and language as any race of savages in existence" (quoted in Lyell 1863:67). His conclusion expressed classically the interrelationship perceived between the physical and technological evolution of man. While not saying that the fossil skulls belonged to the same race as the Aborigines, he continued:

> The marked resemblances between the ancient skulls and their modern Australian analogues, however, have a profound interest, when it is recollected that the stone axe is as much the weapon and the implement of the modern as of the ancient savage; that the former turns the bones of the kangaroo and of the emu to the same account as the latter did the bones of the deer and the ursus; that the Australian heaps up the shells of devoured shellfish in mounds which represent the "refuse heaps" or "Kjokkenmodding" of Denmark; and finally, that on the other side of Torres Straits, a race akin to the Australians are among the few people who now build their houses on pile-works, like those of the ancient Swiss lakes. (Quoted in Lyell 1863:69)

What he found the most interesting was that there was

> this amount of resemblance in habit and in the conditions of existence . . . accompanied by as close a resemblance in cranial configuration. (Quoted in Lyell 1863:69)

Tylor, in his *Researches into the Early History of Mankind and the Development of Civilization* (1865:195), also saw an identity of form and function between a Tasmanian stone scraper recently sent to England and one recovered from the Drift (i.e., middle Pleistocene gravels) near Paris. In a nice reversal, it was the descriptions of Spencer and Gillen (1899) of the ceremonial life of the desert Arunta that finally persuaded Cartailhac (1902) of the authenticity of the Paleolithic cave art of the Pyrenees—the argument being that if Stone Age hunters of the extreme harsh wastes of the Australian interior could so brilliantly integrate religion, dance, music, and art, then so too could the flint masters of Paleo-France, an admission of Gallic pride elegantly expressed in his "Mea culpa d'un sceptic." The Aborigines became living exemplars of the Stone Age, the situation being quite precisely stated by Lubbock (1865:416), de Quatrefages (1884), and many others as can be seen in the very title of Tylor's paper "On the Tasmanians as Representatives of

Palaeolithic Man" (1893). Late in his academic life, Tylor was to muse of Australia and Tasmania that

> It is thus becoming clearer and clearer that the anthropology of this remote district can give us clues to the earliest state of civilization of which traces have reached us and which has been thought to be lost in a past of almost incalculable antiquity. Man of the Lower Stone Age ceases to be a creature of philosophical inference, but becomes a known reality. (Tylor 1899:ix)

The fact that corrupt use was then and later made of these theories by evil men in order to justify usurpation of land and even genocide (e.g., Mulvaney 1981:55–57) does not in my view constitute a sufficient criticism of the theories themselves, which when proposed were the honest expression of sincerely held views by people, some of whom were the foremost liberal reformers of their age.[1] The ironic aspect of this stadial view of prehistory was that although it was predicated on the reality of profound changes in human technology and society over time, within each stadium there was also the tendency to regard the situation as static. Thus if living hunters could be studied in order to elucidate the campsite behavior, stone tool use, cave art, territoriality, hunting strategies, or whatever of Paleolithic man, then an unwritten assumption was that the behavior of these hunters and that of their ancestors had remained constant over all the millennia since the time when they were the contemporaries of those Paleolithic people. Even when more finely controlled archaeological work from the days of de Mortillet onward established different phases within the Paleolithic—Lower, Middle, and Upper (and within the latter the Aurignacian, Magdalenian, etc.)—there was a tendency to see each individual phase as a self-contained entity, and different contemporary hunting societies were assigned to the various phases. Thus the Tasmanians were variously seen as living representatives of the putative eolithic man of the Oligocene period—indeed "un grave problem" as Rutot (1907) put it (but not quite as he saw it)—of archaeolithic (or Lower Palaeolithic) culture (Noetling 1908:1–5), or of the Mousterians (Exteens 1911). In Sollas' *Ancient Hunters and Their Modern Representatives* (1911), various hunting cultures were grouped as being comparable with previous stages of the archaeological record, the Tasmanians with the "earliest relics of Palaeolithic man" (p. 91), the Australian Aborigines with the Aurignacian–Gravettian, and the Eskimos with the Magdalenian.

Since the early 1960s there has been a great resurgence of interest in the ecology, social and cognitive anthropology, and prehistory of hunting and gathering societies. This has in many places brought together once more

---

[1]What was called the "eight-hour day" in Australia—eight hours sleep, eight hours work and eight hours play—was for a long time in England referred to as "St Lubbock's Day" after Sir John Lubbock's efforts to product this social reform.

what at least in the British and Australian tradition of anthropology had for the previous 50 years been increasingly disparate disciplines, into a cooperative research effort. Yet within the very title of the book *Man the Hunter* (Lee and DeVore 1968) is there not an assumption being made that somehow we are dealing with a unitary phenomenon the deep structure of which is essentially changeless in space and time, that the range of behavior of modern hunting and gathering societies spans the possibilities of those of the prehistoric past at least of biologically modern man?

Conjectural History

Australia, as the only continent entirely occupied by hunting and gathering societies into the historically recorded period, has a potential key role to play in these investigations. Although studies of Aboriginal ethnography have been carried out since the days of the first European navigators and colonists and the intensive formal anthropological work of the 1880s, investigation of the past of these Aboriginal societies, that is, the prehistory of Australia, has languished until as recently as the 1960s. There were many reasons for this, which I have discussed previously (Jones 1971, 1982). There were the obvious practical difficulties of a landscape generally of subdued relief with little tectonic movement to initiate erosion and with surviving artifacts largely confined to stone tools, which over much of the known prehistoric period have shown little morphological change and thus do not provide a ready means of setting up relative dating sequences based on typological studies. Some people have argued in fact that a systematic program of investigation into the prehistory of Australia would not have been possible without the use of radiocarbon dating methods. While it is true that radiocarbon and other methods of absolute dating have perhaps been integrated into primary archaeological research programs since the early 1960s to a greater extent in Australia and Melanesia than almost anywhere else, I have argued that it would have been possible to erect a coherent prehistory here using the classic older methods of stratigraphy and comparative typology (although the process would have been more time-consuming and much less chronologically precise; Jones 1982). The greater inhibitory factor in my opinion was an intellectual one: The doctrine of Aborigines as static social relics of a previous stage of human society had so imbued the thought of anthropologists in the early part of this century that direct investigation of this Aboriginal past was seen to have been futile. This was expressed by Radcliffe-Brown soon after taking up the Foundation Chair in the University of Sydney in the late 1920s:

> Meanwhile, the scientific study of such peoples as the Australian Aborigines will make little progress until we abandon these attempts at conjectural reconstructions of a past

about which we can obtain no direct knowledge in favour of a systematic study of culture as it exists in the present. (1930:370)

Although this attack was directed against the proponents of the culture cycle school, in particular D. S. Davidson, a sense of pessimism about the possibilities of direct investigation of the past was also more pervasive. This perceived futility of carrying out diachronic research was in the Australian region widespread. It was clearly expressed in a celebrated phrase by the President of the Anthropology Section of the Australian Association for the Advancement of Science at its Hobart, Tasmania meeting in 1929 when discussing the large shell middens in the caves at Rocky Cape in north west Tasmania (which some forty years later became the subject of my own doctoral dissertation) he said that excavation would be useless since everything "points to the conclusion that they [the Tasmanians] were an *unchanging people in an unchanging environment.*" (Pulleine 1929:310). A case study from western Tasmania that proves the falsity of this statement forms the main topic of this chapter.

Western Tasmania

Of all the places encountered during the Age of Discovery, few were more remote and inhospitable than the west coast of Tasmania. Lashed by southerly gales of the Roaring Forties, ships such as those of Tasman in 1642 were wary indeed of this exposed rock-bound coast with the cliffs and forested mountains rising behind it, and they sought refuge in the calmer waters of Storm Bay to the east in the lee of the mountains. Tasman's track was followed by all of the primary British and French explorers of the region, and so while we have some accounts of the Aborigines living on the coastline of southeastern Tasmania, derived from that classic phase of southern Ocean exploration that included the illustrious names of Cook, Bligh, Du Fresne, D'Entrecasteaux, and Baudin, there are none from the west coast itself (Figure 2.1). In 1798, Flinders and Bass were the first Europeans to sail down the entire west coast of Tasmania, but they held well offshore. It was only in 1816, some thirteen years after the initial British settlement in Hobart, that a whaling boat under the command of a colonial sealer James Kelly made a close examination of the coastline and found two huge harbors in this otherwise hostile coast. Kelly and his crew saw Aborigines and the smokes of their fires several times but made no detailed observations. It was the very remoteness of one of these harbors, Macquarie Harbour, that led the British government to install on a small island there in 1822 the most notorious punishment prison of the entire imperial convict system. Felons attempting to escape got lost in the dense rain forest and finding no food there resorted, on at least one occasion, to can-

FIGURE 2.1   Band of Tasmanian Aborigines as depicted by the late eighteenth-century French artist Piron from the expedition led by D'Entrecasteaux that visited Tasmania in 1792–1793. Tasmanian women are shown diving for shellfish, which they place in woven baskets. People are shown sitting on a shell midden. (Labillardière 1800:facing p. 309.)

nibalism, others were reported as choosing by lot to kill one of their number so that all could commit a religiously acceptable form of suicide by being subsequently hanged. It was here that the Aborigines of the west coast first met European civilization. Within twelve years there was not a single Aborigine left living there.

The main agent for this was an unlikely one, namely a dissenter lay preacher and stone builder with a social conscience, G. A. Robinson (Plomley 1966). At a time when elsewhere in Tasmania there was a Government bounty on the head of every Aborigine captured and periodic declarations of martial law, to say nothing of private killings, Robinson with the support of Governor Arthur felt that there was a better and more humane way of dealing with the situation. He proposed visiting the various tribes and through peaceful mediation persuading them to leave their country and accept relocation in a government settlement on one of the Bass Strait islands where they might be taught the three rudiments of civilization: agriculture, English, and Christianity. This scheme was carried out with immense personal heroism on the part of Robinson himself and many of his Aboriginal assistants but resulted ultimately in total failure since of all the Aborigines taken to Wybelanna on Flinders Island and later settlements none survived the famous Truganini in

1876. Unlike some Tasmanian and mainland Australian Aboriginal women who lived with British sealers on the edge of the law on some of the Bass Strait islands, the relocated Aborigines on the mainland left no issue. Even before reaching their final government decreed destination, many of the Aboriginal bands were almost entirely destroyed by European diseases, such as bronchial pneumonia, within days of reaching the Macquarie Harbour prison for transshipment (Robinson 11.8. 1833. in Plomley 1966:780). Yet such was the zealous determination of Robinson, that he did not stop his self-appointed task until every person he could find had been removed from the land, which until only a few years previously had been theirs alone and which even today along a total stretch of 450 km is almost entirely uninhabited.

Robinson with his small party, which included Aborigines, walked along the entire length of this coast on several expeditions between 1829 and 1834, and he was the first European ever to do so; indeed few have done it since. During his expeditions he kept a voluminous journal (Plomley 1966) that is of immense interest because it was one of the very few times in the history of Australian exploration that an ethnographer of sorts carried out a primary exploration on foot, unarmed, with several Aboriginal companions, and with the main aim of contacting the Aborigines of the country to ascertain their names and those of their relatives, to document the names and sizes of local groups found, and to collect other census or locational data of relevance to his final purpose. I say "ethnographer of sorts" because Robinson came from a London-derived, upwardly mobile, working-class background and had received little formal education. The ethnographic skills he did possess were self-taught; he worked in a period before the science of anthropology had developed systematic field techniques, and his knowledge of the west coast Aboriginal language(s) was sketchy, though he probably had a reasonable working knowledge of a pidgin version of the southeastern Aboriginal language spoken by his main Aboriginal companions Woorady and Truganini, who also spoke some Pidgin English (Jones 1974). He of course also had his prejudices, less so in his first trips when he recorded such phenomena as cremation practices and Aboriginal ideas about cosmology fairly dispassionately, but more so later when, perhaps faced with the ultimate moral collapse of this scheme, he hardened an intolerant streak in his fundamentalist Christian attitudes. Nevertheless, it must be remembered that he did spend five years, more or less, in constant contact with Aborigines, either with members of his own party or in the bush, and that he spent in that period about three years actually traveling within what was virtually an unaffected aboriginal landscape. As to his intellectual makeup, he was not entirely naive of the ethnographic method.[2] For example, he records how he had carried with him and read in the wilds of Tasmania a copy of Ellis's *Polynesian*

[2]This has been naively promulgated by White and O'Connell (1982; see Bowdler 1983:139).

Researches (1829), a book he found rather prolix. His dogged perseverence in writing his field diary, day after day and under immensely difficult field and political circumstances, commands respect whatever ones's views are of his motives. He was the first European to travel on the west coast and was the first of his race that many of the Aborigines were to see.

Yet the Aborigines of the west coast had already felt the impact of the European contact, and this has to be taken into account in any historical reconstruction. Seasonal traditional visits by some of the southern bands of the west coast to the government settlement at Bruny Island and to whaling camps on Recherche Bay in the southeast had led to a number of deaths from pneumonia, and it is possible that carriers of the disease could have taken it back to infect other groups (Jones 1974). A pilot station installed at Hells Gates, the narrow mouth of Macquarie Harbour at the time of the convict settlement, had the incidental effect of being strategically placed so that easy seasonal movement up and down the coast was blocked. There is evidence that some prostitution of Aboriginal women had taken place there before 1833 (Robinson 12.7. 1833. in Plomley 1966:753). In 1828 the Van Diemen's Land Company set up one of their main settlements on the north tip of the coast at Cape Grim and from there had outstations with shepherds pasturing sheep on grassy runs several score kilometers to the south. A series of fights resulting in a massacre of substantial parts of an Aboriginal band had occurred just south of Cape Grim a short time before 1830, when Robinson investigated the killings. Perhaps as great an effect had been the indirect one due to sealers, who since 1799 had launched a massive attack on the Bass Strait seal population. By as early as 1815, this prey population had collapsed to such an extent that many of the prominent operators had moved elsewhere, even to sub-Antarctic islands, leaving small parties to clean up the final colonies. Such was the impact of this onslaught that within Robinson's journals there are only about half a dozen direct observations of seals being caught although his Aboriginal companions many times recalled sealing exploits in their camp fire yarning. Archaeological evidence from the most recent middens on the west coast shows that seal was probably the dominant contributor in gross energy to the diet (see for example Jones 1966; Stockton 1983).

In an opposite direction, the west coast Aborigines were in the process of obtaining dogs when Robinson contacted them, although they only had managed to obtain a few, in contrast to the remnants of the eastern Tasmanian bands where there were two or three dogs per person (Jones 1969). It must be remembered that in Tasmania there were no dingoes, this half-domesticated dog having arrived on the Australian continent some 4000 years ago well after the post glacial inundation of Bass Strait. In Tasmania, the Aborigines very quickly realized the value of European dogs as hunting aids in rounding up game, and they eagerly sought them (Jones 1969). Despite all of these factors, many of these changes had taken place within seven or eight years of Robinson's visits, and none were more than thirty years old. With substantial parts of bands still intact, including senior people, the level of folk memory of the Aborigines was high, and much of Robinson's key ecological and sociological information, such as the names, numbers, individual composition, and seasonal movements of bands, was in the form of testimony to him by groups of Aborigines.

Robinson's journals were never published in his own lifetime, and for over a century they were believed to have been lost or nonexistent. The extent of our knowledge of the west coast Aborigines without these journals is starkly exemplified by J. B. Walker's (1898) very brief account of the western "tribes," the useful information in which is limited only to a couple of lines. Robinson's journals were rediscovered in Britain in the late 1930s and brought back to Australia to the Mitchell Library in Sydney after the war; since then they have been meticulously edited by N. J. B. Plomley and were published in 1966. On the basis of information in these journals, together with that from other colonial historical sources, I compiled a synthesis of what was known about the social organization, distribution of people, population estimates and densities, language groups, seasonal movements, and trade of all of the various groups of Tasmanian Aborigines (Jones 1971, 1974). From these accounts I have drawn the following overview of the ecological relations of the Aboriginal people of the western part of Tasmania at the time of European contact.

Tasmanian Social Organization and Territoriality

The basic social unit in Tasmania can be roughly referred to as a band, defined here as a group of people who call themselves by a particular name. Each of these bands owned a territory, the core of which was often associated with a prominent landscape feature such as an estuary or bay, and in the Pidgin English translations available to us, this territory was referred to as the band's country. The basis for such ownership may have been totemic, that is, based on some form of clan, for it was often stated that the core members of a particular band were prominent men "belonging" to that country although the composition of band members who actually foraged together in the field was flexible and often included men who were said to come from other bands. What scraps of evidence we have about the mythological system of these people suggests a broad similarity to that of mainland Australian Aborigines, as in for example their fire myths (Maddock 1970; Milligan 1858:274), and their concept of an original, inchoate state of the world being given animation by ancestral heroes, now fixed in some stars, who named places and gave to species distinctive aspects of their appearance, such as color of feathers or bends in their legs, and who formed mankind (e.g., Robinson 7.7. 1831. in Plomley 1966:373). There are rock carving sites at the mouths of some west coast rivers with pecked designs of circles and other geometric motifs and bird tracks as well as stone arrangements in the form of paths and mazes similar to those of mainland central Australia (Cane 1980; Jones 1965, 1981). Some songs and dances were recorded that related to particular animals. Finally, there are several tantalizing hints that are consistent with some form of a totemic religious system: men being identified as "belonging" to different trees; certain people not being able to eat certain animals; rules of behavior that had to be observed at particular places, such as caves or ochre quarries, lest *Wraggeowrapper* (the "spirit of the dead" as it is stated in the literature) would be disturbed and punish the transgressors; and rites of the disposal of the dead, which include cremation and the carrying of the ashes and other relics in little bags (e.g., Hiatt 1968:217, 1969; Robinson 24.7. 1834. in Plomley 1966:908). It is thus possible that the basis of land ownership was in terms of clans—probably patrilineal ones related totemically to certain places—and that such clan members formed the core of a foraging group, added to on occasions by other people from other clans, thus forming a de facto foraging band. Perhaps it is to such a clan system that one looks for an explanation of the information that is consistently given that such bands were exogamous, that is, the wife married outside her band and joined her husband's band (e.g., Robinson 14.10. 1829, 19 and 20.11. 1830. in Plomley 1966:83, 280; see also Jones 1974:324). As far as one can tell, marriages were not polygamous (e.g., Robinson 27.8. 1832. in Plomley 1966:644) there is no hint of moieties, the men were not circumcised, and although people carried decorative cicatrices cut into their shoulders and upper arms, which were said to be related in some way to band affiliation, there did not seem to be the great rites of passage and involved men's secret ceremonies that were so prominent a feature of the social and religious life of the mainland Aborigines. I once discussed these facts at length with a senior Aboriginal man from the Kimberley region of northwest Australia who said he thought that while the nineteenth-century Tasmanians had an essentially Aboriginal religious culture and that they must have known something of the "dreaming," they did not fully understand the "business" (i.e., the secret high ritual). They were thus in a state similar to that of uninitiated men, lacking what the Gidjingali of Arnhem Land would call, in an outside term, *mindjak* or meat.

It is a speculation worth pursuing further that in Tasmania there was a survival of an early form of the Aboriginal totemic religious system before it became elaborated by new great cults as on the mainland and there was associated with this a simple form of social organization based on what may indeed have been patrilineal exogamous "hordes" (Rose 1960:234–238). A determined effort by social anthropologists and linguists to analyze the available historical data could still increase our understanding of Tasmanian social structure, but the glass is dark and the effort is like trying to investigate the society of the ancient Britons through the eyes of Tacitus.

Observations from French explorers, Labillardière (1800) and Péron (1807), and other sources at the point of first contact with the Aborigines (Plomley 1983) suggest that the size of the bands numbered between say 35 and 40 people, of whom one third would be children. These were organized into separate hearth groups based on an extended family, each usually occupying a separate hut. In descriptions of individual huts there are several accounts that the huts were occupied by about 5–7 people and that the hearth groups numbered about 3–10; these numbers are consistent with such estimates of the size and composition of bands. Plomley has painstakingly collated from Robinson's vast journals and other papers a list of named bands and, after having winnowed out the cases of double names and other false trails, has listed them and mapped their locations (1966:968–976). My own assessment, taking into account a few corrections to these data and areas from which we have little information (such as the Midland Valley, which by the early 1830s was relatively densely settled by British colonists) is that there were some 70–85 such bands in the whole of Tasmania, most of which are shown in Figure 2.2 (Jones 1971, 1974). This would give a total estimate of the population at between 3000 and 5000 people. This is consistent with Plomley's figure of ca. 4000 and is slightly higher than that of observers at the end of the nineteenth century who tended to underestimate the figures partly because of the almost total lack of information about the west and northeast coasts only available to us in Robinson's journals. Radcliffe-Brown (1930) also estimated a lower figure, ca. 2500 people, again because of the same lack of information. It is interesting to note that Robinson himself in a public lecture he gave at Sydney some five years after he left the field in Tasmania estimated that there had been ca. 7000 Aboriginal people in Tasmania (Jones 1974:330). I believe that we have a good estimate of the order of magnitude.

These bands occupied territories, perhaps comparable with Stanner's (1965) "estates," measuring some 500–800 km² in area, and it appears that in the regions where we have reasonably good coverage, such as the northeast of Tasmania, these territories seem to have been reasonably evenly spaced from each other (Figure 2.2). Where estates fronted the coast, they again seemed well spaced, each occupying some 25–35 km of coastline. In the southeast, there is some evidence that the boundaries of these estates may have corresponded roughly with prominent geographic features such as rivers. However in their seasonal movements, bands traveled away from their named estates into the territories of other neighboring bands.

There was in Tasmania also a higher level of social organization associated

FIGURE 2.2 Tasmania: ●, local residence of bands; (●), approximate central locations of band territories; − − −, ─────, boundaries of tribe-sized groupings; ...., prominent tracks through otherwise unoccupied country. (Following Jones 1971:275; 1974:327.)

with a linguistic community. These linguistic units are very difficult to define precisely because of the very paucity of reliable ethnographic and linguistic data. However, in my 1974 paper, I defined a *tribe* as an agglomeration of bands with contiguous estates, the members of which spoke a common language or dialect, shared the same cultural traits such as burial customs, art, and body and hair decoration styles, usually intermarried, had a similar pattern of seasonal movement, and habitually met together for economic and other reasons. The pattern of peaceful relations between bands, such as marriage and trade, tended to be within such a tribal agglomeration and that of hostile ones or war outside it. Such a tribe occupied a territory that was the sum of the estates of its constituent bands. Movements of bands outside this territory and of alien bands within it were carefully sanctioned, often associated with trade of valuables such as ochre or shell necklaces, and timed to take advantage of seasonally abundant foods—trespass being usually a challenge to war. Such seasonal movements often took place along well-marked roads that in their relative location vis-à-vis tribal territories and prominent geographic barriers such as passes tended to give maximum access with minimum trespass. Later reviews have endorsed these definitions (Bowdler 1982:14; Plomley 1983:168–171; Ryan 1981:7–46).

In my analysis of the literature, I believe that one can isolate nine such tribal units and map their territories with a reasonable degree of confidence (Jones 1974; see also Radcliffe-Brown 1930; Walker 1898). There is linguistic evidence of at least 5 languages or major dialects spoken by the Aborigines (Schmidt 1952), some of which were totally unintelligible from each other (e.g., Robinson 21.5. 1831. in Plomley 1966:726). Research by Crowley and Dixon, which utilizes the word fragments from Robinson's diaries (Plomley 1976) as well as the previously known lexica, suggests that there were at least 8 and possibly 12 Tasmanian languages, the phonological system "accord[ing] exactly with the Australian type" (1981:233). Using analogous data from the mainland, such linguistic tribal communities can be estimated usually to number some 350–500 people; so again this gives a rough estimate of about 3000–5000 people for the total Tasmanian population, which is in general accord with the estimate derived from a count of the named bands.

Population Densities

With Tasmania being 65,000 km² in area, with a coastline some 2500 km long, the figure of 4000 people gives an average density for the whole island of 1 person per 15 km² or 0.6 km of coast per person. Such figures are slightly deceptive however, since, as will be shown below, substantial parts of the western interior of Tasmania were not occupied, so that within the inhabited area of some 45,000 km² the average density was about 1 person per 10–12 km². This figure is of the same order as those in comparable ecological and climatic areas of the southeastern part of the Australian mainland (Meggitt 1964). In the tablelands of New South Wales about 20–25 km² sufficed to support a single person (Flood 1980), whereas in the areas of the Gippsland Coast and around Port Phillip Bay in southern Victoria only 4–10 km² per person was needed (Gaughwin 1983:59; Howitt 1904).

In Tasmania, population densities were not the same all over the island; the population of the more fertile coastal ecosystems being comparatively more dense than that of the productive hinterland. There was a tendency for the population of any tribe to remain constant, so that those with a long coastline had relatively small hinterland areas, and conversely those with only seasonal access to the coast had larger inland territories. Thus I plotted for each tribe the area of territory in square kilometers per person (P_a) against length of coast in kilometers per person (P_c) and found even with the limited data that we have available that they had an inverse and roughly linear relation. The approximate empirical formula for population density (P), in kilometers, thus can be expressed as

$$P = \frac{P_a}{20} + \frac{P_c}{2} .$$

That is, for groups with no coastline it took on average 20 km² to support a person, and for those theoretically living entirely off the coast 2 km would be required to support a person. In practice, however, most groups utilized a combination of both resources, which could be predicted reasonably well using the preceding formula (Jones 1977a:361–362).

One can express these relations slightly differently by plotting for each group on one axis of a graph the density in terms of square kilometers per person, and on the other the ratio of the length of coast to area of land of their territories, as has been shown on Figure 2.3. On this I have plotted the Tasmanian figures and compared them with those derived from excellent, direct, modern census material from a variety of linguistic groups (tribes) from central and eastern Arnhem Land, the latter information coming from the work of Hiatt (1965), Meehan (1982), Neville White (personal communication, 1982), and myself. The two curves are similar in shape and when we are dealing with totally inland groups, the Tasmanian figures are within the range of the Arnhem Land ones. This range is explained in that for the inland Arnhem Land groups the population densities varied proportionally to rainfall as predicted by Birdsell (1953). For coastal groups, the Arnhem Land densities are somewhat greater than those of Tasmania, which may reflect the greater productivity of the tropical estuaries than those of Tasmania and the greater range of foods exploited, especially fish. However, the similarities in the curve gives one some confidence that crude though our Tasmanian data may be, they reflect real ecological relations.

The similarities between the population density figures from Tasmania and those from ecologically comparable areas of mainland Australia have important implications in the debate as to whether Australian hunter gatherer population densities were proportional to some function of gross productivity as proposed by Birdsell (1953, 1957) or whether they were a function of some measure of technological capacity or intensification in the social structure (for the debate see Jones 1977b; Lourandos 1980). The technology of the Tasmanians was much simpler with respect to number and elaboration of

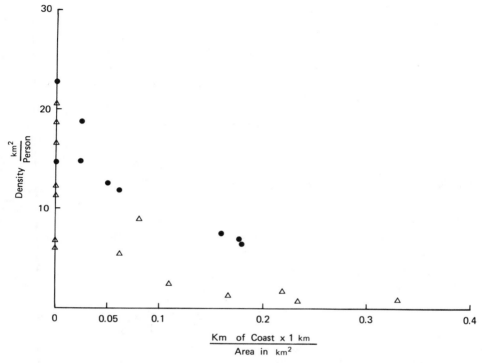

FIGURE 2.3 Population densities of band-sized groups in both Tasmania (●) and Arnhem Land (△), measured in terms of square kilometers needed to support one person plotted against the length of coast per unit area of their respective territories.

tools than that of the neighboring mainlanders, yet it was sufficient to support the same order of population density in similar environments, giving support to Birdsell's ideas about basic ecological relations linking hunters to land (Jones 1977b). Lourandos (1980) denies some of these facts arguing that mainland figures were much higher than Tasmanian ones because of the great extractive capacity of a more complex technology and social system. However, he uses as his yardstick of the mainland, an area—southwestern Victoria—with volcanic soils, steady moderate rainfall, and other factors such as numerous swamps that make it an exceptionally rich region. His claimed population densities from here (i.e., 1–2 people per km²) are also much higher—up to five times higher—than those estimated by officials charged with that task in the 1840's (see Radcliffe-Brown 1930), and they are also higher than population estimates for contiguous areas of southeastern Australia such as Gippsland and the southern New South Wales coast and plains mentioned previously. Either some of the figures are wrong (e.g., see Bar-wick 1983 for a further discussion), or the western Victoria region had an unusually higher population density and should be compared, if we take the Arnhem Land figures, only with those unusually rich and highly localized situations on the floodplain mouths of major rivers (e.g., the Anbarra). Per-haps the only terrain where intensification could take place in the Australian situation was in such wetlands. The debate continues.

The Bands of the West Coast

The west coast of Tasmania measures some 450 km from north to south. It is mostly rocky, with long beaches separated by rocky headlands and offshore reefs and in several parts by steep cliffs. There are only two major indenta-tions, Macquarie Harbour and Port Davey, and there are no large river estu-aries. The sea regime itself is of high energy, with a strong pattern of westerly winds and a swell with a gigantic fetch that reaches back over the wastes of the Southern Ocean to Patagonia. There is a narrow coastal platform a few kilometers wide over much of the coast, but behind this rise rugged moun-tains of Paleozoic rock, which standing square in the track of the oceanic winds receive an annual precipitation of over 2500 mm of rain per year. The coastal plain supports a low heathy vegetation and swamplands, but a short distance inland, this is replaced by dense forests of *Eucalyptus* on the ridge tops and closed-canopy rain forest dominated by the southern beech (*Notho-fagus*) and other trees with circum-Antarctic affinities deep in the valleys. The presence and frequency of fire is an important determinant within this suc-cession; without it the climax vegetation almost everywhere would be rain forest (Jackson 1965).

Along this coast were the estates of at least 12 named bands; those of the northern half of the coast, including those of Hunters Islands, are listed in Table 2.1. These bands probably all spoke a mutually intelligible language, but there is some evidence of dialect differences; so it is probable that there was a dialect chain from one end of the coast to the other (Jones 1974:331). The band estates were all coastal, and in contrast to the eastern half of Tasmania, there were no entirely inland estates. The core areas of these estates were regularly spaced along the coast, and the mean length of coast-line for those of the northern half of the coast for which we have the most precise information was 40 ± 11 km. All of the cultural evidence points to the fact that these people belonged to a single tribal unit, with some differentia-tion into a northwest and a southwest subtribe with somewhat different patterns of seasonal movements. The west coast people could not understand the language of the east coast and in traditional times had no contact with them. However, there was some contact between the Northwest people and

TABLE 2.1

West Coast Aboriginal Bands

Core of band territory	Plomley's number[a]	Name[b]	Coastline (km)
Robbins Island	40a	*Par.Per.Loi.He.Ner*	48
Cape Grim	39a	*Pen.Ne.Muke.Er*	45
Mount Cameron West	38b	*Wob.Ber.Er.Pen.Dur.Rer*	24
West Point	37b	*Pee.Rap.Per*	25
Arthur River	36a	*Mane.Gin*	32
Sandy Cape	35a	*Tar.Kine.Ner*	40
Pieman River	34a	*Loo.Min.De.With.Er.Roke*	56

[a]From Plomley (1966: 971).
[b]Several names often given. See Plomley (1966: 968–1005).

the North tribe, and between the Southwest people and those of Bruny Island and the shores of Storm Bay in the southeast (see Figure 2.2).

To protect themselves from the weather, the west coast people built distinctive dome-shaped houses by sticking into the ground a circle of pliable ti-tree stems (*Leptospermum* sp.) and folding them over and tying or pleating them at the top. This framework was then covered with bark or turf, sealed with vegetation such as moss, and often lined with bird feathers. Measuring some 4 m in diameter and 2.5 m high, with a small 0.8-m high entrance, they were observed to hold about 7 to 10 people each. There are many references in the ethnographies to groups of such huts ranging in number from two to six as villages, and these were said to be the base camps of bands. According to ethnographic observations the floors of these huts were dug into the underlying sand, and the remains of such circular depressions, 3.5–5 m in diameter and grouped together in sets of four or five, are common on the surface of large grass-stabilized shell middens. An open-area excavation of one of a group of three such middens near Sundown Point by Ranson in 1978 showed the structure of a circular hut plan with an annulus of shell discard around a central clear area containing hearths (Ranson 1980). On the surface of two large middens at West Point, a low rocky promontary in the northern part of the west coast, I mapped five and seven such hut depressions respectively, which would indicate a band size of about 50 people. In my excavation of one of these middens, which contained a large number of southern elephant seal bones, other land animals, birds, and shellfish, Coleman (1966) and I calculated that the midden contained the remains of animals that would have provided 3 million kcals of food energy per cubic meter of midden. Given the volume of midden at ca. 1000 m³, there are the remains of enough meat to provide about 70% of daily caloric requirement for 50 people living there for the four or so months of the year indicated by the seasonal indicators once a year for the entire 500 years of the midden deposition, between ca. 1800 and 1300 b.p.

In another study, Stockton (1983) carried out a formal stratified sampling program and calculated the total volume of midden still surviving along a 70-km sector of the coast north of Sandy Cape. Having calibrated for loss of midden due to erosion in measured sand blows and by carbon dating a sample of about 20–30 middens, he established that most were deposited within the past 1000 years. He then used Meehan's estimate (1982) of the volume of shell deposited by the Anbarra community of ca. 35–40 people on the north coast of Arnhem Land during tbe year 1972–1973 when shellfish contributed some 7% of total caloric intake to the diet and established that there is still enough shell midden extant along the northwest coast of Tasmania to account for this rate of shell production per year over this entire period for the same number of bands as was derived from ethnographic sources discussed in the preceding section (Meehan 1982:70). Thus the archaeological data are in accord with the ethnographic ones concerning band sizes, hearth group composition, and indeed general order of population density along the coast in the final phase of Aboriginal occupation.

Technology and Subsistence

The technology on the west coast, as for the rest of Tasmania, was simple. For hunting, men used a single-piece, long, pliable spear sharpened at one end and without hafted tips. The women used a digging stick that could also be used as a club and on the coast as a wedge for removing shellfish. Small game and shellfish were carried in a woven bag made from rushes; they also made a two-ply string from rushes. All stone tools, mostly scrapers and flaked pebble choppers, were hand held. They could carry fire in slow-burning torches but could not make it. For crossing water, they made canoe-shaped rafts by tying together three large rolls of paper and propelled these with a long pole. Items prominent in the technology of southeastern mainland Australia, but absent in the Tasmanian toolkit, included hafted tools of all kinds, edge ground axes, spear throwers, nets, complex woven bags, composite tools, such as barbed spears or mounted adzes, boomerangs, fire sticks, fishhooks, and skin capes. Bone tools of various types had been made in Tasmania in prehistoric times but discontinued after ca. 3000 b.p. (Jones 1971). I have elsewhere characterized the Tasmanian technology as the simplest ever recorded ethnographically (1977b).

With these tools, the west coast Aborigines had a diet based predominantly on exploiting the seashore and the swamps and coastal plains immediately behind. Archaeological sites of the recent past show the great importance of

seal, both fur seal and southern elephant seal, to the diet. These were probably caught by both men and women. It was women's work to dive under the
water to collect shellfish, mostly the abalone (*Notohaliotis*) but also other
rocky coast gastropods, and to catch rock lobsters (Figure 2.1). The men
hunted red-necked wallabies (*Macropus rufogriseus*) and wombats (*Vom-
batus ursinus*). Sea birds such as gulls and cormorants were also caught.
There was a general scarcity of vegetable foods at these temperate latitudes
(Hiatt 1967, 1968), with vegetable carbohydrates being provided by bracken-
fern rhizomes, some orchid bulbs, the heart of tree ferns, and sea kelp
(bashed and braised to make it palatable) (Hiatt 1968; Jones 1971). It is our
opinion that probably less than 30% of the total caloric intake came from
vegetable food, but, at least in the summer season, animal flesh was abundant.
Missing from the dietary inventory were scale fish of all sorts, which were
regarded with abomination (Jones 1978). This proscription existed all over
the island, but archaeological excavations have shown that fish were an
important part of the diet in some sites prior to 3500 years ago (see Jones
1978 for references). Why this happened has been the subject of considerable
speculation that is beyond the scope of this chapter (e.g., Allen 1979; Bowdler
1980; Horton 1979; Thomas 1981; Walters 1981; White and O'Connell 1982),
but I am still of the opinion that no coherent ecological explanation based on
the principles of optimal foraging strategy can be made for it; the explanation
must lie in the realm of culturally proscribed rules of what is defined as food.
Why such rules over such a potentially important class of food should remain
in force over 3000 years is another question, but I have argued that we may
have to look at the effects of isolation on the small Tasmanian community,
separating it from comparative pressures of having coastal neighbors who
were fish eaters and also insulating it from any technical innovations in
fishing technology, which may have been invented by or diffused into communities on the larger social system of the mainland of Australia (Jones 1978).

The available food along the west coast fluctuates greatly according to the
seasons. The winter is the hardest season, and in keeping with Leibig's "law of
the minimum," winter was the time when the bands were spaced at greatest
distances from each other. It was also during winter that shellfish was most
important and an occasional individual young seal was hunted.

With the onset of spring, swans and other birds began laying eggs in the
coastal lagoons and people moved from their winter stations to take advantage of the egging season. Seals congregated at their breeding sites, and,
especially in the case of elephant seals, these breeding and moulting sites
were restricted in number. The large numbers of seals provided a potentially
highly reliable predation target, with successive cohorts of seals—first the
cows to give birth, then young pups, then young moulting adult seals in their
first few years, finally the cows again for their moult—giving an intermittent

sealing season from September or October to early March. Analyses of the growth rings of the seal teeth from West Point show that breeding females and young pups, some foetal, were killed, indicating predation of a breeding colony (S. O'Connor, M. Bryden, and R. Jones, personal communication, 1983). Petrels (*Puffinus tenuirostris*), or mutton birds as they are known in Tasmania, arrive on offshore islands of Tasmania in scores of millions at a highly predictable time in early summer, having returned from a circum-Pacific journey that took them to the Aleutian Islands during the Northern Hemisphere summer, and lay their eggs in the same burrow that they were born in. Chicks are fed during summer and by late March are abandoned by their parents to make the great journey on their own. At that time, the fat young birds with their oily flesh were caught by the Aborigines as they are today by their descendants.

Both seals and mutton birds congregate especially on islands—the Hunters Islands off northwest Tasmania and the Maatsuyker Islands off the southwest tip. Bands used to move along the coast to exploit these resources, crossing the rivers and the dangerous interisland distances of up to 3–5 km using their canoe–rafts. Some bands or parts of them are recorded as having traveled distances of up to 250 km during this summer phase (Jones 1974:336, 1977a). Movement was along the coastline, and extensive firing of the bush was carried out to keep it clear. Such firing has the long-term ecological effect of keeping the vegetation succession at the level of a complex mosaic of heath and scrub, which incidentally has a greater population of marsupials and other game and a greater species diversity of edible plants than the pure rain forest that would eventually replace it if left unburned. During these summer seasonal aggregations, social relations were carried out with other bands. Disputes were settled, fights took place, and trade was transacted. At this time there was also some meeting with bands of other tribes: In the north, people from northern Tasmania would come to the northwest coast with ochre, and in the southwest, west coast bands would travel along the coast and sometimes meet southeastern bands for example from Bruny Island. It must be stressed that all of this movement was linear, the inhabitable country extending inland from the coast only a few kilometers and the only outlet from this coast being by coastal roads along the northwest and southwest corners of it. It was only at these latter points that there was any possibility of contacts with bands of eastern Aborigines.

Savage-Looking Country

The reason for this limitation of contact was geographic. As described previously, a short distance inland from the coast there are the great mountainous walls of western Tasmania. The greatest impediment to travel, however, was not so much the mountains, since there are rivers cutting through them in huge gorges, or the climate, though it is cold and wet, with sleet and snow sometimes even in summer and the number of sunshine hours being the lowest in the whole of Australia, but the vegetation. Choking the valleys and the slopes of the hills is dense, closed-canopy rain forest that constitutes a formidable barrier to any human movement. The major trees are southern beech (*Nothofagus*) and other rain forest species, and there are several species of podocarps, which are similar to pines including the second oldest living trees in the world the Huon pine (*Dacrydium franklinii*). In the understory are tree ferns (*Dicksonia*). It is botanically a primitive forest of liverworts, mosses, ferns, and fungi, with very few flowering plants. The rain forest flourished before the Age of Reptiles and is closely related to the forests of the South Island of New Zealand and of Fuego Patagonia. These similarities are due to the fact that the ancestors of these plants lived when the southern continents still formed a single land mass, and then with the break up of Gondwanaland, more than 100 million years ago, the different continents each took part of the forest with them. In southwest Tasmania conditions have remained wet, so this vegetation has remained relatively unchanged. Elsewhere in Australia, plant forms evolved from these Gondwanic ancestral forms to cope with drought and eventually fire. Fire is the greatest enemy to the southwest Tasmanian rain forest, and with frequent fires, those effective fire weeds—the *Eucalyptus*—move in (Jackson 1965; Jones 1968).

To the hunter in this forest, such botanical thoughts would hardly be uppermost. Because of the lack of decompositors, the peat floor is littered with half-decayed trunks of trees, which fell centuries ago and from which and through which the trees of the present generation grow. Most of the deep valleys have remained unburned for an unknown period, longer than 500 years (Christian and Sharp-Paul 1979:53), a situation unique on the Australian continent. Visibility can be so obscured by vegetation that in places one cannot see another person at a distance of 20 m, and traveling 1 km can take several hours of hard work. The famous "horizontal scrub" forms layers of intertwined boughs, so that one is often walking on a living lattice 5 m above the ground. Except for the raindrops shaking off the canopy, the forest is silent. There is little light and almost no sound of birds. For food for man there is only the heart of the tree fern and some fungi. It is only on the edges of the forest, or where the fall of a massive tree trunk has opened the canopy to the light, that a temporary phase of weeds can support small wallabies or mice.

Jorgen Jorgenson—for a brief while the self-proclaimed King of Iceland, for which he was transported to Tasmania—was a primary explorer for the

Van Diemen's Land Company and in 1827 first encountered the Tasmanian rain forest. In his field journal he wrote:

> Fallen trees in every direction had interrupted our march, and it is a question whether ever human beings either civilised or savage had ever visited this savage looking country. Be this as it may, all about us appeared well calculated to arrest the progress of the traveller, sternly forbidding man to traverse those places which nature had selected for its own silent and awful repose. (Quoted in Binks 1980:75)

Robinson, on one of his journeys along the western coast, decided that he would make a determined effort to enter this country and see whether or not there were any people living there. After a terrible journey, he climbed to a vantage spot near the Arthur Ranges and looked north across the valleys of the Gordon and Franklin rivers. He said that he "saw not the least sign or appearance of natives or of any white man ever being in this part of the country. The natives that accompanied me assured me there was no natives ever went inland" (Quoted in Plomley 1966:128).

It was because of such data that in 1974 on my map of the distribution of Aboriginal bands of Tasmania I labeled the large area encompassed by these western mountains and deep valleys as unoccupied. I believed then that this was a true wilderness. Substantial parts of it have still not been explored on foot by Europeans, and I thought at that time that the canoe journey down the Gordon River in 1958 by Olegas Truchanas was the first crossing of that country from east to west by any human (Angus 1975:14–15) and this was the only part of the Australian continent never to be inhabited by Aborigines.

Expeditions to the Limestone

The Tasmanian Hydro-Electric Commission, wanting to build a highly controversial dam across the Gordon River below its confluence with the Franklin River (an area that in December 1982 was placed on the World Heritage List), used my 1974 map with its designation of the territory in question as unoccupied and stated quite correctly that "There are no known archaeological sites in the project area" (Hydro-Electric Commission [HEC] 1979:80). What they did not add was that no searches had ever been made and that no archaeological component had been included in their environmental survey team. There was in fact some cause for thinking that an archaeological probe could be justified. In 1976, a limestone cave was found in the Florentine Valley, a tributary of the Derwent River on the eastern watershed of Tasmania but still in high rainfall country. Here a few stone tools were found in a breccia deposit initially dated to ca. 12,000 years ago and later corrected to 20,000 years ago (Murray et al. 1980). At about the same time, pollen analytical work being carried out in the central highlands by MacPhail (1975,

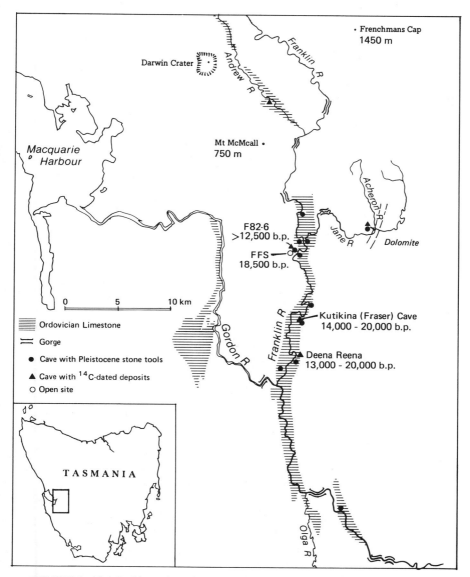

FIGURE 2.4   The Franklin and Gordon rivers of southwestern Tasmania, showing locations of main outcrops of limestone and the distribution of Pleistocene archaeological sites. Where carbon dates are available for the occupation layers, their approximate ages are indicated.

1979)—the first such study attempted—had shown that during the height of the last ice age about 18,000 years ago, the region was vegetated by alpine herb fields similar in some ways to tundra and the rain forest trees were low-lying refugia that only emerged in their present form in the late glacial and early postglacial period beginning some 15,000 years ago. Therefore the present terrain need not represent what this region was like at all times in the past.

With these background considerations, a major factor worth investigating was the 1- to 2-km wide and 40-km long belt of Gordon limestone of Ordovician age that forms the floor of the lower Franklin and middle Gordon river valleys (Figure 2.4). Caves had been discovered in this outcrop in a pioneering expedition organized by the Sydney Speleological Society in 1974, and further expeditions slowly moving higher up river and using rubber dinghies to negotiate various rapids had by 1979 established the existence of about 70 caves in these valleys, most of them in the Franklin (Middleton 1979). Accordingly in January 1981, an expedition jointly organized by the Australian National University and the Tasmanian National Parks Service went to the Gordon River valley and discovered two sites, one an open-terrace site and the other a limestone cave deposit with a few stone tools *in situ*. Three more expeditions were mounted to the Franklin and Gordon rivers in March 1981, 1982, and 1983, and these have resulted in the discovery of 13 limestone archaeological cave sites and two open sites, which together constitute one of the most important provinces in Australian Pleistocene archaeological research (Blain *et al.* 1983; Jones *et al.* 1983; Kiernan *et al.* 1983; Ranson *et al.* 1983).

Men of the Southern Ice Age

Kutikina (formerly Fraser) Cave (F36), in a limestone bluff fronting the Franklin River, has an entrance 12 m wide opening easily into a chamber some 18 m deep and 5 m high. The stalagmite-covered floor is partially eroded, and we carried out a small excavation there (Kiernan *et al.* 1983; Ranson *et al.* 1983) (Figure 2.5). The stratigraphy revealed was complex with a total depth of 1.2 m but can be divided briefly into three main units. The basal unit consisted of alluvial gravels, overlaid by thick sand lenses, the middle part of the deposit consisted of a rubble of angular limestone, and above that the rubble was blackened by charcoal and numerous superimposed *in situ* hearths; the whole deposit was sealed by flowstone. Radiocarbon dates confirmed our field estimate that the rubble dated from the height of the last ice age ca. 18,000 years ago and was formed by ice shattering the roof. The basal date was ca. 19,800 years ago, with the final occupation just under 15,000 years ago, after which the entire floor was covered in calcium

FIGURE 2.5 Interior of F36, Kutikina (Fraser) Cave on the Franklin River, southwest Tasmania. The deposit on the floor of the cave contains rich occupation layers with a top date of ca. 14,500 b.p. and a basal date of ca. 20,000 b.p. (Photograph, Rhys Jones 1982.)

carbonate flowstone. The site was immensely rich, yielding some 70,000 stone artifacts per cubic meter, and in the small excavation of 0.6 m³, there were also some 250,000 bone fragments, more than a third of which were charred or calcined by fire. This was a base camp site as rich as any discovered in Australia and comparable in age and content with some of the classic cave sites of the European Upper Paleolithic.

Some 4 km downstream in another high block of karsitic limestone is Cave F66, Deena-Reena, discovered in 1982, which with almost 700 m of passage is the biggest cave system so far found in the Franklin–Gordon valleys. An entrance 4 m wide opens into a passage 6.5 m high and 40 m long where it joins other passages. At its mouth is a talus 3.5 m high capped with large limestone blocks that overlay a stalagmite capped floor into which natural erosion has cut a gully 3 m deep. In the walls of this gully was a complex section containing stone tools and burned animal bones *in situ*. As at Kutikina, there was a stratigraphic sequence with basal gravels overlaid by a clayey sand, overlain by a rubble, and capped by stalagmites. Most of the charcoal hearths and stone tools were in clayey sand from which radiocarbon dates ranging from ca. 18,000 to ca. 20,500 years ago have been obtained. Further samples still being processed come from a hearth 20 cm below these dates, and stone tools are found 20–30 cm below that. The top date still being processed from a small hearth just underneath the stalagmite has an age of ca. 12,800 b.p. This sequence thus parallels closely that from Cave F36, Kutikina. Another small cave (F82-6) about 8 kms north of Kutikina on the west bank of the river, unnamed as yet, has a top date (which is still being processed) in excess of 12,000 years, and an open site about 200 m away in a river terrace, where stone tools have been found in an iron pan clay, has a date of ca. 18,000 b.p., the first proven Pleistocene open site ever found in Tasmania. In addition to those caves with stone tools already found, there is another dozen or so caves that have a scree-strewn talus on their surfaces, obscuring the underlying deposit.

Even with the limited amount of analytical work having been done, there is a story to tell. At the beginning of the full phase of the last ice age, about 23,000 years ago, the weather began to get sufficiently cold for the polar ice sheets to expand, and the sea level dropped below the 65-m isobath and thus exposed a continuous dry Bassian Plain to Tasmania from the Australian continent (Jones 1977a; see Figure 2.6). Man took this opportunity to expand his range and in the western valleys found great rivers that emanated from glaciers. At the height of the last ice age, say 18,000–17,000 years ago, there were small ice fields on the upper valley slopes and the full wall of the Antarctic ice sheet lay only another 1000 km to the south, indicating that glaciers must have floated north past the Tasmanian coast. The vegetation was dominated on the upper slopes by Alpine herb fields, such as the cushion plant (*Donatia*), and on the richer limestone soils perhaps by grasses. We have no direct evidence of where the rain forest was as yet, but it may have been restricted to its heartland refuges in the ravines and gorges or perhaps out on the now submerged coastal plains to the west. On these relatively open valley flanks, the occupants of the caves hunted predominantly red-necked wallabies, which constituted over 95% of the numbers of animals hunted, and also some wombats. Other species combined, numbered only about 2%. Whether this hunting strategy reflected a high degree of species targeting or whether the range of species on those glacial fields was very much less than in any contemporary ecosystem is a question still to be resolved. Analysis of the age structure of the wallaby population through tooth precession shows the foraging targets to be very similar to that of the West Point midden more than 15,000 years later (K. Geering, personal communication, 1983).

Most stone tools at the basal levels of Kutikina were made from quartzites obtained from river pebbles nearby, and with these the people manufactured nosed and notched scrapers and steep edge scrapers similar to those found at

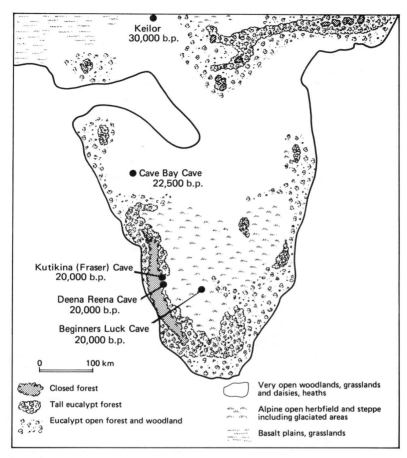

Keilor
30,000 b.p.

● **Cave Bay Cave**
22,500 b.p.

Kutikina (Fraser) Cave
20,000 b.p.

Deena Reena Cave
20,000 b.p.

Beginners Luck Cave
20,000 b.p.

0   100 km

Closed forest

Tall eucalypt forest

Eucalypt open forest and woodland

Very open woodlands, grasslands
and daisies, heaths

Alpine open herbfield and steppe
including glaciated areas

Basalt plains, grasslands

FIGURE 2.6 Environmental reconstruction of the Tasmanian–Bassian peninsula during the
height of the last ice age, ca. 18,000 b.p., showing the location of the main dated archaeological
sites. (Following Kiernan *et al.* 1983:30, and information provided by G. Hope.)

the base of the Rocky Cape sequence in northwest Tasmania, beginning 8,000
years ago and with a direct culture-historical link to the ethnographically
observed Tasmanians. However in the upper levels from about 16,000 or
17,000 to 15,000 years ago there was a great surprise in that, suddenly, the
stone tools consisted almost entirely of tiny, beautifully formed thumbnail
quartz scrapers, some of which were snapped transversely and bore heavy
use-wear edge damage. The assemblage is similar, in many ways, to what was
found in Green Gully near Melbourne (Wright 1970), a site that might have

been contemporary to this Kutikina episode and about 400 km to the north across the dry cold Bassian Plain. What such a sophisticated industry of small tools was doing in the western mountains of the Tasmanian ice age is a question beyond the scope of this chapter. Bone tools (strong points or awls) were made from wallaby fibulae. Similar tools were also found in contemporary, ca. 18,000 years old, deposits in Cave Bay Cave on what is now Hunter Island to the north (Bowdler 1974), and they continued to be made in Tasmania after 8000 years ago as shown in the Rocky Cape sequence, where they disappear at ca. 3,500. No bone tools were used by the ethnographically observed Tasmanians.

In addition to the local raw materials for stone tool making, there was also a small but persistent component of flakes manufactured from Darwin glass, a true glass formed when a meteorite hit the earth's surface and formed a crater some 25 km in a direct line to the northwest of Kutikina. The splash pattern of this glass extends to the west of the crater, so obviously the inhabitants of the cave carried it back there, probably as ready-made flakes. This crater was only discovered by Western science about 8 years ago (Fudali and Ford 1979), but clearly the late Pleistocene hunters of western Tasmania already had an excellent knowledge of the local mineralogy even by 17,000 years ago. Fossils are found in the archaeological layers, which must have been brought in as mementos, and high-quality, heavy, iron ore is found down to the lowest levels, ca. 19,000 years ago. In some caves that members of our team visited, they were the first Europeans even to enter them. Mindful of data recognized from similar primary exploration of some of the inner passages of Pyrenean caves, we were especially on the lookout for parietal art or the evidence of footprints. None were found, and so far there is no evidence that the inner passages beyond the limit of the light were entered by these people (Blain *et al.* 1983:80–81).

At the height of the last ice age, the inhabitants of the Franklin and Gordon valleys were then the most southerly human beings on earth. They alone of our species were witness to life on the edge of the southern ice sheets. It would take another 18,000 years for people to reach comparable conditions in the south in Tierra del Fuego. I have pointed out that the inhabitants of these valleys of southwest Tasmania lived in environmental conditions analogous to those of the Upper Paleolithic hunters of the tundras of northern Eurasia; one hunted red deer, the other red-necked wallaby (Jones 1983; see also Kiernan *et al.* 1983:31).

It is a nice irony, which I only realized as I was writing this chapter, that instead of comparing Paleolithic European man to ethnographic Tasmanians, I had come full circle in comparing Paleolithic Tasmania with Paleolithic Europe.

The Advance of Trees and the Sea

With the warming of the earth's atmosphere and perhaps, at least in Tasmania, with the onset of a wetter climate (MacPhail 1979), conditions were conducive to the spread of the rain forest out of its glacial refuges and onto the slopes of the main valleys of southwestern Tasmania. The archaeological evidence shows that despite the effects of man's fire sticks, which may have served to retard the spread, this occurred in a sense inexorably and by about 12,000–14,000 years ago had blotted out the Franklin Valley as a habitat for human hunters. Occupation of the caves ceased and the deposits became entombed in shiny white flowstone. Nobody entered them for another 12,000 years. Outside in the quiet wet forest, the Franklin became a lost valley of the ice age.

There were other great environmental changes that were profoundly to affect the fate of the Paleo-Tasmanians. The sea level rose and flooding the Bassian Plain, eventually at about 12,000 years ago, separated Tasmania from the mainland from then onwards (Jones 1977a). Higher parts of the plain became islands, and there is good archaeological evidence to show that populations became isolated on them for substantial periods of time. I found a site on King Island (Jones 1979) in the western part of Bass Strait with a radiocarbon date of ca. 7500 b.p., showing that someone was living there about 4000 years after it had become detached from Tasmania. Then this population became locally extinct, leaving a terrain full of food resources, such as seals, but unoccupied by humans when the first European navigators saw it in the latter part of the eighteenth century. I have argued that the size of the population unit so isolated was too small for long-term viability, a circumstance also found in Bassian islands on the eastern parts of the strait in the Kent group and the Furneaux group and on Kangaroo Island off South Australia, which also shared the same fate (Jones 1977a; Lampert 1981; Orchiston and Glenie 1978).

The sea reached the foot of the cliffs of Rocky Cape in northwest Tasmania about 8000 years ago, and people driven back by the rising sea occupied its caves and used them from then until the time that Matthew Flinders sailed his brig just offshore and named the cape. These eight millennia of occupation resulted in the deposition of a total of 7 m of shell midden. In the basal occupation, people seemed to have had an economy almost exclusively based on what they could get in the immediate vicinity of the cave, foraging for food at the edge of the sea and eating predominantly seal, molluscs, and, at that time, also scale fish (Jones 1971, 1978). Later, about 3500 years ago, the cave occupants had stopped eating fish and some 500 years later had stopped making bone tools, and there is evidence that the economy of the people using these caves seasonally became part of a wider articulated system. About 2500 years ago, stone tools were made of materials brought in from 100 km to the west and 30 km to the east, more land animals and particularly birds were eaten, and there is a sense of the hinterland having been used as well as the very edge of the seashore. I have called this the "reestablishment of a regionally co-ordinated economic system" (Jones 1977a:345–347). It is only in this last phase that I saw the archaeological equivalent of the ethnographically observed economic system as outlined in an earlier part of this chapter. Its ramifications can be seen in the integration of the resources of Hunter Island in the period after ca. 2000 b.p. (Bowdler 1982:29–33) and indeed in the fundamental first use of any of the resources of the west coast (Jones 1966; Stockton 1983).

Systematic sampling of west coast middens by Stockton (1983) added to previous work by Jones (1966, 1978, 1981), Vanderwal (1978) and Ranson (1980), shows that no shell middens or indeed any other site older than ca. 4000 b.p. has been found on the actual west coast of Tasmania. Only a few are as old as 2000 years, and the great majority of known shell middens are more recent than 1500 b.p. Along the west coast from 2000 years b.p. onwards one sees many ramifications of what can only be described as the first real utilization of the coast in its present form. Not only do most midden sites only date to ca. 1500–2000 years ago as described previously, but also parts of the region, such as offshore islands, seem for the first time to be occupied and utilized. For example, Vanderwal has shown that the seal colonies of Maatsuyker Island were only first used about 500 or 600 years ago and that the first occupation of the southern coast occurred only ca. 3000 years ago but that the bulk of the evidence dates from much more recently, that is, only 1000 years ago (1978).

Such a new exploitation of the west coast may be attributed to one or all of the several explanations that have been put forward. One of these is that perhaps prior to ca. 2500 years ago, rain forest extended right down to the shoreline and thus blocked travel and prevented any useful economic use of a coastal hinterland. Another explanation is that the distinctive Tasmanian watercraft was invented only about 2000 years ago, and thus for the first time allowing effective crossing of the large river mouths of the west coast and, more importantly access, to the offshore islands in the north and south for the hunting of seals and mutton birds.

Still another theory is that after its postglacial rise, it was only in the past 2000–3000 years that the present coastline has been productive, since it took several thousand years for the litoral ecosystems to adapt to a new level. Proponents of this latter view point to a similar intensification of the use of coastal resources around the Australian mainland at about the same period, Australia and Tasmania being totally isolated culturally from each other at this time. Whatever the reason, the system of hunters linked to land recorded ethnographically, which seemed to have worked like a crystal clock since time immemorial, had on the west coast of Tasmania an antiquity at the very most of only 2500 years and most likely of within the past 1500 years. A great archaeological problem that now faces us is what use if any was made of the coast between ca. 6000–8000 years ago when the sea came up to approximately its present level and the period ca. 2000 years ago when it was utilized in a manner compatible with the ethnographic situation. If people were using the mountains and valleys of ice age Tasmania, why not the coast of the first 4000 years of postglacial stability?

Conclusion

In this chapter I have tried to show how the images drawn from ethnographic sources are deeply embedded in the very origins of Palaolithic archaeology. Often these images are implicit. On a formal level, difficulties may arise because what are being compared are different kinds of data. On the one hand we have observations of the lives and cultures of living peoples and on the other inferences derived from a study of prehistoric material phenomena. Yet contemporary hunters are not static relics from a frozen past; they also have their own past that can be investigated archaeologically.

Tasmania was once seen as the examplar par excellence of the most static and primitive human cultural system to have survived into modern times. Yet the archaeological record investigated since 1981 from western Tasmania shows a dynamic interplay between human societies and great changes in the environment over a period of the past 20,000 years. Rather than comparing horizontally (i.e., using an analogy of behavior drawn from one society and divorced from the historical reasons of why it existed in that society to illuminate some other cultural phenomenon elsewhere), I advocate comparing one history with another history. To return to the central theme of this chapter, rather than comparing the chronologically and ethnographically frozen Tasmania with, for example, a 5000-year time slice of what we call the Magdalenians, I advocate comparing a *history* of the Paleo-Tasmanians over a period of 20,000 years with a *history* of the Upper Paleolithic European people over 20,000 years. In this way, if there are common elements in these histories, they may tell us something fundamental about human behavior.

Acknowledgments

I wish to thank Winifred Mumford, who drew the figures, and Jeanine Mummery, who typed the text.

References

Allen, Harry
1979   Left out in the cold: why the Tasmanians stopped eating fish. *The Artefact* 4:1–10.

Angus, Max
1975   *The world of Olegas Truchanas.* Australian Conservation Foundation, Hawthorn, Victoria.

Aubrey, John
1949   *Brief lives and other selected writings,* edited by Anthony Powell. The Cresset Press, London.

Barwick, Diane E.
1983   *Mapping the past: clan and tribal boundaries of the "Kulin Nation" and their neighbours in Victoria, Australia 1935–1904.* Paper presented at the Third International Conference on Hunters and Gatherers, Werner Reimers Stiftung, Bad Homburg, Germany.

Binks, C. J.
1980   *Explorers of western Tasmania.* Mary Fisher Bookshop, Launceston.

Birdsell, Joseph B.
1953   Some environmental and cultural factors influencing the structuring of Australian Aboriginal populations. *The American Naturalist* 87:171–207.
1957   Some population problems involving Pleistocene man. *Cold Spring Harbor Symposium on Quantitative Biology* 22:47–69.

Blain, Barry, R. Fullager, Don Ranson, Jim Allen, Steve Harris, Rhys Jones, Eric Stadler, Richard Cosgrove, and Greg Middleton
1983   The Australian National University—Tasmanian National Parks and Wildlife Service Archaeological Expedition to the Franklin and Gordon Rivers, 1983: A summary of results. *Australian Archaeology* 16:71–83.

Bowdler, Sandra
1974   Pleistocene date for man in Tasmania. *Nature* 252:697–698.
1980   Fish and culture. *Mankind* 12:334–340.
1982   Prehistoric archaeology in Tasmania. In *Advances in world archaeology* (Vol. 1), edited by Fred Wendorf, pp. 1–49. Academic Press, New York.
1983   A white prehistory. *Australian Archaeology,* 16:134–143.

Burridge, Kenelm
1973   *Encountering Aborigines.* Pergamon Press, New York.

Cane, Scott
1980   *Stone arrangements in Tasmania.* Unpublished M.A. qualifying dissertation, Department of Prehistory and Anthropology, Australian National University, Canberra.

Cartailhac, Emile
1902   ". . . Mea culpa d'un sceptic." *L'Anthropologie* 13:348–354.

Christian, C. S., and Sharp-Paul, A.
1979   Description of the biophysical environment. *Lower Gordon Scientific Survey.* Hydro-Electric Commission, Hobart.

Coleman, Emily
1966   *An analysis of small samples from West Point shell midden.* Unpublished B.A. dissertation, Department of Anthropology, University of Sydney.

Crowley, T., and Dixon, R. M. W.
1981   Tasmanian. In *Handbook of Australian Languages,* (Vol. 2), edited by R. M. W. Dixon and B. J. Blake, pp. 394–421. Australian National University Press, Canberra.

Daniel, Glyn
    1967   *The origins and growth of archaeology.* Penguin Books, Harmondsworth.
de Quatrefages, A.
    1884   *Hommes fossiles et hommes sauvages: etudes d'anthropologie.* Paris.
Ellis, William
    1829   *Polynesian researches during a residence of nearly six years in the South Sea is-*
           lands . . . Dawsons of Pall Mall, London.
Exsteens, M.
    1911   Note sur les instruments de pierre des Tasmaniens eteints. *Bulletin Société An-*
           thropologie, Bruxelles 30:286–288.
Flood, Josephine
    1980   *The moth hunters.* Australian Institute of Aboriginal Studies, Canberra.
Frere, John
    1800   Account of flint weapons discovered at Hoxne in Suffolk. *Archaeologia* 13:204–205.
Fudali, R. F., and Ford, R. J.
    1979   Darwin glass and Darwin crater: a progress report. *Meteoritics* 14:283–296.
Gaughwin, Denise
    1983   *Coastal economics and the Western Port catchment.* Unpublished M.A. dissertation,
           Division of Prehistory, La Trobe University, Melbourne.
Gunther, R. T.
    1945   *Life and letters of Edward Lhuyd.* Oxford University Press, Oxford.
Hiatt, Betty (Meehan)
    1967   The food quest and economy of Tasmanian Aborigines. *Oceania* 38:99–133.
    1968   The food quest and economy of Tasmanian Aborigines. *Oceania* 38:190–219
    1969   Cremation in Aboriginal Australia. *Mankind* 7:104–119.
Hiatt, Lester R.
    1965   *Kinship and conflict: a study of an Aboriginal community in northern Arnhem Land.*
           Australian National University, Canberra.
Horton, David R.
    1979   Tasmanian adaptation. *Mankind* 12:28–34.
Howitt, Alfred William
    1904   *The native tribes of south-east Australia.* Macmillan, London.
Hydro-Electric Commission of Tasmania (HEC)
    1979   *Report on the Gordon River Power Development, Stage Two.* Hydro-Electric Commis-
           sion of Tasmania, Hobart.
Jackson, W. D.
    1965   Vegetation. In *Atlas of Tasmania,* edited by J. L. Davies, pp. 30–37. Lands and Surveys
           Department of Tasmania, Hobart.
Jones, Rhys
    1965   Excavations on a stone arrangement in Tasmania. *Man* 65:78–79.
    1966   A speculative archaeological sequence from north west Tasmania. *Records of the*
           Queen Victoria Museum Launceston 25:1–12.
    1968   The geographical background to the arrival of man in Australia and Tasmania. *Ar-*
           chaeology and Physical Anthropology in Oceania 3:186–215.
    1969   Fire stick farming. *Australian Natural History* 16:224–228.
    1971   The demography of hunters and farmers in Tasmania. In *Aboriginal man and en-*
           vironment in Australia, edited by Derek John Mulvaney and Jack Golson, pp. 271–87.
           Australian National University Press, Canberra.
    1974   Tasmanian Tribes. Appendix to *Aboriginal Tribes of Australia* by Norman B. Tindale,
           pp. 319–354. University of California Press, San Francisco.

1977a   Man as an element of a continental fauna: the case of the sundering of the Bassian bridge. In *Sunda and Sahul: prehistoric studies in Southeast Asia, Melanesia and Australia*, edited by Jim Allen, Jack Golson and Rhys Jones, pp. 317–386. Academic Press, London, New York, San Francisco.

1977b   The Tasmanian paradox. In *Stone Tools as cultural markers: change, evolution and complexity*, edited by Richard V. S. Wright, pp. 189–204. Australian Institute of Aboriginal Studies, Canberra.

1978   Why did the Tasmanians stop eating fish? In *Explorations in ethnoarchaeology*, edited by Richard A. Gould, pp. 11–48. University of New Mexico Press, Santa Fe.

1979   A note on the discovery of stone tools and a stratified prehistoric site on King Island, Bass Strait. *Australian Archaeology* 9:87–93.

1981   Rocky Cape, West Point and Mt. Cameron West, north west Tasmania. In *The heritage of Australia: the illustrated register of the national estate*, pp. 86–90. Macmillan, Melbourne.

1982   Ions and eons: some thoughts on archaeological science and scientific archaeology. In *Archaeometry: an Australian Perspective*, edited by Wallace Ambrose and P. Duerden, pp. 22–35. Department of Prehistory, Research School of Pacific Studies, Australian National University, Canberra.

1983   Standing where they stood. *Hemisphere* 28:58–64.

Jones, Rhys, Don Ranson, Jim Allen, and Kevin Kiernan
1983   The Australian National University—Tasmanian National Parks and Wildlife Service archaeological expedition to the Franklin River, 1982: a summary of results. *Australian Archaeology* 16:57–70.

Kiernan, Kevin, Rhys Jones, and Don Ranson
1983   New evidence from Fraser Cave for glacial age man in south west Tasmania. *Nature* 301:28–32.

Labillardière, Jacques Julian de
1800   *Voyage in search of La Pérouse*. Translated from the French. John Stockdale, London.

Lampert, Ronald, J.
1981   *The great Kartan mystery*. Research School of Pacific Studies, Department of Prehistory, *Terra Australis* 5. Australian National University, Canberra.

Lee, Richard B. and Irven DeVore (editors)
1968   *Man the hunter*. Aldine, Chicago.

Lourandos, Harry
1980   Change or stability? hydraulics, hunter–gatherers and population in temperate Australia. *World Archaeology* 11:245–264.

Lubbock, Sir John
1865   *Pre-historic times as illustrated by ancient remains and the manner and customs of modern savages*. Williams and Norgate, London and Edinburgh.

Lucretius
1695   *De rerum naturae* 6 vols, edited by Thomas Creech. In the Sheldonian Theatre, Oxford.

Lyell, Charles
1863   *The geological evidence of the antiquity of man*. John Murray, London.

MacPhail, Michael K.
1975   Late Pleistocene environments in Tasmania. *Search* 6:295–300.
1979   Vegetation and climate in southern Tasmania since the last glaciation. *Quarternary Research* 11:306–341.

Maddock, Kenneth
1970   Myths of the acquisition of fire in northern and eastern Australia. In *Australian*

Aboriginal Anthropology, edited by Ronald M. Berndt, pp. 174–199. University of Western Australia Press, Perth.

Meehan, Betty
    1982   *Shell bed to shell midden.* Australian Institute of Aboriginal Studies, Canberra.

Meggitt, Mervyn J.
    1964   Indigeneous forms of government among the Australian Aborigines. *Bijdragen tot de Taal, Land en Volkerkunde* 120:163–180.

Middleton, G. J.
    1979   Wilderness Caves: a preliminary survey of the caves of the Gordon–Franklin river system, south-west Tasmania. *Centre for Environmental Studies, Occasional Paper* 11. University of Tasmania, Hobart.

Milligan, J.
    1858   Vocabulary of the dialects of some of the Aboriginal tribes of Tasmania. *Papers and Proceedings of the Royal Society of Tasmania* 3:239–274.

Morgan, Lewis Henry
    1877   *Ancient society; or researches in the lines of human progress from savagery through barbarism to civilization.* Holt, New York.

Mulvaney, Derek John
    1971   Aboriginal social evolution: a retrospective view. In *Aboriginal man and environment in Australia,* edited by Derek John Mulvaney and Jack Golson, pp. 368–380. Australian National University Press, Canberra.
    1981   Gum leaves on the golden bough: Australia's Palaeolithic survivals discovered. In *Antiquity and man: essays in honour of Glyn Daniel,* edited by John D. Evans, Barry Cunliffe, and Colin Renfrew, pp. 52–64. Thames and Hudson, London.

Murray, Peter, Albert Goede, and J. Bada
    1980   Pleistocene human occupation at Beginner's Luck Cave, Florentine Valley, Tasmania. *Archaeology and Physical Anthropology in Oceania* 15:142–152.

Noetling, Fritz
    1908   Notes on the Tasmanian amorpholithes. *Papers and Proceedings of the Royal Society of Tasmania for 1906–7* :1–37.

Orchiston, D. Wayne, and R. C. Glenie
    1978   Residual Holocene populations in Bassiania: Aboriginal man at Palana, Northern Flinders Island. *Australian Archaeology,* 8:127–141.

Péron, Francois
    1807   *Voyage de découvertes aux Terres Australes* (Vol. 1). Primerie Royale, Paris.

Plomley, Norman James Brian
    1966   *Friendly mission: The Tasmanian journals and papers of George Augustus Robinson 1829–1834.* Tasmanian Historical Research Association, Hobart.
    1976   *A word-list of the Tasmanian Aboriginal languages.* The Author, Hobart.
    1983   *The Baudin expedition and the Tasmanian Aborigines 1802.* Blubber Head Press, Hobart.

Pulleine, R. H.
    1929   The Tasmanians and their stone culture. *Report of the Australian Association for the Advancement of Science* 19:294–314.

Radcliffe-Brown, Alfred Reginald
    1930   Former numbers and distribution of the Australian Aborigines. In *Official Year Book of the Commonwealth of Australia* pp. 687–686. Government Printer, Melbourne.

Ranson, Don
    1980   Open area excavation in Australia: a plea for bigger holes. In *Holier than thou: Proceedings of the 1978 Kioloa Conference on Australian Prehistory,* edited by Ian

Johnson, pp. 77–90. Department of Prehistory, Research School of Pacific Studies, Australian National University, Canberra.

Ranson, Don, Jim Allen, and Rhys Jones
  1983   Australia's prehistory uncovered. *Australian Natural History* 21:83–87.

Rose, Frederick G. G.
  1960   *Classification of kin, age structure and marriage amongst the Groote Eylandt Aborigines.* Akademie-Verlag, Berlin.

Rousseau, Jean Jacques
  1754   *Discourse . . . on the origin of the inequality among men, and is it authorized by natural law,* Edited by J. H. Brumfilt and J. C. Hall 1973. J. M. Dent, London.

Rutot, A.
  1907   Un grave probleme. Une industrie humaine datant de l'epoque Oligocene. Comparison des outils avec ceux des Tasmaniens actuels. *Bulletin Socété Belge Géologique* 21:439–482.

Ryan, Lyndall
  1981   *The Aboriginal Tasmanians.* University of Queensland Press, Brisbane.

Schmidt, W.
  1952   *Die Tasmanischen sprachen: quellen, gruppierungen, grammatik, wörterbücher.* Spectrum, Utrecht.

Smith, Bernard
  1960   *European vision and the south Pacific 1768–1850. A study in the history of art and ideas.* Oxford University Press, Oxford.

Sollas, William Johnson
  1911   *Ancient hunters and their modern representatives.* Macmillan, London.

Spencer, W. Baldwin and Frank J. Gillen
  1899   *The native tribes of central Australia.* MacMillan, London.

Stanner, William E. H.
  1965   Aboriginal territorial organisation: estate, range, domain and regime. *Oceania* 36:1–26.

Stockton, Jim
  1983   The prehistoric population of northwest Tasmania. *Australian Archaeology* 17:67–78.

Thomas, Nicholas
  1981   Social theory, ecology and epistemology: theoretical issues in Australian prehistory. *Mankind* 13:165–177.

Thomsen, Christian J.
  1848   Of the different periods to which the heathen antiquities may be referred. In *Guide to Northern Archaeology by the Royal Society of Northern Antiquaries of Copenhagen,* edited for use by English readers of The Earl of Ellesmere, pp. 63–71. James Bain, London and Berling Brothers, Copenhagen.

Tylor, Edward Burnett
  1865   *Researches into the early history of mankind and the development of civilization.* John Murray, London.
  1893   On the Tasmanians as representatives of Palaeolithic man. *Journal of Anthropological Institute of Great Britain and Ireland* 23:141–152.
  1899   Preface. In *Aborigines of Tasmania* (second ed.), edited by Henry Ling Roth, pp. v–ix. F. King & Sons, Halifax, England.

Vanderwal, Ronald L.
  1978   Adaptive technology in southwest Tasmania. *Australian Archaeology* 8:107–127.

Walker, J. Backhouse
    1898   Some notes on the tribal divisions of the Aborigines of Tasmania. *Papers and Proceedings of the Royal Society of Tasmania.* Hobart, 1897:176–187.
Walters, I. N.
    1981   Why the Tasmanians stopped eating fish: a theoretical consideration. *The Artefact* 6:71–77.
White, J. Peter, and James F. O'Connell
    1982   *A Prehistory of Australia, New Guinea and Sahul.* Academic Press, Sydney.
Wright, Richard V. S.
    1970   Flaked stone material from SSW-I. *The Green Gully Burial, Memoirs of the National Museum of Victoria* 30:79–92. Melbourne.

3

Interactions of Past and Present in Arnhem Land, North Australia

CARMEL SCHRIRE

Introduction

A century ago, a scholar asked to picture Australian Aborigines at first contact with the European world might have drawn a great glass bell jar on the very verge of shattering from a massive blow. Through the racing cracks lay a perfect, pastoral scene, with the eternal foragers poised like brilliant butterflies against the trees and meadows. Of course, our Victorian savant knew, as we do, that Southeast Asian visitors had breached the Aboriginal world long before European settlement took place. Yet Western invasion was seen as the paramount force that burst the protective caul and shattered the ancient and timeless Aboriginal world beyond retrieval. The only records of its lengthy existence are the traces we call the archaeological data; the only written accounts come from the earliest explorers and ethnographers, whose first footsteps broke the protective and insulating bell jar. Hence, ethnographic accounts made a bridge between past and present, being a mirror of the timeless past and a yardstick by which to judge the degree of modern dislocation.

The impression of prehistoric stability strongly influences interpretations of Australian prehistory even today. It is often expressed subtly in that authors pay constant lip service to the evidence they do not have about innumerable changes in the past. They speak of perturbations and dislocations but end up concentrating most on the impact of the only major change they can find, namely the rise of the postglacial sea. This transgression changed the coastline of the land, sundered Australia from New Guinea and Tasmania, and altered the environment of the present coastline profoundly. It has acquired a similar status to the disruption caused by European invasion, and nowhere can this be seen more clearly than in White and O'Connell's textbook of Australian prehistory, where two stable periods are separated neatly at 10,000 b.p., when the sea rose (1982:97).

On the other side of the fine line separating past and present lies the body of modern ethnographic data that deals with many aspects of Australian Aboriginal life since European settlement in the late eighteenth century. In contrast to the stability conferred on the millennia of prehistoric existence that we did not record on film and paper, the dynamics of historic time are considered to be exceedingly volatile, produced by European interaction, and of little resemblance to the traditional system. Arguments on this issue have largely focused on aspects of land use (see Lee and DeVore 1968:209–216), while prehistorians have tended to pick over the traces, selecting aspects that fit their particular needs. A startling realization came with the detailed probings of the land rights hearings, when a well-integrated system of land use, management of resources, and personal interchanges was seen operating up north in the modern context, almost regardless of the massive external changes in Aboriginal life.

This chapter uses the concepts outlined above to analyze and review a problem regarding prehistoric land use and management systems in the Alligator Rivers region of north Australia. It examines the notion of prehistoric stability using current evidence of changing land–sea relations as reflected in the geological and archaeological record to show that the man–land interactions observed at first contact with Europeans could not have existed here for more than the past 1000 years. Likewise, it shows that the human ecology of this region has changed markedly as a direct consequence of European settlement, so that modern plant and animal distribution patterns and human responses differ somewhat from those recorded about a century ago. Finally, it brings modern and traditional Aboriginal behavior back into the picture, showing how the indigenous perception of the land as a physical and spiritual entity is reflected in the prehistoric record of human adaptation.

A Problematic Dichotomy

The Alligator Rivers region of western Arnhem Land, which lies about 1300 km south of the equator, is a land of political, topographic, and climatic contrasts. It is made up of three political units. The largest is the Arnhem Land Reserve, lying between the East Alligator River and the Gulf of Carpentaria and owned and managed by Aboriginal people under the mandate of the

Aboriginal Land Rights (Northern Territory) Act of 1976 (henceforth called the Land Rights Act of 1976). Then there is the Kakadu National Park, lying west of the reserve, declared in 1979 and placed on the World Heritage List under the UNESCO convention in 1981. Finally, in both the reserve and the park are excised leases used for cattle raising, scientific research, and uranium mining (Figure 3.1).

Topographically, the region is divided into a plateau and adjacent plain separated by the ecotone of the Arnhem Land escarpment. The plateau is wild, rugged, and faulted. Rivers originate here, flowing through rocky defiles and over cliffs until they reach the low-lying plain. Much of the plateau is bare, with patches of spinifex and grasses on occasional sandy exposures, but there are also broad valleys carved through the rocks, where trees and shrubs grow in deeper soils, fed by seasonal streams. The edge of the plateau is marked by the escarpment, a dramatic series of buttresses that rise 25–250 m above the plain, with sandstone cliffs glowing like ochred battlements at dawn and dusk. Innumerable caves, shelters, and overhangs here house the imprint of prehistoric occupation in stratified floors and rock paintings. The retreat of this scarp to its present position is marked by a series of outliers scattered over the plain. The plain itself comprises foothills, lowlands, and alluvial and coastal elements. The coastal element, a "legacy of postglacial shoreline progradation" (Clarke *et al.* 1979:92), is made up largely of estuarine sediments laid down in drowned river valleys after the sea reached its present level 6000 years ago. Vegetation here is closely related to elevation and drainage. *Eucalyptus,* monsoon forest patches, and grasses grow on hills and along the edge of the wetlands, while paperbark trees (*Melaleuca* spp.), waterplants, and reeds throng the freshwater floodplain. Estuarine conditions extend inland, sometimes up to 50 km upriver, due to a combination of high tides and low relief.

These topographic contrasts are echoed in the faunal distributions. A wide variety of terrestrial forms is found, and the native mammal suite of marsupials, rodents, and bats is the richest in terms of the number of species known so far for any region in Australia. The floodplain and estuaries sport a rich and varied fauna including crocodiles, turtles, tortoises and goannas, water snakes, fish, and waterfowl. Insects abound, as do molluscs, with freshwater mussels being popular throughout the wetlands and estuarine forms concentrating in mudflats and mangrove thickets.

The physical variations are mirrored in the strong seasonality of this sub-humid savanna environment. There are high average annual temperatures and a high-intensity seasonal rainfall. Northwest monsoon winds and cyclones bring summer rain (up to about 1300 mm) between November and March, and the southeast tradewinds blow during the dry season from April to September. Rivers are full and the plain is flooded at the peak of the wet

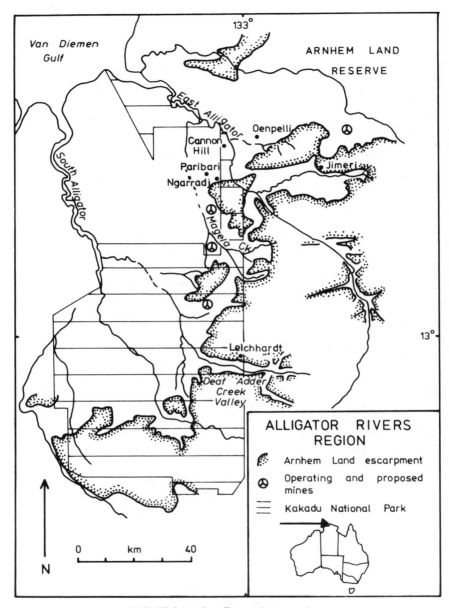

FIGURE 3.1 The Alligator Rivers region.

season, whereas swamps drain and shrink to dusty wastes as the dry season takes its toll. Today, as in the past, natural fires are most prevalent at the end of the dry season when lightning storms herald the monsoons. Obviously, the observed Aboriginal fire regime, which lasts from May to December, has a far greater impact on the land than do natural fires. Some authors (Haynes 1978, 1982; Jones 1969, 1980) assume that this type of regime prevailed in the past and was therefore a profound determinant of the present landscape. Others (e.g., Clark 1983:32) argue that fire frequency must have been lower in the past to produce the current structure. Today Aboriginal people recognize the details and intricacies of seasonal changes and divide the year into seasons according to rain, heat, winds, flowering plants, availability of animals, and grass fires in a system that betrays great familiarity and closeness to their land (Chaloupka 1981; Jones 1980).

Archaeological research here always tended to rely on local traditional owners to help locate sites and, to a greater or lesser degree, to condone their excavation. The earliest work was that of the 1948 joint American–Australian Scientific Expedition to Arnhem Land, whose efforts were concentrated on excavating sites overlooking Oenpelli (McCarthy and Setzler 1960). In 1964–1965, I excavated two series of shelters, one on the plain near the East Alligator River and another in a broad plateau valley southeast of Oenpelli (Schrire 1982; White 1967a, b, c, 1971; White and Peterson 1969). In 1973 a regional survey of 120 sites in the Kakadu Park region lying east of the East Alligator River was undertaken as part of a wider environmental fact-finding program (Barton 1979; Kamminga and Allen 1973). The latest survey and excavations were carried out from 1980 to 1981 as part of the process involved in establishing the Kakadu National Park (Kakadu Archaeological Working Group 1980) (see Figure 3.1).

Prehistoric sequences show that people reached this region at least 24,000 years ago. Other Australian evidence suggests that the continent was occupied for almost twice as long (Pearce and Barbetti 1981). Around this time, the last ice age was in play, and its lowered seas exposed a land bridge extending from Arnhem Land to the mountain chain of New Guinea. The plain was dryer then than it is today, and it was probably cut by deep river channels. When the grip of glaciation relaxed and the sea rose to its present level about 6000 years ago, the landscape was transformed as the Holocene plain was created (Chappell *et al.* 1982; Jones and Bowler 1980:14). The land–sea gradient here is so slight that the lateral transgression was rapid, with saltwater moving inland at a rate of several hundred meters per year (Schrire 1982:9; J. Chappell, personal communication). In a single lifetime, people must have seen their former estates disappear beneath the waves. Old river beds were filled with estuarine clays, and saline swamps spread across the plains bringing vast estuarine foraging grounds to the inhabitants (Allen 1977, 1978). At the same time, clay, mud, and sand were washed down to block some outlets to the sea. The interplay of these processes created a variety of different environments, with the most important shift being a succession from estuarine flats to the freshwater swamps we find today. One has therefore to regard the plain as a labile ecosystem within which foraging strategies shifted and adapted through time.

Remains older than 6000 years are very scant, comprising mainly fragments of former hearths and associated stone tools. We have no direct indication of how people looked or what they ate. The only items that betray their origins are numerous edge-ground axes, the chief parallels of which to date occur in Japan (Oda and Keally 1973). In contrast to this, some sites dated from 6000 years ago onward register the human perception of the arrival of estuarine conditions in the vicinity. They contain dense middens made up principally of mangrove–mudflat shells, which changed the pH of the otherwise slightly acidic soils and buffered finer elements against decay. Thus plains sites contain a rich record of the organic component of human behavior, which allows us to elaborate on the diet and culture of prehistoric foragers.

One problem we are concerned with here involves a distinction between plain and plateau sites occupied after about 6000 years ago. Plain sites contain abundant organic remains such as shells but very few stone tools, which though highly characteristic in form were apparently made elsewhere. Despite the fact that they sometimes lie only 20 km away from plains sites, plateau valley sites such as those at Jimeri and the Leichhardt site have no organic remains other than charcoal but abundant evidence of stone tool making that produced scores of the same tool types lying so sparsely in the plains sites. The absence of organic remains in the plateau sites is easily explained in that they have been destroyed by slightly acid groundwater moving through a coarse, sandy matrix. Such considerations do not, however, apply to stone artifacts, the differential distribution of which through plateau and plain therefore constitutes an important cultural issue.

From 1964 to 1965, my field crew and I questioned local site owners carefully about site use in the past. Previous expeditions had been told that people used the shelters near Oenpelli as refuges in the wet season, and that the mangrove snails there had been gathered on the East Alligator River (McCarthy and Setzler 1960:270). Our informants gave the same reply at first, but when we pointed out the rarity if not total absence of mangrove–mudflat habitats in the vicinity today, they deferred, insisting that the shells had been washed into the shelters by a catastrophe, specifically, Noah's flood. They were less equivocal about stone tools, however, and maintained the same stance for two years, saying that the patterns of differential stone working on plain and plateau sites reflected the presence of two technologically different tribes. Stone tool makers lived on the plateau and traded their wares to shell and bone tool makers living on the plains. This accounted for the presence of stone points and scrapers in plains sites and provided a framework for interpreting cultural and environmental variations across the escarpment.

This dichotomy has been explored repeatedly since 1964, and the changing interpretations reflect how scholars have gradually widened their view of the ecology of local hunter gatherers beyond mere technological concerns. The impact of social, political, and ecological changes on Aboriginal demography and foraging patterns takes us beyond the bones and stones of the past into present concerns. Thus, the background for understanding Arnhem Land prehistory now demands an outline of regional history and ethnography to set the stage for our observations and inferences about Aboriginal hunter gatherers.

The Documentary Sources

Written accounts of Aboriginal land use and resource management in Arnhem Land go back over 300 years and range from mere sightings of smoke to detailed accounts of foraging behavior and ceremonial matters. Most records describe indigenous efforts to cope with problems that arose from European invasion, the devastation of new diseases, the environmental impact of feral animals, and the social consequences of sudden depopulation and loss of political power. Archaeologists tend to try to separate traditional aspects of behavior from those that seem to have arisen as a direct consequence of European contact in order to create useful models of past behavior. There is considerable merit in this exercise, although two aspects of this particular study suggest that it should not be the chief preoccupation in using ethnohistoric records. First, it forces prehistorians to be overly particularistic, insisting that endemic diseases or environmental degradation were peculiar to the postcontact scene, whereas similar pressures might well have evoked responses in the past. Second, our latest documentary sources, the massive claim books prepared under the aegis of the Land Rights Act of 1976, show a stronger persistence in the Northern Territory of traditional links with the land and with the past. These links are so pervasive that they override the outward impression that contact has destroyed all aspects of life as witnessed in the past century. They suggest that Aboriginal identity is strong but subtle and that modern testimony about traditional land use systems has to be treated carefully and analytically in order to derive the richest possible impression of forager behavior.

The earliest known visitors to the north coast of Australia were Southeast Asian trepangers, who sailed here on the northwest monsoon and spent the wet season camped on the beach to process their catch (MacKnight 1976). Up to 1500 "Macassan" men are thought to have visited the shores each year, and their effect on Aborigines is seen in trade, genetics, rituals, and language (Berndt and Berndt 1954; Kirk 1971; MacKnight 1969, 1976; Thomson 1949; Urry and Walsh 1981). Written accounts of the Aborigines themselves begin with scrappy sightings by early Dutch explorers from 1623 to 1644 and go on to accounts by British navigators such as Matthew Flinders at the turn of the nineteenth century. More detail emerges between 1824 and 1849 when the British established a series of outposts on this southern rim of their Asian interests with an eye to colonizing the whole north coast (Allen 1980). Stockades rose up, only to be abandoned as Royal Marines succumbed to the tropics. The last outpost at Victoria on Port Essington was following this pattern when, late in 1845, a meticulous diarist crossed the plain at the end of a two-year trek from Brisbane: He was Ludwig Leichhardt, a master explorer who would later be immortalized by Patrick White as "Voss." With his customary angst quieted by the joy of witnessing the original Noble Savage at first hand, he breasted the cliffs of the South Alligator River near Jim Jim Falls and saw people fishing, fowling, hunting, and harvesting amid the smoke and dust that wreathed the shrunken swamps. The annual magpie goose hunt was on, revealing a strong division of labor. Men speared *Anseranas semipalmata* with multipronged bone-tipped spears launched from flat spear-throwers or *wommelas*. Women gathered shellfish near the coast, harvested fruits and cabbage palms, and dug for tubers in the hot sun. Both sexes uprooted the sweet rhizomes of the spike rush (*Eleocharis dulcis*) in the dried hearts of former swamps. Paths crisscrossed the region, leading from one resource to another and epitomizing the strategies that promoted a varied diet (Leichhardt 1847:504–505). A particularly revealing section of the account shows the kind of compromises that people were willing to make to achieve their ends. Surface water was scarce at that time, yet some chose to camp atop a hill away from mosquitos and were willing to carry their water uphill in small wooden basins to do so (Leichhardt 1847:506). Others chose to camp near shellfish beds, even though it meant painfully gouging a succession of wells in the hard clay to get enough water there (Leichhardt 1847:504–505, n.d.a:414, n.d.b:35). Though Leichhardt was not looking for anomalies in land use, he certainly noted the total absence of people in the rocky plateau as opposed to the densely settled plains, where groups of 200 people were seen at one time. He assumed that people lived on the plain all year round, because he saw sapling and bark huts near the coast that seemed to be awaiting occupancy once the rains started in earnest (Leichhardt 1847:495–496, 526–527). This might be a reflection of postcontact habits, associated with a desire to camp near sources of iron and cloth. These objects were widespread when Leichhardt crossed the plain, and a few words of English had penetrated even to the foothills of the plateau by then (Leichhardt 1847:502).

Shortly hereafter, in 1849, Victoria was abandoned and two processes ensued. First, Asian water buffalos freed from their stockades fanned out over the plains to begin a course of environmental degradation the severity of which has only recently been realized. Second, with the last of these British outposts came a new era of colonialism as the Australian government turned its attention away from Asia and toward the north. A strong wave of ill will emanated from the South Australian outpost at Escape Cliffs near Darwin and infiltrated the Alligator plains. Only two decades after Leichhardt was met with smiles, shrieks and spears greeted McKinlay when he struggled through the swamps of Cannon Hill in 1866 (Hill 1951:84; McKinlay 1866; South Australian Parliamentary Papers [SAAP] 1867). Later, hostilities grew as when John Lewis phlegmatically shot down scores of Aboriginal spearmen as he crossed the East Alligator River in 1874 (Lewis 1922:141–143).

By the time Paddy Cahill, a buffalo shooter, established a station next to the permanent lake at Oenpelli around the turn of the century, things seemed to have quieted down. Numerous groups swarmed in from the east for the food, tobacco, and medicine doled out each day. The local people seemed subdued, except for what Cahill called an "astonishing" incident, when, in a singular expression of Aboriginal feeling about loss of land and authority, Cahill's most trusted helper tried to murder him and his family with strychnine (Cahill n.d.:10.10. 1917, 20.6. 1918). It was to Cahill's "paradise" that Baldwin Spencer, professor of zoology turned anthropologist, came in 1912 to record the customs and ceremonies of what he believed were rapidly disappearing groups of local people. Spencer would later become "Protector of Aborigines" and set up the Arnhem Land Reserve to enclose the endangered folk, but for now he was after what he feared was a dwindling Aboriginal culture. This Cahill provided for him, until Spencer sighed with relief for a day's rest (Spencer 1914, 1928). Yet his fears for the local people seemed justified, because contact with buffalo shooters and gold miners brought smallpox, venereal diseases, and leprosy, the spread of which was enhanced by people living in large, settled groups (Cook 1966; Hargrave 1983). All visitors documented the toll in mournful detail as the locals became infertile and died young (Cahill n.d.).

The Arnhem Land Reserve was gazetted in 1920, and a mission was established on its eastern border, at Oenpelli, in 1925 (Cole 1975). It became a focal point for Aborigines traveling to work on small cattle stations, buffalo shooting camps, and towns farther afield (Levitus 1982). When heads were counted as part of the investigations of the Land Rights Act of 1976, processes observed in the past had been almost concluded. Many traditional owners still retained detailed and coherent memories of their lands and their resources, providing insights into the way they were used when these adults were children. Today, many such individuals have been incorporated into the staff of the Kakadu National Park to serve as rangers, in a land where buffalo herds graze on the shimmering plain and uranium mines release radon gas into the air and mirror the sacred cliffs of Mount Brockman in their toxic and leaking retention ponds.

We can discern three threads in the ethnographic accounts of Aboriginal land use that interact to produce certain aspects of behavior witnessed today as well as to provide a basis from which prehistoric patterns might be inferred. They concern seasonal patterns of foraging, demographic shifts, and changes in ecosystem productivity and diversity.

Starting with foraging patterns, all reports confirm the marked response to seasonal gluts, such as the abundance of geese in the dry and goose eggs in the late wet season. Spencer described a generalized round, with people moving in small groups across the plains in search of local flushes of food, from lakeside to hillside to escape mosquitos at night, and from one side of the hill to another to avoid the squalls of the wet season (Spencer 1914:31–32, 1928:744–745, 823–824). Spencer was only at Oenpelli during the dry season, but he obviously drew heavily on Cahill for the action he missed (Cahill n.d.). The only seasonal movements Cahill actually observed were those made by people living on his station, who depended heavily on their daily ration of food and medicine. For the record, neither Cahill nor Spencer recorded patterns of fire management.

Things become somewhat more complicated as we move to the nature of actual land-owning groups. Most of our information comes from the detailed and painstaking research that was done in connection with the demands of the Land Rights Act of 1976, which sought to define such groups, to explain how they worked, and to identify their present living members (see Fox *et al.* 1977; Keen 1980; Northern Land Council [NLC] 1980). Today, as in the recalled past, there were two different types of land-owning groups in the Alligator Rivers region. For the most part, the land-owning group is called the *gunmogurrgurr,* which translates as "clan," and its members are drawn from one or more patrilineages and have common rights on a contiguous area of land that includes a set of dreaming sites (NLC 1980:71). In the east, language and clan are not synonymous. Several clans might speak the same shared language, and within a clan, members may speak different languages. Thus identifying oneself according to the language spoken may be misleading as far as land and site ownership are concerned. In contrast, west of the South Alligator River land ownership apparently *did* reside in a language group containing one or more lineages.

This rather mechanistic view is moderated by showing how sites and resources were used. The clans were and still are, exogamous entities. People maintained links with other clans through marriage and the fact that men often spoke their mothers' tongue. Clans met to share ceremonies and to trade in items such as ochre, stone blades, and spears, and one clan might assume responsibility for the land and sites in another area should the need arise. In other words, though norms were defined, they could be bent to facilitate cooperation and interaction in a highly diverse and labile ecosystem. There were no rigid rules to threaten the viability of small clans; instead there were mechanisms to ensure affiliation of more than one group per person. Likewise ties of marriage, customs, ceremonies, language, and trade ensured widespread access to scarce resources, maximizing the material and spiritual diversity of small groups. According to Altman (1980:91), the long tenure of Aborigines in North Australia proves that their economic system worked efficiently, "proof" being simply a reiteration of the concept of prehistoric stability mentioned at the outset of this essay. Perhaps a more interesting inference concerns the apparent effectiveness of the Aboriginal land-use system in coping with perturbations. In what appears to be the greatest stress Aborigines have ever known—the dislocation of their lives and radical depopulation of their land as a direct consequence of European invasion—the strength of their traditional land-use system emerges as a key to maintaining spiritual identity and links to the land while the impact of contact took its dreadful toll.

This toll, in point of fact, has been measured.[1] Processes of disease and depopulation observed by Cahill (n.d.) and Spencer (1914) 70 years ago moved inexorably toward the present situation, where Keen estimates a reduction to a mere 3–4% of the population observed at first contact (Keen 1980:171–172; NLC 1980:35–44). Similarly, in other parts of Arnhem Land today, where disease has not ravaged the population, the average land-owning group numbers 38 individuals as opposed to 5 in the Alligator Rivers region (Keen 1980:172). Most of the people living in the Alligator Rivers region today are immigrants who are recorded as moving from the south and east to European stations since the turn of the century. Their perceptions of prehistoric land use in this particular region are often much less detailed than those of the few remaining traditional owners.

Finally, there is a process involving reduction of species diversity and of overall biomass in the region. Cahill observed that game was sharply reduced around Oenpelli due to indiscriminate use of guns by people operating intensively around this permanent settlement (Cahill n.d.:9.10. 1913). The spread of feral buffalos and pigs is documented not only in head counts but also in the corresponding decline of indigenous plants and their dependent animals (Ford and Tulloch 1977; Letts 1979; Warburton 1934). Despite cull-

[1]The situation in Victoria and New South Wales has been reassessed in a study that argues that precontact populations may have been considerably larger than conventional sources suggest (Butlin 1983).

ing, herds whose ancestors were released to graze only 150 years ago numbered upwards of 200,000 head in the 1970s (McKnight 1971:760, 1976:83, Stocker 1971). Their spectacular ecological success is due in large part to their appetite for water plants like *Hymenachne,* which once formed a floating carpet beneath which crocodiles nested and on which birds, and even humans, could walk to the water's edge. Its removal has significantly encouraged soil erosion by water and wind. Continued grazing and trampling has stripped the land of less-favored vegetation too. Today, the net effect emphasizes the impact of seasonality. Floods of the wet season bring swirling lakes to the foot of the outliers and sheet erosion to the soil. The late dry season reveals endless stretches of hoof-pitted plains covered with smoke from the last grass fires set by the Aborigines as part of their seasonal regime (Haynes 1982; Jones 1969, 1975, 1980).

One might argue that the factors outlined in the preceding pages simply show the present overlaying the past, with social and ecological consequences of European invasion neatly superimposed on traditional patterns such as seasonal transhumance and firing of the bush, but it is nowhere near as straightforward as this, as the impact of Aboriginal firing of the bush so aptly illustrates. There is a popular tendency to project current burning patterns backward in time in order to reconstruct prehistoric human resource management (Australian National Parks and Wildlife Service [ANPWS] 1980:193; Hallam 1975; Haynes 1978, 1982; Jones 1975, 1980; Lewis 1982). In contrast, an analysis of the Alligator Rivers vegetation suggests that prehistoric fires were less intense than modern ones (Clark 1983). Yet we should not automatically conclude that Aborigines burned differently in the past, or that they burned less or over smaller areas, because their modern fires burn in a buffalo-impacted landscape and therefore have a different impact from those that smouldered before the introduction of feral buffaloes and pigs (see Schrire 1982:16). In short, the synergistic effect of feral depredation and fires is probably unique since about 1950, underscoring the difficulties of using the present to create the past. The following analyses show how each archaeological inference demands careful scrutiny to avoid unwittingly transposing the altered present back into the past.

The Archaeological Sources

The first effort to reconstruct the past was based on the 1948 excavations in shelters on two hills flanking Oenpelli (McCarthy and Setzler 1960). The work was dispatched with such vigor that gas masks were needed to cope with the dust. In the rush, the excavators ignored all food debris, including the shells that littered the floors, and concentrated on finished stone tools.

They interpreted five different tool types as reflecting successive waves of prehistoric immigration into Australia. Thus Oenpelli became the Les Eyzies of the Antipodes, a cultural meeting place from which colonists spread forth.

I first tried to synthesize the Aboriginal past in 1967 in an analysis of material from a dry cave called Paribari that stands high on an outlier on the plain (White 1967b). A shallow, dusty deposit accumulated there over about 3500 years and protected recesses and niches in the rock wall were stuffed with straw, leaves, and paperbark that cushioned shells, bones, and eggshell as well as smashed and ochred human bones. Tools of shell, wood, bone, and stone lay associated with their manufacturing debris, such as wood shavings and occasional waste flakes. The assemblage correlated almost perfectly with the lists that Spencer drew up in 1912 for the local Kakadu people (Spencer 1928), including wooden fire sticks, message sticks, woven baskets, spear-throwers knobbed with wooden prongs set in beeswax, and trident fish spears tipped with bone bipoints. His observation that they seldom used stone tools but cut and scraped with shell instead (1928:774), was confirmed by finding very few stone tools as opposed to numerous mangrove clam shells with chipped and use-polished edges. Stone tools included small, finely worked unifacial and bifacial points, scrapers, and flakes with use polish on their sharp edges and mastic on the blunt ones. Very few associated waste flakes suggested that these tools were generally made elsewhere and carried into Paribari for refurbishing, use, or discard. Spencer (1928:821–823) acknowledged that the Kakadu had stone blades, which had been traded from afar, and that they also had the occasional stone ax but observed their increasing enthusiasm for iron. This was confirmed at Paribari in the summer of 1982 when, revisiting the cave, I stuck my hand into a recess in its darker depths and found a rusty, iron spearhead that no one had come to reclaim.

In 1967, I was bolstered by Aboriginal informants' confirmation of Spencer's data and saw this assemblage as reflecting an unchanging cultural presence in this area. I published a paper entitled "The Prehistory of the Kakadu People" in which additional data were incorporated to suggest a continuous presence of shell-using, non–stone tool making people in the region since the registration of estuarine conditions 6000 years ago (White 1967a, b). Continuity was inferred from material objects, such as stone tools and bone points, that seemed to occur throughout the middens and that were also documented to have been made and used by local Aboriginal people early this century. On a more subliminal level, I began to infer other aspects of continuity in the use of shelters to store bark-wrapped bones, axes, and spearheads pending later retrieval. The central assumption, therefore, was that distinct groups of people had operated in different environments under stable conditions for 6000 years. It was this concept that needed closer scrutiny.

In 1969, Peterson and I presented a new synthesis based on a broader view of documentary sources relating to foraging along an ecotone in a region of high seasonality (White and Peterson 1969). We started out with two propositions. First, we reviewed a number of accounts of Aboriginal behavior and settlement patterns made by early observers in and around Oenpelli, as well as other parts of Arnhem Land, and concluded that the degree of transhumance recorded was so similar to that observed by Thomson in Cape York that his famous object lesson concerning the material expression of seasonal movements could apply to our area as well (Thomson 1939). Second, we pondered the matter of Aboriginal insistence that culturally different groups had always occupied the plain and plateau and figured that this was not necessarily an empirical fact but rather a metaphor expressing the relative distance, both geographic and cultural, between the more-sophisticated plains people and their isolated counterparts in the "stone country" hinterland (White and Peterson 1969:58). We concluded that the archaeology resulted from seasonal movements of people between high and low country, partly through choice—to take advantage of seasonal flushes in game and plants—and partly through necessity—when the climate forced them to leave the flooded plain in the peak of the wet season and the desiccated plateau in the peak of the dry. This was no automatic response, but rather a complex set of well-orchestrated decisions, the archaeological expression of which could be read in the presence of artifacts for fowling, fishing, and foraging on the plain as opposed to hunting tools on the plateau. Once settled, people relied on shell knives and scrapers on the plain and stone ones in high plateau valleys.

Critics, drawn to the apparent neatness of this solution, have since attacked it on several fronts. White and O'Connell (1982:42–43) would prefer to see the seasonality proven by direct archaeological evidence of dietary changes. Gould (1980:34–35) labels our conclusions a fine example of "discontinuous analogy," claiming that they rest too strongly on Wik Munkan behavior as reported by Thomson (1939, 1949) as a model for people living 900 km east of Oenpelli in modern times. He amplifies his objections (Gould and Watson 1982:373) by describing our reasoning as "a fallacy of affirming the consequent" and explains further that "The seasonal transhumant model only seems to be the most parsimonious . . . because it has not considered other, possibly more parsimonious alternatives not reported ethnographically for monsoonal Australia."

These comments have considerable merit, but all demand direct evidence that we simply do not possess. For instance, it would be extremely interesting to try to reconstruct the diet of prehistoric people by studying the "isotopic signature" of food in their skeletal remains (van der Merwe, 1982). This would enable us to establish whether people foraged mainly on the plain, the plateau, or regularily used both regions. Unfortunately however, weathering processes seem to have destroyed almost all prehistoric bones buried in plateau shelters, so that we are forced to compare dietary practices in the two regions according to currently available resources rather than direct pre-historic evidence. However, the notion that the entire venture rests on Thomson's model is not altogether true. We admired Thomson's insights and drew strong parallels between his findings in Cape York and ours, but we were also able to present comparable ethnographic evidence of Oenpelli people re-sponding to seasonal changes shortly after the establishment of the first European station in the area (Spencer 1914, 1928). As for the hypothetical "more parsimonious alternatives" that we do not have, lacking these we must proceed willy-nilly with the available data.

However Gould's (1980) accusation that we took modern observations and simply threw them back into the past, like a seine net, to encompass all our data, is a point well taken. Our seasonal transhumance paper (White and Peterson 1969) ignores the possibility that major environmental changes might have altered peoples' behavior through time. It is the famous hedge-hog's view of a problem, where, following Isaiah Berlin (1953), the hedgehog sees everything in terms of one great explanatory mechanism, whereas the fox appreciates complexity to such a great extent that he risks losing sight of the original issue. There is something appealing about interpreting the past in terms of single, driving force, such as environmental or seasonal change, because it masks all the annoying contradictions that crop up when new data are revealed. On the other hand, new data often reveal the inadequacy of an interpretation and help to resolve the problem. This is exactly what a new series of investigations in the area provided: a wealth of new sites that chal-lenges the proposition that this was an unchanging environment for 6000 years.

In 1972 and 1973 a massive survey of more than 120 sites testified to the depth and diversity of prehistoric land use (Kamminga and Allen 1973). Spreads of stone artifacts on the present floodplain, pointed to some degree of stone tool making in dry season camps near concentrations of fish and fowl. Several stone arrangements suggested ceremonial sites. Along outliers and the edge of the escarpment and into plateau valleys, scores of shelters attested to recent and ancient use. Their floors were crammed with food debris and stone tools, while cracks and niches in the walls were stuffed with the bark-stripped bones of humans and a dog and with the ochred bones of kangaroos. Red, gold, and white paintings glowed from the walls. Some overhangs were scarred by quarrying; other outcrops showed where ax blanks were made. Wooden spears, woomeras, and stone blades lay cached in crannies, and wet season stringy bark shelters still stood in some sheltered spots.

Detailed excavations by Allen at Ngarradj Warde Djobkeng (henceforth termed Ngarradj), alters our view of the prehistoric dichotomy (Allen 1977; Barton 1979). This site lies about 5 km from both the East Alligator River and Magela Creek, along the catchments of which other archaeological sites register the presence of hypersaline mud flats over the past about 6000 years (Schrire 1982:230–31). Ngarradj was occupied first about 9000 years ago and was used continuously (Kamminga and Allen 1973:30) or intermittantly (Schrire 1982:229–231), as the case may be, until recent times. Yet, despite the proven presence of nearby estuarine flats, no middens appeared at Ngarradj until about 3500 years ago (Gillespie and Temple 1976:100). Unlike coterminous plain shelters, many stone points and scrapers were made here over the past 4000 years, but their incidence began to decrease after the appearance of mangrove shells (Schrire 1982:251). Thus Ngarradj, though it lay near shell beds, was treated as a plateau site lying beyond the reach of estuarine flats but within the cultural province of intensive stone tool making until about 3000 years ago.

In the same way as Tasmanian avoidance of scale fish acquired its deeper implications through prehistory (Jones 1978), the archaeological findings at Ngarradj questioned our original simple dichotomy between plain and plateau and forced us to enquire more closely into the cognitive aspects of site identity and usage. We turn therefore to a review of how sites were used and perceived and how they functioned in the ecosystem as a whole.

Reconciling Past and Present

Starting with the sheer density of residues as a guide to intensity of site use over time, and making allowance for past depositional deflation, it seems clear that very little garbage was ever dumped in these shelters. Confirmation comes from Meehan's yearlong observation of modern Aboriginal foraging inter alia for shellfish in the mud flats of the Blyth River mouth in eastern Arnhem Land. She watched 34 people, for whom shellfish constituted 2.5–8.9% of the total calories consumed per year, and estimated that if people with this diet were to drop all their empty shells in one place, it would generate an 8-m^3 pile in a year (Meehan 1982:165–166). The Alligator Rivers middens accumulated over 6000 years, but we have nowhere near that amount of shells in any shelter found so far, suggesting that they were never repositories for significant amounts of waste. Nor should they be regarded as monuments in a prehistoric landscape, reflecting all aspects of forager life. Rather, to judge from the small heaps of crab claws, shells, bones, bedding, and secondary burials, they were pit stops, offering shade and shelter as an alternative to normal, outdoor camping. We may infer a night's sleep on a paperbark mat, an overladen forager caching a ground ax head deep into the loose, hot sand at the back of the shelter for later retrieval, and a possum grilled and eaten at midday, its small bones scattered for a nocturnal predator's feast. Even the heaps of mangrove shells reflect how far a person was willing to lug a bag of unshucked clams, before resting to roast them in the shade.

This brings us to the shells themselves. Estuarine species from mangrove–mudflat habitats, make up most of the middens in the sites to which we have referred. They flourish in intertidal environments, burrowing into the salty mudflats and clinging to the roots and stems of mangrove tangles. Given the large number of middens on the Alligator Rivers plains, it comes as a surprise to find that although there are muddy intertidal flats along rivers such as the East Alligator near the sites today, there are very few mangroves and certainly no extensive stretches of hypersaline flats to provide a niche for such fauna today. The nearest shell beds lie some 40 km away near the present shore (Wilkes 1978). Therefore, unless we postulate that people lugged shellfish for vast distances from their source to the shelters, we must reject the notion that the environment has been unchanging for 6000 years (White 1967a, b) and envisage instead a major environmental shift from extensive estuarine to freshwater swamp conditions sometime in the past six millennia.

The questions now are what was the nature of the change, and when did it occur. With the rise of postglacial sea, rivers were drowned and salt flats spread out widely over the plain. The transgression is reflected in muds at the mouth of the East Alligator River (Negerevitch *et al.* 1980:107–109), with geological profiles at various localities on the coastal plain showing estuarine muds and clays covered with several feet of freshwater clays (Williams 1969:74–75). Drainage basins such as Magela Creek possibly felt the first tidal influences 9000 years ago (Allen 1977, 1978) and hypersaline flats extended well beyond in the banks by 6500 b.p., registering that the sea had reached, and possibly even exceeded, its present level by then (Chappell and Thom 1977:282). The full extent of saltwater swamps possibly conformed closely to that of freshwater ones, as is suggested by innumerable slight rises that mark the presence of eroded old estuarine shell heaps on the modern black soil plain between the East Alligator River and Oenpelli. It is difficult to pinpoint the date of this shift because our current field evidence is rather limited. What does seem likely is that it was not an absolute switch, but rather a gradual and patchy change in dominance until the present wetlands, with no readily accessible patches of estuarine forms, were established. The clearest absolute date for succession comes from a profile on the upper reaches of the South Alligator River, where estuarine muds gave way to freshwater deposits about 800 years ago (R. Jones, personal communication, 1983). In the same area, a deep and dense midden of freshwater mussels has been estimated to have accumulated over several thousand years (Kamminga and Allen 1973:54–66).

Nearby, in a number of shelters between the East Alligator River and Magela Creek, we find a strong predominance of estuarine over freshwater mussels until historic times. Mangrove shells are tougher than freshwater species, so that their relative scarcity on the surface of shelters represents a real change in the dietary patterns of people using the shelters. Occasional heaps of estuarine shells did occur on the surface at Paribari (Schrire 1982:51–52) and at another site near Oenpelli (McCarthy and Setzler 1960:207), but their scarcity contrasts markedly with the numbers that must have littered the floors of shelters around 1000 years ago. One inevitably looks for the antecedents of this change in the middens themselves. The earliest indication of some perturbation in this niche may be a significant shift from predominantly large clams and snails to small mud whelks in some middens around 3000 years ago (Schrire 1982:232–334). This change cannot at present be linked to a specific cause, though Meehans' work among littoral foragers (1982) raises a number of interesting speculations. First, modern Aboriginal shellfish eaters favor juicy clams and snails over whelks, suggesting that the change might not reflect a deliberate switch to tastier food. Second, modern shell beds show shifts in species dominance due to tides, seasons, and cyclones, but these are short-lived changes that revert to the norm after a year or two. The persistence of the prehistoric Alligator River changes suggest that there was a real drop in species availability in response to a number of possible stresses including overpredation, reduction of habitat, and environmental change.

Whatever the timing of the shift from estuarine to freshwater dominance, the total absence of mangrove–mudflat shell beds in the region today is somewhat puzzling. Patches of these shells must have occurred only a century ago, when iron and glass was known. It is tempting to link this change with the general pattern of species reduction due to the environmental impact of feral buffalo. It is not that buffalos eat mangroves but rather that they disrupt existing swamp systems by creating swim channels and denuding the plant cover so that freshwater flows into saline areas and vice versa. Intertidal mangroves may well have been destroyed by persistant freshwater incursions. Certainly their disappearance from well-attested localities such as the East Alligator River crossing since about 1950 coincides so neatly with the disappearance of other edible plants that we hazard inferring a cause and effect relationship there.

The bottom line then, is this: whatever the age, rate, or agent of change, the environment within which people operated has changed over the past 500–1000 years from a predominantly estuarine to freshwater wetlands. If modern counterparts are any indication, freshwater swamps are biotically more productive than saltwater flats. Today, wetlands in Arnhem Land that are unaffected by feral animals, support a richer, denser, and more varied flora and fauna than do hypersaline flats. In human terms, this means that until 500–1000 years ago the Alligator Rivers plains probably did not support human hunter gatherer densities comparable to those witnessed by Leichhardt in 1845. In addition, over the past century the wetlands have changed from thickly vegetated swamps and woodlands to a denuded and relatively impoverished plain. This obviously raises doubts about the dependability of current Aboriginal accounts of land-use patterns and the distribution of sacred sites such as water holes for anything but the relatively recent past. We were unaware of these reservations when we formulated our notion of 6000 years of unchanging Aboriginal response to seasonality (White and Peterson 1969). Moreover, in ignoring the twentieth-century impact of buffalos, we assumed that people had always been faced with sheets of water rather than carpets of weed in the wet season and envisaged a marked human response of moving to high ground at that time. Had we made allowance for the impact of feral animals, we might have envisaged more flexibility in seasonal response with concomitantly wider ranges used by people and animals throughout the year.

Prehistorians often describe human behavior as being "flexible" and leave it to the reader to imagine what that actually means. What makes the Arnhem Land case rather different from others is that here in a complex compendium of facts relating to traditional land-use systems we have some indication of how people managed their resources before the region was strongly affected by missionaries, parks, roads, and buffalos. The data to which I refer come largely from the findings of the land commissions the purpose of which was to interrogate local people in order to establish traditional land ownership in the region. They started out with the usual notions about a long, unchanging past and a volatile, dislocated present but ended up showing a patent link between the two in the existence and persistence of well-recognized owners, managers, and landmarks. They showed clearly that what earlier ethographers such as Spencer thought were land-owning entities, were really linguistic divisions, so that the time-honored Kakadu people were in reality Gagadju speakers, distributed widely over the land according to the gunmogurrgurr to which marriage and alliance had consigned them (NLC 1980:88). Further insight into the relationships of land-owning groups may be gained from oral history, specifically from a cautious reading of one particular person's recall of life in this region in about 1920 (Chaloupka 1981). The man in question belonged to a gunmogurrgurr whose estate was centered in the broad plateau valley of Deaf Adder Creek. A condensed version of their annual round suggests that people made four main journeys each year, the longest of which lasted some 6 months and covered a track of about 450 km. During this trip they moved in a broad arc across the plateau catchments and then cut down to the plain at Oenpelli to return home along the escarpment. En route, they performed ceremonies and traded in stone blades, ax blanks, and ochre. Other journeys were shorter, covering about 70–100 km: On one they went to the South Alligator wetlands in the late dry or early wet season for the annual goose hunt and on another they went to the same place in the late wet season to harvest goose eggs. Both ventures yielded bamboos, which were carried inland in the wet season to be made into spear shafts (Figure 3.1).

It goes without saying that this account is an idealized rendition of actual events. Although certain perturbations such as specific marriages, births, and deaths are mentioned, each year's peculiarities are glossed over to allow the story to flow. In addition, Chaloupka's efforts to discover these patterns were goaded by the demands of the land rights commissions, and probably his work induced the informants to create certainties where time had blurred some recollections. Some facts cannot be confirmed, but others, such as the marked abundance of geese on the plains, support the ecological findings that densities there have decreased markedly since the impact of feral buffalos took its toll.

Leaving specifics aside, the general aspects of this account provides interesting insights that amplify the interpretation of our prehistoric data. It confirms that in historic times at least, small land-owning groups of around 35 people interacted in ceremonies and trade exchanges in a confined area. The groups ranged widely throughout the year, depending on a multiplicity of circumstances, but were certainly not bound to the plateau in the wet season or to the plain in the dry season. Taking our impressions beyond the well-used epithet of hunter gatherer flexibility helps us spell out in archaeological terms how resources may have been used. People responded to localized availability of food and raw materials such as ochre, diorite, and bamboos by crossing ecotones. In addition they assumed what they perceived to be an appropriate material cultural identity when the occasion warranted. When people who made stone tools in the hills traversed the plains they could and did replace stone with shell. Thus far we are on firmer ground than we were with our original interpretation of Arnhem Land seasonality (White and Peterson 1969) but not far enough along to understand prehistoric perceptions of the land. To advance beyond that rather mechanistic view we need to understand from a closer reading of this account as well as certain others, that the seasonal pattern was not invariable; nor was the use of all sites entirely dependent on their access to food and on their position in a Western, geographic landscape.

In Chaloupka's account we find that decisions to go from one place to another depend on what might have happened the previous year, or what ceremony might be planned for the following month. Movements were not inevitable but contingent. In this way, sites acquire two roles: one as landmarks in a physical landscape and another as landmarks in the minds of the people using them. The two roles do not always converge comfortably. Meehan (1982) illustrated this point in her discussion of the factors that influenced the frequency with which shellfishing occurred from base camps near the Blyth River in eastern Arnhem Land in the early 70s. She points to three interrelated factors, namely, distance of the camps from the shell beds, season of the year, and ceremonial obligations. The first two factors may be seen as elements in the physical landscape, but the third is a cognitive aspect of human life. Their interaction is illustrated in this description of one apparently paradoxical site:

> At first sight Njalidjibama presents us with a paradox. It was occupied during the dry season, and while it is situated only 1 km from the sea the main shell beds . . . lay about 3 km away. Yet there is a higher frequency of shellfish gathering from this camp . . . than from any of the other sites. There is a cultural explanation for this high frequency which over-rides spatial and seasonal factors. The duration of my observations . . . coincided with the last few weeks of a Kunapipi ceremony. . . . During this time the population was increasing daily and . . . the men had little time to hunt for food. The heavy responsibility for providing substenance for everybody fell upon the mature women, who responded to the challenge in two main ways—by preparing *Cycas media* bread and by collecting shellfish. (Meehan 1982:66)

It is precisely this kind of consideration that helps us to spell out the details of prehistoric land-use patterns in a seasonal environment. The case in point concerns Ngarradj, a plains site the contents of which are anomalous when compared with neighboring shelters. For about 2500 years, from 6000 until about 3500 years ago, this plains site was used like a plateau one. Instead of being littered with estuarine shells from nearby mangrove mud flats, its occupants seem to have eaten land animals and manufactured stone, rather than shell, tools. Bone is rarely preserved in shelters such as this, other than in the protective context of a shell midden. Fortunately, however, it is present in pre-midden levels at Ngarradj and a cremated human cranial fragment was dated here to 3990 ± 195 b.p. (Gillespie and Temple 1976:100). Assuming that the person buried here also lived in the shelter at some time, it would be exceedingly interesting to test the "isotopic signature" of his diet in order to confirm that he ate nearby estuarine foods such as shellfish (see van der Merwe 1982:604).

Lacking such confirmation at present, we might try to rationalize the situation by investigating the precise locality of prehistoric shell beds and arguing that 5, 4, or even 3 km were too far for people to carry intact shellfish back to a camp site. We certainly know, without further testing, that people using shelters a mere 3–5 km from Ngarradj carried shellfish to their sites and deposited midden debris there for 2500 years before Ngarradj was used in this way. In other words, it seems that our problem is not one of diet so much as it is one of prehistoric peoples' perceptions and consequent uses of their sites.

The site therefore serves to reconcile an apparent anomaly in our neat scheme of prehistoric land-use patterns by having encoded within it two operating principles. The first is human response to environmental change, an issue that can be established by systematic investigation of landforms and stratigraphic sequences in a given area. This is the standard way in which hunter gatherer prehistory has been studied and written. People are seen as intelligent predators in a changing landscape, with environmental change being the engine that drives human response through technological and dietary changes. Ethnographic studies of living Aboriginal people provide an important new dimension at this point, however, by stressing that human perception of resources is intimately linked with their views on creation and identity as regards the land, its yield, and its monuments. Sites may be both mundane elements in a rational landscape—high caves, deep holes, and shaded shelters—as well as points in a cognitive landscape or markers in a mythic world (cf. Leone 1982). Their use is related to actual historical events as well as to mythic ones. These concerns in turn interact with the perception of that site in relation to food resources, bamboos, goose eggs, or water plants to produce the archaeological record.

Recognizing this complexity helps to shift archaeological views from environmental determinism into another gear. In the particular Arnhem Land case with which we are concerned the apparent anomaly of the Ngarradj deposit is best understood by seeing the site's identity changing over time as people's view of its use shifted. This broader view exposes the limits of our earlier explanation of the cultural dichotomy between plain and plateau by introducing a stronger element of human decision making and self-perception as elements operating within the ecosystem.

Acknowledgments

The research on which this chapter is based was funded at various times by the Research School of Pacific Studies, Australian National University, Canberra, Australia, the Australian Institute of Aboriginal Studies, Canberra, Australia, the Faculty Assisted Study Plan, Rutgers University, New Brunswick, New Jersey, the Department of Archaeology, University of Cape Town, the Werner Reimers Stiftung, the Max-Planck-Society, and the Maison des Sciences de l'Homme. I thank all these institutes for their support. In addition, I thank Professor Jack Golson, my teacher and editor at the Australian National University, for his dedicated help and kindness over the past 20 years.

References

Allen, Harry
　　1977　Archaeology of the East Alligator River region, western Arnhem Land. Unpublished typescript on file, Department of Anthropology, University of Auckland.

1978   The Jabiluka Project draft environmental statement comments. Unpublished type-
        script on file, Department of Anthropology, University of Auckland.
Allen, Jim
    1980   Head-on: the early nineteenth century British colonisation of the Top End. In *North-
            ern Australia: options and implications,* edited by Rhys Jones, pp. 33–39. *Australian
            National University, Research School of Pacific Studies, School Seminar Series* 1,
            Canberra.
Altman, Jon C.
    1980   The Aboriginal economy. In *Northern Australia: options and implications,* edited by
            Rhys Jones, pp. 87–107. *Australian National University, Research School of Pacific
            Studies, School Seminar Series* 1, Canberra.
Australian National Parks and Wildlife Service (ANPWS)
    1980   *Kakadu National Park plan of management.* Commonwealth of Australia, Canberra.
Barton, Gerald
    1979   *Ngarradj Warde Jobkeng rock shelter, western Arnhem Land, Australia: an analysis
            and assessment of the flaked stone assemblage.* Unpublished MA dissertation, Depart-
            ment of Anthropology, University of Auckland, Auckland.
Berlin, Isaiah
    1953   *The hedgehog and the fox: an essay on Tolstoy's view of history.* Simon and Schuster,
            New York.
Berndt, Ronald M., and Catherine H. Berndt
    1954   *Arnhem Land: its history and its people.* Cheshire, Melbourne.
Butlin, Noel
    1983   *Our original aggression.* George Allen and Unwin, Sydney.
Cahill, Paddy
    n.d.   Letters to Sir W. Baldwin Spencer, 1913–1921, manuscript on file, Australian Institute
            of Aboriginal Studies, Canberra.
Chaloupka, George
    1981   The traditional movement of a band of Aboriginals in Kakadu. In *Kakadu National
            Park educational resources,* edited by T. Stokes, Appendix I, pp. 162–171. Australian
            National Wildlife Parks and Wildlife Service, Canberra and Darwin.
Chappell, John, M. A., and Bruce G. Thom
    1977   Sea levels and coasts. In *Sunda and Sahul, prehistoric studies in Southeast Asia,
            Melanesia and Australia,* edited by Jim Allen, Jack Golson, and Rhys Jones, pp. 275–
            291. Academic Press, New York.
Chappell, John, M. A., Eugene G. Rhoades, Bruce G. Thom, and Eugene Wallensky
    1982   Hydro-isostasy and the sea level isobase of 5500 B.P., in north Queensland, Australia.
            Marine Geology 49:81–90.
Clark, Robin L.
    1983   Pollen and charcoal evidence for the effects of Aboriginal burning on the vegetation
            of Australia. *Archaeology in Oceania* 18:32–37.
Clarke, Michael F., Robert J. Wasson, and Martin A. J. Williams
    1979   Point Stuart chenier and Holocene sea levels in northern Australia. *Search* 10:90–92.
Cole, Keith
    1975   *A history of Oenpelli.* Nungalinya Publications, Darwin.
Cook, Cecil Evelyn
    1966   Medicine and the Australian Aboriginal: a century of contact in the Northern Territo-
            ry. *The Medical Journal of Australia* 1:559–565.
Ford, Brian D., and Donald G. Tulloch (editors)
    1977   *The Australian buffalo: a collection of papers.* Department of the Northern Territory,
            Animal Industry and Agriculture Branch, Canberra.

Fox, Russell Walter, Graeme G. Kelleher, and Charles B. Kerr
1977 *Ranger uranium environmental inquiry second report.* Australian Government Publishing Service, Canberra.

Gillespie, Richard, and Richard B. Temple
1976 Sydney University natural radiocarbon measurements III. *Radiocarbon* 18:96–109.

Gould, Richard A.
1980 *Living archaeology.* Cambridge University Press, Cambridge.

Gould, Richard A., and Patty Jo Watson
1982 A dialogue on the meaning and use of analogy in ethnoarchaeological reasoning. *Journal of Anthropological Archaeology* 1:355–381.

Hallam, Sylvia
1975 *Fire and hearth.* Australian Institute of Aboriginal Studies, Canberra.

Hargrave, John
1983 Leprosy in Australian Aborigines. *Aboriginal Health Project Information Bulletin* 3:10–15.

Haynes, Christopher
1978 Fire in the mind: Aboriginal cognisance of fire use in north central Arnhemland. Manuscript on file, Australian National Parks and Wildlife Service, Darwin, Northern Territory.
1982 *Man's firestick and God's lightning: bushfire in Arnhemland.* Paper presented at ANZAAS 52nd Congress, Section 25 A. Sydney.

Hill, Ernestine
1951 *The Territory.* Angus and Robertson, Sydney.

Jones, Rhys
1969 Fire-stick farming. *Australian Natural History* 16:224–228.
1975 The Neolithic, Palaeolithic and the hunting gardeners: man and land in the Antipodes. In Quaternary Studies: selected papers from the IX INQUA Congress, Christchurch, New Zealand, 2–10 December, 1973, edited by R. P. Suggate and M. M. Cresswell, pp. 21–34. *Royal Society of New Zealand, Bulletin* 13.
1978 Why did the Tasmanians stop eating fish? In *Explorations in ethnoarchaeology,* edited by Richard A. Gould, pp. 11–47. University of New Mexico Press, Albuquerque.
1980 Hunters in the Australian coastal savanna. In *Human ecology in savanna environments,* edited by David R. Harris, pp. 107–146. Academic Press, New York.

Jones, Rhys, and Jim Bowler
1980 Struggle for the savanna: northern Australia in ecological and prehistoric perspective. In *Northern Australia: options and implications,* edited by Rhys Jones, pp. 3–31. *Australian National University, Research School of Pacific Studies, School Seminar Series* 1, Canberra.

Kakadu Archaeological Working Group (editors)
1980 *Archaeological research in the Kakadu Park. A consultancy report to the Australian National Parks and Wildlife Service.* Department of Prehistory, Research School of Pacific Studies, Australian National University, Canberra.

Kamminga, Johann, and Harry Allen
1973 *Report of the archaeological survey.* Alligator Rivers Environmental Fact-Finding Study, Canberra.

Keen, Ian
1980 The Alligator Rivers Aborigines: retrospect and prospect. In *Northern Australia: options and implications,* edited by Rhys Jones, pp. 171–86. *Australian National University, Research School of Pacific Studies, School Seminar Series* 1, Canberra.

Kirk, Robert L.
    1971   Genetic evidence and its implications for Australian prehistory. In *Aboriginal man and environment,* edited by Derek John Mulvaney and Jack Golson, pp. 326–43. Australian National University Press, Canberra.
Lee, Richard B., and Irven DeVore (editors)
    1968   *Man the hunter.* Aldine, Chicago.
Leichhardt, Ludwig
    n.d.a   Continuation of my log from the Abel Tasman to Port Essington: the 8 September 1845. Manuscript (MS c. 155) on file, State Library of New South Wales, Mitchell Library, Sydney.
    n.d.b   Report of the expedition of L. Leichhardt, Esq. from Moreton Bay to Port Essington. Manuscript (MS c. 157) on file, State Library of New South Wales, Mitchell Library, Sydney.
    1847   *Journal of an overland expedition in Australia from Moreton Bay to Port Essington.* T. and W. Boone, London.
Leone, Mark P.
    1982   Some opinions about recovering mind. *American Antiquity* 47(4):742–760.
Letts, Gough A. (chairman)
    1979   *Feral animals in the Northern Territory: report.* Government Printer, Darwin.
Levitus, Robert
    1982   *Everybody bin all day work.* A report to the Australian National Parks and Wildlife Service on the social history of the Alligator Rivers region of the Northern Territory, 1869–1973. Australian Institute of Aboriginal Studies, Canberra.
Lewis, Henry T.
    1982   Fire technology and resource management in aboriginal North America and Australia. In *Resource managers: North American and Australian hunter–gatherers,* edited by Nancy M. Williams and Eugene S. Hunn, pp. 45–67. *AAAS Selected Symposium* 67, Westview Press, Inc., Boulder.
Lewis, John
    1922   *Fought and won.* W. K. Thomas, Adelaide.
McCarthy, Frederick D., and Frank M. Setzler
    1960   The Archaeology of Arnhem Land. In *Anthropology and nutrition, records of the American–Australian scientific expedition to Arnhem Land, 1948* (Vol. 2), edited by Charles Percy Mountford, pp. 215–295. Melbourne University Press, Melbourne.
McKinlay, John
    1866   Exploration of the Northern Territory. *South Australian Parliamentary Papers 1865–6,* (Vol. II, No. 131). Government Printer, Adelaide.
MacKnight, Campbell C. (editor)
    1969   *The farthest coast: a selection of writings relating to the history of the northern coast of Australia.* Melbourne University Press, Melbourne.
    1976   *The voyage to Marege: Macassan trepangers in northern Australia.* Melbourne University Press, Melbourne.
McKnight, Thomas L.
    1971   Australia's buffalo dilemma. *Annals of the Association of American Geographers* 61:759–773.
    1976   *Friendly vermin: a study of feral livestock in Australia.* University of California Press, Berkeley.
Meehan, Betty
    1982   *Shell bed to shell midden.* Australian Institute of Aboriginal Studies, Canberra.

Negerevitch, Tia, contributions from Geoffrey Hope and Philip Hughes
    1980   Review of environmental sources relevant to the region. In *Archaeological research in the Kakadu Park: a consultancy report to the Australian National Parks and Wildlife Service,* edited by the Kakadu Archaeological Working Group, pp. 91–128. Department of Prehistory, Research School of Pacific Studies, Australian National University, Canberra.

Northern Land Council (NLC)
    1980   *Alligator Rivers stage II land claim* (prepared by Ian Keen). Northern Land Council, Berrimah, Northern Territory.

Oda, Shizuo, and Charles T. Keally
    1973   Edge-ground stone tools from the Japanese preceramic culture. *Busshitsu Bunka* (Material Culture) 22:1–26.

Pearce, Robert Harwood, and Michael Barbetti
    1981   A 38,000 year old archaeological site at Upper Swan, Western Australia. *Archaeology in Oceania* 16:173–178.

Schrire, Carmel
    1982   *The Alligator Rivers: prehistory and ecology in Western Arnhem Land.* Research School of Pacific Studies, Department of Prehistory, *Terra Australis* 7. Australian National University Press, Canberra.

South Australian Parliamentary Papers (SAPP)
    1867   Report of commission appointed by the Governor-in-Chief to inquire into the management of the Northern Territory Expedition, together with minutes of evidence and appendix. *South Australian Parliamentary Papers 1866–7* (Vol. 2, No. 17). Government Printer, Adelaide.

Spencer, Baldwin
    1914   *Native tribes of the Northern Territory of Australia.* Macmillan, London.
    1928   *Wanderings in wild Australia* (Vol. II). Macmillan, London.

Stocker, Geoffrey C.
    1971   Water buffaloes and conservation in the Northern Territory. *Wildlife in Australia* 8:10–12.

Thomson, Donald F.
    1939   The seasonal factor in human culture, illustrated from the life of a contemporary nomadic group. *Proceedings of the Prehistoric Society* 5:209–221.
    1949   *Economic structure and the ceremonial exchange cycle in Arnhem Land.* Macmillan, Melbourne.

Urry, James, and Michael Walsh
    1981   The lost "Macassar language" of northern Australia. *Aboriginal History* 5:91–108.

Van der Merwe, Nikolaas J.
    1982   Carbon isotopes, photosynthesis and archaeology. *American Scientist* 70:596–606.

Warburton, Charles
    1934   *Buffaloes: life and adventure in Arnhem Land.* Angus and Robertson, Sydney.

White, Carmel (Schrire)
    1967a *Plateau and plain: prehistoric investigations in Arnhem Land Northern Territory.* Unpublished Ph.D. dissertation, Department of Prehistory, Australian National University, Canberra.
    1967b The prehistory of the Kakadu people. *Mankind* 6(9):426–431.
    1967c Early stone axes in Arnhem Land. *Antiquity* 41:147–152.
    1971   Man and environment in northwest Arnhem Land. In *Aboriginal man and environment,* edited by Derek John Mulvaney and Jack Golson, pp. 141–157. Australian National University Press, Canberra.

White, Carmel (Schrire), and Nicolas Peterson
   1969   Ethnographic interpretations of the prehistory of western Arnhem Land. *Southwestern Journal of Anthropology* 25:45–69.
White, John Peter, and James F. O'Connell
   1982   *A prehistory of Australia, New Guinea and Sahul.* Academic Press, New York.
Wilkes, E. (Ted) T.
   1978   Training in archaeological techniques. *Australian Institute of Aboriginal Studies Newsletter* 10:28–29.
Williams, Martin A. J.
   1969   Geomorphology of the Adelaide–Alligator River area. In Lands of the Adelaide–Alligator area, Northern Territory. *Commonwealth Scientific and Industrial Research Organisation, Land Research Series* 25:71–94. Commonwealth Scientific and Industrial Research Organisation, Melbourne.

4

Forager Resource and Land Use in the Humid Tropics: The Agta of Northeastern Luzon, the Philippines

P. BION GRIFFIN

Introduction

The purpose of this chapter is to analyze foraging adaptations in humid tropics with a view to making a model of possible prehistoric foraging adaptations. One way to achieve this is to review the several ethnographically known foraging societies in similar environments, whether in Africa, Southeast Asia, or the Americas. We, however, closely look at one extant foraging population, paying special attention to the relations of human behaviors to the environment. Since land and resource use in the present and the past is at issue, the dynamic aspects of the natural environment as they affect the eventual food resource base of people should be a major focus. The social environment of a foraging society will also be pertinent to foragers' land and resource relations, since it indicates something of the range of possibilities in the past.

The Agta of northeastern Luzon, the Philippines, provide the data for detailed analysis of land control and use and serve as a model for reconstructing alternative earlier adaptive systems. Through these reconstructions, we suggest tentative principles of the evolution of foraging and incipient-farming economic systems in the humid tropics and address the possibilities of intergroup communication, exchange, and dependence.

Past and Present in Hunter Gatherer Studies 95

Once there were only hunter gatherers, but this world has not existed in the tropics since the early Holocene in most of Southeast Asia. A multiplicity of adaptations focusing on variation in economic organization seems to have been the rule. Certainly modern foragers are diverse in strategy and degree of "purity" of hunting and gathering, as witnessed by comparing the Tasaday of Mindanao (Yen 1976), the Jarawa and Onge of the Andamans (Pandit 1976), and the Agta (Estioko and Griffin 1975) and the Ayta (Brosius 1981) of Luzon. We do, however, find three interrelated conditions that stand up under some scrutiny. First, many humid-tropics foragers operate in environments rich in animal protein resources. Second, wild plant food resources, such as carbo-hydrate staples, are less abundant and present serious environmental limita-tions to forager growth. In other words, unlike the arid tropics, the humid tropics may be game rich and plant-food poor (Griffin *et al.* n.d.a, b; Hutterer 1982, 1983). Third, modern foraging is not limited to collection of wild resources; it often includes incipient horticulture and exchange with non-foraging peoples within or adjacent to the foragers' own collection ranges.

Case Study: The Agta

Agta are dwellers of the Sierra Madre, a rugged and broken forest-covered range of mountains that runs nearly the entire length of the island along the Pacific coast (Figure 4.1). Agta hunt the largest game of the Philippine forests, wild pig and deer, and fish the short and steep rivers that run into the Pacific and the Cagayan Valley to the west. They gather plant and animal foods, either for consumption or exchange, and they sometimes plant small swiddens of root crops, vegetables, rice, and corn. Today they have constant social and economic intercourse with non-Agta farmers and loggers and are as depen-dent on trade as on the acquisition of wild fauna. In other words, although they generally forage, the Agta are not primitive isolates, and their life-style (including subsistence) is partially influenced by world economic and politi-cal systems.

Agta have for decades, and possibly centuries, engaged in trade of forest products, usually meat, for domesticated roots and cereal grains, cloth, metal, and ornamentation. These exchange patterns have intensified and diversified as new options have appeared. No longer is simple trade of meat for rice and sweet potatoes the rule; a complex reciprocity of goods and services is uni-versal. In addition, the area is now experiencing new elements such as jet aircraft, videotapes, television, insecticides (used to kill riverine fish), arma-lites (to kill people), antibiotics, and lipstick. Still, a consideration of their adaptation that focuses on control of resources and land may tell us much of value in looking for generalizations concerning present and past foraging adaptations in and out of Southeast Asia.

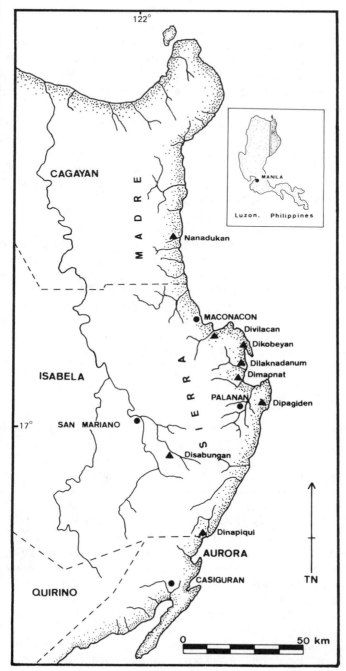

FIGURE 4.1 The research area, northeast Luzon: (– – –) provincial boundary; (●) munici-
pality; and (▲) Agta campsite.

Brief and unpublished visits were made to Palanan between 1954 and 1972 by Robert Fox of the National Museum of the Philippines. He was followed by Bennagen (1976) and Peterson (1978), who both focused on Agta–lowland farmer economic exchange among relatively settled groups. Thomas Headland has been working among the Casiguran Agta since 1962, and his doctoral research should add to the insights gained by Rai (1982).

Work among the less settled Agta began in 1972, when I conducted a survey of hunting bands north and south of Palanan on the Pacific coast. At this time the first observations of women hunting were made and the diversity in Agta adaptations perceived (Estioko and Griffin 1975). A brief visit in 1973 examined the impact of Philippine martial law and conflict between the government and insurgents. Between June 1974 and June 1976, about 15 months of research was completed under the guise of ethnoarchaeology (Estioko-Griffin and Griffin 1981a; Griffin 1981; Griffin and Estioko-Griffin 1978). Again, brief summer visits in 1978 and 1979 allowed further examination of women's activities and contact with different Agta bands (Estioko-Griffin and Griffin 1981b). Between October 1980 and June 1982 we again worked in Isabela and Cagayan provinces, mostly at Nanadukan, Cagayan. These researches focused on women as hunters. In research design and analyses we have been joined by Goodman and Grove (Griffin *et al.* n.d.a), while Allen and Mudar worked in ethnobotany and ethnozoology, respectively (Allen 1985; Mudar 1985).

The Natural Environment

The forests and mountains of Isabela and Cagayan provinces lie almost on the equator, between 16 and 18°30′ north latitude. As is the case for most of Southeast Asia, these are humid tropics. Climate and topography together produce a slightly seasonal cycle of environmental change, with alternating rainy and dry seasons and a crosscutting typhoon season.

The climate of northeastern Luzon is not completely understood. The Philippine Atmospheric Geophysical and Astronomical Services Administration (PAGASA), as well as meteorologists (Flores and Balagot 1969) and anthropologists (Hutterer 1983; Rai 1982), feel the region has little seasonal variation as marked by rainfall and as felt by floral and faunal communities. Personal experience suggests that we should not consider monthly averages of rainfall, but rather days per month with no rain, and then correlate days with rainfall in the drier months with the occurrence of tropical cyclones (depressions through typhoons). We then discern a new view of the supposedly nonseasonal climate and its impact on the biotic community. Drier months have a larger number of days without rainfall (Figure 4.2) and much of the rainfall during these months is caused by storms (PAGASA 1978).

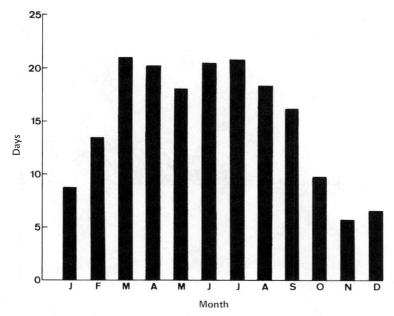

FIGURE 4.2   Mean monthly days without rain, Maconacon, Isabela, 1975–1982.

Runoff is immediate and the degree of forest saturation quite different from that experienced during the months of the northeast monsoon. Clearly seasonality exists: a wet season begins in late October and extends into March. April and May are relatively dry. June through September are dry except when typhoons pass (Figure 4.3).

Storms are not dispersed evenly throughout the dry season. Of 212 tropical cyclones impacting the Philippines between 1968 and 1978, 91 (43%) directly affected northeastern Luzon. Since the weather bureau and the Acme Lumber Company data show a consistent dry season association of rainfall and storms, we conclude that northeastern Luzon does experience cyclical wetter and drier periods, which can best be treated if considered as a seasonal cycle.

Temperature and humidity covary with rainfall. The mean annual relative humidity is 87%, the second highest of the entire Philippines. The high humidity is a product of evaporation of the nearby Pacific Ocean, of rainfall, and of the forest cover throughout the area. The annual temperature, ranging from 36.8 to 13.8°C (PAGASA 1975) with an average of 25.4°C, is only slightly lower than the Philippine average (PAGASA 1974). Following the pattern indicated for dry and wet seasons, May, June, and July are hottest and December, January, and February are coolest.

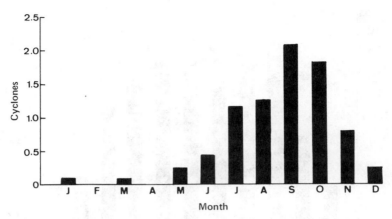

FIGURE 4.3 Mean monthly frequency of tropical cyclones, northeast Luzon, 1968–1978.

Northeastern Luzon therefore falls within the definition of the humid tropics, being a region with high temperatures and at least 100 mm of rainfall each month. Critical to understanding the nature of the floral and faunal community and its human foraging adaptation is the unique configuration of the Sierra Madre environment and its mildly seasonal tropical forest ecosystem. The cyclical nature of the climate, including its major typhoons, produces, in part, the resource base to which the foragers adjust their economic and social systems. The dynamics of the tropical forest are central to understanding how plant foods for human consumption are scarce whereas animal sources are abundant.

The general and human ecology of the humid tropics are poorly known. Tropical rain forests are the most complex ecosystems on earth, and are both difficult and expensive to study. Generalizations are difficult to make and when we consider Luzon we are indeed on tenuous ground. Little ecological research has been attempted there, and it has only been since 1980 that our University of Hawaii team started a survey of the flora and fauna. Many plants and animals remain uncollected, unidentified, and unnamed. Nevertheless, hypotheses may be advanced using available data.

Tropical rain forests have been romantically characterized as lush paradises, full of roots, fruits, nuts, and berries. An opposite view suggests green deserts, devoid of harvestable plant foods and edible game. Both views reflect popular Western views of jungles and the state of current ecological research. Deserts may be bountiful to the knowledgable exploiter yet hostile to the uninitiated. The truth probably lies somewhere in between providence and impoverishment where human resources are concerned, and the best generalization to date is one that asserts a typically game-rich condition.

Rain forests have the greatest standing biomass of all terrestrial ecosystems, but most of the mass is in plant growth above the ground in wood and leaves. Hutterer, in a consideration of tropical ecosystems (1982), points out that both New and Old World tropical forests tend to provide plant foods for a great variety of animals. While the percentage of biomass of animals may be low, especially compared with a more seasonal or savanna tropical environment, the overwhelming amount of plants per unit of land supports many animals and great species diversity. Herbivores are not sustainable in large numbers or densities, but browsers, such as deer, are common, and omnivores, of which the pig (*Sus* spp.) is a good example, may comprise a fair portion of the humanly procurable animals.

The tropical rain forest of northeastern Luzon, with the Sierra Madre range of mountains, varies seasonally according to elevation and topography. The Sierra Madre makes up for its lack of elevation (higher peaks reach about 1800 m) with an extremely rugged and broken topography and a steepness of nearly all slopes. The highly eroded, landslide-scarred surfaces are cut by streams that flow during the rains but are often dry at higher elevations otherwise. Water flows from the divide eastward to the Pacific and westward to the Cagayan Valley. While few rivers are long, their volume of runoff and rapidity of descent contribute to their special characteristics.

A variety of biotic zones, from mangrove swamp to submontane stunted forest, is found. Most of the lower mountain slopes are covered with dipterocarps, the large and tall commercially valuable hardwoods of Southeast Asian tropics that dominate both foothill and interior mountain terrains to about 500 m (Allen 1985). Today rolling western foothills are covered with secondary growth, bamboos, and swiddeners' settlements. To the east, foothills often terminate in narrow ridges and in sea cliffs. Unlike the drier hills on the west, these are covered with dipterocarps and smaller, storm- and wet-adapted plants. Rattans, palm trees, and a multitude of fruiting shrubs and trees are ubiquitous.

The northeastern Luzon forest is not a single-layered, high-canopy forest. Steep gradients of slope and disruptions due to landslides, typhoons, and seasonality permit a two- or three-storied floral community, with intense competition for sunlight at all levels. Dipterocarps and other large trees usually are the highest community members, with many palms interspersed. Rattans are common; their thorn-laden stems lie at all angles in most terrains. All trees and shrubs support vines, parasitic plants, and orchids. On the forest floor, the young shoots and saplings of many species compete with small shrubs, tubers, and mosses and fungi, and everywhere, the rotting remains of dead plants host plant and animal life.

Two points need stressing. First, the ground cover is mostly immature growth. Plants lying on the ground itself include a few edible fungi but are otherwise largely useless to humans. Edible roots are scattered in patchy growths. Second, from beneath the subsurface of the ground to the canopy of the second story, most leaves, blossoms, fruits, and seeds are edible only to animals other than humans. Several of these animals, however, form the basis of Agta foraging and involve a significant portion of Agta energy expenditure and intake. In addition, the nutritional impact of wild tubers may be less than that seen today in cultivated tubers such as taro, cassava, and sweet potato. An abundance of animal protein, taken with the advantages of domesticated root crops, may be significant considerations for Agta foragers.

Deer (*Cervus philippinus*) and wild pig (*Sus barbatus*) are the two largest mammals of the Luzon forests. While once locally plentiful, no feral bovines remain today in the Sierra Madre. No large carnivorous cats are known, and the Philippine macaque (*Macaca philippinesis*) is the only recorded higher primate. Civet cats (*Viverra* sp., *Paradoxurus* sp.) and several large rodent-like tree-dwelling mammals are common. Fruit bats (*Ptenochirus jagorii*) are the largest of many species of bats. Amphibians and reptiles are well known, yet of minor importance here, since their exploitation is not energy efficient. The monitor lizard and the crocodile are prey animals, but only the former is frequently killed. The Philippine eagle, giant hornbill, numerous hawks and kites, and a plethora of other birds range from the sea to the mountain crests.

The wild pig (*Sus barbatus*) is an omnivore found in nearly all habitats, cooling itself in the littoral waters by sand beaches, feeding throughout the lowland dipterocarp and lower montane forests, and sleeping as high as the montane forest. While pigs may on occasion venture into agricultural fields, they prefer the fallen fruits of the lowland dipterocarp forest and roots found at all elevations. An opportunistic forager capable of eating seasonally available foods, the pig flourishes both with the late dry season fruit abundance and with the reproductive cycle of the dipterocarps. *Sus barbatus* appears to resemble the feral *Sus scrofa* of New Guinea, as discussed by Morren (1979:6–7), yet may be less inclined to seek food in agricultural fields. Boars of *Sus barbatus* do not perform the breeding functions of the New Guinea feral male and hence are unlikely to be drawn to domesticated sows. When pigs intrude on fields, they are hungry due to lack of forest foods.

Pigs generally put on fat before the wet season begins and retain it in good years until the following early dry season. In poor years with little fallen fruit or excessive monsoons, pigs may be lean and in poor health by February. New piglets tend to be born in the middle of the dry season when fruit is appearing in greater abundance. Size of litter and survival apparently depends on quantity and quality of fodder available to sows both during and after gestation. Our observations, based on numbers of fetuses in sows killed by hunters and on forest observations of family groups of pigs, suggest that litters seldom count more than four or five fetuses and live births. Given human and python predation, accident, and disease, we suggest one or two pigs per litter survive to maturity.

Abundance of wild pigs is difficult to state in quantitative terms. Pig and deer have been considered very plentiful throughout the Philippines since the earliest Spanish colonial efforts and subsequent recorded observations. The Agta believe game to have been once abundant throughout the Sierra Madre and to be still plentiful in the remoter regions far from human presence. Since the dynamics of wild pig populations and concomitant human predation is the subject of some concern (Peterson 1981, 1982; Rai 1982), we explore the issue of abundance of wild pigs as we review Agta exploitation of game. For now, pigs are numerous enough to be sought year-round and nearly daily by each residential group of Agta, though their abundance is partly determined by cyclical variations in plant fodder. The determination of the abundance of the tropical rain forest's game populations remains based on inferences from kill numbers rather than from studies of living game populations.

Male deer often reach over 50 kg, as opposed to less than 50 kg for pigs. Deer are similar to pigs in variety of habitats exploited but are browsers as well as fructivores. Deer travel alone as a rule, except when a doe is accompanied by her fawns, when parties of two or three may be found. Like pigs, deer tend to gravitate to water courses where fallen fruits have clumped, where patches of trees drop fruits on the ground, or where other plant foods are plentiful. They seem to be slightly less subject to perturbations in the floral environment than pigs, probably because of their ability to digest leaves and shoots. Relative abundance of deer, as opposed to pig, remains a problem. We observed that Agta kill more pigs than deer, partly because they prefer wild pig meat and possibly because of idiosyncracies in the environment during the period of observation.

Riverine and marine fauna are varied and plentiful where pollution, overharvesting, and wanton destruction have not yet reached. Fish and shellfish abound since the rivers are rich in nutrients. The littoral zone is also well populated with the usual tropical fish, crustaceans, molluscs, and other fauna. The coasts alternate sand beaches, cobble beaches, live or uplifted dead corals, and sea cliffs, each of which has its own set of flora and fauna and its relations with the seasonal climate, storms, and human populations.

The Social Environment

The social environment of the Agta is as complex as their natural environment. Since World War II, rapid change has seen increasing immigration of farmers, loggers, and many others; missionaries and anthropologists are among the more recent arrivals. Today northeastern Luzon contains several indigenous non-Agta groups. The Casiguranin and Paranan speakers (lowland dialects related to Agta; Headland and Headland 1974) are centered in farming communities on the coast in Isabela, while swiddeners are scattered to the west on the river drainages flowing into the Cagayan. North of these swiddeners are Itawis and other small groups. Ilokanos, Ibanags, Ifugao, Tinggian, and Itneg swiddeners and wet-rice farmers have expanded into Agta territory. Logging and mining industries are bringing in thousands of new migrants, almost all of whom are insensitive to Agta customs and needs. As agricultural and industrial populations grow, other stressful elements appear, such as soldiers and their insurgent counterparts, petty entrepreneurs, and even a few tourists.

The social environment contains diverse resources exploitable by varied tactics. Resources differ in availability according to season, geographic location, and conditions in the resource loci. Farmers' stores of exchangeable roots and grains vary according to seasons and storms. The logging industry and its laborers are highly seasonal as a resource base. Some firms only operate between February and August, when trucks can reach the forest, but others, having access to permanent roads, may encounter some, though not all, Agta groups during all months.

As we consider the social environment of the Agta in terms of the Agta foraging adaptation and use of land, we must note that the non-Agta peoples are both exploited by the Agta and exploiters of the Agta. Exchanges are necessarily two-way. Agta efforts to maintain themselves on their own traditional land are hampered by competition from non-Agta groups.

Agta in Space

Settlement, dispersal for subsistence, and social identification all begin with flowing water. Rivers, or sections of rivers and their tributary streams, are the principal foci of identification of one's origins and belonging. Rights to live along the river, to exploit it and surrounding areas, and to restrict other Agta who are not so identified follow from location of one's own birth, of one's parents' births, and of one's childhood years. Each Agta regards himself as coming from a certain river drainage system, and though residence in adulthood may not coincide with this system, one nevertheless remains associated with it, though not with a clearly defined territory.

Dialect groups do not covary with explicitly defined and delimited sets of rivers but do amalgamate units of extended families residing on adjacent rivers (for another discussion see Rai 1982). At this level the Agta system exhibits its greatest fuzziness and allows no clear boundaries to be marked. Some clarification may be obtained by moving back to the single-river system, where one or more extended families may reside, depending on the size of the river, fortune and misfortune of the local populations, and external environmental impacts. The extended family lives in nuclear-family residential dwellings, either small rainy season pole houses or lean-tos, and two to six houses comprise the cluster. The basis of organization of the extended joint family is the unity of siblings and the strength of parent–children bonds. Since grandparents are rare, core sibling units are often the device used to group people together. Rai (1982) argues that links between sisters are most important, though cousin ties are frequently considered.

The extended family is not a stable, enduring entity as far as localized membership is concerned. Flexibility and fluidity is the rule. At first, in-marrying spouses do not permanently leave their birthplace but only temporarily relocate. When a couple is young, and sometimes even when old, frequent residence shifts between both spouses' families is the rule. Should one's siblings be split up, movement among different groups on several rivers is typical. Movement is not random but planned among known and named campsites and among close consanguineal and affinal kin. No Agta couple would willingly sleep a single night among nonkin.

Although there are exceptions, most mates are found among the people of a single dialect group. Since the dialect boundaries are ill defined and highly permeable, marriage ties are most complicated in these transition zones. Social identity is a consideration however, since people outside the existing network are considered to be bad, to have customs of a dubious sort, and to make poor spouses. As a result, sections of the mountain range are felt to be the home of specific groups of people.

The settlement system involves kin arrangements and a way of mobilizing the community for subsistence and maintenance activities. During the wet season, nucleation of related people usually occurs. Residence cluster size increases slightly, and movement and readjustment decrease. Work parties operate from the seasonally permanent base camp, seldom setting up the one or two nuclear-family dwelling sites known in the dry season. Dry season residence is usually dispersed, returning periodically to a single base camp site to check the swidden and prevent theft by non-Agta groups. Subsistence activities, since they are more varied, force nuclear families to occupy seasonal, specialized campsites and to operate in semi-independence, but few single families ever do so for more than one or two nights.

Given one or two extended families per river (and today not all rivers are inhabited by Agta), we see that population density is low, about 0.35–0.50 people per km². People are widely scattered, numbers per square kilometer are difficult to calculate since distribution is uneven, proximity to non-Agta centers is critical, and annual changes are considerable.

Though Agta do not cluster into large groups, non-Agta groups live in towns with several thousand occupants and on outlying farmsteads that may be scattered or clustered depending on ethnic affiliation of the farmers. Seasonal logging camps inside the forest are often inhabited by several dozen men and a few of their wives.

Control of People and Space

Moving outward from the river, the Agta follow the network of tributaries into the foothills and upriver into the mountains until the slopes become so difficult that hunting is not feasible. The area where men and women from one river drainage system often hunt may be considered their home range. Nonrelatives are unwelcome, and if they are found foraging or traveling without permission, they may be attacked.

Our data indicate that intergroup raiding, which often resulted in death, was once far more prevalent than it is today. Agta do not raid to acquire territory or to gain access to resources; nor do they regard it as a population control device. Rather, Agta see raiding as a means of combating sorcery by other Agta. All Agta therefore maintain (or did until the 1960s) a defensive guard against outsiders. All strangers are highly suspect and may be killed.

Since the 1970s, as they are forced into less traditional work, Agta have had to travel over greater distances to interact with non-Agta groups. Today, should difficult times impact one area, Agta may move close to unrelated Agta, but they reside adjacent to farmers' houses and fields. On arrival in new territory, contact is made with the local Agta, perhaps through a non-Agta intermediary, in order to seek permission to reside in the area as well as to provide an explanation as to why this is necessary. Thereafter, depending on personalities and past actions, all the Agta might frequently interact, share resources, and find new marriage partners, for without strong affinal ties, the cooperation does not last after the economic problems or opportunities of the incoming group are resolved.

Fear still is the major device used to keep Agta apart and in their respective ranges. Even new spouses, especially males, may be quite afraid of in-laws for a time, suspicious of intentions and dreading hostility. Agta oral history and present-day behavior is full of concern for raiders and for the evil potential of "bad Agta." Foraging parties often are wary of possible conflict in distant areas of dialect transition. Hunters are especially aware of the chance of illegal trespassers and assume that they may be bent on raiding. In the remotest forest hunting zones, where hunters from more than one dialect group may range, precautions are taken and one would seldom hunt alone.

The Agta of the 1980s are somewhat less fearful of intruders than they say they were 20 years earlier, but they are nevertheless suspicious for new and more complicated reasons. The recent history of involvement with government–insurgent conflict has left many wounds and causes for revenge. Agta have been coerced into serving both the military and the antigovernment forces, and resulting deaths have now confused and sometimes strengthened old lines of conflict.

In spite of these problems of control of land and of distribution of people in space, the practicalities of everyday subsistence efforts more closely determine Agta use of the environment. As hunter gatherers and incipient farmers, they may depend on fear, aggression, and custom to keep others out of their ranges, but they utilize a well-established set of strategies to guarantee their own access and success in exploitation of the land's resources.

The Organization of Resource Acquisition

People get food using bow and arrow hunting, spearfishing, diversified gathering, incipient swidden horticulture, barter exchange, and sporadic wage labor. While dependence on or importance of each of these is partially a subjective or at least a localized matter, most Agta males clearly consider themselves, first and foremost, hunters.

Outside the areas of concentration of lowlanders, all Agta men and, in some places, many Agta women are hunters of the wild pig and deer (Estioko-Griffin 1984; Estioko-Griffin and Griffin 1980, 1981b; Griffin et al. n.d.a). Agta also hunt macaque when, in the rainy season, these are fat and complacent. They seldom enter the forest to hunt lesser game, civet cats, monitor lizards, large birds, and fruit bats will be killed if seen and are desirable when animal protein is scarce.

The bow and arrow is the most elaborate Agta technology and is well developed and well suited for use in the dense forest environment and on the variety of game available. The organization and composition of hunting parties, as well as the tactics chosen, depend in part on the potentialities of bow and arrow use and on the requisites of the game on which they are preying. Traps and guns may be used to secure pig and deer, but only infrequently and under special circumstances.

Dogs are used to assist in the location, driving, and killing of game. Usually two or three hunters work together with one or two teams of dogs, often pursuing game for long distances before the kill. This small-team tactic is especially favored by women, who hunt in groups of two or three, combining either husbands and wives, sisters, or older and younger women. Large teams often include all capable youths and adults and all compatible dogs. These hunts are quite exciting but last only a few hours at best, and one or two kills is a satisfactory catch. Participation of teenagers is especially likely in team hunting with dogs. Women generally use dogs, but all men can and do hunt without them, since men hunt constantly and dogs are often unavailable.

Forest stalking is the main tactic of dogless hunting. Stalking is often a solitary enterprise, although two or three may work in concert, following a plan of movement and rendezvous. The hunter slowly walks through the forest, following trails and lines of ambush and heading toward wallows, thickets, and sleeping and feeding areas. Hunters often choose to lie in ambush by a trail to a watering spot or by a well-used line of movement; ambush from above, while hidden in a tree adjacent to fallen fruit, is also a favorite.

Both stalking and use of dogs are somewhat seasonal. In the dryer months when human steps in the forest are noisy, dogs may move quietly, follow spoor, and brave the elements better. They move through flooded waters poorly, cannot track, and lack spirit and courage when wet and cold. On the other hand, stalking is a wet season tactic. The forest floor is saturated and quiet as one walks slowly up and down slopes looking for spoor or hoping to encounter an animal. At that time, pigs, which are usually fat and less agile, may be approached from downwind and stalked within two or three meters. Often Agta men combine stalking with ambush tactics, since lengthy immobility during cold rain is more uncomfortable than slow but constant movement.

Hunting demands great mobility. Trips start within a kilometer of residential location and continue in remote, lightly hunted ranges a day's walk distance. During a stalk, one may walk up and down mountainsides all day and return to a hunting camp in the late afternoon. Driving with dogs consumes less time, but is a high-speed activity demanding great endurance and the ability to run through the jungle. Distance and mobility favor the establishment of hunting camps, either all male or mixed male–female teams and even occasionally two or three entire families. These camps are placed far into the forest, are occupied from one night to a week, and are used sporadically during a single season.

Personnel used in the several tactics of hunting depend on the numbers and health of adult and near-adult members of a single residential cluster. The number of children, newly lactating mothers, and able teenagers is important. Of course groups adjust as much as possible, especially when numbers are low, but obviously individuals on hand in a given day affect tactics of hunting.

Among some of the Agta groups, women participate in hunting in regular and predictable fashions, usually without consideration as to numbers of men. Nearly all women have some experience hunting. Furthermore, many women are successful hunters (Estioko-Griffin 1984, 1985; Estioko-Griffin and Griffin 1981b; Griffin *et al.* n.d.a).

The numbers of game killed by the Agta living at Nanadukan (Table 4.1), as recorded between the beginning of the 1980 wet season and the middle of the 1982 dry season, illustrate two points: The Agta are regular, successful preda-

TABLE 4.1

Recorded Game Kills by the Nanadukan Agta[a]

	Wet season[b] 1980–1981 58 days (11/11/80–1/7/81)	Dry season[b] 1981 179 days (3/16/81–6/25/81; 9/2/81–11/20/81)	Wet season[c] 1981–1982 116 days (11/21/81–3/13/82)	Dry season[c] early 1982 77 days (3/15/82–6/1/82)
Deer				
adult male	0	12	N.A.	N.A.
adult female	3	16	N.A.	N.A.
subadult	1	10	N.A.	N.A.
Pig				
adult male	2	6	5	5
adult female	4	13	18	14
subadult	8	8	22	23
Minor game				
monkey, adult	9	2	N.A.	N.A.
monkey, subadult	3	0	N.A.	N.A.
civet cat	3	4	N.A.	N.A.
One pig killed every:	4.1 days	6.6 days	2.6 days	1.9 days
One pig or deer killed every:	3.2 days	2.7 days		

[a] Average number of Agta at Nanadukan was 30, with a range of 15–50.
[b] Adulthood is as determined in the field by Agta (see, however, Mudar 1985). Field observations were made by anthropologists.
[c] Data in part from skulls saved from kills. The figures should be increased about 20% to include skulls not collected.

tors of large game, and success rates vary. The problem is to account for these fluctuations. Obviously, sampling error or environmental fluctuations might account for the data. Sampling error is always a problem when working with a small number of people for a short period of time. For example, some of the data collected between November 21, 1981 and June 1, 1982 were gained by asking Agta to save skulls of kills. We calculate that 20% of the kills were abandoned or were lost to dogs. We first asked that only pig skulls be saved then later asked for skulls of all animals killed. Confused by our requests, the Agta did as they saw fit, providing only minimum numbers of kills. We might also ask whether the fluctuations are due to idosyncracies of this particular group. Every group of Agta we know could produce somewhat different figures, depending on many factors. At Nanadukan, some women are active hunters; an adjacent group has few women who hunt. Nevertheless, we feel that the data are an acceptable characterization of hunting strategy of all of the less-settled Agta of northeastern Luzon.

Environmental fluctuations, not seasonality, seem to explain the data best. Between May and July 1980, two unusually serious typhoons hit northeastern Luzon. Loggers and Agta report that the flowering fruit trees were stripped of blossoms. As a result, the fruit did not develop and game animals were diminished in numbers and quality. Our first wet season experience verifies these data. Pig and deer were seldom killed and most of those killed were lower in body fat than we have observed in other years. Seldom did a kill have more than 2 cm of fat over the loins. Pigs remained lean throughout the wet season. At the end of the wet season, the number of available breeding sows was low due to the small numbers of surviving piglets born during the times of the bad typhoons. Hunting pressure further diminished the numbers. The game population characteristics reported by the Agta are corroborated by the wild pig adult–subadult kill ratios. The adult–subadult ratio was completely reversed in the 1980–1981 wet season and the 1981 dry season, amounting to 1:2 in the former and 2:1 in the latter. This ratio changed to approximately 1:1 until the following farrowing period in mid-1982. Throughout late 1981 and 1982 the pigs remained fat, healthy, and numerous.

An unusual dry season in 1981 followed the disastrous one of 1980. For the first time in about 5 years, the dipterocarps blossomed. The entire lower dipterocarp forest and lower montane forest and part of the montane forest blossomed (Allen 1985). There were no typhoons during this flowering or in the subsequent critical fruiting weeks. By the late dry season quantities of fallen fruit were feeding pig, deer, and smaller animals. More piglets per litter seem to have survived into youth and adulthood. The adult–subadult kill ratios may be accounted for by the providence of the cyclical reproduction of the dipterocarps and by the lack of damage to all fruiting trees throughout the critical period. Between 2 and 4 cm of fat was found on wild pig kills throughout early 1982.

While our counts of deer kills are less reliable, we may safely say that more deer were killed after the period of dipterocarp fruiting. Deer seemed to be fatter and healthier. Forest spoor were common, and Agta reported a general abundance. Agta prefer to secure wild pigs and given a choice will so select. While never fussy enough to ignore deer, Agta do, in a time of abundance of pig, hunt in localities most likely to yield them. While our data are tentative, we suggest that during the dry season of 1981 Agta were favoring deer due to their relative abundance and condition, having responded negatively to bad conditions less than did the pig population.

Partial testing of an hypothesis concerning the relations of Agta hunting, game behavior, and expansion of non-Agta agricultural fields has resulted in a model of Agta adaptation based on exploitation of ecotones and advantage in trade with farmers (Peterson 1981, 1982). This hypothesis argues that an ecotone rich in game, especially pig, exists between forests and agricultural fields. Agta, it is said, intensively hunt this ecotone, which is expanded as new swiddens are created and as old swiddens are converted into permanent fields by a rapidly growing farming population. The Agta subsistence system benefits from new swiddens; hence the expansion of non-Agta farmers is, by and large, positive. Subsequent examination of the hypothesis has, however, cast serious doubt on its veracity (Griffin *et al.* n.d.b; Rai 1982).

First, close examination of several field systems found in northeastern Luzon and of the forest itself indicate no ecotone exists and the ecotone concept itself may be inappropriate. Second, lowland-farmer dependence on Agta-procured animal protein is strongly contradicted by examination of the Peterson data (1981:3, 1982:34, 38) since farmers kill enough pigs in traps and do not need to trade (but see Griffin *et al.* n.d.b). Last, and most important, extended fieldwork among two separate Agta groups indicate that Agtas hunt most successfully far from agriculturalists' fields (Griffin 1981; Rai 1982).

Rai (1982:233) spent 64 days counting 48 hunts by Agta on the Disabungan River, San Mariano, Isabela (Figure 4.1). Thirty-seven trips were made beyond a 3-km perimeter around swiddeners, and 11 trips were made within. Only 11% of game killed during this time came from within the 3-km zone. In addition, Agta resided between 7 and 13 km from farmers' fields (Rai 1982:187). Likewise, in a sample of 122 hunting trips at Nanadukan, we found that little effort was expended in hunting in either their own or farmers' fields (Table 4.2).

Agta seldom bothered hunting near the fields of farmers. Of course, at Nanadukan and Disabungan, farmers are several kilometers distant from Agta camps, and at Nanadukan, Agta seldom hunt in their own swiddens. During

TABLE 4.2
Location and Distance of Agta Hunting Trips

	Number	Percentage
Location		
adjacent to swidden	1	0.8
interior mountain	36	29.0
near river	13	10.5
near stream	5	4.0
seashore	1	0.8
foothills	65	52.5
Agta swidden	2	1.6
beach terrace	1	0.8
Distance (km)		
1	2	1.6
1–5	48	38.7
6–10	62	50.0
11–15	10	8.1
16–20	2	1.6

1980 and 1982 only one pig was killed by Agtas hunting in a swidden. Another was killed when dogs hunting by themselves drove their quarry into a rice field during harvesting. When Agta do hunt in their swiddens, they do so at night with flashlights and the primary aim is to keep game wary and away from the crops. In addition, in 1982, the Agta placed no traps in or adjacent to cultivated areas. In short, perhaps ecotones and expanding swiddens do not seem to be at all helpful to Agta hunters.

Considerable variation does, it is true, exist among the many Agta groups throughout northeastern Luzon. The Agtas of the Dimapnat area of Palanan may not be as committed to hunting as are more isolated groups. They live close to farmers, often within only a few minutes walk from their dwellings to a lowlander's house. Our sporadic research between 1972 and 1982 in Palanan indicates that even these people hunt deep in the forest (see Bennagen 1976:40; Griffin *et al.* n.d.b). While the hunting emphasis may generally dominate Agta foraging strategies in and out of Palanan, tactics vary from place to place, group to group, and year to year, and much greater understanding of the tropical ecosystem is necessary before Agta hunting may be fully understood.

Although Agta consider themselves hunters, quantitative analyses of time expenditure and reliability and regularity of catch suggest that fishing is a basic source of food. Nearly all Agta are capable of fishing, and fish are found in most locations where Agta reside. The technology is simple and effective, requiring minimum outlay for purchased materials, which are all readily available from lowlander traders. Even in the rainy season some fishing is possible, especially in coastal areas. Spearfishing is the main tactic and is most concentrated in rivers and large streams. It involves the use of a pair of goggles made of wood, glass, and rubber bands, a metal wire propelled by a heavy rubber band, and occasionally a small steel barbed head attached to a line and a wooden shaft. Agta fisherman swim underwater, spearing fish and crustaceans as they encounter them.

The rivers have an abundance of fish, many of which live in varied microhabitats. Agta seasonal camps occasionally are placed far upriver during the dry season, when different fish are available. Indeed, much of the mobility, flexibility, and variability in Agta subsistence strategies and group organization is dependent on the reliability and providence of fishing resources. Agta are perhaps more conscious of the need to control access to riverine fish than any other forest food. In fact, Agta are most likely to be provoked to action over trespass of fishing domains.

Marine fishing is more diversified; modernized spearfishing, line fishing, and net fishing are all known, but they are all, we suspect, twentieth-century introductions. Agta are adapting well to the new technologies but rely on simple spearfishing. Some Agta (exceptions are found mainly among the Pahanan speakers) are afraid of the ocean and its fauna. Only close, inshore spearfishing is regularly undertaken. While some Agta fish from boats, most only accompany lowlanders. Nets, nylon line, and fishhooks are expensive but desired. Throughout the coastal portions of northeastern Luzon, a progression is found from Agta who are very reticent to enter the ocean at all to those who depend regularly and heavily on its fish and shellfish.

The Agta do not depend heavily on plants and in fact use them even less now than before World War II. Several classes of plant food are conspicuous: wild roots, greens and fruits, and the starch of the caryota tree (*Caryota cumingii*), a sago-like palm. All, excepting fruit, are supplements or lean-period foods. Fruits are eaten in quantity whenever in season. Throughout the dry months a range of wild fruits become available, sometimes in abundance and sometimes not, depending on the particular year concerned. Edible fruits, like most forest resources, are patchy, scattered, and seldom abundant in consecutive years. Rattan fruit is a main exception, yielding abundantly every dry season.

Agta do not often move to collect plant foods, especially fruits and greens or vegetables. Infrequently a brief move is made in order to reach good growths of roots, and more frequently temporary rainy season camps are placed far up remote streams adjacent to stands of *Caryota* palm. Generally, task groups simply forage during the day and return home by evening.

Honey collection and marine littoral-zone shellfish gathering are seasonal activities differing little from other gathering. While parties of both men and women search for honey in the dry season, usually only women and children collect the molluscs found on dead, uplifted coral beds and adjacent live corals. As with the procurement of plant foods, parties leave the base camp whenever the resources are desired.

Agta are easily termed "incipient farmers." All are aware of plant cultivation and claim to have prepared swidden in the past, even if they are not actively doing so when queried. Dependence on self-generated crops is variable indeed. Most Cagayan Agta seem to be interested and, after a fashion, successful small-scale swiddeners. In Isabela, much less interest, dependence, and success has been observed (Estioko-Griffin and Griffin 1981b; Rai 1982). In any case, Agta attempts to become successful farmers account for shifts in settlement and changes in social organization and subsistence strategies discernible today.

Agta are occasional root crop cultivators: sweet potato, cassava, and lesser cultigens are easily grown in the alluvial flats and slopes of the region's rivers. Indigenous Taro, a traditional Old World crop, demands more attention than introduced sweet potato and cassava and is less productive. Cassava and sweet potato are well suited to the mobility patterns and competing subsistence strategies of the Agta; after clearing and burning the small trees and shrubs, shoots are planted; then little further attention is given, and they are harvested sporadically and when convenient. Wild pig and deer may damage a crop, but usually with little effort a return is certain. The only real problem is theft of cleared land by the politically dominant non-Agta lowlanders.

Agta farming today is not just a supplemental source of food. The cultivation of roots and cereals is an explicit and overt attempt to control land in order that future options will include ownership and use of land. The Agta recognize that, given the power of others, they must play the game of identification with and maintenance of fields. Settlements must be located in field systems, sedentism is necessary to preclude theft, and a farming commitment must be made to ensure long-term survival. As the Agta say, "What will our grandchildren have if our cultivable lands disappear?"

Many Agta are unable to follow such a commitment. They cannot adjust to the immediate demands of their nonhorticultural resource procurement systems, cannot keep their fields from being stolen, and prefer to hunt and subsist on a day-to-day basis. They all try to balance out the several strategies and do choose to emphasize one or another combinations.

The Agta aim to acquire a quantity of plant foods sufficient for twice or thrice the daily consumption. While animal flesh is always desired, a diet so limited is never favored. Animal fat is especially prized, perhaps for the nutritional advantages that Hayden (1981; see also Speth and Spielman 1983) suggest, but lack of roots, grains, or other staples is considered deprivation.

Agta secure plant foods as situations permit. Since hunting usually brings the greatest return for time and energy invested (caloric return for caloric expense; Rai 1982), securing and exchanging fish and game for domesticated crops is the basic Agta subsistence strategy (Estioko and Griffin 1975; Headland 1978; Peterson 1978). Gathering almost always supplements and diversifies cultivated foods. Gathering occurs when farmers are unable or unwilling to exchange, when travel to exchange locations is impossible, and when traditional foods to accompany a good supply of fatty wild pig are desired.

The Agta in Time

To what extent does our understanding of contemporary Agta foragers relate to our knowledge and assumptions about prehistoric humid tropics foragers, including the Agta, since the early Holocene? We attempt to broaden the base for reconstruction of the past, visualizing reasonable past forager uses of a tropical rain forest setting, including variants of interaction systems between farmers and foragers (Peterson 1974).

The prehistory of the Agta and of Southeast Asian foragers is usually viewed as an evolution from only hunting and gathering to symbiotic relations with farming populations (Griffin 1985). An intensification of both food-getting efforts and socioeconomic interactions between two populations has been posited (Peterson and Peterson 1977). This model is built directly on today's observed forager–farmer exchange system and on the notion that the relation works to the advantage of both parties. This system may, however, be neither ancient nor in the long run adaptive, and several alternatives may be advanced for consideration.

Our basic premise is that since forager adaptations are highly flexible and the tropical rain forest allows diversity, a wide range of foraging economic strategies may have come and gone as specific conditions of population, group contact, and resource availability fluctuated. More precisely, nonhorticultural foragers may not have existed in the past several thousand years. Farming societies emphasizing cultivation over hunting may or may not have any great antiquity, and foragers need not have intensified trade relations with farmers until this century. Indeed, they may not have traded foods at all in past millennia, since they may have grown their own roots. The populations of the Sierra Madre may have gone through cycles of growth, intensification of food procurement, and collapse, during which one society's trajectory of change may have fluctuated from primarily hunting, gathering, and fishing to a concentration on swiddening.

If, as we hypothesize, the tropical rain forest is game rich and plant-food poor, a hunting gathering strategy may be fine only for very low population densities. Scarcity of wild roots as well as the difficulty involved in processing them and the low quantities of usable starch yielded by them (Allen 1985), coupled with the problems foragers would meet in the reproductive characteristics of the caryota palm, force us to suggest that experimentation with plant manipulation would be advantageous. The Agta do today often replant the top of tubers and their vines. They return to harvest new tubers when they calculate maturity. Taro and yam are well suited to foragers' manipulations (Harris 1972, 1977). If Agta are any example, such handling of wild plants would be widespread in past foraging tactics.

As Agta populations slowly increased, one option available would always be additional plant production. The knowledge was present, the land was plentiful, the capacity for work was certain, and necessary game resources were nearby. In other words, we do not have to assume that the Agta were dependent on their farming neighbors, because the Agta themselves were the farmers! Nor do we have to account for the presence of pottery-bearing archaeological sites by assuming that an association of visible house remains, pottery, and plant-harvesting stone tools belonged to a non-Agta population.

Without question, non-Agta swiddeners and permanent field cultivators have lived and do now live along the watercourses of the Sierra Madre. Numerous "neolithic" sites are found in the Cagayan Valley and adjacent foothills. Expansion across the mountains to the Pacific coast from the Cagayan Valley occurred before historic contact, inasmuch as the Spanish found and conquered farming peoples at Palanan (Keesing 1962). This expansion may have been encouraged by trade with Philippine coastal dwellers, always expert sailors, who ranged along the coasts of Luzon trading, slaving, and in general extracting a variety of resources.

Non-Agta populations resembled the Agta economically speaking. Horticulturally inclined people were always able to hunt. Given the game-rich forest and the minimal amounts of time necessarily invested in swiddening activities, adults would have been able to hunt and acquire all their needed meat. Fishing is likewise easy and reliable. Why grow crops to trade for meat and fish when both are readily available with little effort? The Ilongot in the mountains of Quirino, south of Isabela, certainly exemplify this argument (Rosaldo 1980). In other words, instead of having distinct populations of foragers and farmers in the past, prehistoric northeastern Luzon might have been occupied by generalists who hunted, fished, and planted root crops in swiddens for thousands of years, adjusting the degree of dependence on various subsistence systems according to local short-term perturbations like those found in the region today. The exchange systems that maintain variations between groups who concentrate on farming and those who hunt today might have been more varied in the past.

What then are the reasonable hypothetical models to be generated? The models must grant the flexibility inherent in Agta economic behaviors. A

game-rich yet plant-food-poor rain forest is a possibility, and seasonal providence of riverine fish and shellfish is a given. Marine or littoral fauna are
abundant. Probably forest game and fish buffer each other as each cycles
through its own fluctuations. Human predators should never have felt serious
depletion in both resources simultaneously. The critical factor may be a
general scarcity of edible plant foods; this lack has a direct relation to the
most variable resource system, horticulture.

Our original model suggests a history of changing intensities of trade
relations between foragers and farmers. Generally the model posits that over
time intensification increased until the system we observe today was realized.
The central focus of the relation was the exchange of forest game products
and fish for cultivated foodstuffs. The second model trajectory is one of Agta,
or any foragers in the humid tropics, passing through emphases on swiddening, on hunting and gathering, and, perhaps, on exchange of foods and goods
with other ethnic groups.

We favor the latter model because it conforms more comfortably to our
understanding of subsistence within this particular ecosystem. Of course, we
are considering only the past few thousand years, during which no major
climatic variations have apparently altered the Luzon land. As for perturbations induced by human activities, before 1960s, when industrial developments began, the chief man-made effect was that of fire, specifically by swiddening. Given the rugged nature of the mountains and hills and the absence
of broad valleys comparable to those that were intensely cultivated over the
past 6000 and possibly 9000 years in Highland New Guinea (Golson 1977),
we suggest that the impact of fire in northeastern Luzon has not markedly
altered the environment for the past 4000 years.

Within this ecosystem lived generalists who farmed, fished, hunted, and
husbanded. The mix of strategies was adjusted according to a multiplicity of
factors, including seasons that inhibited fruiting and destroyed crops, local
landslides, erosion, bad breeding seasons for wild pigs, and a run of good
years for fruit trees. The Agta we see today might not always have practiced
the same mix of strategies: Had we come here 500 years ago, their ancestors
might have been making numerous swiddens. Likewise, the non-Agta groups
of today might have been hunting intensively 150 years ago. Twentieth-century development has accelerated trends and has frozen a formerly fluid
system into a single time frame, maintained as a model of the past for some,
but containing within it, in its ecological aspects, the indications of a far more
important fluidity in the past for others.

We hypothesize that at least until non-Agta groups moved into the Sierra
Madre, Agta foragers experimented with reliance on whatever economic
strategy fed the largest number of people. Swiddening commitments could
have included less mobility in the settlement system than we see at present.

Scattered residential clusters of extended families would have been found as they are today among both the Agta and the hunting–swiddening Ilongot (Rosaldo 1980). Each family may have farmed swidden, hunted, and fished in adjacent resource zones, and maintained cooperation, visitation, and mate exchange among kin in a bounded dialect group. Again, both the Agta and the Ilongot exemplify this organization.

Our notions of what Asian foragers might have been are colored by what we want them to be. We may want them to be "real" hunter gatherers like the !Kung and other famous groups, but we are learning that even the !Kung were and are less static and less "pure" than supposed (Denbow this volume; Schrire 1980). Perhaps as we closely examine the special conditions of the humid tropics we will achieve fresh insights concerning rain forest foragers. As we move our view from a close understanding of the single foraging society and from Southeast Asia and compare adaptation of foragers in central Africa and the Americas, we may begin to understand human foraging adaptations in the humid tropics. The Agta, with their variability and in their specific environment, point the way to a few new possibilities.

Acknowledgments

As in all my Agta research, Agnes Estioko-Griffin has collaborated in writing this chapter. Data collected together and ideas generated over the years cannot be separated. Much of this chapter, therefore, reflects her work. In addition, Madeleine J. Goodman, Melinda S. Allen, Karen Mudar, and John Grove all helped in this research. Navin K. Rai continues to provide insightful criticism; his help on earlier drafts of this chapter is acknowledged, as are comments by Carmel Schrire and Polly Weissner. Any faults remain those of the author.

I thank Acme Plywood and Veneer, Inc. and its owner, managers, and staff for years of kind assistance. Mr. Alfonso Lim, Jr., Ms. Morgan Uytiepo, Mr. Pete Galimba, and Mr. Isabelo Miguel are especially thanked. Mr. Nick Cerra and Mr. Pat Jackson of Goodwood Management Corporation, Ltd. are thanked for constant help, interest, and encouragement.

Special thanks go to the Agta of Nanadukan, and directly to Galpong, Taytayan, Littawan, and Heting Taginod. Their favor has been indispensible to our research efforts. Dr. Jesus Peralta and Assistant Director Alfrado Evangelista of the National Museum of the Philippines are thanked for their assistance and guidance over the years. This research was funded by the National Science Foundation (grant numbers SOC73-09083-A01 and BNS80-14308) and by the National Endowment for the Humanities (grant number RO-00168-80-0123). We thank the foundations and the American taxpayers for their support. An earlier version of this chapter was given as a paper at the Third International Conference on Hunter–Gatherers, June 13–16, 1983, Bad Homburg, West Germany. Support assistance was provided by the University of Hawaii Foundation and the Werner Reimers Stiftung. *Aloha nui loa.*

References

Allen, Melinda S.
    1985   Ethnobotany of the Agta of Nanadukan. In *The Agta of northeastern Luzon: recent studies,* edited by P. Bion Griffin and Agnes Estioko-Griffin. Humanities series, University of San Carlos, Cebu City, Philippines.

Bennagen, Ponciano L.
1976 *Kultura at Kapaligiran: Pangkulturang Pagbabago at Kapanatagan ng mga Agta sa Palanan, Isabela.* Unpublished M.A. dissertation, Department of Anthropology, University of the Philippines, Diliman, Quezon City.

Brosius, James Peter
1981 *After Duwagan: deforestation, succession and adaptation in upland Luzon, Philippines.* Unpublished M.A. dissertation, Department of Anthropology, University of Hawaii, Honolulu.

Estioko, Agnes A., and P. Bion Griffin
1975 The Ebuked Agta of northeast Luzon. *Philippine Quarterly of Culture and Society* 3:237–244.

Estioko-Griffin, Agnes A.
1984 *The ethnography of southeast Cagayan Agta hunting.* Unpublished M.A. dissertation, Department of Anthropology, University of the Philippines, Diliman, Quezon City.
1985 Women as hunters: The case of an eastern Cagayan Agta group. In *The Agta of northeastern Luzon: recent studies,* edited by P. Bion Griffin and Agnes Estioko-Griffin. Humanities series, University of San Carlos, Cebu City, Philippines.

Estioko-Griffin, Agnes A., and P. Bion Griffin
1980 *Subsistence, sexual division of labor, and male–female relations among the Agta of northeastern Luzon.* Paper presented at the Second International Conference on Hunting and Gathering Societies, September 19–24, 1980, Quebec City.
1981a The beginnings of cultivation among Agta hunter–gatherers in northeast Luzon. In *Contributions to the study of Philippine shifting cultivation,* edited by Harold Olofson, pp. 55–72. Forest Research Institute, College, Laguna, Philippines.
1981b Woman the hunter: the Agta. In *Woman the gatherer,* edited by Frances Dahlberg, pp. 121–151. Yale University Press, New Haven.

Flores, J. F., and V. F. Balagot
1969 Climate of the Philippines. In *Climate of northern and eastern Asia,* edited by H. Arakawa, pp. 159–213. Elsevier, Amsterdam.

Golson, Jack
1977 No room at the top: agricultural intensification in the New Guinea highlands. In *Sunda and Sahul: prehistoric studies in Southeast Asia, Melanesia and Australia,* edited by Jim Allen, Jack Golson, and Rhys Jones, pp. 601–638. Academic Press, London.

Griffin, P. Bion
1981 Northern Luzon Agta subsistence and settlement. *Filipinas* 2:26–42.
1985 Agta subsistence strategies and the origins of tropical horticulture. In *Recent advances in Indo–Pacific prehistory,* edited by V. N. Misra and Peter S. Bellwood, Oxford and IBH, New Delhi.

Griffin, P. Bion, and Agnes Estioko-Griffin
1978 Ethnoarchaeology of Agta hunter–gatherers. *Archaeology* 31:34–43.

Griffin, P. Bion, Madeleine J. Goodman, Agnes Estioko-Griffin, and John Grove
n.d.a Agta women hunters: Subsistence, reproduction, and child care. Manuscript on file, Department of Anthropology, University of Hawaii.

Griffin, P. Bion, Thomas N. Headland, Navin K. Rai, Melinda S. Allen, and Karen Mudar
n.d.b Agta hunting, ecotones, and wild pigs. Manuscript on file, Department of Anthropology, University of Hawaii.

Harris, David R.
1972 The origins of agriculture in the tropics. *American Scientist* 60:180–193.
1977 Alternative pathways to agriculture. In *Origins of agriculture,* edited by Charles A. Reed, pp. 179–243. Mouton, The Hague.

Hayden, Brian
  1981   Subsistence and ecological adaptations of modern hunter/gatherers. In *Omnivorous primates: gathering and hunting in human evolution,* edited by Robert S. O. Harding and Geza Teleki, pp. 344–421. Columbia University Press, New York.
Headland, Thomas N.
  1978   Cultural ecology, ethnicity, and the Negritos of Northeastern Luzon: a review article. *Asian Perspectives* 21:128–139.
Headland, Thomas N., and Janet D. Headland
  1974   *A Dumagat (Casiguran)–English Dictionary.* Department of Linguistics, Research School of Pacific Studies. The Australian National University, Canberra.
Hutterer, Karl Leopold
  1982   *Interaction between tropical ecosystems and human foragers: some general considerations.* Working paper, Environment and Policy Institute, the East–West Center, Honolulu.
  1983   The natural and cultural history of Southeast Asian agriculture: ecological and evolutionary considerations. *Anthropos* 79:169–212.
Kessing, Felix M.
  1962   *The ethnohistory of northern Luzon.* Stanford University Press, Stanford.
Morren, George E. B.
  1979   Seasonality among the Miyanmin: wild pigs, movement, and dual kinship organization. *Mankind* 12:1–12.
Mudar, Karen
  1985   *Sus barbatus* (wild pig) and the Agta hunting in coastal Cagayan. In *The Agta of northeastern Luzon: recent studies,* edited by P. Bion Griffin and Agnes Estioko-Griffin. Humanities Series, University of San Carlos, Cebu City, Philippines.
Pandit, T. N.
  1976   The original inhabitants of the Andaman and Nicobar Islands. *Yojana* 20:1–16.
Peterson, Jean Treloggen
  1978   The ecology of social boundaries: Agta foragers of the Philippines. *Illinois Studies in Anthropology* 11. University of Illinois Press, Urbana.
  1981   Game, farming, and interethnic relations in northeastern Luzon, Philippines. *Human Ecology* 9:1–22.
  1982   The effects of farming expansion on hunting. *Philippine Sociological Review* 30:35–50.
Peterson, Jean Treloggen, and Warren Peterson
  1977   Implications of contemporary and prehistoric exchange systems. In *Sunda and Sahul: prehistoric studies in Southeast Asia, Melanesia and Australia,* edited by Jim Allen, Jack Golson, and Rhys Jones, pp. 533–564. Academic Press, New York.
Peterson, Warren
  1974   Summary report of two archaeological sites from north-eastern Luzon. *Archaeology and Physical Anthropology in Oceania* 9:26–35.
Philippine Atmospheric Geophysical and Astronomical Services Administration (PAGASA)
  1974   *Mean dry bulb temperature of synoptic stations.* Climatological Division, PAGASA, Quezon City.
  1975   *Extremes of temperature, rainfall, winds and sea level pressure of the Philippines as of 1972.* Climatic Statistics Section, Climatological Division, PAGASA, Quezon City.
  1978   *Tropical cyclone summaries from 1948 to 1978.* PAGASA, Quezon City.
Rai, Navin K.
  1982   *From forest to field: a study of Philippine negrito foragers in transition.* Unpublished Ph.D. dissertation, Department of Anthropology, University of Hawaii, Honolulu.

Rosaldo, Renata
  1980   *Ilongot headhunting, 1883–1974: a study in history and society.* Stanford University Press, Stanford, California.
Schrire, Carmel
  1980   An enquiry into the evolutionary status and apparent identity of San hunter–gatherers. *Human Ecology* 8:9–32.
Speth, John D., and Katherine A. Spielmann
  1983   Energy source, protein metabolism, and hunter–gatherer subsistence strategies. *Journal of Anthropological Archaeology* 2:1–31.
Yen, Douglas E.
  1976   The ethnobotany of the Tasaday: (Part III) Notes on the subsistence system. In Further studies on the Tasaday, edited by Douglas E. Yen and John Nance, *Panamin Foundation Research Series* 2, Panamin Foundation, Makiti, Rizal, Philippines.

5

Punan Foragers in the Trading Networks of Southeast Asia*

CARL L. HOFFMAN

Punan in the Mind

There is a vivid and time-honored conception of hunter gatherers in Borneo known as the Punan. Four generations of Western travelers, traders, colonial officials, and anthropologists have maintained a fascination with these people that persists to the present day. In its general outlines, the prevailing Western conception of the Punan has depicted an inordinately primitive hunting and gathering people who are widely dispersed in small bands scattered throughout the island of Borneo, wander through the deepest recesses of the rain forest, sleep in caves and in rude shelters of sticks and leaves, and are sickened by direct sunlight and fearful of other human beings. It is said that the Punan are seldom seen, hard to find, and considered to be savages and barely human wild men by the sedentary agricultural Dayak tribes of the longhouses and villages. The notion that somewhere in the dark inner forests of Borneo there lives a people more primitive, more exotic, and more remote than the sedentary Dayak headhunters has been an idea that has persistently whetted the imagination of Western visitors to the island for well over 100 years.

While brief references to these people began appearing in scholarly journals of one sort or another in the mid–nineteenth century, Punan achieved

*Portions of this chapter have appeared elsewhere in somewhat different form. Those wishing a broader and more detailed treatment of some of the issues raised in this chapter, as well as a general ethnographic overview of several hunting and gathering groups in Indonesian Borneo, are referred to Hoffman (1983).

123

genuine notoriety in the Western world in the year 1882 when a small group of them were documented and described as "the wild people of the woods" in a travel narrative by explorer and naturalist Carl Bock (Bock 1882:69–76). Bock encountered several male members of a Punan band at Long Wai, a village of the sedentary agricultural Modang Dayaks on the Mahakam River in eastern Borneo. He noted that these Punan were "on friendly terms with the Dayaks" of Long Wai (Bock 1882:76) and that the two groups were regular trading partners. Punan men appear to have been present at Long Wai throughout the course of Bock's stay:

> I had ample opportunity of observing the customs of the men during my stay at Long Wai, as I made several hunting excursions with different parties of them from time to time. (1882:71–72)

Bock had heard numerous stories and rumors about the wild people of Borneo's rain forests prior to his arrival, but evidently his observations of these Punan visitors to Long Wai did not quite match his expectations. He seems to have been particularly surprised at finding Punan in this relatively large and easily accessible agricultural village:

> I had often heard of the Orang Poonan, and of their alleged ferocity, and the state of utter savagedom in which they lived; and, though I had hoped to be able to see them in the course of my journey, I little expected to have been confronted with them so early. (1882:61–62)

Like so many Western travelers who would trek through Borneo in later years, Bock was intrigued by these people, and he promptly began entreating them to take him to their encampment in the forest. The Punan, he said, were a mystery that had to be solved (Bock 1882:69). His efforts were eventually rewarded with a one-day excursion to a Punan encampment in the forest:

> We started at sunrise, taking a small prau up the river—the Poonan chief, myself, Sariman, and four of the tribe. After paddling some twenty miles up the stream, the canoe was turned to the left into a narrow creek, up which we proceeded for a couple of hours. Suddenly the prau was stopped, and the Poonan made signs that we must land and go through the forest. I could see no trace of a landing-place; and, though I had kept an anxious look-out for any indication of human habitation, I had seen none. There was nothing to show that the spot at which we had stopped was different from any other point throughout the whole distance we had travelled—no trace of a path, not even a broken branch or other indication of traffic could I see, as a sign that human foot had ever trodden there before. I was afterwards told that the Poonans make marks on trees to show their movements and resting places to each other. After struggling with a bamboo thicket, which, to all appearance had never before been disturbed by human hand or foot, we found ourselves in the dense forest. The chief made a curious cry, *Hio! hio!* which was answered by another voice in the distance; and a few moments later I was led up to a tall tree, where, sitting under an awning of attap, supported by four bamboo sticks, were three young women, one of them with a baby in a sort of cradle slung on her back; while a fourth woman, much older, was

roasting the thick hide of a long-nosed monkey (*nasalis larvatus*) before a fire. Just beyond were two men, who came forward as we approached. . . . My stay among these primitive wild people of the woods was limited to a single afternoon. (1882:69–71)

The single afternoon in this Punan encampment appears to have exerted a rather profound effect on Bock's thinking. His reaction to this handful of people, their appearance and dress, the stark simplicity of their material accoutrements, and the seeming remoteness of their small settlement apparently far outweighed his earlier observations of Punan at the village of Long Wai. For when he emerged from this experience and, later, published his memoirs, Bock introduced a notion about the Punan that has remained with us ever since: that they are evolutionarily antecedent to the sedentary agricultural peoples of Borneo—the dwindling remnants of an earlier stratum of human life on the island:

> I believe these savages to be the true aborigines of Borneo. They live in utter wildness in the central forests of Borneo, almost entirely isolated from all communication with the rest of the world. (1882:75–76)

Bock's evolutionary perspective on the Punan spread. Charles Hose, speaking from experience with Punan groups in northern Sarawak, soon declared: "I have no doubt in my mind that this wandering race of people are the aboriginals of the country" (1893:157). Hose subsequently claimed that Punan "do not count beyond three" (Hose and McDougall 1912:211), and impressions of their childlike status proliferated as in this description of Punan in eastern Borneo:

> Inche Abdallah bin Nakhodah is my authority for the following information concerning these weird people. He is a Malay trader of Tawao. The Punans live in the dense jungle beyond the Sagai, in the interior of Bolongan, on the east coast of Borneo. They are a hunter tribe (corresponding somewhat to the Dorobo of East Africa), and will not come into a village, but always live in the jungle, as they are unable to bear the heat the glare of the sun. . . . They wear no clothes except the bark of trees; they have no houses or property, but wander about and sleep in trees. They are rapidly becoming extinct.
>
> They have a curious method of leaping three or four yards at a time, instead of walking, and their celerity of movement is astounding.
>
> Those who have had the opportunity of seeing the [sic] dance have told me that the performance is quite marvellous, their bodies seeming to be made of elastic and to contain no bones. (Beech 1911:17)

Despite these descriptions and various later embellishments (Andreini 1924; Miller 1942; Rubenstein 1973), a small number of more sober observations on Punan groups throughout Borneo also appeared. These were more often than not put forth by colonial officials, both British and Dutch, whose experience on the island enabled each of them to speak with authority about a specific Punan group in some specific locale (Hoffman 1983:113–116). The general perception that emerged from these reports was that the so-called Punan of Borneo were not quite what they appeared to be at first glance and that the prevailing idea of their status as dwindling representatives of Paleolithic man was flawed. The crux of the matter of who exactly the Punan were and the state of knowledge about their way of life was expressed in 1949 by Tom Harrisson, government ethnologist of Sarawak:

> No outside investigator has ever made a protracted study of any Punan group, and we do not even know if the persons so termed really represent a culturally, a linguistically or physically related people, or whether they have several origins and are uniform only in a common habit of nomadism. (1949:131)

Harrisson outlined this position more explicitly later:

> are the nomadic Punans or Pennans (or whatever it is) really so peculiar, so separate, just because they are nomadic and have (at present) a very special way of life? It is my own view that the Punans or Pennans (or whatever they are) do not differ fundamentally from the Kenyahs, Kayans and Kelabits, and that any one of these so-called "people," or all of them, could easily, under altered circumstances of nature, push out into the jungle and become nomadic as Punans. And, conversely that the people we talk of as Punans today do not stem from one simple and separate stock, but are themselves a reflection of not one but some of the now resident peoples around and among them. (1959:133)

Fantasies have a self-perpetuating force, however. Harrissons' opinions notwithstanding and in spite of the detailed and precise ethnography of nomadic groups in Sarawak by Needham (1954, 1955, 1972), it was still possible for the following profile of the Punan to appear in a popular Western tourist guidebook of 1977:

> The Punan: These tribesmen are the original inhabitants of Borneo who even preeceed the Dayaks. Very elusive aboriginals, the Punans run when they *smell* you coming. . . . It's better if you arrange to go with a government party, they could be defensive and hostile. They are fearless because they don't know any better. (Dalton 1977:352)

Punan in Space

Today, groups who are presently or were formerly nomadic hunters and gatherers and who are known as Punan, or by the dialectical variant Penan, are widely distributed across the island of Borneo (Figure 5.1). Overtly at least, they are racially identical to the surrounding and far more numerous sedentary agricultural Dayak peoples, sharing with them the same proto-Malay somatological characteristics of medium stature, prominent muscularity, and Mongoloid facial features and hair form. Punan are present in all but one of the four provinces of Indonesian Borneo, throughout much of

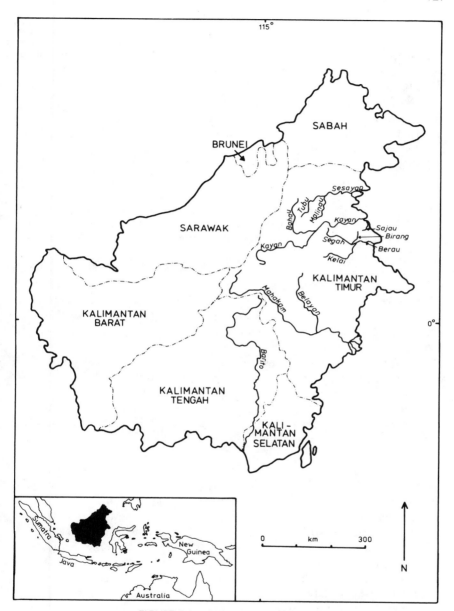

FIGURE 5.1 Punan research region.

Sarawak, and in Brunei. There are presently no known hunting and gathering groups in Sabah.

The ethnographic situation is complicated somewhat by the fact that there are groups called Punan who are not nomadic, and who have no tradition of every having been nomadic. Aside from the Punan Ba described by Needham (1955), there are the Punan Biau and the Punan Tepaling of the Belaga district in Sarawak, who have been described as "longhouse dwellers and sophisticated agriculturalists" for whom "there is no evidence, within living memory, to indicate that they were nomads" (Langub 1975:45).

In addition, several nomadic groups are known by names other than Punan or Penan. In Sarawak, some of these have been called Ukit, Bukit, Bukitan, Bukat, Pakatan, and Sian. In Indonesian Borneo, or Kalimantan as it is now called, there is a group known variously as Kareho and Penyabung who were nomadic until around the 1920s; and there are, moreover, two groups who are presently nomadic known as Basap (Hoffman 1983:22–23, 30–31, 154–164, 175–177). It can nonetheless be stated that the overwhelming majority of nomadic groups in Borneo are referred to as Punan or Penan and that in Kalimantan the term of reference is almost always Punan.

When people in Borneo speak of any one Punan group, the term *Punan* is invariably used in conjunction with some sort of toponym denoting the name of a river, tributary, or specific location at which the group is known to reside. A group called the Punan Berun, for example, are thus the Punan of the Berun River and the Punan Benyawung are the Punan of the Benyawung. These are largely terms of identification used by sedentary people to refer to a specific Punan group and by one Punan group to refer to another. A term such as this is rarely a label of identity by which people refer to themselves: A Punan of the Berun River, for example, is most unlikely to call him- or herself a Punan Berun, but he or she might, however, speak of Punan of the Kelai River as Punan Kelai.

As a term that denotes groups of nomadic hunters and gatherers, *punan* seems originally to have been an exonym—a name by which a group is referred to by other peoples. It was my observation in Kalimantan that the word *punan* was far more commonly a term of reference applied to nomads by sedentary peoples than an actual label of identity for the nomads themselves. The latter will on occasion refer to themselves as Punan, particularly when speaking to outsiders, but they are usually more prone to speak of themselves using some local lexeme meaning "us." In either case, *punan* is rarely a meaningful ethnic name in the minds of peoples so termed.

The precise meaning and derivation of the word itself is unclear. Harrisson (1949) maintained that in several of the Dayak languages with which he was familiar, *punan* is synonymous with the Malay word *hulu,* meaning "upriver" or "headwaters of a river." When I asked the various sedentary agricultural peoples I met to relate their own definitions of *punan,* the responses included "people who live up at the source of the river," "people who live deep within the forest," "people always moving from place to place," and "people who do not plant gardens and swiddens and must hunt for their food." Moreover, I was informed by Kenyah at the village of Long Nawang and by Ot Danum at Muara Joloi that in each of their respective languages *punan* is a verb meaning "to assemble, pile up, or gather things together." What seems to emerge from these various definitions is the probability that, for native peoples of Borneo, the use of the word *punan* to designate groups of people involves more a description of the geographic location and behavioral characteristics of the peoples so termed than a label of ethnic identity.

In many instances throughout Borneo, linguistic evidence strongly suggests that a certain ethnic label does in fact reflect a uniform, discreet ethnic group. Such is the case, for example, with the ethnic category *Iban.* Although widely dispersed throughout Sarawak, the various Iban subgroups share a common, relatively homogeneous language in which internal variation is minimal (LeBar 1972:180–181). The term *Kayan* similarly represents a group whose scattered segments "everywhere speak closely related dialects" (1972:169). Each of these peoples is moreover characterized by both a high degree of cultural uniformity and a strong sense of ethnic identity. The various groups known as Punan, however, do not share a single, common language. There is no Punan language spoken overall by the various people so termed. Nor do the many widely dispersed Punan groups exhibit either cultural uniformity or any sort of cohesive ethnic ideology. Instead, the evidence suggests that any one Punan group is almost always closer in language and customs to a specific sedentary agricultural people than it is to other Punan groups living in other regions of the island. This somewhat surprising state of affairs becomes particularly evident when we consider the traditional pattern of land tenure and residence in areas where Punan groups are found.

Contrary to the impression one derives from reading any number of early published accounts of Punan groups, one discovers on close inspection that these scattered groups do not wander freely across the length and breadth of Borneo's forested interior. What is instead the case is that each and every Punan group tends to confine itself to a somewhat loosely bounded territory that the group regards as its home range. We can fully understand the precise nature of a Punan group's home range by considering its two most significant characteristics. These two characteristics show us what essentially a home range is and where it is located.

Stated simply, the traditional home ranges of Punan groups are invariably tracts of primary forest. A primary forest area is either one that has never been cleared for cultivation or a previously cultivated area left fallow for so long that the resulting forest has returned to full growth. In either case, the area is one in which a wide array of different species of botanical life has grown to maturity. A primary forest topography is the first characteristic of a Punan group's traditional home range.

So far so good. The observation that Punans concentrate in primary forest should come as a surprise to no one. Yet it is important to realize just where it is that a Punan group's primary forest home range is situated. For while all Punan groups traditionally have lived within tracts of primary forest, it is not conversely the case that all tracks of primary forest have had Punan groups living within them. Vast uninhabited expanses of primary forest exist throughout Kalimantan. However, each group known as Punan has tended to confine itself to a tract of primary forest adjacent and contiguous to an area occupied by a specific sedentary agricultural people. In actual terms, this has usually entailed a Punan group living at the headwaters and tributaries of a river that is occupied in its lower reaches by a specific sedentary agricultural people with whom the Punan group is affiliated. This Punan group and this sedentary people thus share the same drainage area, in which the former hunt and gather in primary forest upriver and the latter practice agriculture and live in villages on cleared land downriver. Relative proximity to a specific sedentary agricultural people is thus the second characteristic of a Punan group's traditional home range.

The actual boundaries of such a home range have relatively little to do with topography, but are essentially cultural in nature. Today, as in the historic past, dispersed households of a Punan group have ranged about in an area of primary forest adjacent to an area occupied by a specific sedentary people with whom this group is culturally affiliated and with whom it is involved in a symbiotic trading relation. Every member of the Punan group has in his or her mind a cognitive map of the larger region around him or her that shows an area belonging to *orang macam kita*, "people of our kind," which grades somewhat vaguely and indefinitely into surrounding areas occupied by *orang macam lain*, "people of other kinds." "People of our kind" include a Punan group and the specific sedentary people with whom this group is economically interdependent and with whom it shares similarities in customs, historical traditions, and sometimes language as well. "People of other kinds" are culturally and historically different; and the members of the Punan group have perceived them as being *jauh*, "distant"—culturally as well as geographically.

The group's home range is thought of as the maximal spatial area claimed (and, in former times, defended) by both the group and its affiliated sedentary neighbors. Families moving about in the forest do not want to stray too far from "our kind" of people and too close to the various "other kinds" of people. It is this mental constraint that above all else furnishes the actual boundaries of a group's home range in the traditional pattern of residence.

The traditional conception, however, of just where it is exactly that the territory belonging to "our kind" ends and that belonging to "other kinds" begins has usually been rather vague. And indeed in former times it was largely putative. Disputes over territory and encroachment by "other kinds" of people were among the major causes of intergroup warfare, not only between a Punan group and some "other" sedentary people, but also between that group and some "other" Punan group as well.

In addition to the proximity of Punan and their sedentary agricultural neighbors are their social interactions. Each of these groups traditionally has stayed within a loosely demarcated area—the group's home range—located upriver from a sedentary people to whom the Punan group is well known. Local Punan are not a mystery as far as their sedentary neighbors are concerned: Punan and the villagers maintain close personal relations, individuals know one another quite well, and they address each other by name.

Not surprisingly, the Punan group resembles its sedentary neighbors in customs, traditions, and usually language. Thus in the Apo Kayan area of East Kalimantan, one of the Kenyah Lepo Tau legends tells tells how they and the nearby Punan Oho are both descended from one common ancestor. The Kenyah Lepo Tau find this perfectly acceptable since they and the Punan Oho speak similar dialects and are culturally almost identical. These two peoples have been economically symbiotic for as long as anyone can remember. The Kenyah told me that they have, on occasion, traded also with members of such groups as the Punan Aput, but that the conditions are never as friendly—or, as they expressed it, as "normal"—as when they trade with the Punan Oho. Likewise, the Punan Kelai claim to be descended from the same ancestor as gave birth to the sedentary Segai. As one Punan Kelai man expressed it, *"Segainya hampir sama bangsa dengan kita"* (The Segai are almost the same people as us."). In the Malinau district, both Tebiluns and Meraps say that their neighboring Punan are "the same as us—same people," a judgment with which every Punan group I visited in that area concurred. Tebiluns were particularly eager to clarify the point that the distinction between Tebilun and Punan was largely irrelevant to them. As far as they were concerned, they and their neighboring Punan were "People of the Tubu," some of whom lived downriver while others lived upriver. Finally, in a village of the Ot Danum people on the upper Barito River, I was told by one man to stop worrying about who was Ot Danum, who was Siang, and who was Punan Murung. He explained that while language varies slightly from one small village to the next along the upper Barito, all of the area's inhabitants nonetheless comprise a single, uniform type of people, with similar customs and historical traditions.

None of these sedentary, agricultural Dayak people feel any sort of kinship with Punan in general. The feeling of close affiliation that, say, the Tebilun have for the Punan of the Tubu does not extend to other groups throughout Borneo who are also known as Punan. A sedentary group's sense of affiliation is directed only to specific, neighboring Punan to whom those sedentary people are culturally similar. For example, in the Peso district at the middle Kayan River, the Kayan Malaran people refer to the Punan Berun and Punan Benyawung as "our little brothers." These Kayan Malaran abandoned their old swiddens and villages around 1940 and migrated to their present location down the Kayan River. They say, that inasmuch as they were moving to a new place downriver, it was only natural that their Punan brothers, who were known in those days as the Punan Bahau, should move right along with them. As such, when these Kayan moved downriver and built their present villages at Long Telenjau and Long Naha Ayah, "their" Punan staked out new primary forest territories nearby and formed two groups, each of which interact with one of the villages today.

The corollary to this proximity and affiliation between specific Punan groups and specific sedentary agricultural peoples is that any one Punan group is almost always closer in customs and language to its affiliated sedentary people than it is to other Punan groups living in other regions. In Kalimantan alone, one is struck by the profound differences among Punan groups, relating to almost everything other than their common hunting and gathering adaptation. Particularly striking is the broad divergence in customs pertaining to marriage, divorce, death and burial, and the treatment of the sick (Hoffman 1983:79–95). Many Punan are themselves aware of these cultural differences, and they will forcefully bring them to the attention of anyone who tries to tell them that all Punan are the same.

But what Punan themselves find especially significant are the profound linguistic differences evident among the various groups known as Punan. While the Punan Murung, for example, have no difficulty speaking and understanding the languages of the neighboring Siang and Ot Danum, they are completely at a loss in trying to communicate with Punan they occasionally meet from the upper Mahakam River. A Punan Murung man informed me that the speech of Punan from the Mahakam sounds to him like the "singing of birds." Likewise, two Punan informants from the Tubu River told of an incident that occurred as the two were traveling one time through the upper Mahakam. They met some Punan of a type they had never encountered before. My informants were not certain of who these Punan were or where they had come from. They related to me, in somewhat humorous detail, their difficulties in trying to communicate with these people. They said that they and the other Punan were totally unable to make themselves understood either in their respective languages or in any native language the two parties were familiar with. They finally found recourse in Malay and explained that the only thing they held in common with these strange Punan was their name.

Like Dayaks generally, most of the Punan groups of my acquaintance engaged in frequent warfare in former times. Many of these wars took the form of territorial disputes against other (different) Punan. Perhaps the most warlike Punan group were the Punan Lisum of the upper Belayan River, who by their own accounts were willing to fight practically anyone and everyone for any reason. As they expressed it, *"Asal ketemu, langsung membunuh"* ("If we met them, we killed them"). They went up against other Punan with no less vigor and determination than that expended in wars against people of other tribes. When I asked them if there was not at least one people, somewhere, with whom the Punan Lisum were usually at peace, I was told that they never made war against the Kenyah Lepo Timai. I asked why this was so and was told, "Punan Lisum and Kenyah Lepo Timai have always had the same customs and almost the same language. We speak their language and they speak ours. We and they are the same people."

In summary, therefore, *punan* appears to mean something quite different to native people of Borneo than it has to numerous Western visitors to the island. The term seems to encompass a widely diverse and unconnected array of peoples who differ considerably in language and customs and who appear also to derive from diverse ethnic origins. We noted earlier that Harrisson was of the opinion that "the people we talk of as Punans today do not stem from one simple and separate stock, but are themselves a reflection of not one but some of the now resident peoples around and among them" (Harrisson 1959:133). This perspective is developed more broadly in the work of historical linguist Robert Blust. After fieldwork in Sarawak—a comparative linguistic analysis that led him to declare that "there are no linguistic grounds for regarding Penan dialects as distinct from Kenyah" (1972:13)—Blust widened his focus to explicate some larger issues in Southeast Asian culture history. He has argued (1976) that the cultivation of rice was already firmly established as a mode of subsistence among Austronesian speakers prior to their migration and expansion. As such, Blust asserts the Punan of Borneo and such hunting and gathering peoples as the Kubu of Sumatra, the Toala of Celebes, the Tasaday of the Philippines—indeed all Austronesian hunters and gatherers—were at one time sedentary agriculturalists who subsequently became nomadic. This sentiment, as far as it concerns the Punan, was shared not only by Harrisson but also by a growing number of anthropologists specializing in Borneo today.[1]

The major question that arises, however, is *why* this return to nomadic hunting and gathering occurred and prevailed. In my opinion the answer can best be sought not among the Punan themselves but rather in a broader

[1]This view was widely accepted at the meeting of the Borneo Research Council at the American Anthropological Association Annual Meeting, Washington, D.C., 1982.

geographic perspective. The Punan, I believe, are the result of certain historical and economic forces that are larger than Borneo itself.

Punan in Time

> As soon as the Chinese polity extended its boundaries southwards, it gained control of
> a subtropical region of forested hills, with abundant rainfall and a year-long growing
> season. Although the animal and vegetable products of this environment were profuse
> and various, there came a time when a developing desire for luxuries in a unified
> Chinese state could be satisfied only by the import of products alien to the soil of the
> country. At first these were brought in over the north-western frontier, but even as
> early as the reign of Emperor Wu (141–87 B.C.) of the Former Han, Chinese imperial
> envoys with the help of men of Nan-yueh were exploring the South Seas in search of
> precious merchandise. (Wheatley 1959:18–19)

> The South China Seas have always been a Chinese lake. . . . Wave after wave of people
> who had made their homes in China, including Indo-China, moved southward. There
> was never any political barrier in the prehistoric and early historic days. The only
> incentive was to make a living, especially when people were unable to do so in their
> homeland. The search for such an opportunity took them to all the havens and lands
> that they knew, and they did not hesitate to exploit any possibilities which they
> happened to encounter abroad. (Cheng 1969:19)

> I would guess that wherever you go in the world, there will probably be Chinese. (An
> elderly Kayan from the village of Long Naha Ayah, middle Kayan River)

There is an unfortunate tendency among ethnographers to regard Borneo
as an island unto itself, isolated from the rest of Asia. As a result of this narrow
and limiting perspective, Borneo is approached conceptually as though it
were another New Guinea, and its peoples are studied as though their
cultures were pristine. Yet while the interior of New Guinea has apparently
indeed been inhabited by culturally isolated groups—many of whom remained uncontacted and undisturbed by outside influences until well into
the present century—the ethnographic situation in Borneo presents quite
another picture. Since the earliest centuries of the present millennium, the
island of Borneo has been a heavily trafficked and well-trodden crossroads
for many of the major civilizations of the East. Borneo and its peoples have
played host to Indians, Arabs, Persians, and, perhaps most notably, Chinese.

It is not known precisely when the Chinese first appeared in Borneo.
Robert Heine-Geldern thought that Chinese contacts with insular Southeast
Asia in general could be traced at least to the first century B.C., and cited
evidence from Borneo to support his opinion:

> Taking all into account, one may come to the conclusion that direct Chinese influence
> in Indonesia goes back at least to the early Han period, that is at the very latest to the
> 1st century B.C. However, the ornamental designs of the Dyak tribes of Borneo and of

the Ngada of Flores are so clearly related to Chinese designs of the late Chou period that one can hardly avoid the inference that Chinese contacts started as early as the beginning of the third century B.C., and probably earlier. (1945:147)

More specifically pertaining to Borneo, another historian has argued:

both *a priori* reasoning and such data as we possess lead to a very early knowledge of Borneo on the part of the Indians and Chinese and that in the case of both of them probably, but the latter certainly, they must have been familiar with Borneo before they became familiar with Java, the navigation to which was far more difficult and more dangerous. (Braddell 1941:72)

While such views remain a matter of speculation, certain points are a matter of record and quite beyond doubt. Chinese coins of the Chin and Han dynasty have been discovered at the mouth of the Sarawak River, and coins dating from the Sung period have been unearthed throughout the island (Runciman 1960:13). Sepulchral pottery vessels from the Han period have also been unearthed (Purcell 1951:15), and hoards of Chinese pottery, some of it dating from the T'ang and Sung periods (Runciman 1960:13), are kept as heirlooms by Dayak peoples throughout Borneo. Excavations at Santubong in Sarawak attest to the existence of Chinese mining and smelting activity in that area during the T'ang and Sung periods (Cheng 1969:12–22). Furthermore, by the ninth century A.D., the kingdom of Brunei—from which the island of Borneo derives its name—was already a prosperous trading entrepôt known to the Chinese as Po-ni. Chinese historical sources document its existence as well as its gifts of tribute to the Chinese court in A.D. 977 and again in A.D. 1082.

The long-term presence of Chinese in Borneo is further reflected in such place-names as Kinabatangan, meaning the "Chinese River," and Kinabalu, meaning the "Chinese widow," the name of Borneo's highest peak. Numerous stories and legends dispersed throughout the island concern the alleged Chinese ancestry of certain Dayak tribes. Statements to the effect that the Murut and Dusun peoples of northern Borneo have been heavily infused with "Chinese blood" were recorded by such early travelers to the island's interior as St. John (1862:Vol. 2, p. 313), Low (1894:172), and Beccari (1904:253). Ascertaining the historical accuracy of these legends, and the precise degree of Chinese genetic contribution to Dayak peoples is beyond the scope of our discussion, but what is significant is that these stories are very widespread and enduring. I myself heard several legends of this nature, some of which concerned the Punan. Allegations that one or another Punan group is *campur dengan Cina,* "admixtured with Chinese," are often part of the folklore about Punan that one hears from coastal Malays. Whatever their merit, these stories, along with the other evidence noted previously, attest to a lengthy and continued Chinese presence in Borneo that has persisted to the present day.

We turn now to the anthropological implications of the Chinese influence.

> Tangible evidence of Chinese contact with Sarawak is afforded by the "sacred jars,"
> undoubtedly of Chinese origin. The "jar cult" played an important role not only in
> Borneo but also among the Moi of southern Indochina, in the Philippines, in Formosa,
> and various other parts of the Indonesian region. (Purcell 1951:27)

The importance of these sacred jars to the native peoples of Borneo has been documented and described in great detail by travelers to the island since the time of St. John (1862). It is well known that wherever one travels throughout Borneo, one cannot help but notice the many ceramic jars that are highly regarded and prominently displayed in Dayak villages by families of rank. Those that I saw most often in central and eastern Kalimantan were large stoneware urns, often well over a meter tall, invariably covered with a smooth brown glaze, and further ornamented with a dragon design in relief slightly below the rim. In addition to these dragon jars are brass gongs, of different sizes but of the same general type as those used in Indonesian gamelan orchestras.

Aside from having numerous practical uses, these famous heirloom items are symbols of rank and prestige and are often the preferred goods for bridewealth and indemnity payments. Formerly in many areas of the island, the jars served as the final resting places of the dead. These jars and gongs are not items of local manufacture. Dayak obtain these tokens of wealth in trade with peoples from "outside." Dayak peoples attest to the fact that *dari jaman nenek moyang dulu* ("from the time of our ancestors long ago"), they have been trading with *Orang Luar* ("people from outside") who have come to their areas from places downriver. More often than not, these outsiders have been coastal Malays and, more recently, Buginese. It is from these traders, the Dayaks say, that they have received their precious gongs and jars.

It is also from these traders that many Dayak peoples have obtained various items in addition to the gongs and jars. One such item has been salt. While a few Dayak groups, such as the Kelabit and Lun Daya, have been fortunate enough to have their own sources of salt within their respective territories, most groups elsewhere have been largely dependent on trade as the source for this essential commodity. This has also been the case with regard to metal. While such peoples as the Kenyah of the Apo Kayan area were able in former times to extract and work their own metal, most Dayak groups have had to rely on trade to obtain metal for their weapons and implements. For most Dayak groups, trade has also been the source for such items as cloth, tobacco, and, since about the 1960s, money. Indeed throughout the areas of Kalimantan that I visited, trade was the major, if not only, source of cash income for Dayak peoples.

As such, trading relations with downriver and coastal Malays and Buginese have served as the principal means by which most Dayaks have obtained not only such socially important status items as gongs and jars, but also a variety of essential commodities. It is important to note, however, that these Malay and Buginese traders have merely been acting as middlemen within a much broader trading network. For while most sedentary agricultural Dayak groups have, by and large, traded directly with these downriver merchant–traders, the ultimate source of the trade goods involved have been the Chinese.

By the twelfth century A.D., Chinese sources describe regular Chinese trading activity in Borneo (Purcell 1951:27–28). This trade was also observed by some of the earliest European visitors to the island. Antonio Pigafetta, who had formerly sailed with Magellan, visited Brunei in 1521 and made note of the Chinese silks and porcelains that he saw there, as well as of the natives' adoption of Chinese weights and money (Purcell 1951:448). Daniel Beeckman, trading at Banjermasin in the year 1714, recorded his observations of Chinese ships and their cargoes (1718/1973). Thomas Forrest, visiting Brunei in 1776, recorded his perceptions of that busy port:

> At Borneo town the Chinese sometimes build junks which they load with the rough produce of the Island of Borneo, and send thence to China. I have seen a dock close to town in which a Chinese junk of 500 tons has been lately built.
>
> Imagine a fleet of London wherries, loaded with fish, fowls, grain, &c., floating up with the tide from London Bridge towards Westminster: then down again, with many buyers floating up and down with them; this will give some idea of the Borneo market. (Quoted in Purcell 1951:487)

Carl Bock, traveling through eastern Borneo a century later, made similar observations about the coastal town of Samarinda:

> The commerce of Samarinda is very considerable. Everyone is a trader, even the Pangerans and the Hadjis. Here, as everywhere, John Chinaman musters in great force, and the greater part of the export trade is in his hands. At the time of my arrival there were five vessels—three of them barques of considerable size—all belonging to Chinamen, being loaded with the produce of the country, which is brought down the river on long rafts. Rattan is the staple product; but gutta-percha, timber, beeswax, and edible birds' nests (*Sarong boerung*) . . . are also exported in considerable quantities. (1882:25–26)

Aside from attesting to the volume and bustle of Chinese economic activity in eastern Borneo during the past century, Bock's observations provide us with a brief glimpse of the type of export commodities that have attracted the Chinese to Borneo. The Chinese have come to Borneo for centuries not as tourists but as traders, seeking certain raw natural commodities found primarily within large tracts of primary forest. These include the following:

Aloes wood: Called *kayu gharu* throughout Borneo, this is the pathologically diseased portion of several different species of trees of the genus *Aquilaria*. When burned, this wood gives off a rather pungent fragrance, and thus it has been used as incense by Chinese, Indians, and Arabs.

Rattan: A modification of the Malay word *rotan,* this term covers several species of climbing plant that has been utilized for everything from basket-making to housebuilding throughout Borneo and for furniture elsewhere in Asia and in the rest of the world.

Camphor: A modification of the Malay word *kapur,* this substance is obtained in Borneo from the tree *Dryobalanops aromatica,* where it is found in hardened, crystalline form. Camphor has long been used in the making of medicines and incense and in embalming.

Resin: Known throughout Kalimantan by the Malay word *damar,* resin is collected from various dipterocarpaceous trees and used chiefly as an adhesive, as caulking putty, and as a base for varnish.

Gutta percha: A resinous latex obtained from the sap of certain trees of the genus *Palaquium,* this multipurpose substance has traditionally been used by the Chinese as an adhesive and as waterproof caulking for sailing vessels. Less frequently, it was also utilized in the making of medicines. Gutta percha continues to be used throughout the world for various purposes, most notably as electrical insulation and in dentistry.

Beeswax: As its name implies, this is a wax secreted by bees. Among the many uses to which it has traditionally been put by the Chinese, beeswax has long been utilized in the making of base substances for a variety of ointments and medicines for external use.

Edible birds' nest: These nests are made entirely of a gelatinous, translucent, beige-colored substance secreted through the saliva of a small swift (*Collocalia nidifica*). Another type, regarded as quite inferior, consists of smaller quantities of this substance mixed with moss and other impurities and is made by *Collocalia linchii,* a related species of swift. Called *sarang burung,* these small nests are found deep within caves attached to the upper sections of the walls close to the roof. Long valued by Chinese for the preparation of various culinary dishes, especially soups, they are also claimed by some Chinese to have various medicinal uses as well.

Bezoar stones: Generally referred to as *guliga* throughout central and eastern Kalimantan, the use of these for medicinal purposes has been a pan-Asian phenomenon, encompassing Chinese, Indians, Persians, and Arabs. Generally speaking, bezoar stones are the hardened concretions occasionally found in the internal organs of certain animals, especially ruminants. Borneo, however, has long been the source of two rather unusual and very valuable types of bezoar, the more common being *batu monyet* (gallstones from monkeys). These are found, I was told, in the gallbladders of any one of three varieties of monkey, and in perhaps no more than one out of a hundred of these monkeys that are hunted. Ranging usually anywhere in size from that of a pea to a lima bean, *batu monyet* has been known to occur in sizes reaching that of a small chicken's egg. They are inordinately valuable to traders; the larger the gallstone the higher the value. Even more valuable, however, is the second type of bezoar found in Borneo, called *batu landak*. These are concretions that form around external wounds in porcupines, and they are extremely rare. I was informed that only one out of hundreds of porcupines are to be found with such a concretion, and that porcupines themselves are encountered only occasionally—most often at night. *Batu landak* are always very small, extremely light in weight, and able to fetch fantastic prices at all times. These bezoars from Borneo, *batu monyet* and *batu landak,* have been valued for centuries by Chinese who hold them in very high regard as medicinals. Indeed, both varieties have been, and continue to be, the raw sources of an extensive array of pharmaceutical remedies for everything from stomachache to asthma.

Rhinoceros horns: Like bezoar stones, the horns from wild rhinoceros, called *tanduk badak,* have been thought for centuries to possess enormous curative properties. As such they have been pounded, pummeled, and ground into a wide variety of Chinese medicines, including aphrodisiacs and treatments for impotence.

Illipe nuts: Known throughout Borneo as *buah tengkawang,* the illipe nut when fully grown is roughly the same size and shape as an avocado. It grows wild in primary forests in several species of trees of the genus *Dipterocarpus*. The Chinese, and coastal Malays as well, have long valued illipe nuts as the raw source of a popular type of cooking oil. Illipe nuts have also been used to make tallow, candle wax, and lubricating oil as well as a base substance in certain modern cosmetics.

With the probable exception of illipe nuts—a relatively recent entrant to the list—the items just listed were the principal forest products of Borneo sought after for centuries by the Chinese. It has been these items, many of them serving as basic ingredients in the traditional Chinese pharmocopoeia, that attracted the Chinese to Borneo possibly ever since their maritime trading activity began. And it has been these items for which the Chinese brought not only culturally important status items, but also essential goods and commodities, to trade with the native peoples of the island's interior.

For most of these native peoples—sedentary, village-dwelling, swidden agriculturalists—this crucial trading activity was associated with a rather serious problem. All of the forest product items just noted are found chiefly within large tracts of primary forest. The sedentary agricultural peoples of Borneo, by and large, tend to be situated often considerable distances from large areas of primary forest. An agricultural village is surrounded by its gardens and swiddens, which are in turn surrounded by broad expanses of secondary forest growing up over previously cleared land. Primary forest, where it exists at all, is usually limited to small patches at the outer periphery of the village's land.

This feature has been studied in close detail, and has even been quantified, in parts of Borneo that I did not visit. Dove, studying the Kantu people of western Kalimantan, made some interesting observations concerning the nature of the 10 km² held by the Kantu village of Tikul Batu (Dove n.d.). Approximately one quarter is given over to rubber trees, fruit trees, burial grounds, dwellings, and the combined surface area of trails and waterways. The remaining land is forest, 92% of which is secondary growth. Primary forest comprises only the remaining 8%, and much or perhaps all of this was cleared and farmed during the nineteenth century. Dove estimates, moreover, that each household in the village clears an average of 2.3 new swiddens every year.

In many areas in east and central Kalimantan today, there are few if any patches of primary forest to be seen at all. Immense tracts of shadeless, tangled, secondary scrub stretch for miles in all directions, forming the outer boundaries of one village and sprawling outward to meet identically denuded tracts at the borders of another village. This is particularly true for districts such as Malinau, Peso, Kelai, and Tabang but quite different in places such as the Apo Kayan, where tracts of primary forest close to the villages are actually kept as reserves (C. Mackie, personal communication, 1984). The general degree of deforestation means that many sedentary peoples are forced to travel great distances from their villages in order to gather forest products in sufficient quantities for trade. Undertaking such journeys involves an expenditure of time that most of these sedentary agriculturalists simply do not have.

Thus the dilemma faced by many of the native peoples of Borneo, especially those living far from primary-forest tracts, is that they need the goods and commodities offered by the Orang Luar in exchange for primary-forest products but might find themselves unable to expend the necessary time and effort needed to collect these products in quantities sufficient for trade.

This last point is important and worthy of some emphasis. Sedentary agricultural people in Borneo today can and do gather forest products to varying degrees. They certainly gather rattan, if nothing else. The essential question, however, is whether sedentary agricultural groups are able to find and collect sufficient quantities of products from the primary forest to exchange for needed amounts of salt, metal, cloth, etc. I noted that most sedentary groups are indeed unable to accomplish this beyond the occasional, haphazard, one-shot excursion to the nearest stand of rain forest. In short, one cannot be in two places at once. This dilemma, I believe, is the point we ought to keep in mind when attempting to speculate on the origins of the so-called Punan. I suggest that it was precisely this inability of sedentary agricultural groups adequately to exploit two distinct environmental zones that led to the type of hunting and gathering we see in Borneo in the ethnographic present. For in many parts of the island, this problem appears to have been alleviated, and in some places resolved. In many parts of Borneo, and perhaps at many times in the past, the Dayak peoples of the interior tended to specialize. And having done that, they presented the ethnographic picture that greeted Bock on his arrival at the Modang village of Long Wai over a century ago. It is a picture that has greeted the arrival of visitors in some areas since: a sedentary agricultural village community tending its gardens and swiddens and receiving forest products from a culturally related group of hunters and gatherers from the forests upriver whom the villagers refer as Orang Punan.

This is not to say that individuals and families have not switched from concentrating on the forest to the swiddens time and again. The point I want to stress, however, is that specialization at the group level has resulted in a form of intergroup economic interaction that has persisted to the present day. A Punan group trades raw commodities from a distant primary forest with sedentary agricultural people with whom it shares a historical tradition of alliance and cultural affiliation. The nomads bring their forest products to their sedentary neighbors downriver, receiving in exchange primarily such items as salt, tobacco, cloth, and iron machetes. On rarer occasions the Punan group might also receive such coveted wealth tokens as dragon jars and gongs; nowadays some groups receive money.

These goods and commodities that the sedentary agricultural people give to their Punan are themselves the returns from trading relations carried on between these sedentary people and non-Dayak traders. After receiving forest products from their Punan, the sedentary villagers subsequently trade these products with Malay traders from farther downriver in exchange for salt, tobacco, cloth and clothing, metal, household implements, gongs, jars, and also cash. It is from these traders that the sedentary agricultural people receive these goods and commodities on a fairly regular basis. In Kalimantan, these itinerant traders have been members of the various local coastal Malay ethnic groups (e.g., Orang Bulungan, Orang Berau, Orang Kutai, and Orang Banjar), although Buginese from Celebes have also been conspicuous participants. This century many sedentary groups have also traded directly with small-scale Chinese shopkeepers operating out of downriver market towns (see Krohn 1927:315–316).

Whomever the trader might be, however, it is important to note again that his position is that of middleman. His role in the trade network is essentially to accumulate and assemble the primary-forest products for eventual transport and resale to coastal Chinese exporters.

We are thus now able to perceive the outlines of numerous traditional trade networks, involving rain forest hunters and gatherers, sedentary swidden agriculturalists, itinerant middlemen traders, and coastal mercantile exporters, that has persisted intact to the present day. While widely scattered across Borneo, these many regional networks have all had in common the same basic function of moving forest products out of the island while moving trade goods and commodities in.

The popularily held, frequently invoked assumption that Punan live deep within the jungle in order to hunt animals for food is refuted by the fact that wild pigs and other game animals are often just as plentiful in downriver areas and near large towns as they are in the primary forest. In fact, pigs are often more common near villages than in the forest due to their attraction to the gardens and swiddens of the villagers (see Griffin, this volume). Dayaks living downriver in or near such towns as Malinau, Long Peso, Tabang, and Tumbang Kunyi often told me of having to guard their swiddens against foraging wild pigs and mentioned the difficulty of preventing the pigs from ravaging their gardens at night. Likewise, wild deer are often found drinking at riverbanks no more than 5 km outside of any one of these towns. In short, Punan groups have scant cause to dwell within primary forest areas for hunting alone. It is possible that some tracts within the forest were selected for vegetable foods like sago, but in general I would argue that Punan groups have dwelled and still do dwell in tracts of primary forest because that is where most of the raw commodities that they collect and trade are to be found.

Ironically enough, the specialized economic role of these groups is clearly stated in the earliest published reference to nomadic Punan of which I am aware:

> In the neighbourhood of the Kanowit, and scattered about these countries, are the wandering tribes of Pakatan and Punan, which seldom build regular houses, but prefer running up temporary huts. . . . They are the great collectors of wax, edible birds' nests, camphor and rattans. (St. John 1862:Vol. 1, p. 45)

Considering the often colorful descriptions of Punan that were to follow in subsequent decades (e.g., Bock 1882:69–76; Beech 1911:17; Andreini 1924:76–77; Miller 1942:266–272; Rubenstein 1973:1330–1337), it is somewhat surprising to find these people described in the first known report of their existence as simply collectors of forest products.

In nearly all of the literature on Punan that has followed, however, forest product collection and trade are mentioned only parenthetically, if at all, as being just another thing that Punan do. Invariably, trade is described as a subsidiary activity in which Punan groups engage on the side, out of sheer necessity, to support their life-style as hunters. This view of the Punan is expressed most succinctly by Needham: "They need to trade with the settled peoples . . . in order to remain nomads" (1972:177–178).

My observations in 1980–1982 of Punan suggest precisely the opposite. They do not trade in order to remain nomads, but rather, I suggest, they remain and possibly even became nomads in order to trade. This is not to say that sedentary horticulturalists do not gather forest products. What is at issue here is a degree of specialization. In historic times the level of warfare kept horticulturalists more bound to their regions than they are today, thus reducing their opportunities to engage in extensive forest exploitation. This must have been more noticeable in regions far from extensive primary-forest tracts, though areas such as Apo Kayan, being close to the primary forest, probably always housed people who move easily and frequently from fields to forest as they do today (C. Mackie, personal communication, 1984). Punan do not collect forest products to support themselves while hunting; they hunt, gather, and fish to support themselves while collecting forest products. Trade is not just another thing the Punan do; it is the thing that Punan do most. The collection and trade of forest products, not hunting, is the historic raison d'être of nomadic, primary-forest groups known as Punan. Both the demand for these forest products and the local need for the goods they bring in exchange have led to the hunting and gathering adaptation that modern-day Westerners observe in groups called "Punan."

Punan in General

The publication of *Man the Hunter* (Lee and DeVore [editors] 1968) was unquestionably a milestone in the anthropological study of hunters and gatherers. The overall impact of this volume was profound. As a state-of-the-art compendium, *Man the Hunter* rapidly became a staple feature of undergraduate reading lists and an almost inevitable contribution to university training in anthropology. For many anthropologists in the 1970s, this volume has been both a touchstone and fact of life, but, like all comprehensive books, *Man the Hunter* has led to the codification and entrenchment of certain questionable ideas that ought now to be rethought.

The original symposium drew on the expertise of some 75 social anthropologists, physical anthropologists, and archaeologists, as well as specialists in demography, ecology, and human ethology. In synthesizing the available data on hunting and gathering societies, the sponsors hoped not only to explicate various ethnographic issues, but also to shed some new light on hunting and gathering as a once universal stage in the evolution of man. Thus for most of the symposium's participants, the study of surviving hunters was perceived as a crucial means toward understanding and illuminating mankind's long-term hunting and gathering past (Lee and DeVore 1968:4). Perhaps the most eloquent statement of this perception was that expressed by Murdock:

> Many of the peoples who subsisted by hunting and gathering at the time of Columbus have disappeared entirely and been replaced by stronger peoples. Others have been reduced to dependency—on reservations or as servants or outcaste groups. Still

others have made a transition, in some form or another, to modes of subsistence based on agriculture, animal husbandry, or industrial employment. Only a handful still live an independent life of hunting and gathering, nearly all of them under markedly altered conditions. It is time—indeed, long past time—that we took stock of these dwindling remnants, for it is only among them that we can still study at first hand the modes of life and types of cultural adjustments that prevailed throughout most of human history. (1968:13)

Murdock seems to have been stating the majority opinion and also a major running theme of the symposium, namely that present-day groups of hunters and gatherers are "dwindling remnants" of the once universal Paleolithic phase of human evolution and that they comprise isolated pockets of human-kind's pre-Neolithic, preagricultural past. The conviction that modern for-agers are somehow leftover relics from the Pleistocene was, of course, well established in anthropology long before the appearance of *Man the Hunter*. Yet here it was expressed most articulately and systematically. The impact of this volume on subsequent thinking has been such that the perception of contemporary hunters and gatherers as living representatives of Pleistocene man is now usually accepted as an article of faith. It has remained the basic underlying premise of not only many new ethnographies of hunting and gathering groups, but also of any number of theoretical studies in which the literature on contemporary hunters and gatherers is used to advance argu-ments in issues ranging from Pleistocene subsistence strategies (Martin 1983) to the evolution of human sex roles (Tanner 1983).

The time has come to rethink this premise and place it in its proper perspective. We need to reexamine the ethnographic record and draw a distinction between two quite different types of hunters and gatherers, types that might be termed *primary* and *secondary*. Primary hunters and gathers would be those groups who do in fact appear to be the aboriginal, autoch-thonous peoples of their respective regions, groups for whom there exists at present no cultural, historical, or linguistic evidence of a prior agricultural adaptation. This would include such well-known examples as the Andaman Islanders, most if not all Australian Aborigines, and the Pygmy peoples of central Africa.

Secondary hunters and gatherers are those groups that clearly appear to derive from sedentary agricultural peoples. These are groups for whom hunt-ing and gathering is essentially a readaptation to a specialized ecological niche. Some examples of this type would obviously be the Punan of Borneo and other nomadic groups of Borneo known by different names (Hoffman 1983:20–21, 23, 30–31, 175–176) as well as groups such as the Kubu of Sumatra, the Tasaday of Mindanao (Hoffman 1983:117), and the Phi Tong Luang of northeastern Thailand (Hoffman 1983:183–188; cf. Bernatzik 1951). Moreover, a careful reexamination of the ethnographic literature might also suggest the inclusion of most or all of the hunting and gathering groups of the

Indian subcontinent as well as most if not all of the hunting and gathering groups of the tropical forest zone of South America. It is indeed not inconceivable that we may ultimately have to include the majority of the hunting and gathering peoples of the ethnographic present.

Under no circumstances, however, should this distinction between primary and secondary hunters and gatherers be interpreted to imply, even faintly, a distinction between "real" hunters and gatherers and groups that are somehow "unreal" or "impure." Such a conception would be not only spurious but also quite counterproductive. The fact that a hunting and gathering group appears to derive from a former sedentary agricultural adaptation does not mean that it is in any way less genuine, less interesting, or less instructive with regard to hunting and gathering as a way of life. I mention this point in response to a particularly unfortunate legacy of *Man the Hunter* and its pervasive evolutionary perspective. While a small handful of nomadic groups were cited in this volume as having derived from agricultural peoples, they were, predictably, depicted as being the "wreckage of evolved agricultural societies" and the result of "cultural devolution" (Lathrap 1968:29). This was expressed by the editors:

> A further consideration was introduced by Lathrap (Chapter 3) and others who cited a number of hunting peoples who were "failed" agriculturalists. This *readaptation* to hunting, or "devolution" as it has been called, characterized such classic "hunters" as the Siriono of South America and the Veddas of Ceylon. (Lee and DeVore 1968:4)

I would like to suggest, however, that the apparent "devolution" of these peoples is a function of nothing more than our insistence on imposing the paradigm of evolution on everything we see. Consider the case of the Veddas of Ceylon. While there is probably little doubt that these people did in fact derive from sedentary, agricultural Sinhalese at some time in the past, there is, I think, no good reason to suspect that failure or devolution had anything to do with their readaptation to hunting and gathering. As for what did, a quick perusal of the Seligmanns' prodigious ethnography on the Veddas (1911) is repaid with such notable observations as these:

> The wilder Veddas of those days built no houses but lived entirely in caves; trading places called *wadia* near the caves, but out of sight of them, under a tree or rock, were used for bartering, where all strangers would stop and shout and then wait until their calls had been answered from the caves. (Seligmann and Seligmann 1911:32–33)

> The few necessities of life which the forest does not supply, such as steel and iron for their arrowheads and axes, and the very scanty clothing which they wear, they obtain by barter, their wax, and honey, elk flesh and ivory, being eagerly sought after by the neighbouring Sinhalese. (1911:94)

These observations should, by now, have a somewhat familiar ring. The picture that emerges is not one of cultural retrogression, but of economic specialization. We are dealing here with people not unlike the Punan, who, rather than being the "wreckage" of sedentary societies, appear to be ones who opted to specialize in the collection of resources that could best be obtained in primary-forest areas.

There is perhaps no more illustrative an example of economic specialization at the group level, in which hunters and gatherers were involved, than that which prevailed in the Nilgiri Hills of South India at the time of Rivers' classic study (1906). For there on the same plateau lived the pastoral Todas, the agricultural Badagas, and the artisan Kotas along with whom Rivers (1906:6) called "two wild, dwarfish tribes" of hunters and gatherers (the Irulas and Kurumbas), who ranged through the plateau's forested slopes. Living together in close economic interdependence, these tribes presented what for all intents and purposes was a caste system, with accompanying *jajmani* relations, but without the overarching ideology of Hinduism.

In addition to distinguishing between two fundamentally different types of hunters and gatherers, it might also be useful to note the distinction between two quite different types of hunting and gathering adaptation. We ought to recognize the clear and profound difference between subsistence hunting and gathering on the one hand, and what has been called "commercial" hunting and gathering on the other (cf. Woodburn 1980:98–99). Subsistence hunting and gathering is the type that by definition prevailed universally throughout the Paleolithic and that continued into modern times among such groups as the Andaman Islanders and the Aborigines of Australia. Commercial hunting and gathering, which probably has a long history, is an adaptation in which the collection of natural commodities for trade forms a major, if not primary motivation for hunting and gathering.

Commercial hunting and gathering may well turn out to be far more important an issue than many of us ever imagined in both historical as well as anthropological terms. For example, we know that the seventh-century Indonesian kingdom of Srivijaya, on the island of Sumatra, developed into statehood from its role as a major commodities entrepôt for the China trade.

> Srivijaya's rise to power depended upon trade and upon China's sponsorship. Put in a rather simplified form, the international trade pattern that was of greatest importance in the early period of Southeast Asian history was the east–west trade between China and the region including India but stretching further west to Persia and beyond. Precious Western goods, including forest products believed to have medicinal qualities, were exchanged in China for silks and porcelain, lacqueurs and other manufactured items. By the seventh century control of much of this trade, at least for the trade passing backwards and forwards between the Indonesian islands, was in the hands of Malays whose chief center of power was somewhere in southern Sumatra, on the eastern coast of that island.
>
> How this came about is still uncertain. (Osborne 1979:29)

An even earlier kingdom, indeed the earliest known Indonesian kingdom, was that of Kutai in eastern Borneo. This fifth-century state was situated at the lower reaches of the Mahakam River, where, as we have seen in modern times,

> the produce of the country . . . is brought down the river on long rafts. Rattan is the staple product; but gutta-percha, timber, beeswax and edible birds' nests (*Sarong boeroeng*) from the interior, and trepang, tortoise-shell, and turtle eggs from the coast, are also exported in considerable quantities. (Bock 1882:25–26)

It may of course be purely coincidental, but one cannot help but notice that the two islands that provided the setting for the earliest Indonesian kingdoms are the same two islands in Indonesia on which may presently be found full-time, specialized nomadic hunting and gathering groups collecting forest products for trade. Thus, a particularly intriguing question is the extent to which hunters and gatherers may have contributed, however unknowingly, to the formation and maintenance of complex states.

A serious reexamination of the ethnographic record in its historical perspective may well indicate that commercial hunting and gathering not only accounts for most hunter gatherer groups of the ethnographic present, but also explains why the hunting and gathering adaptation has persisted to the present day. If this is proved to be the case, then the seemingly endless array of new studies on hunters and gatherers that focus on such matters as optimal foraging strategies, cost–benefit ratios, patch use models, and other aspects of subsistence really tell us very little about these people.

Acknowledgments

Research for this study was made possible through the support of the National Institutes of Health (N.I.M.H. grant number 5 F31 MHO7995-03) and through the approval and cooperation of Lembaga Ilmu Pengetahuan Indonesia (LIPI).

I thank my thesis supervisor and mentor, Professor W. Davenport; greatest Punan of all, he expanded my vision beyond structure and description into the wider view of foragers in the mercantile world. Finally my thanks to Carmel Schrire for helping to edit this chapter and to Cynthia Mackie for helpful criticism and comments on Apo Kayan.

References

Andreini, E. L.
    1924   The gypsies of Sarawak (Punans). *Journal of the Malayan Branch of the Royal Asiatic Society* 2:76–77.
Beccari, Odoardo
    1904   *Wanderings in the great forests of Borneo.* Archibald Constable, London.
Beech, Mervyn W. H.
    1911   Punans of Borneo. *Man* 11:17–18.
Beeckman, Daniel
    1973   *A voyage to and from the island of Borneo in the East-Indies.* Dawsons of Pall Mall, Folkstone. (Original work published 1718.)

Bernatkik, Hugo Adolf
    1951   *The spirits of the yellow leaves.* Robert Hale, London.
Blust, Robert A.
    1972   Report on linguistic field work undertaken in Sarawak. *Borneo Research Bulletin* 4:12–14.
    1976   Austronesian culture history: some linguistic inferences and the relations to the archaeological record. *World Archaeology* 8(1):19–43.
Bock, Carl
    1882   *The head-hunters of Borneo: a narrative of travel up the Mahakkam and down the Barito.* Sampson Low, Marston, Searle and Rivington, London.
Braddell, Sir Roland
    1941   An introduction to the study of ancient times in the Malay Peninsula and the Straits of Malacca. *Journal of the Malayan Branch of the Royal Asiatic Society* 19(1): 21–74.
Cheng, Te-K'un
    1969   *Archaeology in Sarawak.* W. Heffer and Sons, Cambridge.
Dalton, Bill
    1977   *Indonesia handbook.* Moon Publications, Franklin Village, Michigan.
Dove, Michael
    n.d.   Swidden systems, and their potential role in agricultural development: a case study from Kalimantan. Manuscript on file, Gadjah Mada University, Java.
Harrisson, Tom
    1949   Notes on some nomadic Punans. *Sarawak Museum Journal* 5:130–146.
    1959   *The peoples of Sarawak.* Sarawak Museum, Kuching.
Heine-Geldern, Robert
    1945   *Prehistoric research in the Netherlands Indies.* Southeast Asia Institute, New York.
Hoffman, Carl L.
    1983   *Punan.* Ph.D. dissertation, University of Pennsylvania, Philadelphia. University Microfilms, Ann Arbor.
Hose, Charles
    1893   The natives of Borneo. *Journal of the Royal Anthropological Institute* 23:156–172.
Hose, Charles, and William McDougall
    1912   *The pagan tribes of Borneo* (2 vols.). Macmillan, London.
Krohn, William O.
    1927   *In Borneo jungles: among the Dyak headhunters.* Bobbs-Merrill, Indianapolis.
Langub, Jayl
    1975   Distribution of Penan and Punan in the Belaga district. *Borneo Research Bulletin* 7:45–48.
Lathrap, Donald W.
    1968   The "hunting" economies of the tropical forest zone of South America: an attempt at historical perspective. In *Man the hunter,* edited by Richard B. Lee and Irven DeVore, pp. 23–29. Aldine, Chicago.
LeBar, Frank (editor)
    1972   *Ethnic groups of insular Southeast Asia* (Vol. 1). Human Relations Area Files Press, New Haven.
Lee, Richard B., and Irven DeVore
    1968   Problems in the study of hunters and gatherers. In *Man the hunter,* edited by Richard B. Lee and Irven DeVore, pp. 3–12.
Lee, Richard B., and Irven DeVore (editors).
    1968   *Man the hunter.* Aldine, Chicago.

Low, Sir Hugh
    1894   Discussion. In The natives of Borneo, by Charles Hose, pp. 171–172. *Journal of the Anthropological Institute of Great Britain and Ireland* 23:156–205.
Martin, John F.
    1983   Optimal foraging theory: a review of some models and their applications. *American Anthropologist* 85:612–629.
Miller, Charles C.
    1942   *Black Borneo*. Modern Age Books, New York.
Murdock, George P.
    1968   The current status of the world's hunting and gathering peoples. In *Man the hunter,* edited by Richard B. Lee and Irven DeVore, pp. 13–20. Aldine, Chicago.
Needham, Rodney
    1954   Penan and Punan. *Journal of the Malayan Branch of the Royal Asiatic Society* 27(1):173–183.
    1955   Punan Ba. *Journal of the Malayan Branch of the Royal Asiatic Society* 28(1):124–136.
    1972   Penan. In *Ethnic groups of insular Southeast Asia* (Vol. 1), edited by Frank LeBar, pp. 176–180. Human Relations Area Files Press, New Haven.
Osborne, Milton
    1979   *Southeast Asia; an introductory history.* George Allen and Unwin, Sydney.
Purcell, Victor
    1951   *The Chinese in Southeast Asia.* Oxford University Press, Oxford.
Rivers, William Halse Rivers
    1906   *The Todas.* Macmillan, London.
Rubenstein, Carol
    1973   Poems of the indigenous peoples of Sarawak: some of the songs and chants. *Sarawak Museum Journal* 21(42) Part 2:Special Monograph 2.
Runciman, Steven
    1960   *The white rajahs: a history of Sarawak from 1841 to 1946.* Cambridge University Press, Cambridge.
St. John, Spenser
    1862   *Life in the forests of the Far East* (2 vols.). Smith, Elder and Co., London.
Seligmann, Charles G., and Brenda Z. Seligmann
    1911   *The Veddas.* Cambridge University Press, Cambridge.
Tanner, Nancy M.
    1983   Hunters, gatherers, and sex roles in space and time. *American Anthropologist* 85:335–341.
Wheatley, Paul
    1959   Geographical notes on some commodities involved in Sung maritime trade. *Journal of the Malayan Branch of the Royal Asiatic Society* 32(2):115–140.
Woodburn, James
    1980   Hunters and gatherers today and reconstructions of the past. In *Soviet and Western anthropology,* edited by Ernest Gellner, pp. 95–117. Columbia University Press, New York.

6

Soaqua and Bushmen: Hunters and Robbers

JOHN E. PARKINGTON

Introduction

This chapter investigates a problem with two facets, one specific to the archaeology carried out in the southwestern Cape of South Africa since 1968, the other more basic to the understanding of hunter gatherer subsistence in historic and protohistoric times. The specific question concerns the identity of people known to early travelers in the Cape as Soaqua or Sonqua. A more general concern is that our static view of hunter gatherer existence combined with an often detailed historical record may seduce us into misreading historical accounts as representative of the prehistoric past and thereby obscuring the real situation.

As a starting point I describe a life-style that emerges fairly clearly and consistently from the diaries and travelogs of seventeenth- and eighteenth-century literate visitors to the southwestern Cape. The people observed are referred to as Soaqua or more rarely Sonqua and only later, apparently, as Bosjesmen or Bushmen. Next I suggest that there is a clear archaeological manifestation of the Soaqua in the uppermost excavated levels of caves and rockshelters that corresponds with the eyewitness accounts in the same area. This allows us to study the time depth of the behavior involved and adds aspects of material culture and land use to the details noted historically. Thus we can ask and expect to be able to answer the question: Who were the Soaqua? Were they pastoralists engaged in some special or atypical subsistence task such as hunting? Were they pastoralists who had temporarily lost their stock holdings and were reduced to a largely hunting and gathering existence? Or were they simply hunter gatherers living on the fringes of pastoralist society, coping with the problems of living in a pastoralist-dominated landscape? I believe the last to be the case.

At this point a more general question arises. Can we take the short-term and relatively uninformed observations of the early travelers as a reflection of a long-term pattern that persisted unchanged since precontact times? Or should we assume fluid transformations among and between segments of the prehistoric populations, intercepted almost randomly by the movement of exotic visitors? Written reports of these encounters would then reflect an amalgam of misunderstandings, misrepresentations, and ethnocentrisms. How are we to contextualize the useful but partial comments of eyewitnesses at the end of the prehistoric trajectory? The Soaqua are a case history in the study of protohistoric hunter gatherers, and allowing them a changing past is the main challenge.

Archaeological work in the southwestern Cape since the 1960's demonstrates some correlation between the appearance of the Soaqua pattern and the appearance of sheep bones and ceramics in stratified deposits. There is little doubt that settlement patterns were quite different in the millennia before domestic stock appear in the archaeological record and hence imply a very different life-style. The intrusion of domestic animals drastically changed the potential of the landscape, even for those who retained an essentially nonherding existence. The archaeological evidence of these subsistence changes reminds us that many versions of the basic hunter gatherer economy are viable at this latitude, perhaps making us nervous about global generalizations. After reviewing the sequence in the southwestern Cape, I suggest that the relation between historical or ethnographic observations and the archaeological sequences that precede them should be viewed as a trajectory of change in which the past leads to, but does not simply mirror, the present.

Before getting down to details, the geographic setting and the contact-period literature in the southwestern Cape are briefly reviewed (see Figures 6.1 and 6.2).

The physiography of the southwestern Cape is dominated by the parallel ridges of mountains known as the Cape Folded Belt (Figure 6.1). These are quartzites, sandstones, and shales that, as the name suggests, have been folded into ridges that parallel the present western and southern Cape coastlines and impart great topographic variety to the landscape. Between the mountains and the sea lie low undulating coastal plains, broken and defined by massive outliers of the mountain chains to the east. The Cape Peninsula is such an outlying string of mountains separated from the mainland by a broad sandy isthmus known now as the Cape Flats. The soils of the coastal plains are formed on sands or shales, whereas in the mountains, little soil formation has taken place except in the bottoms of the intermontane valleys. Beyond the

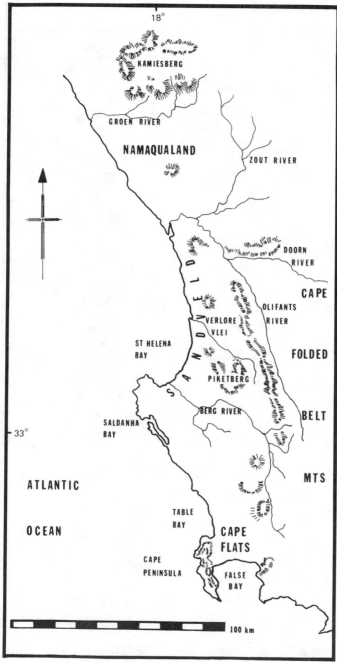

FIGURE 6.1   Physiography of the southwestern Cape.

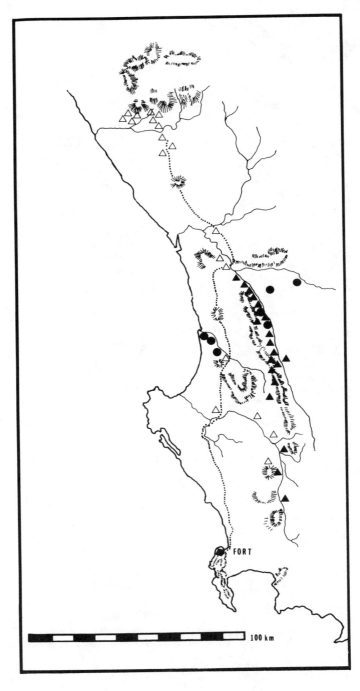

FORT

100 km

Cape Folded Belt is a shale-dominated landscape of little relief with a rather monotonous character of endless plains dotted with more resistant, rocky, flattop hills. In parts, substantial mountains of the escarpment form a second barrier to penetration of the continental interior.

Climatically the Cape differs from the rest of the subcontinent in experiencing winter rainfall, derived from east-moving cyclonic depressions in the southern Atlantic. These rain-bearing lows clip the Cape in winter but track farther south in the summer. Thus the southwestern Cape shows a rainfall gradient with higher rainfall at the Cape, decreasing northward as the northern limits of the winter rainfall belt are reached; rainfall is highest in the folded ranges, fairly low at the coast, and very low in the rain shadow east of the Cape Folded Belt.

These geological and climatic patterns generate a varied but patterned set of vegetation communities. The core of this is the Cape fynbos ("fine-leaved bushes"), a shrub-dominated flora best represented in the better-watered regions of the Cape Folded Belt. East and west of the mountains are related communities that share many genera and species but are adapted to more arid circumstances. On shale soils, vegetation with a greater grass component exists, but overall, the fynbos suit browsing ungulates rather than the grazers of the drier karoo interior. The broken terrain of the Cape Folded Belt with great geological, climatic, and vegetational variety offers a wide range of habitats for all kinds of animals, in contrast to the relative monotony of the karoo plains.

Turning to historical matters, Portuguese sailors rounded the Cape at the end of the fifteenth century, ushering in 150 years of almost exclusively coastal contact between literate observers and indigenous groups (Raven-Hart 1967, 1970). Though many details of the customs and material culture of indigenous people are listed in these interactions, an ambiguous picture emerges as to population distributions or land-use patterns. The impression gained is that the coast and coastal plains were occupied by sheep- and cattle-herding pastoralists who lived in settlements of various sizes but a fairly consistent structure. Pastoralist encampments featured circular arrangements of dome-shaped houses made of reed mats lying over a hemispherical framework of saplings. Since people moved regularly in search of pasture, they needed portable dwellings that could be packed on the backs of oxen. Visiting sailors were interested in trading sheep and cattle from these pastoralists, and they occasionally met indigenous people without domestic stock; this dichotomy was neither explored nor explained at this time.

FIGURE 6.2 Soaqua–European contact in the southwestern Cape: (●) rockshelters; (△) Bergh or Van der Stel expedition contact locations; (▲) Van Riebeeck expedition contact locations; (.....) Bergh expedition route.

In 1652 when the Dutch established a refreshment station at the Cape, it became possible for Europeans to develop more intimate relations with indigenous people. The diaries of Jan van Riebeeck, first commander of the Fort at the Cape, illustrate this transition very clearly. They show a growing awareness of intergroup relations that highlights the importance of stock owning and stock theft among rival groups (Elphick 1977; Thom 1952). The picture, however, is complicated by the very presence of the Europeans, in that visits by ships to Table Bay had become predictable and reliable events to be exploited for resources. Precontact situations, by definition, cannot be historically documented, so it is a challenge to unearth from Van Riebeeck's comments vestiges of the prehistoric settlement pattern. Interpreters like Harry, Doman, and Eva, members of the local cattle-less Strandloper (beach-comber) peoples who had kin among local cattle-owning groups, were influential at this time as entrepreneurs, exploiting an increasing European presence and an ever more dependable supply of exotic goods. Yet they were far from being unbiased commentators on the details of indigenous life-styles; nor can their responses be taken out of the context of the contact situation.

Within a few years of the founding of the Cape settlement, Van Riebeeck began to use new terms, obviously derived from indigenous usage, to describe the local people. Until then the word *Hottentot,* or some version of it, had been ubiquitous. Permanent settlement allowed regular observations to be made over several years and informants began to explain, presumably not dispassionately, the distinctions between segments of the local population. Pastoralist groups began to be referred to by their specific names (Namaqua, Chariguriqua, Hessequa) or by the names of their leaders (Oedesoa's people, Gonnema's people), sometimes with the word *Hottentot* tacked on (as in the Namaqua Hottentot). Other herd-owning peoples were confusingly referred to as *Saldanhamen,* a term that creates problems in that Saldanha was the original name for what is now called Table Bay but was later transferred to what is presently Saldanha Bay. Apart from names, less clear to Van Riebeeck were the relations among groups occupying the Cape Peninsula, some of whom did not own stock but lived, apparently permanently, as Strandlopers along the shores.

Van Riebeeck noted great variability among Cape peoples but reported no local hunter gatherers until his soldiers began to penetrate north in search of raw materials. The people they encountered here, specifically the Soaqua, were arguably hunter gatherers. These groups (Figure 6.2) had no domestic stock and were given their name by pastoralist interpreters. As the European presence grew, explorations into the interior became more frequent, and interaction with the Soaqua increased. In 1682 Olof Bergh, journeying north to find the sources of copper ornaments worn by Namaqua, referred to some "Somquaas, alias Bushmen" (Mossop 1931:85), and a new link in the chain of terminology was added. Before the end of the seventeenth century the term *Bushmen* or *Bushmen Hottentot* complemented and replaced *Sonqua Hottentot* to describe people living to the north and east beyond the Cape settlement. Finally, by the end of the eighteenth century, observers, naturalists, and botanists, traveling to the borders of the colony some 250 km from the Cape, generated more extensive descriptions of indigenous peoples. By then groups near the Cape had been severely disrupted, decimated by disease, and largely incorporated as a work force into the growing colony (Marks 1972; Elphick 1977).

Ethnographic Evidence

The increased documentation of Soaqua life by the Dutch settlers makes interesting reading, though Sherlock Holmes' talents are needed to discriminate between the false impressions and intentional misrepresentations by settlers and informants. Van Riebeeck made a start on November 13, 1652 by questioning his resident interpreter Harry (or Herry), who only spoke "a little broken English," as to the relations among people living near Table Bay. As Van Riebeeck understood, there were

> three tribes of people, similar in dress and customs. One is called the Strandlopers, or as they call themselves in the broken English they have learned, Watermen, because they live on mussels which they find on the rocks and some roots from the earth. As far as we have observed they are not above 40 or 50 in number and, in any case, have no cattle. The second kind are those from Saldanha, called by them Saldanhamen, who arrive here every year with countless cattle and sheep. The third kind were called by him Fishermen, who after the departure of the Saldanhamen, arrive here with cattle only and no sheep, and who subsist by fishing, without boats, from the rocks with little fishing lines. (Thom 1952:80)

Harry made it clear that there was considerable enmity between these Fishermen and other local peoples, but as Thom observes in an editorial note, the stock-owning character of the Fishermen may have been a misunderstanding since "Van Riebeeck and his people would surely have experienced some difficulty in understanding the mixture of gesticulations, clicks and broken English" (Thom 1952:80 Footnote 1).

Only two months later a second discussion revealed that the Fishermen were also known as Soaqua and that they lived by stealing and robbing from pastoralists. "After all they lived on nothing else but what they stole: none of their possessions were their own. Everything had been stolen from the Saldanhars" (Thom 1952:127). The Saldanhars, Harry added, "consequently pursued them at every opportunity and when they caught any of them killed them without mercy and threw them to the dogs" (Thom 1952:127). Soaqua is thus the first Dutch usage of an indigenous term to describe local people, and as such, deserves some comment. The suffix -*qua* is a masculine dual ending, indiscriminately adopted thenceforth by the Dutch to refer to people of both sexes, to individuals, and to groups of any size. The root *soa* is probably a version of a verb meaning to gather, particularly to gather wild foods, as is the word *sa* in the Nama language (Vedder 1938:124; Ernst Westphal, personal communication, 1983). An alternative meaning (Hahn 1881:3) suggests that the root may have been a nasalized *sa,* referring to aboriginal people. Although an exact etymology is impossible in the absence of detailed knowledge of Cape Peninsula grammar, it is likely that Soaqua and the currently fashionable term *San* share the same root. It seems certain too that Harry did not intend the word *Soaqua* to have been capitalized, in the sense of referring to named communities, but meant it as a reference to a particular, and widespread, life-style. Soaqua seems not to be a word of equivalent status to Namaqua or Chainouqua (see Hoffman this volume on the usage of punan).

Our present grasp of the connotations of Soaqua is strengthened immeasurably by the Dutch account of meeting some Fishermen on April 3, 1655, almost exactly three years after Van Riebeeck's arrival. Jan Wintervogel spent almost three weeks traveling about 340 km north and reported that "they had come across a certain people of very small stature, subsisting very meagrely, quite wild, without huts, cattle or anything in the world, clad in small skins like these [Table Bay] Hottentots and speaking almost as they do" (Thom 1952:305). After describing encounters with cattle-owning Saldanhars, Wintervogel added, somewhat confusingly, that he and his men had "also met some Souquas, named Fishermen, who had no cattle and were enemies of the Watermen and Saldanhamen" (Thom 1952:305). The official who transcribed this report does not expressly connect the "people of small stature" with the "Souquas, named Fishermen" but subsequent traveler accounts make it highly likely that these two brief mentions refer to the same, Soaqua, life-style.

After 1655 the word *Soaqua* (occasionally *Soanqua*) replaces *Fishermen* as the term to describe robbers or thieves, and the distinction between them and stock-owning pastoralists becomes entrenched in the written record. On July 16, 1656, after a quarrel between Harry and Table Bay pastoralists, three sons of a local leader arrived at the Fort and demanded that Harry be seized for cattle theft, arguing that

> He is a good-for-nothing and was already conspiring with the robbers, named Soanqua, with a view to enlarging his following, and for that purpose had already gathered many around him, none of them being of his own people. . . . He had gathered these about him, a course he still daily pursued in order by that means and by propagation to become in due course as powerful in followers as he was rich in cattle. This was very obvious, they said, as we knew that when we first came here he did not even have a skin to cover his naked body or a hut to live in, but had to sleep under the brushwood at night. (Thom 1954:50)

This passage illustrates, inter alia, two technological attributes of Soaqua as the Table Bay pastoralists saw it. They had no mat-covered huts, and they had less access to domestic animal skins from which to make clothing. It is possible that Harry and his Strandlopers were originally clients of local pastoralists, whom Van Riebeeck called Capemen to distinguish them from Saldanhamen, but that Dutch patronage helped him aspire to pastoralist status. Whatever the prior trajectory of the Strandlopers, we have to see these statements as a self-centered definition of stock ownership as a standard of wealth as opposed to the lack thereof, whether due to tradition or loss.

In March 1659, explorers returned to the Fort, having apparently traveled to the mouth of the Berg River some 200 km to the north, and referred to the "Souquas (or bandits, a most barbarous people possessing neither homes nor livestock, but well armed with assegais, bows and arrows)" (Thom 1958:24). This raises the interesting point that the possession, even the wearing on the person, of bows and arrows is almost synonymous with Soaqua but is rarely considered worthy of mention in descriptions of stock-keeping peoples. It is as characteristic as not having cattle, stealing, not having huts, and wearing less attractive clothing, and it probably reflects the difference between habitual hunting as a subsistence pattern and occasional hunting trips made by pastoralist men. Two other observations relate to this same point. The dangers of being struck by the poisoned arrows of the Soaqua are often mentioned, but in the long and detailed record of Dutch interactions with pastoralists at Table Bay, there is no reference of any such mishap from pastoralists' weaponry. In contrast, the impression is gained that stock owners seldom hunted bovids for food but most frequently hunted carnivores in organized drives, partly to obtain desirable skins and partly to rid their herds of troublesome predators.

Many of the Soaqua attributes are inextricably linked in an informative passage that describes meetings between Jan Danckaert's explorers and indigenous people between November 1660 and January 1661. The account is complicated by the fact that two explorers returned to the Fort early and gave a brief verbatim report, while the leader handed in a much fuller, but in some ways different, account later. Van Riebeeck's diarist noted that

> They had come across a poverty-stricken band of tiny people, who had helped them to cross the first range and had been very friendly to them, giving them some honey and dried fish. These small people, who have already been encountered somewhat nearer here by previous exploring parties, live in a state of poverty in shabby, low huts made of branches. Our explorers found some of these standing empty here and there and it seemed to them that these little fellows use them during the night. They are well provided with bows and arrows, and they are adept at using these for shooting all kinds of game for food. Honey also forms part of their diet. They dress like the Hottentots, but they use very poor skins of wild animals. They are not so greasy as the Hottentots, for greasiness is a sign of prestige and of wealth in cattle, etc. (Thom 1958:299–300)

This is an extremely interesting summary that establishes a package of traits, both physical and behavioral, by which these small people may be distinguished from the "Hottentots." Immediately following this and still referring to "these small people," the diary has "They are rather modest, but in their speech they also cluck like turkey-cocks, the more so as one goes further into the interior. Among the Hottentot race there is also one language which all their great ones understand but which the common people do not" (Thom 1958:300). Although somewhat enigmatic and open to several interpretations (Elphick 1977:29), this phrasing, taken with Wintervogel's "speaking almost as they do," seems to suggest language differences between stock owners and stock thieves. The word *Soaqua* is not used in this paragraph summary taken from the comments of the two explorers who returned early, but in the Danckaert journal reported in full some pages later, the word *Soaqua* appears on six occasions and is clearly synonomous with "these small people." Their association with mountainous regions and their knowledge of the mountain passes is reflected in a series of subsequent references to Soaqua as "mountain people," "the Soaqua, a mountain tribe," and "the Soaquas, or Mountain Hottentots" (Thom 1958:304, 306, 321).

A series of expeditions follow Danckaert's, all clearly crossing the Cape Folded Belt mountains into the Olifants River valley, named after 200–300 elephants that Danckaert counted when he first arrived. There were many encounters with the Soaqua in the valley, and explorers regularly used abandoned windbreaks or, as they called them, Soaqua huts. On February 18, 1661 the Dutch made contact in this area with the Namaqua, whose clothing, artifacts, and life-style, as noted in some detail, were easily distinguishable from those of the Soaqua. These Namaqua numbered about 700, had 4000 cattle and 3000 sheep, and moved their settlement of mat-covered huts regularly every few days in search of pasture. Interestingly, the explorers noted that "there is a circle of 73 huts, and outside this kraal there are three huts whose occupants have no cattle but are like messengers, who run from one kraal to another at the king's command" (Thom 1958:353). This is a hint by the expedition leader Pieter van Meerhoff here, of a form of clientship more fully described by Van der Stel in 1685 (Waterhouse 1932).

Perhaps the most interesting report of these expeditions, in terms of stock ownership and stock theft, is that of April 1661, which relates a sequence of hostilities among three of the pastoralist groups, the Namaqua, the Chariguriqua, and the Cochoqua. Oedasoa, chief of the Cochoqua, had hired out some of his cattle to the Chariguriqua for them to graze, but the latter refused to return them. Oedasoa then took back his cattle by force, "whereupon the Chariguriquas had gone off to join the Namaquas, who had provided them with some of their own cattle to be pastured on similar terms, so that they now kept the Chariguriquas as their tributaries" (Thom 1958:373). This illustrates clearly that one response of pastoralists to stock loss was to borrow from kinsmen or allies until such time as natural increase and good management allowed herd replacement. There is no suggestion here that on losing their animals the Chariguriquas ever thought of going off and becoming Soaqua and no reason for expecting them to assume the package of generally derogatory characters subsumed under that description.

The eyewitness accounts of Van Riebeeck's explorers are complemented and in effect synthesized by the description of the Sonquas given by Olfert Dapper in 1668 (Schapera and Farrington 1933). Although Dapper never visited the Cape, it is supposed that he got his information reliably from a German student, George Frederick Wreede, who was there between 1659 and 1662 (Schapera and Farrington 1933:1–2). Wreede's observations, like those of Wintervogel, Danckaert, and Van Meerhoff, are invaluable because they precede wholesale trading and European hunting in the western Cape interior and predate the expeditions of Bergh and Van der Stel by a generation. Dapper noted:

> The Sonquas are a people dwelling in massive mountainous country. They number several thousands, and are very small in size, both men and women. They have no cattle, but live by shooting rock rabbits with the bow and arrow, which they use with remarkable skill. . . . They also go out hunting big game, especially wild horses and mules. . . . The meat of the rock-rabbits constitutes a pleasant food for the Sonquas, who live principally on it and on certain roots growing in the ground. They also keep many hunting dogs, trained to hunt the rock-rabbits which are their principal food, and knowing how to drag these animals out of their holes.
>
> They are extremely great plunderers and marauders. They steal from other Hottentots all the cattle they can get, with which they then flee immediately to the mountains, where they cannot be found in their retreats and hidden caves by anybody, not even by other Hottentots.
>
> Their huts, made only of branches twined together, without woven mats, and covered solely with rushes, are several thousand in number; for they move about from one place to another, and never break up the huts, but erect still others wherever they camp.
>
> Their little cloaks are sewn together from the skins of the wild oxen [presumably he means wild ungulates such as the klipspringer] which live on the rocks. (Schapera and Farrington 1933:31–33)

This initial and informative phase of northward penetration from the Cape was interrupted in the mid-1660s when Dutch attention was drawn by rich pastoralists in the east, with whom trade now increased. By 1673, pastoralist groups near the Cape were largely dispossessed, and the Cochoqua under Gonnema were at war with the Dutch, partly the result of the deaths of European hippopotamus hunters (Elphick 1977:130). These animosities, which cost the Cochoqua at least 1765 cattle and 4930 sheep (Elphick 1977:133), prevented peaceful interaction and further reporting in this direction. After 1679, however, more or less cordial relations were reestablished, and the alleged presence of copper ore induced Van der Stel to send a series of expeditions north to Namaqualand, including one under his own leadership in 1685. Olof Bergh's trips in 1682 and 1683 resulted in few direct observations of people called Soaqua, but he did note that in November 1682 "we came to some Hottentots, they being Somquaas alias Bushmen. They were armed with assegais and bows and arrows" (Mossop 1931:85). It is not clear precisely how the equation between Somquaas and Bushmen, or Bosjesmen, was made, but the new term appears regularly from the mid-1680s on, sometimes in the form *Bosjesman Hottentots.*

Van der Stel's own diary, recounting a five-month expedition to the copper deposits of Namaqualand, is more informative on Soaqua life and Soaqua–Namaqua relations (Serton *et al.* 1971; Waterhouse 1932). Moving north along the Berg River toward the Piketberg, he saw "very high rocky mountains on the far side of the Berg river, at times covered with snow but nevertheless inhabited by a tribe of Hottentots called Obiquas, who subsist by raiding and robbing other Hottentots, since they have no cattle at all nor anything to live from, and thus they seize the cattle of their neighbours" (Serton *et al.* 1971:233). Three days later he passed "various little huts belonging to the above-named marauders called Obiquas [the editors replaced this with Sonquas], built in the same manner as those of the other Hottentots, with the difference that these cover them with branches and bush whereas the others use mats" (1971:237). Soon afterward he met a group of five who, speaking through Cape Hottentot interpreters,

> said that they were Sonquas, the aforesaid marauders, and that they were come here in search of an eland which they had shot with a poisoned arrow the day before, such as a rule dying only the next day. They carry bows and arrows and assegais. They have not cattle and live on honey and the wild animals they shoot. (Serton *et al.* 1971:241)

The origin of the word *Obiqua* (sometimes *Ubiqua*) is obscure (Elphick 1977; Maingard 1935), but occasionally clearly serves as a synonym for *Soaqua,* especially east of the Cape. In the rest of his journal van der Stel refers regularly to Sonqua, including finding the campsite of the five people mentioned earlier, with no mention of their possessing stock.

Crossing the Olifants River at its confluence with the Doorn, Van der Stel

> understood from the Gregriquas [that the Doorn] has its source in the Hessiqua mountains, and is inhabited by the aforesaid Sonquas. By enquiry and information given we found that these Sonquas are like the troops[1] in Europe, of whom each tribe of the Hottentots has its own, used by them to give warning should they hear of [the approach of] any strange tribe. They steal nothing whatever from the kraal which they

[1]Waterhouse (1932:122) translates the Dutch *armen* here as "poor," not "troops." Raven-Hart (Serton *et al.* 1971:259) justifies "troops" according to the context he perceives, but, clearly, controversy exists.

serve, but they indeed steal from other kraals, whether in war or peace, since, as was already said, they have nothing but what they get by this. (Serton *et al.* 1971:257, 259)

North of the bend in the Olifants River Van der Stel entered an extremely arid landscape, which he noted "is not inhabited except by the Sonquas that roam across it, subsisting on the game, of which little is found here. These Sonquas here are in the service of the Amacquas [Namaqua] and made use of by them, of which tribe they also form a part" (Serton *et al.* 1971:271). During one of several more encounters with Sonqua he described them as

all very thin and lightly built, owing to the great hunger and hardship they suffer. They eat only the bulbs of a flower which they call ajuintjes, and tortoises, and certain large caterpillars, as also locusts, which are found here in abundance. (Serton *et al.* 1971:277)

To complete this brief survey of the transfer of meaning between words it is worth mentioning the comments of Landdrost Starrenburg, who, in 1705, followed roughly the route of Van der Stel in a trading expedition to the Olifants River (Raidt 1973:15–57). By this time cattle-trading expeditions by free burghers, as distinct from those of the Dutch East India Company, were common and had resulted in the loss, often by violence, of thousands of animals by pastoralist groups. At the modern Verlore Vlei stream some pastoralists explained to Starrenburg

that a certain freeman, generally called Dronke Gerrit was come to their kraal a few years previously, accompanied by some others, and without any parley fired on it from all sides, chased out the Hottentots, set fire to their huts, and took away all their cattle, without their knowing for what reason, since they had never harmed any of the Dutch. By this they lost everything they had, and were compelled to betake themselves to the Dutch living further out, and there steal cattle again, and, if they could get anything, rob their own compatriots; and with these cattle they then ran off into the mountains and feasted on them until it was all finished, and then getting more, several times succeeding in this, from which they still have a few beasts today. (Raidt 1973:25)

Somewhat farther north Starrenburg saw more of the impact of Dutch free-booters and concluded about the indigenous pastoralists that "from men who sustained themselves quietly by cattle breeding, living in peace and content-ment, divided under their chiefs and kraals, they have nearly all become Bushmen, hunters and brigands, dispersed everywhere between and in the mountains" (Raidt 1973:41). Starrenburg illustrates how stock had been lost to the indigenous people through trade with colonists, causing widespread impoverishment and leading to a minor version of the well-known *Difa-qane*.[2] The Dutch were a stock "sink," and their intrusion had the effect of

---

[2]*Difaqane* means "forced migration." It describes the period of widespread chaos that prevailed on the high veld of southern Africa in the 1820's when Nguni invaders disrupted local Sotho peoples and set in train a pattern of war, famine, and flux (Thompson 1969:391).

lowering the carrying capacity for the indigenous peoples in the same way as the intrusion of pastoralism into a hunters' world had reduced the viability of an exclusively foraging economy.

This profile of early contacts, while not complete, allows us to reconsider the meaning of four interrelated terms: *Fishermen, Soaqua, Obiqua,* and *Bushmen.* Even allowing for some inconsistency in usage, there seems to be a clear sequence in which the status of non–stock-owning peoples is first recognized, then described in patterned comments, and finally complicated by the increasingly serious effects of a European presence on indigenous subsistence and settlement. The term *Fishermen* is least relevant, as it precedes any real understanding of groupings by the Dutch. By contrast Soaqua is used fairly systematically and has physical as well as behavioral connotations. These small people were very widely distributed in the western Cape, lived in caves or windbreaks, and supplemented their hunting and gathering existence by stealing occasional sheep or cattle from nearby herds. They almost always carried their bows and quivers, knew the mountain routes intimately, and may even have spoken languages different from those of the "Cape Hottentots," who clearly despised and feared them. This substantial evidence supports their status as residual hunter gatherers who had survived the appearance of pastoralism by a combination of economic and distributional responses while nonetheless living in the interstices of pastoralist society. Almost certainly, Soaqua should be referred to not as a title but as a description of set of strategies that varied from almost complete independence to clientship, depending on local circumstances. There is little evidence that Cochoqua, Namaqua, or Guriqua became Soaqua when they lost their stock.

Obiqua is less easily dealt with because it seems partly to be a synonym for *Soaqua.* Its usage may be related to a time when increased Dutch interference was causing massive, and irreversible, changes in indigenous group relations. *Bushmen* relates more clearly to these changes. As pastoralist groups were increasingly disrupted by traders, hunters, and freebooters, more stock owners were dispossessed and took up a life-style superficially similar to that implied by the term *soaqua* (used not as denoting a tribe, but rather, in lower-case letters as denoting a behavioral complex). By this time, however, the growing colony was shedding a range of misfits, former pastoralists were moving off into the interior, and escaped slaves were looking for a living away from Dutch control; the word *Bushman,* as John Goodwin noted some time ago (Goodwin and van Riet Lowe 1929:147), became a wastepaper basket term for all those who lived by hunting, gathering, and stealing. Guriqua and Cochoqua probably did become Bushmen when they lost their stock and took to stealing the animals of others. I suggest that whereas the soaqua life-style was the original hunter gatherers' response to a pastoralist presence in the western Cape, the Bushman life-style, as used in the same area, was that led by former pastoralists and foragers as a result of increased Dutch disruption. It thus represents a more labile mode that encompasses a less coherent set of behaviors and a variety of physical types. Diachronically speaking, the term *soaqua* was a category that later became transformed into *bushman* with some loss of content and coherence.

Archaeological Evidence

Excavations in the southwestern Cape provide archaeological materials that can be compared directly with the historical record. At de Hangen and other rockshelters in the mountains flanking the Olifants River valley, a distinct pattern of debris is clearly the physical residue of the behaviors referred to in the preceding as soaqua (Parkington 1977a, b, 1979, 1980; Parkington and Poggenpoel 1971). From these sites have come food remains that reflect an economy dominated by the collection of underground corms (van der Stel's "ajuintjes" (Serton *et al.* 1971:277), other plant foods, tortoises, dassies (rock rabbits), and small browsing ungulates. Much less frequently we find the bones of a wide range of larger game, such as eland, elephant, and hartebeest, and of domestic animals, mostly sheep and in one case cattle.

Although to date only four such sites have been excavated in detail, our surveys show over 100 such sites lying undisturbed in the region bounded by the Berg and Olifants rivers and extending from the Atlantic Coast to the Doorn River karoo. Most of these sites are small shelters in rugged, broken regions, which may have been only marginally attractive to herders but which offered a range of resources and maximum protection to small foraging groups. The four excavated sites exhibit a consistent pattern of use, marked by grass-lined sleeping hollows placed around a central ash deposit. Hollows of exactly these dimensions and design described by Wikar in his travels along the Orange River were made for him by his Bushmen companions (Mossop 1935:39), and Stow reported identical patterns of bedding in caves north of the Orange River, apparently still then occupied by Bushmen (Stow 1905:44). From the bedding grasses and associated ash deposits at de Hangen and elsewhere came a range of arrow parts, sinew bowstring fragments, pieces of quivers, and parts of wooden digging sticks (Parkington and Poggenpoel 1971). Leather goods made from the skins of wild animals have also been found, and a bundle of grass bedding that inclosed a piece of leather clothing has been dated to about 400 years ago, which coincides fairly well with the date of soaqua entry into the historical record (Pta 346, 390 ± 45 b.p. in Parkington and Poggenpoel 1971:31, footnote).

There are some aspects of this archaeological pattern that are not mentioned in the historical accounts. Stone toolmaking, for example, is very conspicuously absent from the early journals, perhaps partly because Europeans rarely visited campsites and apparently never saw, or recorded, cave sites in use. The surfaces of excavated caves and rockshelters are littered with stone tool debris of assemblages that are dominated by small convex scrapers and adzes, thought to have been used for skin scraping and woodworking, respectively (Deacon and Deacon 1980; J. N. F. Binneman personal communication, 1982). In addition, alongside wooden tools such as digging sticks, handles, fire drills, and some arrow parts are innumerable wood shavings in and among the bedding grasses. The mix of plant food debris with extractive stone and wooden plant-food gathering tools is repeatedly encountered.

Unmistakably associated with these stone tools are potsherds of the kind now normally referred to as Cape Coastal (Rudner 1968). These are always very fragmentary, thin-walled sherds that occasionally include lugs, spouts, and conical bases that seem to reflect isolated remnants of many pots rather than the pieces of a few pots scattered at the sites. Kolb (1731) made the most specific reference to pot manufacture in the early years of European settlement when he noted, among people he called Hottentots, that "the richer among them make pots" (Kolb 1731). Given the habit of European observers of using the words *rich* and *possessions* to refer to stock owning, it is tempting to conclude that pastoralist groups made and perhaps traded pots. The synchronous appearance of pottery and domestic stock in archaeological contexts in the western Cape is fairly well established.

There is, also, the interesting question of rock paintings. Most, if not all, rockshelters containing the debris pattern I refer to as soaqua have painted walls, yet there is absolutely no mention prior to the middle of the eighteenth century of any such tradition among indigenous people in this area. It must be admitted, though, that the association between the paintings, tools, and food-waste patterns is as yet only circumstantial. They exist in the same places. It is possible that like regular hunting, stone tool making, and poisoned arrow use, painting was not a central or obvious feature of stockkeeping communities most frequently encountered and described by Europeans in the southwestern Cape.

Our excavations also allow us to amplify historical records by extending the pattern to littoral situations that early explorers never witnessed. The site-use pattern documented at de Hangen is found in small rockshelters across the coastal plain and at or near the coast. The rash of postpottery occupations at shelters in the mountains is repeated in the many shell middens scattered along the coastal fringe, nearly all associated with the same Cape Coastal pottery. What distinguishes these coastal sites are two patterns of debris: First, the food debris is dominated by shellfish remains rather than underground plant food parts, and second, the paucity of digging-stick use near the coast is accompanied by a change in stone tool assemblage composition, with fewer adzes being made and discarded here. Given the relative density of soaqua sites and assuming that the coastal and inland patterns are versions of the same underlying cave-use behavior since about 2000 or 1800 years ago, what is striking is that large numbers of open and cave localities across the landscape were visited regularly only from that time on. Most of these sites are along the coast or in the Cape Folded Belt.

Excavations in the southwestern Cape provide no evidence as yet for extending this pattern of debris back before the appearance of pottery and domestic animal bones. Small though the sample is, it seems to point to a distinct change in settlement patterns coincident with the local introduction of pastoralism. Assemblages of plant food debris associated with adze-dominated stone toolkits in arrangements of ash and bedding in small rockshelters either sit directly on bedrock or lie on deposits much older in time or quite different in content. Before interpreting this situation as evidence for settlement pattern change we must first consider the possibilities that it is caused either by preservation problems or by a research design that has emphasized small shelters with shallow deposits. Given the absence of a major environmental event, it is inconceivable that increasing preservation problems with age would regularly produce dramatic changes exactly at the pottery–prepottery interface in a series of sites of varied size, depth, and exposure. Then too, some components such as ash concentrations and stone tools are not affected by biological decay such as might destroy plant materials. In any case the change is often as basic as that between a shelter not having been occupied and it being regularly visited. The second suggestion, that we have tended to favor for reasons of research design and an interest in spatial patterning shallow shelters that simply do not penetrate back as far as the early stages of the pattern, is equally unsatisfactory. It is true that de Hangen seems to have been occupied regularly only after about 1800 years ago (this is part of the patterning at issue here), but we have correctly predicted and excavated substantial deposits in Klipfonteinrand and Diepkloof, neither of which show the soaqua pattern to have obtained prior to that time. In addition, material from deep coastal sequences at Elands Bay Cave and Tortoise Cave substantiate the observation of artifactual and cave-use changes coincident with the local appearance of domestic animals.

I conclude that the appearance of pastoralism, reflected archaeologically in the inclusion of ceramics and particularly sheep bones into prepastoral contexts, resulted in the reorganization of hunter gatherer life into a pattern that survived to be historically described as soaqua. The visible elements of this life-style were greater use of isolated and fairly rugged parts of the landscape and the broadening of the resource base (Smith 1983) to include, or perhaps to emphasize, reliable and widespread but small food parcels such as underground geophytic corms, caterpillars, locusts, termites, a variety of shellfish, tortoises, and rock rabbits. In some parts of the landscape alliances, or arrangements, were made with local pastoralists, and a certain amount of stock raiding helped supplement protein inputs from game hunting. The alternative, favored by Elphick (1977) and Schrire (1980), sees much more continuity between the stock-owning and soaqua lifeways and less between aboriginal hunter gatherers and those referred to historically as soaqua. I suggest that the most economic view of the archaeological and written records renders soaqua behavior as that of residual communities while not denying the shadowy quality of intercommunity boundaries. Moreover, instead of viewing the soaqua pattern as the "natural" form of hunting and gathering at this latitude, we should regard it as a response to the domination of the landscape by sheep- and cattle-owning pastoralists, because the archaeological record of the area prior to 1800 years ago shows quite unequivocally that hunter gatherer settlement had been markedly different from that of the soaqua.

Perhaps the most significant difference is the distribution of sites before, as compared with after, the appearance of domestic stock and ceramics. Both at the coast and in the mountains, the number of sites occupied between about 1800 and 4000 years ago is very low when compared to the later pattern, whereas by contrast the number of open sites in the coastal plain is much higher. It is my impression from the site distributions that when there were only hunter gatherers in the landscape, they concentrated on the undulating coastal plain, choosing to camp in the open, presumably in windbreaks of the kind still in use in the seventeenth century. We have little evidence of group size or of the duration of occupation of individual campsites, but many sites from this period now look like deflated hollows in the sand and are littered with innumerable stone tools ranging to and beyond 250,000 pieces per site. A small number of caves in the mountains or at the coast were also used, as were a few select open locations at the coast, but settlement systems may have been focused on the resources of the plains. Stone toolkits from these sites have few adzes, many scrapers, and high percentages (between 15 and 35) of small backed microliths. This extreme contrast with the composition of later assemblages tempts us to seek behavioral shifts, with less emphasis on hunting and a greater role for plant food gathering through time (Parkington 1980, 1984). Unfortunately the surface nature of deflation hollows has not encouraged the preservation of faunal or plant materials such as would have aided the reconstruction of subsistence patterns. Two sites do, however, reflect something of the prepastoralist subsistence. At Klipfonteinrand, on the eastern edge of the Cape Folded Belt, there are occupation horizons dated to 5000 years ago (Thackeray 1977) in which virtually no plant foods were preserved, despite favorable circumstances. Instead the debris clearly mirrors hunting of a wide range of largish game, including zebra. More pointedly, at

Tortoise Cave, a coastal plain site, the stone tool sequence changes from backed piece to adze domination in good stratigraphic order, with constant emphasis there on estuarine and marine foods (T. Robey, personal communication, 1983).

We favor the explanation that the local appearance of pastoralism some 1800 years ago forced those hunter gatherers who remained to shift the focus of their settlement into the more broken topography of the mountains where pasture was less attractive for herders. Here they lived more frequently in caves or small rockshelters and laid greater emphasis on plant foods and small but abundant animals such as tortoises and rock rabbits and less on the larger more mobile game species such as eland, hartebeest, and zebra. This change is, of course, one of emphasis not of total range, the economy retaining its mixed hunting and gathering character. Shellfish, too, assumed a greater role in the dietary mix to the extent that people became essentially gatherers who hunted large animals more infrequently than before. The nature of this later soaqua subsistence pattern meant that it was better to camp in more places for shorter periods and to stay close to widespread but localized resources rather than to mount hunting expeditions from fewer sites. The earlier emphasis on the manufacture of small backed points (perhaps missile tips) may point to greater hunting activity then, and the use of small shelters in later times may reflect a decrease in mean group size, but neither is very strongly supported archaeologically as yet. When pastoralists arrived, if indeed that is what happened, there would have been a drop in biomass among wild herbivores, competition by people for the areas with the highest grazing potential, and a subsequent lowering of the hunter gatherer carrying capacity as the pastoralists prevailed.

Conclusions

Hunter gatherer groups have been observed in many parts of the globe by literate explorers, missionaries, and settlers, some of whom have left valuable and detailed accounts of aboriginal societies. The Soaqua example has been pursued here. A few groups even survived long enough to be studied by professional observers in recent times (in southern Africa the ethnographies of Lee (1979), Silberbauer (1981), Marshall (1976), and Tanaka (1980) are probably the best known). Archaeologists studying the prehistory of areas where such survivals have occurred need to integrate ethnographic or historical records into their own findings. The potential richness of the observational record and the possibility of very specific analogies in which temporal, geographic, and cultural distance is minimized make written records seductively attractive. The temptation is to endow the eyewitness accounts of recent times with rather more time depth than they deserve and to force the fragmentary and pliable archaeological data to fit the ethnographic model. Unless the ethnographic or historical observations are seen, at best, as end points in a trajectory of change and taken as situations with which contrasts must be sought, the negative characteristics of the linkup between present and past will outweigh any advantages, and an ahistorical version of the past will emerge.

There is good reason to suppose that the soaqua and bushman patterns of behavior witnessed at the Cape have come about through regular changes over the millennia. Archaeologists, however, have read observed patterns into the past because some elements of the well-described contact period (similar sets of animal bones, occasional underground plant food parts, fragmentary polished bone points, similar ranges of stone tools, rock paintings) can be found farther back in the archaeological record. But the discovery of some humified plant remains does not necessarily illustrate the soaqua plant food dependence; nor do pieces of polished bone mean that an emphasis on hunting with the light bow and poisoned arrows, as in the ethnography, can be inferred for the early Holocene. In the southwestern Cape we have found paintings of triple-curved bows and of nets strung up to catch small herbivores, neither of which are mentioned or even hinted at in historical or ethnographic records for this far south in Africa (A. Manhire and R. Yates, personal communication, 1983). This might mean that interesting subsistence strategies were not seen by early visitors. Alternatively, and perhaps more likely, such technological devices may have characterized earlier phases in hunter gatherer adaptations than were observed historically.

There has been little attempt to demonstrate quantitative and structural parallels between historical observations and archaeological remains and almost no attempt to develop the concept of a trajectory of subtle but directional change. Thus in some texts (Deacon 1976; Inskeep 1978; Parkington 1977b) soaqua is taken to have characterized much of the "Wilton" Holocene sequence and is sometimes described as a plateau of relatively stable behavior. Similarly the interpretation of rock art, which is largely based on ethnographic and nineteenth-century historical information, is used to account for sets of paintings several thousands of years old (Lewis-Williams 1981, 1983, this volume).

The time depth of many of the technological and social devices observed historically needs critical attention, with particular regard for the changing use intensities of devices already known. Change may obviously take the form of reemphasis or reorganization. The sorts of devices that may have been involved at the Cape are the uses of mastic hafts, poison, nets, snares, bows and digging sticks, the institutions of food sharing and periodic fusion and fission, group size and dispersal, and the role of painting in social and economic life. It remains a challenge to archaeologists of southern Africa to document the transformation of foraging society from its prehistoric form to the sort of system rather fragmentarily reported in the so-called contact period. Some suggestions are made in Figure 6.3.

One way to approach the reconstruction of a Holocene sequence would be to list systematically differences between the historical pattern and the more distant past, and from these to try to restructure the settlement arrangements at various time slots. Site distributions from about 4000 years ago are different from those coincident with the appearance of pastoralism about 1800 years ago. They seem to be few and far between in the mountains but abound in the coastal plains. The soaqua pattern produces many sites scattered across the landscape through high residential mobility, but sites in earlier periods seem to be larger and more widely dispersed. The set of plant, insect, and small animal foods noted by early travelers is not repeated at occupation levels in the early or middle Holocene. Reed arrow shafts and bone or wooden components of composite arrows are much more common in post–3000-year-old levels than they are earlier, where, by contrast, small backed microliths dominate the stone tools. In each of these cases we could argue that poor preservation, the accidents of site discovery, or the often-mentioned imperfection of

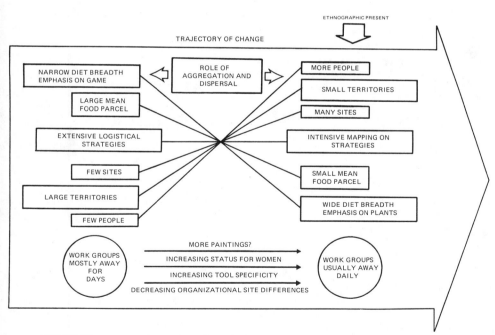

FIGURE 6.3 Suggested trajectory of transformation of South African foraging society from its prehistoric form to that reported in the so-called contact period.

the archaeological record are the main causes of differences, but I suggest that this is not the case. Prehistoric people behaved differently. It may well be that these variations reflect a fairly drastic reorganization of hunter gatherer existence in response to both internal and external pressures. We have good evidence for climatic change during the Holocene (Butzer 1974; Parkington 1984), and there is little doubt that pastoralism was yet another perturbation in the list of externally introduced influences. Equally we must suppose that any technological innovations and borrowings may have set up internal inconsistencies that ultimately required some response. This may have included rescheduling of site locations, increased implementation of previously little-used devices, greater emphasis on exchange relations or food sharing, and even altered roles for painters or trancers.

In summary, then, the soaqua pattern of greater emphasis on gathering than on hunting arose at least in part as a response to the appearance of pastoralism in the landscape. A more general question presents itself now. Certain syntheses of hunter gatherers in southern Africa (for example Lee 1968) argued that the mix was understandable for this latitude and formed part of a global pattern in which hunting, gathering, and fishing contributions varied consistently with distance from the poles. We know now (Denbow this volume; Schrire 1980) that all hunter gatherers in southern Africa have shared the landscape for at least 1500 years with pastoralists or agriculturalists. The impact of the introduction of domestic plants and animals on hunter gatherers in this enormously varied subcontinent is something archaeologists are only now starting to investigate in detail. What we must do is "de-!Kung"—or in the case of the southwestern Cape, "de-Soaqua"—our efforts by using the historical accounts critically as a challenge, not a model, of the past. Until we expect that things were different, we will always discover that they were the same.

Acknowledgments

I thank Antony Manhire, Tim Robey, Royden Yates, Cedric Poggenpoel, and Bill Buchanan for allowing me to make use of our joint fieldwork data, Johanna Parkington and Royden Yates for help with illustrations, Stanley Ambrose for many stimulating discussions, and Carmel Schrire for some substantial and very helpful editorial suggestions.

References

Butzer, Karl W.
    1974   Reflections on the stability of Holocene environmental zonation in South Africa. *South African Archaeological Society Goodwin Series* 2:37–38.
Deacon, Hilary John
    1976   *Where hunters gathered. South African Archaeological Society Monograph Series* 1:1–232.

Deacon, Hilary John, and Janette Deacon
    1980   The hafting, function and distribution of small convex scrapers with an example from
            Boomplaas Cave. *South African Archaeological Bulletin* 35:31–37.
Elphick, Richard
    1977   *Kraal and castle: Khoikhoi and the founding of white South Africa.* Yale University
            Press, New Haven.
Goodwin, Astley John Hilary, and Clarence van Riet Lowe
    1929   The stone age cultures of South Africa. *Annals of the South African Museum* 27:1–
            289.
Hahn, Theophilus
    1881   *Tsuni-//Goam, the supreme being of the Khoi-Khoi.* Trubner, London.
Inskeep, Raymond R.
    1978   *The peopling of Southern Africa.* David Philip, Cape Town.
Kolb, Peter
    1731   *The present state of the Cape of Good Hope.* W. Innys, London.
Lee, Richard B.
    1968   What hunters do for a living, or how to make out on scarce resources. In *Man the
            hunter,* edited by Richard B. Lee and Irven DeVore, pp. 30–48. Aldine, Chicago.
    1979   *The !Kung San: men, women and work in a foraging society.* Cambridge University
            Press, Cambridge.
Lewis-Williams, J. David
    1981   *Believing and seeing: symbolic meanings in southern San rock paintings.* Academic
            Press, New York.
    1983   Introductory essay: science and rock art. In *New approaches to Southern African rock
            art,* edited by J. David Lewis-Williams. *South African Archaeological Society Goodwin
            Series* 4:3–13.
Maingard, Louis Fernand
    1935   The first contacts of the Dutch with the Bushmen until the time of Simon van der Stel
            (1686). *South African Journal of Science* 32:479–487.
Marks, Shula
    1972   Khoisan resistance to the Dutch in the seventeenth and eithteenth centuries. *Journal
            of African History* 13:55–80.
Marshall, Lorna
    1976   *The !Kung of Nyae Nyae.* Harvard University Press, Cambridge.
Mossop, Ernest E. (editor)
    1931   *Journals of . . . Bergh (1683) and . . . Schrijver (1689).* The Van Riebeeck Society,
            12, Cape Town.
    1935   *The journal of Hendrik Jacob Wikar (1779) (translated by A. W. van der Horst) and
            the journals of Jacobus Coetsé Jansz (1760) and Willem van Reenen (1791).* The Van
            Riebeeck Society, 15, Cape Town.
Parkington, John E.
    1977a   Soaqua: hunter–fisher–gatherers of the Olifants River, Western Cape. *South African
            Archaeological Bulletin* 32:150–157.
    1977b   *Follow the San.* Unpublished Ph.D. dissertation, Department of Archaeology,
            Cambridge University, Cambridge.
    1979   *Soaqua.* Report distributed at the South African Association of Archaeologists, Cape
            Town.
    1980   Time and place: some observations on spatial and temporal patterning in the Later
            Stone Age sequence in Southern Africa. *South African Archaeological Bulletin* 35:73–
            83.

1984   Changing views of the Later Stone Age of South Africa. In *Advances in world archaeology* (Vol. 3), edited by Fred Wendorf, pp. 89–142. Academic Press, Orlando.

Parkington, John E., and Cedric Poggenpoel
1971   Excavations at de Hangen 1968. *South African Archaeological Bulletin* 26:3–36.

Raidt, Edith H. (editor)
1973   *François Valentyn. Description of the Cape of Good Hope with the matters concerning it. Amsterdam 1726. Part II.* Van Riebeeck Society, Second Series, 4. Cape Town.

Raven-Hart, Ronald
1967   *Before Van Riebeeck: callers at South Africa from 1488 to 1652.* Struik, Cape Town.
1970   *Cape Good Hope, 1652–1702* (2 vols.). Balkema, Cape Town.

Rudner, Jalmar
1968   Strandlooper pottery from South and South West Africa. *Annals of the South African Museum* 49:441–663.

Schapera, Isaac, and B. Farrington (editors)
1933   *The early Cape Hottentots.* The Van Riebeeck Society, 14, Cape Town.

Schrire, Carmel
1980   An inquiry into the evolutionary status and apparent identity of San hunter–gatherers. *Human Ecology* 8:9–32.

Serton, Petrus, Ronald Raven-Hart, Willem Johannes de Kock, and Edith H. Raidt (editors)
1971   *François Valentyn. Description of the Cape of Good Hope with the matters concerning it. Amsterdam 1726. Part I.* The Van Riebeeck Society, Second Series, 2. Cape Town.

Silberbauer, George B.
1981   *Hunter and habitat in the central Kalahari desert.* Cambridge University Press, Cambridge.

Smith, Andrew B.
1983   Prehistoric pastoralism in the southwestern Cape, South Africa. *World Archaeology* 15(1):79–89.

Stow, George
1905   *The native races of South Africa.* Swan Sonnenschein, London.

Tanaka, Jiri
1980   *The San hunter–gatherers of the Kalahari: a study in ecological anthropology.* University of Tokyo Press, Tokyo.

Thackeray, Anne I.
1977   *Stone artefacts from Klipfonteinrand.* Unpublished B.A. Honours thesis, Department of Archaeology, University of Cape Town, Cape Town.

Thom, Hendrik Bernardus (editor)
1952   *Journal of Jan van Riebeeck* (Vol. I). Balkema, Cape Town and Amsterdam.
1954   *Journal of Jan van Riebeeck* (Vol. II). Balkema, Cape Town and Amsterdam.
1958   *Journal of Jan van Riebeeck* (Vol. III). Balkema, Cape Town and Amsterdam.

Thompson, Leonard
1969   Co-operation and conflict: the high veld. In *The Oxford history of South Africa,* edited by Monica Wilson and Leonard Thompson. I: pp. 391–446. Clarendon Press, Oxford.

Vedder, Heinrich
1938   *South West Africa in early times.* Oxford University Press, London.

Waterhouse, Gilbert
1932   *Simon van der Stel's Journal of his Expedition to Namaqualand, 1685–6.* Longmans, Green, London.

7

Prehistoric Herders and Foragers of the Kalahari: The Evidence for 1500 Years of Interaction

JAMES R. DENBOW

Introduction

Although the first investigations into the recent prehistory of Botswana were carried out in the 1970s, the time has nonetheless come for a reassessment of the antiquity and presumed evolutionary status of contemporary foragers in the Kalahari. In the early 1970s Toutswemogala, on the eastern side of the country, was the only documented and dated Iron Age settlement in Botswana: no Late Stone Age sites with comparable first-millennium dates had been excavated (Lepionka 1971, 1978, 1979). For the most part, little Iron Age research was carried out in Botswana because it was assumed that the low and unpredictable patterns of rainfall along the margins of the Kalahari would have precluded early settlement by Iron Age agriculturalists:

> much of southern Africa, particularly in the western regions, is climatically unsuited to farming settlement. Recent economic patterns tend to support this view and it is likely that climatic change during the last two thousand years has not been on a sufficient scale radically to change this picture. The available evidence suggests that most of Botswana was occupied largely, if not exclusively, by hunting–gathering peoples of Late Stone Age stock until very recent times. (Phillipson 1969:35)

The current picture of Khoisan foragers in Botswana (Lee 1979; Lee and De Vore 1976; Silberbauer 1965, 1981; Tanaka 1974, 1980) reflects and reinforces these earlier misconceptions about the lack of antiquity for agropastoral settlement in the country. Khoisan peoples have been treated almost as pure survivals from another age, people who for millennia have lived out of touch with the outside world. Contemporary foragers have therefore been viewed by some anthropologists as providing unique opportunities to study a way of life that was once practiced by all humankind. Thus one anthropologist chose to study the /Gwi of the central Kalahari because

> even nowadays most of them still live a life of hunting and gathering away from the influence of modern civilization, relying on primitive "stone age" techniques. . . . The fact that a group of people with a population of several thousand is still living in the same fashion as human societies of almost 10,000 years ago is a miracle. (Tanaka, 1974:iii)

Because of the presumed continuity in life-style from the Stone Age to the twentieth century, elements of Khoisan territorial organization, family and group structure, and demography have served as direct models of what life may have been like at some earlier stage in humankind's cultural development. Distortions in this evolutionary picture due to contact and interaction with more complex societies have been treated as recent overlays on this fairly pure hunter gatherer base, transparencies that could be easily removed through judicious use of oral traditions reaching back to precontact times (Lee 1979:xvii, 76–77, 403–406; see also Schrire 1980:12).

Most studies of Khoisan people were made before anything was known about the prehistory of Botswana. Consequently, they present a static picture of pre–nineteenth-century foragers, a caricature set in a timeless dimension with no social or cultural change until recent times. While Lee (1979:76–77) cites archaeological evidence to argue that hunters and gatherers have lived in the Dobe area for the past 11,000 years, most generalizations about their past are based on extrapolations from the present rather than on concrete data. It is only since 1973 that excavations in Botswana have begun to fill the gap between 10,000 years ago and the nineteenth century. In other areas, such as the central Kalahari, we still do not know for certain whether any prehistoric foragers lived there in the past under conditions such as those described for modern /Gwi by Silberbauer (1965, 1981) and Tanaka (1974, 1980). In fact, it is entirely possible that these adaptations are fairly recent phenomena that developed only within the past 1500 years in response to the settlement of agricultural and pastoral peoples in the more favorable parts of the country.

In this chapter a summary of the archaeological data for forager–agropastoral interaction is presented that draws on data from 400 surveyed sites as well as the results of detailed excavations at 16 selected localities. This work has produced a sequence of radiocarbon dates spanning much of the past two millennia. These dates are documented in Table 7.1, while Table 7.2 displays the chronological ordering of excavated sites by geographic location. Figure

TABLE 7.1

Radiocarbon Ages for Archaeological Sites in Botswana[a]

Sample	Age	Excavator	Date (a.d.)	Site	Depth (cm)	Association
Northern sandveld						
SI-4098	110 ± 50	Brooks	1840	Xgi	00–35	Late Stone Age with Iron Age
I-12,163	195 ± 75	Denbow and Campbell	1755	Kwebe Hills	20–35	Late Iron Age, Khoi
I-11,824	305 ± 75	Campbell	1645	Depression Cave	15–20	Late Stone Age with Iron Age
I-12,798	800 ± 80	Denbow	1150	Serondella	30–45	Early Iron Age
Wits 836	970 ± 50	Denbow and Campbell	980	Outpost 1	40–60	Early Iron Age with Late Stone Age
I-11,411	1100 ± 80	Denbow and Campbell	850	Society	25–40	Early Iron Age with Late Stone Age
I-12,165	1120 ± 190	Denbow and Campbell	830	Hippo Tooth	10–20	Late Stone Age with Early Iron Age
Beta 3971	1150 ± 60	Wilmsen	800	Nxai Nxai	50–60	Late Stone Age with Early Iron Age
I-12,800	1190 ± 80	Denbow	760	Chobe	30–45	Early Iron Age
I-12,799	1220 ± 80	Denbow	730	Serondella	110–123	Early Iron Age
Beta 3970	1230 ± 50	Wilmsen	720	Nxai Nxai	90–100	Late Stone Age with Early Iron Age
I-12,801	1270 ± 80	Denbow	680	Matlapaneng	40–55	Early Iron Age with Late Stone Age
Northeastern hardveld						
GX-3775	450 ± 95	Lepionka	1500	Toutswe	—	Late Iron Age
GX-3772	645 ± 95	Lepionka	1305	Toutswe	±25	Early Iron Age
GX-3773	750 ± 95	Lepionka	1200	Toutswe	±75	Early Iron Age
I-11,412	755 ± 75	Denbow	1195	Toutswe	40–50	Early Iron Age
I-11,415	840 ± 75	Denbow	1110	Thatswane	30–40	Early Iron Age
GX-3774	860 ± 105	Lepionka	1090	Toutswe	—	Early Iron Age
Pta-2526	960 ± 50	Denbow	990	Maiphetwane	90–100	Early Iron Age with Late Stone Age
I-11,413	990 ± 75	Denbow	960	Toutswe	110–120	Early Iron Age
I-11,409	995 ± 75	Denbow	955	Taukome	15–25	Early Iron Age with Late Stone Age
I-11,414	1025 ± 80	Denbow	925	Thatswane	130–140	Early Iron Age with Late Stone Age
I-11,410	1240 ± 80	Denbow	710	Taukome	90–105	Early Iron Age with Late Stone Age
I-12,708	1240 ± 80	Denbow and Campbell	710	Bisoli	30–60	Early Iron Age
I-11,407	1265 ± 80	Denbow	685	Taukome	140–150	Early Iron Age with Late Stone Age
Wits 1099	1340 ± 50	Denbow and Campbell	610	Bisoli	30–60	Early Iron Age
Southeastern hardveld						
Wits 837	590 ± 50	Denbow	1360	Broadhurst	20–30	Early Iron Age
I-11,823	855 ± 75	Denbow	1095	Moritsane	70–80	Early Iron Age

[a]From Denbow and Wilmsen 1983: 406.

TABLE 7.2

Radiocarbon Chronology in Botswana[a]

Date (a.d.)	Northern sandveld	Northeastern hardveld	Southeastern hardveld
1900			
	Xgi		
1800			
	Kwebe Hills		
1700			
	Depression		
1600			
1500		Toutswe	
1400			
			Broadhurst
1300		Toutswe	
1200		Toutswe	
		Toutswe	
	Serondella		
1100		Thatswane	
		Toutswe	Moritsane
1000		Maiphetwane	
	Outpost 1	Toutswe	
		Taukome	
		Thatswane	
900			
	Society		
	Hippo Tooth		
800	Nxai Nxai		
	Chobe		
	Serondella		
700	Nxai Nxai	Bisoli and Taukome	
	Matlapaneng	Taukome	
600		Bisoli	

[a]From Denbow and Wilmsen 1983: 407.

7.1 maps the location of dated sites in Botswana. Although continuing studies will certainly expand and alter details in our knowledge, coherence of our present data set suggests that the basic framework of settlement sequences should remain intact.

The excavations and reconnaissances amplify historical evidence from southern Africa (Elphick 1977; Schrire 1980) by showing that foragers and food producers have been enmeshed in networks of interaction and exchange for 1000 years longer than was previously suspected. Over 1200 years ago, these networks reached into the heart of the Dobe area and into other presently isolated parts of Botswana. Although the archaeological evidence does not point to complete displacement of foragers, it does appear that population groups in Botswana have been more opportunistic and open to changes in subsistence strategies and, likely, social systems than the standard anthropological categories of hunter gatherer or herder farmer would suggest. Some hunters and gatherers in the Kalahari apparently vacillated between foraging and food production in the past; others became herders and potters at a relatively early date and are now almost indistinguishable, both genetically and culturally, from their Bantu-speaking neighbors. Thus, the association of particular types of subsistence strategies with specific ethnic or linguistic groups is not straightforward, and the relations among Khoi, San, and Bantu seem to have been both of longer duration and greater complexity than was formerly thought to be the case.

FIGURE 7.1   Botswana: map of dated prehistoric sites described in this chapter. (Denbow and Wilmsen 1983:405.)

The Prehistoric Past

Since 1977, archaeological reconnaissances bordering the eastern fringes of the Kalahari have located more than 300 Early Iron Age sites (Caister 1982; Denbow 1979, 1981, 1982, 1983). Radiocarbon dates from excavations at seven sites (Bisoli, Taukome, Thatswane, Maiphetwane, Toutswe, Moritsane, and Broadhurst) range from the seventh to the fourteenth centuries A.D., while a date from the upper level at Toutswe extends this chronology forward into the sixteenth century. Cultural materials include Early Iron Age ceramics of both Gokomere and Eiland types (Evers 1977; Huffman 1974, 1978, 1982), tools and ornaments made of iron and copper, smelting slag, and remains of pole and daga houses. Cane glass beads and cowrie and conus shells were found at four sites and constitute evidence for participation in exchange networks that reached the east coast. Interaction with surrounding Late Stone Age peoples is indicated at two sites (Maiphetwane and Taukome) by finds of small scrapers, crescents, and other lithics typical of Late Stone Age deposits in other parts of southern Africa (Sampson 1974). The fact that such stone tools were found only on some Iron Age sites and not on others and that they are identical to types found in Late Stone Age contexts suggests that these artifacts were not necessarily manufactured and used by Iron Age peoples, but rather that they reflect interactions between Iron Age and Stone Age groups who may have ranged in the sandveld of the Kalahari to the west.

Over three-quarters of the 320 Iron Age sites located on the eastern margins of the Kalahari possess visible accumulations of animal dung marking the remains of prehistoric kraals (Butterworth 1979; Denbow 1979). These deposits range from 30 to 100 m in diameter and from 25 to 150 cm in depth. The deposits are so extensive that they have induced permanent changes in the associated soils and vegetation—changes that are easily recognizable on 1:50,000-scale aerial photographs of the region. Faunal samples from two first-millennium sites (Taukome and Toutswe) suggest that domesticated cattle, goats, and sheep made up approximately 80% of the meat eaten there (Plug 1982; Welbourne 1975). Identification of springbok in the assemblages—a species that does not live in the region today (Smithers 1968)—suggests either a major shift in environmental zones or, more probably, hunting and trading links with the Kalahari to the west.[1] Carbonized sorghum and cowpeas from Thatswane provide direct evidence of agriculture.

Research leads us to hypothesize that a tripartite hierarchy of settlements in

[1]Springbok and impala compete for the same resources and thus tend to have mutually exclusive territories—springbok in the dryer regions and impala in wetter areas. Only impala are found in the better-watered Toutswe area today. Impala, but not springbok, are also reported for this area in the historic past.

terms of size, location, and length of occupation had already developed along the eastern edge of the Kalahari by A.D. 1000 (Denbow 1982, 1983). Three major long-term centers, surrounded by shorter-term satellite communities, were found during the reconnaissance. Middens at these centers average between 80,000 and 100,000 m² in extent, which are substantial when compared with middens of even the largest satellite communities, which are only about 10,000 m² in area. Likewise, social organization of Iron Age communities in this area was possibly differentiated in a manner similar to—but not necessarily identical with—that of historic southern African pastoralists. Site densities along watercourses in the region average about four sites per km², indicating that the area was heavily utilized by herding and farming communities by the end of the first millennium A.D.

We may therefore conclude that firm evidence for dense agropastoral settlement of the eastern Kalahari goes back almost 1500 years. It is still commonly assumed, however, that similar Iron Age settlement of the northern Kalahari occurred only about 250 years ago with the arrival of the Tswana, Herero, and Hambukushu (Lee 1979; Schapera 1952; Sillery 1952; Tlou 1972, 1976). Lee (1979:76–77, 404) argues that there was little likelihood of contact and interaction between foraging and food-producing peoples in the Dobe area and other parts of Ngamiland prior to the nineteenth century. Archaeological excavations carried out since 1979 in northern Botswana and Namibia, however, indicates this is wrong.

Eight sites in the northern Kalahari with Early Iron Age and Late Stone Age affinities have yielded radiocarbon dates in the first millennium A.D., ranging from a.d. 680 ± 80 (I-12,801) at Matlapaneng to a.d. 980 ± 50 (Wits-836) at Outpost 1 (Denbow 1980; Denbow and Wilmsen 1983; see Tables 7.1 and 7.2). Four of these sites are on the drainage systems of the Okavango and Chobe rivers (Matlapaneng, Serondella, Chobe, and Hippo Tooth), two are in the Tsodilo Hills 60 km west of the Okavango Delta (Society and Outpost 1), and one, Nxai Nxai, is situated 160 km into the sandveld near the Namibian border. A final site, dated to a.d. 840 ± 50 (Pta-234), is reported by Sandelowsky (1979) from Kapako along the Okavango River in northern Namibia.

With the exception of Nxai Nxai and Hippo Tooth, charcoal-tempered Early Iron Age ceramics dominate the artifactual assemblages at these sites. Iron and copper tools include cutting implements, projectile points, beads, linked-chain segments, and pendants. Smelting slag was recovered from Matlapaneng, Society, Serondella, and Chobe, and a grinding stone was found at Matlapaneng. Pole-impressed daga fragments from typical Iron Age structures were found at Serondella and Outpost 1. Cowrie shells from Society and Outpost 1 have an ultimate coastal origin, and cane glass beads found at Society and Matlapaneng provide further evidence that transcontinental trade networks stretched as far as western Botswana by the seventh century A.D. All sites except Kapako also produced small numbers of typical Late Stone Age artifacts, including backed bladelets, crescents, steeply retouched segments, and small scrapers.

As one moves away from the Okavango Delta, the nature of the prehistoric deposits changes. Proportions of Late Stone Age lithics increase, whereas ceramics and metal tools decrease in frequency. In levels dated to the eighth and ninth centuries A.D. at Nxai Nxai and Hippo Tooth, Late Stone Age artifacts form the largest part of the assemblages, though Early Iron Age ceramics and iron tools also occur (Denbow and Campbell 1980; Wilmsen 1979). Since these sites do not possess the full range of Iron Age attributes (Huffman 1970, 1982) and are dominated by Late Stone Age lithics, they should be seen in a similar light to Early Iron Age sites, being probably best classified as Late Stone Age sites with evidence for contact and exchange with Iron Age communities.

The proportion of wild to domesticated fauna increases as one moves into the sandveld. Cattle remains have been identified from all sites except Kapako, and sheep and goats are recorded at Society, Outpost 1, Serondella, and Matlapaneng. At Society and Outpost 1, cattle dominate all other species and even outnumber remains of sheep and goat by a factor of 2:1 (Voigt 1982). Fish bones from Matlapaneng, Society, Serondella, Chobe, and Hippo Tooth as well as hippo bones from Kapako and Hippo Tooth show that aquatic resources were utilized by all these groups. The fish at Society must have been obtained from the river drainage to the east. In contrast to sites closer to the Okavango swamp, faunal remains from Nxai Nxai and Hippo Tooth are dominated by hunted species. Yet even at Nxai Nxai, cattle teeth were recovered by Wilmsen in association with a hearth 60–70 cm below surface, dated to a.d. 800 ± 60 (Beta-3971) (E. Wilmsen 1979, personal communication, 1984).[2]

Since Nxai Nxai lies only 45 km from Dobe, it can no longer be argued that contact between foragers and food producers in the region began only recently. Not only were ceramics and iron tools being traded into the sandveld during the first millennium A.D., but also the cattle teeth from Nxai Nxai indicate that at least some Late Stone Age foragers here were associated with domesticated animals at this time. We do not know the precise nature of this interaction, or whether the cattle at Nxai Nxai were hunted or herded. It is, however, clear that not all foragers in western Ngamiland subsisted entirely

---

[2]Some controversy exists about the antiquity of cattle here (Yellen 1983). Unfortunately, the original announcement (Wilmsen 1979) inadvertently omitted the crucial table relating the position of these teeth. The intimate association here of the teeth and charcoal-tempered pottery, like that found in Early Iron Age sites, supports the antiquity suggested by the radiocarbon date.

on wild foods until the 1950s or 1960s, as has been suggested. Moreover, it is likely that fluctuations in subsistence patterns, analogous to those observed among foragers in the 1970s, have been taking place in the region for more than a thousand years.

Other evidence for changes in the economy of Khoisan peoples is found in the Tsodilo Hills 110 km north of Dobe. Excavations at Society and Outpost 1 have dated the establishment of Iron Age settlements to the ninth and tenth centuries A.D. Over two thousand prehistoric rock paintings have also been recorded at Tsodilo (Campbell *et al.* 1980; Rudner 1965), which is one of the few places in all of western Ngamiland where rock outcrops occur. These paintings are stylistically similar to thousands of others attributed to Khoisan artists in southern Africa. Current views on rock art suggest paintings such as these were not produced for purely decorative reasons but rather played a role in the religious and ritual symbolism of prehistoric foragers (Lewis-Williams 1981; Pager 1971; Vinnicombe 1976). The rock outcrops at Tsodilo may therefore periodically have attracted Late Stone Age people from a wide area who would then have come into contact with Iron Age herders and new ways of life over a thousand years ago. In point of fact, a few paintings reflect contact and interaction by portraying cattle. One scene shows men raiding or tending these animals. There is no indication here that the herders or raiders are ethnically distinct from the painter, and the style of painting is identical to other, more typical, outlines of wild animals and human figures found in the hills. The paintings therefore provide direct evidence of contact and interaction between foraging and agropastoral peoples in the region and suggest that concomitant changes in economic organization may have occurred at the same time.

While we do not know the precise age of the Tsodilo paintings, some must have been made after the introduction of cattle to the region in the first millennium A.D. No rock art is produced in the area today, nor can current informants recall painting in the past. The San living there today attribute the art to God, and it is tempting to suggest that rock painting ceased to be produced after the arrival of Iron Age groups. We have neither confirmation of this hypothesis nor any details about the mechanisms involved in such a change, but given the abandonment of rock art, it is possible that aspects of ritual and religious behavior a thousand years ago may have been significantly different from that observed by anthropologists in the twentieth century.

The Recorded Past

Evidence for interaction between Khoisan- and Bantu-speaking populations in historic times in southern Africa has been outlined by others (e.g.,

Lee 1979; Elphick 1977; Wilmsen 1982). Both historical and archaeological sources provide a better understanding of the processes that underlay present economic patterns in the Kalahari. Excavations at Depression Cave, also in the Tsodilo Hills, indicate that interaction between later Stone Age and Iron Age peoples was not confined to the first, but continued well into the second millennium. The upper levels of this shelter are dominated by Late Stone Age materials but also contain charcoal-tempered pottery down to depths of 50 cm below the surface; beneath this level only Late Stone Age lithics occur. Charcoal from a hearth 10 cm below the surface is dated to the seventeenth century A.D. Since no decorated sherds were found, it is uncertain whether these ceramics are stylistically Iron Age wares, or whether they are indigenous Khoisan ceramics,[3] such as those produced around Lake Ngami in the late nineteenth century.[4] This places a new light on Lee's comment (1979:76) that, "Old people I interviewed stated that their grandfathers had these things [pottery and tobacco] before the first non-San came to the interior." At this point, we cannot rule out the possibility that the pottery mentioned was of San, not Bantu, manufacture.

At the Kwebe Hills 40 km south of Lake Ngami, both Tswana ceramics and decorated, lugged Khoi pottery (Rudner 1968, 1979; Sampson 1974) were recovered from excavations in a midden dated to the middle of the eighteenth century (Denbow, field notes 1981). According to oral tradition, this midden relates to the first settlement of Ngamiland by the Tawana, a Bantu-speaking group who split off from the Ngwato on the eastern side of the country toward the end of the eighteenth century (Schapera 1952; Tlou 1972). Eighteenth-century glass beads, iron and copper tools and ornaments, cattle, goat, and sheep remains, and carbonized sorghum were also recovered, along with remains of nondomesticates.

Between Lake Ngami and Lake Dow similar Khoi ceramics have been found on the surface of more than 50 sites. On some of them, Khoi ceramics and Late Stone Age tools occur together; on others only Khoi ceramics and later Iron Age wares, but no stone tools, are found. The lithics from these sites are identical to those from the first millennium site of Hippo Tooth, where Early Iron Age ceramics were recovered, and are very similar to assemblages from earlier nonceramic Late Stone Age sites in the area dating to 2000–4000 b.p. (A. Brooks, personal communication, 1983). Although none of these ceramic Late Stone Age sites have been dated, their differential distribution suggests that indigenous Khoi pot manufacture is of some antiquity in the region.

[3]Phillipson (1976) records similar charcoal-tempered pottery in association with backed blades and other Late Stone Age lithic debris from the upper level of the Kandanda site at the eastern end of the Caprivi Strip in Zambia. No faunal remains were preserved, but a storage pit containing mongongo nuts (*Ricinodendron rautaneii*) was uncovered. Dates of a.d. 1460 ± 90 (GX-1579) and 1485 ± 85 (SR-200) were obtained from this level.
[4]Examples may be seen in the Albany Museum, Grahamstown, Republic of South Africa.

Dete Khoi informants living in the area today say that their forefathers made pottery prior to the movement of Bantu-speaking groups into the area in the eighteenth century. The pottery they describe looks very like the ceramics found on archaeological sites, as well as on the surface of a known, late nineteenth-century Dete village. None of these groups make pottery today, but Schwartz provides a description from the early twentieth century that illustrates its similarity to known Khoi wares from Namibia: "The Batete . . . make, or used to make, quite nice pottery, usually small pots pointed at the bottom, to be carried by thongs around the mouth. The were unglazed, but quite smooth and polished" (Schwartz 1923:150).

It is clear that Late Stone Age populations along the Botletli River were in contact with Iron Age agropastoralists living along the margins of the Okavango Delta in the first millennium A.D. Linguistic data suggest that the Dete and other Khoi groups in the region today have occupied the area for a considerable period. Their languages, however, are divergent from western ceramic groups such as the Nama in Namibia, leading some authors (Elphick 1977; Westphal 1963, 1979) to postulate that northern Botswana may have been a proto-Khoi nuclear area from which other Khoi speakers expanded in the distant past. Present evidence suggests at least the possibility of an early autochtonic development of a Khoi pot-making industry along the Botletli. Alternatively, knowledge of pot making and herding may have moved from west to east along the river systems from Namibia to the Botletli at a later date.

Informants also stated that the Dete had lived for a long time as herders, fishermen, and hunters prior to the settlement of Bantu-speaking peoples along the river. They offered a folktale describing the origins of pastoralism among them (Denbow, interview with Brai Ozai; Rakops, December 1980), which has a widespread distribution in the Kalahari, cutting across major Khoisan ethnic and linguistic boundaries (Denbow, //gana interview, Kwebe Hills, September, 1981; Biesele 1975:122–123). Livingstone confirms aspects of this tale with his account of Khoi herders a century ago:

> We had no idea that the long-looked for Lake [Ngami] was still more than three hundred miles distant. One reason for our mistake was, that the river Zouga was often spoken of by the same name as the Lake, vis *Noka ea Batletle* ["river of the Batletli or Dete"] . . . but at last we came to the . . . Zouga. . . . A village of Bakurutswe [a Bantu-speaking group] lay on the opposite bank; these live among the Batletle, a tribe having a click in their language, and who were found by Sebituane [ca. 1829] to possess large herds of the great horned cattle. They seem allied to the Hottentot family. [Sebituane] . . . twice lost all his cattle by the attacks of the Matebele. . . . He stocked himself again among the Batletle on Lake Kumandau [Dow]. (Livingstone 1958:72–73)

Livingstone also met other speakers of what was probably a Tshukwe language living along the dryer, northern side of the Makgadikgadi. He noted that these groups also spoke a click language, but referred to them as Bushmen rather than as Hottentots, probably since they were hunters and gatherers. The way of life he records represents yet another point along a continuum from forager to herder in the Kalahari:

> At Rapesh we came among our old friends the Bushmen, under Horoye. . . . [They] were at least six feet high, and of a darker colour than the Bushmen of the south. They always have plenty of food and water; as they frequent the Zouga as often as the game in company with which they live, their life is very different from that of the inhabitants of the thirsty plains of the Kalahari. The animal they refrain from eating is the goat, which . . . is significant of their feelings to the only animals they could have domesticated in their desert home. (Livingstone 1958:183)

Serogenetic studies of Khoi speakers who forage and herd in the area today conclude that they are closer to Bantu than to San populations, despite their language and economy (Chasko *et al.* 1977). Once again, the ability of people to transcend the expectations of conventional anthropological categories emerges, with strong suggestions that this flexibility has a long history in Botswana (see Elphick 1977; Schrire 1980). The swiftness of the transitions is noted in historical accounts and is particularily well illustrated by Hitchcock (1982:60), who found Kua foragers hunting and gathering wild foods in 1975, living on a cattle post herding and drinking milk in 1976, and back subsisting on wild foods the following year! Although one may discover the detailed reasons and rationalizations for these changes among modern groups, such matters have been impossible to discern for prehistoric ones. Nevertheless, the facts of long-term interactions between different groups in Botswana goes a long way toward dispelling that static picture of Kalahari hunter gatherers.

Conclusions

Rapid increases in the number of cattle, goats, and sheep in the Dobe area since the rinderpest epidemic of 1896 and a chronic shortage of labor to tend these large herds are some of the major incentives cited by Lee (1979:408) for the incorporation of present-day San into contemporary Tawana and Herero agropastoral economies. The same economic processes are noted by Hitchcock (1978) as underlying the incorporation of Khoi peoples into the cattle post economy of the eastern Kalahari. In exchange for their labor, whether seasonal or permanent, meat, milk, grain, and other surplus goods are obtained from the agropastoral economy. Visiting, settlement of disputes, and other social activities also form part of the mosaic of Khoisan–Bantu interaction in the region today.

In the recorded past, Khoisan labor was highly valued and sought after by neighboring Bantu groups. During the later part of the nineteenth century, external markets for veld products, such as skins and ostrich feathers, served further to link agropastoral and forager economies into an interdependent economic system (Gordon, this volume). Even remote foragers were not simply left to lead their lives in isolation but were actively sought out and incorporated into wider economic networks:

> The contest for the possession of certain villages of Bakalahari or Bushmen is a fruitful source of strife in Bechwana towns. The vassals with all their possessions are the subject of litigation and endless jealousies; and it needs all the skill of a chief to settle these matters between greedy and plausible rivals. . . . When one Bechwana tribe attacks another, the Bushmen and Bakalahari belonging to both are placed in the same category with cattle and sheep—they are to be "lifted" or killed as opportunity offers. In such cases, therefore, all Bakalahari and Bushmen flee into wastes and inaccessible forests, and hide themselves until the commotion is past. (MacKenzie 1883:62–63)

It has been argued (Howell 1979; Lee 1979; Tanaka 1980) that this intermeshing of forager–herder life-styles and the compound economies that result is a product of the recent past. Anthropologists have thus felt justified in analyzing one component of this dual economy—foraging—as if it were independent from, and unaffected by, the activities and decisions of other sectors of a wider regional network. Oral traditions collected from independent foragers in the twentieth century, however, all pertain to a period when livestock numbers in Botswana were at a low ebb due to the rinderpest epidemic and postdate the collapse of a European market for game products. The economic independence of some foragers in the 1960s, and the shifts from forager to herder recorded for the 1970s, therefore, may not simply represent a unique shift from "Stone Age" to "Iron Age" production strategies but rather are events that mark points along a much longer continuum of cyclical interaction and change.

Archaeological data from a large number of sites in Botswana suggest that the ecological processes that resulted in rapid increases in herd size in the twentieth century also occurred in the past, as indicated by the development of pastorally oriented economies in the first millennium A.D. Most of the 300 Early Iron Age sites examined along the eastern side of the country contain extensive deposits of vitrified cattle, goat, and sheep dung, showing a rapid and intensive commitment to pastoralism. Faunal analyses of these sites, as well as Early Iron Age sites in the Tsodilo Hills, confirm the economic importance of domesticated stock to these societies.

Late Stone Age lithics occur on many of these Iron Age sites, indicating that contact and interaction between Iron Age and Stone Age populations was taking place over a wide geographic space during the first millennium A.D. The presence of ceramics and metal artifacts on sites further into the sandveld, as well as cattle teeth at Nxai Nxai and Hippo Tooth, reflect the other side of this interaction and exchange network. The evidence does not support an argument for the complete displacement of indigenous foraging economies, however, and it is likely that herding intermeshed with foraging to form compound economies that linked both herders and foragers into widespread social and economic systems. The present distribution of Khoi-, San-, and Bantu-speaking populations in Botswana is, thus, "clearly a product of a very long process of interaction, interaction which has involved congruent social concepts and economic systems that were complimentary" (Wilmsen 1982:107).

While the inhabitants of the Kalahari 5000 years ago were undoubtedly hunters living in a world of hunters, over the past 2000 years all cultural and ethnic groups in the region have been in some form of contact with food-producing peoples, with the result that the economic and social decisions of all groups have become, to some degree, interdependent. Even though hunting and gathering continued to be the primary basis for subsistence among some Late Stone Age groups throughout this period, the potential influence of nearby food-producing societies on the organization of subsistence and other activities cannot be ignored—even if indicators like pottery and cattle remains are not found in all archaeological deposits. Anthropologists have tried to get around this problem by searching for independent foraging groups, but in fact there has probably been no such thing here, in an historical or processual sense, for almost 1500 years.

Lee (1979:414–420) noted the rapidity with which present-day !Kung have begun to integrate themselves into a wider, world economy. Though in some cases the outcome of these decisions may be unfortunate (e.g., the incidence of drunkeness and soldiering for the South African army), these examples highlight how quickly groups have been able to respond to new opportunities and resources in their area. The myth of isolated Dobe, separated from the outside world by the sandy "middle passage," breaks down when we learn that Dobe men are quite willing, and able, to walk the 100 km to the road at Nokaneng in order to work in the South African mines (Lee 1979:416).[5] The Tsodilo Hills with their Early Iron Age settlements are no farther away than this, and we should expect similar, though perhaps not identical, responses to the presence of new opportunities and ways of life to have taken place in the past. In fact, Lee's principle of "uniformitarianism" supports the case (Lee 1979:434).

Contact and interaction between Early Iron Age and Late Stone Age peoples began more than a thousand years ago over large parts of Botswana. The repercussions of this contact on hunting and gathering societies is beginning to be specified in detail by the archaeological data. Excavations at all sites in the sandveld, for example, indicate that hunting and gathering continued to play a predominant role in subsistence activities for some groups through the twentieth century. In addition, dates from ≠Gi (Helgren and Brooks 1983) show that Late Stone Age tools continued to be made and used up to the nineteenth century. But stone tools and potsherds alone provide only a gross index of socioeconomic status. More subtle changes in social and economic

---

[5]During the good rains of 1975–1976, even a hippopotamus managed to navigate the sandy "middle passage" in the opposite direction, to take up residence at !Qubi waterhole.

organization may be inferred from the abandonment of rock painting at Tsodilo, the presence of cattle teeth at Nxai Nxai, and the evidence for Khoi herders and pot makers along the Botletli River. Until more detailed excavations and reconnaissances are carried out, with more age assays and faunal analyses, these data will remain somewhat tentative signs of alternative interactive processes. The archaeological, historical, and ethnographic evidence suggests that a frontier situation may have existed for more than a thousand years in Botswana. Rather than representing a zone of geographic separation between peoples, however, this frontier may reflect "people either subject to different political authorities and/or engaged in different modes of production" (Marks and Atmore 1980:8).

In other parts of southern Africa the effects of such long-term interaction between different social and economic systems seem to have resulted in considerable changes in strategies of resource use, territory size, and settlement patterns through time (Parkington, this volume). It would probably be naive to assume that the Khoisan and other peoples of Botswana have not been influenced by similar processes. People are decision makers and, as such, are capable of using the same environment in a number of different ways and of inventing new strategies and technologies to adapt to changes in ecological and social conditions through time. If one attempts to condense these dynamic characteristics into a distinctive, but static, core of features unique to all foragers, one runs the danger of focusing on locally distinct attributes that appear to differentiate foragers from their neighbors rather than on those factors that unite these populations into wider, interregional and interdependent systems (Wobst 1978:304).

It would thus appear that the historical trajectory of all peoples in Botswana—whether foragers or food producers—has included participation and incorporation in wider systems of interaction and exchange. Moreover, this interaction has proceeded for so long that its effects cannot be easily factored out by simple recourse to local histories or oral traditions. The validity of evolutionary generalizations about these societies should therefore, perhaps, be judged by Lee's own standards:

> Although our ultimate goal is to use data on hunter–gatherers to illuminate human evolution, we must acknowledge that nowhere today do we find, in Sahlins apt phrase, hunters living in a world of hunters. All contemporary hunters are in contact with agricultural, pastoral, or industrial societies and are affected by them. Therefore, the first order of business is carefully to account for the effects of contact on their way of life. Only after the most meticulous assessment of the impact of commercial, governmental, and other outside interests can we justify making statements about the "hunter-gatherers" evolutionary significance. (Lee 1979:2)

The archaeological evidence summarized in this chapter indicates that a large gap exists in our understanding and historical assessment of the impact of outside influences on the San. Both the archaeological data and recorded events suggest that contemporary life-styles in the region have been characterized by convergent regional relations and periods of economic flux. In such dynamic circumstances, to fix on one segment of this wider mosaic (whether a particular commodity, group, or archaeological site) as an anthropological isolate may lead to serious distortions in our grasp of past and present processes of stability and change.

Acknowledgments

Support for the research on which this chapter is based came from a number of sources. Doctoral dissertation grants from the National Science Foundation (BNS 77-22784) and Fulbright-Hays financed the archaeological reconnaissances and excavations in eastern Botswana. Further funding was provided by the Botswana Society and Debswana. Excavations in northern Botswana were carried out as part of the National Museum of Botswana's archaeological research program begun in 1979. Without the ongoing support of the Botswana Government, and of Alec Campbell and Doreen Nteta in particular, much of this work could not have been completed. Radiocarbon dates provided by Dr. B. Verhaggen and Dr. J. Vogel are gratefully acknowledged. I would like to thank Alison Brooks, Alec Campbell, Mike Crowder, Tom Huffman, David Mulindwa, Leonard Ngcongco, Neil Parsons, Larry Robbins, Tom Tlou, Ed Wilmsen, and John Yellen for comments on earlier versions of the chapter. I would also like to thank Carmel Schrire for her comments and editorial assistance. Dr. I. Eibl-Eiblesfeld deserves special credit for his efficient organization of the conference on hunter gatherers for which this chapter was initially prepared.

References

Biesele, Megan
> 1975   *Folklore and ritual of !Kung hunter–gatherers.* Unpublished Ph.D. dissertation, Department of Anthropology, Harvard University, Boston.

Butterworth, John
> 1979   Chemical analysis of archaeological deposits from the Thatswane hills, Botswana. *South African Journal of Science* 75:408–409.

Caister, Daniel
> 1982   Archaeological perspectives on settlement patterns in south-east Kweneng district. In *Settlement in Botswana,* edited by Renee Hitchcock and Mary Smith, pp. 87–91. Heinemann, Johannesburg.

Campbell, Alec, Robert K. Hitchcock, and Michael Bryan
> 1980   Rock art at Tsodilo, Botswana. *South African Journal of Science* 76:476–478.

Chasko, W., Henry Harpending, Trefor Jenkins, and George Nurse
> 1977   Sero-genetic studies on the 'Masarwa' of north-eastern Botswana. *Botswana Notes and Records* 11:15–24.

Denbow, James R.
> 1979   *Cenchrus ciliaris:* an ecological indicator of Iron Age middens using aerial photography in eastern Botswana. *South African Journal of Science* 75:405–408.
> 1980   Early Iron Age remains from the Tsodilo hills, north-western Botswana. *South African Journal of Science* 76:474–475.

1981   Broadhurst: a 14th century A.D. expression of the early Iron Age in south-eastern Botswana. *South African Archaeological Bulletin* 36:66–74.

1982   The Toutswe tradition: a study in socio-economic change. In *Settlement in Botswana,* edited by Renee Hitchcock and Mary Smith, pp. 73–86. Heinemann, Johannesburg.

1983   *Iron Age economics: herding, wealth and politics along the fringes of the Kalahari Desert during the early Iron Age.* Unpublished Ph.D. dissertation, Department of Anthropology, Indiana University.

Denbow, James, and Alec Campbell

1980   National Museum of Botswana: archaeological research programme. *Nyame Akuma* 17:2–9.

Denbow, James, and Edwin N. Wilmsen

1983   Iron Age pastoralist settlements in Botswana. *South African Journal of Science* 79:405–408.

Elphick, Richard

1977   *Kraal and castle: Khoikhoi and the founding of white South Africa.* Yale University Press, New Haven and London.

Evers, Timothy

1977   Recent progress in studies of the early Iron Age in the eastern Transvaal, South Africa. *South African Journal of Science* 73:74–77.

Helgren, David, and Alison Brooks

1983   Geoarchaeology at Gi, a Middle Stone Age and Later Stone Age site in the northwest Kalahari. *Journal of Archaeological Science* 10:181–187.

Hitchcock, Robert K.

1978   *Kalahari cattleposts.* Government Printer. Gaborone.

1982   Prehistoric hunter–gatherer adaptations. In *Settlement in Botswana,* edited by Renee Hitchcock and Mary Smith, pp. 47–64. Heinemann, Johannesburg.

Howell, Nancy

1979   *Demography of the Dobe !Kung.* Academic Press, New York.

Huffman, Thomas N.

1970   The early Iron Age and the spread of the Bantu. *South African Archaeological Bulletin* 25:3–21.

1974   The Leopard's Kopje Tradition. *Memoirs of the National Museums and Monuments of Rhodesia* 6. Salisbury.

1978   The origins of Leopard's Kopje: an 11th century Difaquane. *Arnoldia* (Rhodesia) 8:1–23.

1982   Archaeology and ethnohistory of the African Iron Age. *Annual Review of Anthropology* 11:133–150.

Lee, Richard B.

1979   *Kalahari hunter–gatherers: men, women and work in a foraging society.* Harvard University Press, Cambridge.

Lee, Richard B., and Irven DeVore (editors)

1976   *Kalahari hunter–gatherers: studies of the !Kung San and their neighbours.* Harvard University Press, Cambridge.

Lepionka, Larry

1971   A preliminary account of archaeological investigations of Tautswe. *Botswana Notes and Records* 3:22–26.

1978   Excavations at Tautswemogala. *Botswana Notes and Records* 9:1–16.

1979   Ceramics at Tautswemogala, Botswana. *South African Archaeological Society Goodwin Series* 3:62–71.

Lewis-Williams, J. David
    1981   *Believing and seeing: symbolic meanings in southern San rock art.* Academic Press,
            London.
Livingstone, David
    1858   *Missionary travels and researches in South Africa.* Harper and Brothers, New
            York.
MacKenzie, John
    1883   *Day dawn in dark places.* Cassel and Company, London.
Marks, Shula, and Anthony Atmore
    1980   Introduction. In *Economy and Society in pre-industrial South Africa,* edited by Shula
            Marks and Anthony Atmore, pp. 1–43. Longman, London.
Pager, Harold
    1971   *Ndedema.* Akademische Druck, Graz.
Phillipson, David
    1969   Early iron using peoples of southern Africa. In *African societies in southern Africa,*
            edited by Leonard Thompson, pp. 24–49. Heinemann, London.
Phillipson, Laurel
    1976   Survey of the stone age archaeology of the upper Zambezi valley: II. Excavations at
            Kandanda. *Azania* 2:49–81.
Plug, Ina
    1982   The faunal remains from Taukome, a Zhizo site in Botswana. Unpublished report on
            file, Department of Archaeozoology, Transvaal Museum.
Rudner, Ione
    1965   Archaeological report on the Tsodilo hills, Bechuanaland. *South African Archae-
            ological Bulletin* 20:51–70.
Rudner, Jalmar
    1968   *Strandloper pottery from South and Southwest Africa.* Annals of the South African
            Museum 49:2.
    1979   The use of stone artefacts and pottery among the Khoisan peoples in historic and
            proto-historic times. *South African Archaeological Bulletin* 29:3–17.
Sampson, C. Garth
    1974   *The stone age archaeology of southern Africa.* Academic Press, New York.
Sandelowsky, Beatrice
    1979   Kapako and Vunga Vunga: Iron Age sites on the Kavango River. *South African Archae-
            ological Society Goodwin Series* 3:52–61.
Schapera, Isaac
    1952   The ethnic composition of Tswana tribes. *Monographs on social anthropology* 11.
            London School of Economics and Political Science, London.
Schrire, Carmel
    1980   An inquiry into the evolutionary status and apparent identity of San hunter–
            gatherers. *Human Ecology* 8:9–32.
Schwartz, E. H. L.
    1923   *The Kalahari and its native races.* H., F., and G. Witherby, London.
Silberbauer, George B.
    1965   *Report to the Government of Bechuanaland on the Bushmen survey.* Government
            Printer, Gaborone.
    1981   *Hunter and habitat in the central Kalahari desert.* Cambridge University Press, New
            York.
Sillery, Anthony
    1952   *The Bechuanaland Protectorate.* Oxford University Press, London.

Smithers, Rhey
    1968   A checklist and atlas of the mammals of Botswana. *National Museums of Rhodesia Memoir* 4, Salisbury.

Tanaka, Jiri
    1974   *The Bushmen,* translated by D. Hughes and G. Barnes. Shisakusha, Tokyo (mimeograph).
    1980   *The San hunter–gatherers of the Kalahari: a study in ecological anthropology,* translated by David W. Hughes. University of Tokyo Press, Tokyo.

Tlou, Thomas
    1972   The taming of the Okavango swamps. *Botswana Notes and Records* 4:147–160.
    1976   The peopling of the Okavango Delta, c. 1750–1906. In *Symposium on the Okavango Delta,* edited by the Botswana Society, pp. 49–54. Botswana Society, Gaborone.

Vinnicombe, Patricia
    1976   *People of the Eland.* Natal University Press, Pietermaritzburg.

Voigt, Elizabeth
    1982   Tsodilo hills, Botswana: report on identifiable faunal remains. Unpublished report on file, Department of Archaeozoology, Transvaal Museum.

Welbourne, Robert
    1975   Tautswe Iron Age site: its yield of bones. *Botswana Notes and Records* 7:1–16.

Westphal, Ernst
    1963   The linguistic prehistory of southern Africa: Bush, Kwadi, Hottentot, and Bantu linguistic relationships. *Africa* 33:237–264.
    1979   Languages of southern Africa. In *Perspectives on the southern African past,* edited by the Centre for African Studies, pp. 37–68. University of Capetown Press, Capetown.

Wilmsen, Edwin N.
    1979   Prehistoric and historic antecedents of a contemporary Ngamiland community. *Botswana Notes and Records* 10:5–18.
    1982   Exchange, interaction and settlement in northwestern Botswana: past and present perspectives. In *Settlement in Botswana,* edited by Renee Hitchcock and Mary Smith, pp. 98–109. Heinemann, Johannesburg.

Wobst, H. Martin
    1978   The archaeo-ethnology of hunter–gatherers, or the tyranny of the ethnographic record in archaeology. *American Antiquity* 43:303–309.

Yellen, John E.
    1983   The integration of herding into prehistoric hunting and gathering economies. Paper presented at the Southern African Association of Archaeologists conference, Gaborone, July 1983.

8

The !Kung in the Kalahari Exchange: An Ethnohistorical Perspective

ROBERT J. GORDON

Introduction

Lorna Marshall was speaking metaphorically when she said that the !Kung have been at Nyae Nyae since time began (1960:325), because specific evidence of !Kung people cannot be dated before hearing them speak. Unfortunately she has been taken at face value, and the presence of prehistoric artifacts at Nyae Nyae has been used further to encourage this misconception (Lee 1979:76). Having dismissed the !Kung past as timeless and endless, their historic presence begins around the turn of the century; it is epitomized as a series of exploitative interactions with whites and unfortunate dealings with blacks, and a rather unsatisfactory resolution of matters leaves the !Kung straddling an uncomfortable border between Botswana and Namibia, under the effective thumb of the South African government. They emerge as relics of the past, trapped in a fast-moving present frame that supports the notion that they have, until very recently, been traditional hunters and gatherers.

This essay explores the historical records relating to Bushmen in the Kaukauveld to reveal their complex interrelations with numerous other people through time. It is designed to complement the prehistoric findings outlined in Denbow's study (this volume) that suggest several millennia of interaction between Bushmen foragers and local pastoralists. In addition, by presenting a record that goes beyond generalizations about economic modes and into the actions and aspirations of individuals, it describes a situation of complex interactions between different groups that is probably analogous to that which pertained several centuries earlier in the southern tip of Africa, the structure of which is recorded in the early colonial Dutch records analyzed by Parkington (this volume).

The picture of Bushmen that emerges is complex and changing. The old notion of these people as passive victims of European invasion and Bantu expansion is challenged. Bushmen emerge as one of many indigenous people operating in a mobile landscape and forming and shifting their political and economic alliances to take advantage of circumstances as they perceived them. Instead of toppling helplessly from foraging to begging, they emerge as hotshot traders in the mercantile world market for ivory and skins. Rather than being victims of pastoralists and traders who depleted game, they appear as one of many willing agents of this commercial depletion, operating as brokers between competing forces as hired shots. Instead of being ignorant of metals, true men of the Stone Age who knew nothing of iron, they were fierce defenders of rich copper mines that they worked for trade and profit. If this essay has a central theme, it is to show how ignorance of archival sources helped create the Bushman image that we, anthropologists, wanted to believe, and how knowledge of these sources makes sense of the Bushmen we observe today.

First Historic Contact

The term *Bushman* has had a rather checkered history in the portals of academe, and various alternatives have been suggested. I will, however, continue to use the term because according to Hahn (1870) and Nienaber (1952), who is probably the foremost etymologist of the Afrikaans language, the term is derived from the Dutch *Bossiesman,* which meant "bandit," a term that they did not achieve by living in the splendid invigorating isolation of the Kalahari. I continue to use the term *Bushman* because I think that it is necessary to make banditry respectable again.

Research on the Bushmen has a long tradition. Already in 1929 a traveler, W. J. Makin, was moved to complain that

> As is usual with any disappearing race, the Bushmen have now become an absorbing ethnological study to many pundits in the professional world. Every year whites come to the edge of the Kalahari desert, camp out there with an array of cameras and scientific impediments, and try to entice the nomads of the desert to visit the camp. Tobacco is scattered lavishly as crumbs to ensnare birds. And the few Bushmen who are in touch with civilization, a type that like a nameless dog will hang about the place where a bone may be flung at them, come into the camp and are scientifically examined. (1929:278).

One consequence of their scientific commoditization, as I have shown elsewhere (Gordon 1984), is that the officials responsible for censusing or estimating population size would progressively inflate the figures for the demographic growth of the Bushmen. This has resulted in some scientists believing that the Bushmen are in no danger of extinction, a conclusion clearly at odds with my own ethnohistoric research.

From possibly being the hospitable inhabitants of the whole land mass now known as South West Africa or Namibia (Vedder 1938), the Bushmen have been engulfed, subjugated, humiliated, exterminated, and driven out of most of the country so that now they are found mostly in the northeastern corner, in an area known as the Kaukauveld, on land that is not especially usable for pastoral activities for either white ranchers or Herero cattle raisers. While it has a comparatively high rainfall, the presence of large waterless tracts and, more important, the presence of lungsickness and horse-sickness served to inhibit any permanent predatory expansionist tendencies of ranchers. This did not prevent the movement of commercial hunters and some traders into the area, but generally speaking the history of penetration by outsiders into an area that would today include the magisterial districts of Tsumeb and Grootfontein, extending to the Okavango River in the north and the Botswana border in the east, is of recent vintage. Indeed, historical records suggest that it first occurred just over a century ago (Figure 8.1).

The first white traveler to visit Ovamboland from the south, Sir Francis Galton, reported that on his journey in 1851 the northernmost Herero cattle outpost was at Okamabuti, near the present-day Grootfontein; beyond that was a large tract of land of considerable breadth that belonged to the Bushmen (Galton 1889:103). Schinz, who was perhaps the most reliable and informative early scientific explorer of this area, reported that the Hereros were at Okamabuti on sufferance from the Ovambo king who had taken pity on them as a result of their losses suffered from marauding Oorlams in the south. Shortly thereafter, residential permission was withdrawn and the Herero retreated to the Waterberg (Schinz 1891:351). In 1857 the Reverend Hahn passed through the area en route to Ovamboland and referred to the area around Otjituo (now a major center in the government-proclaimed Herero ethnic homeland), Grootfontein, and the Otjitjika Mountains as Bushmanland (Moritz 1980; Vedder 1938:308). There were no Herero or Khoi in the area. The Ovambo lived to the north of the Etosha Pan, but used to trade with the Bushmen who mined copper at what is now Great Otavi. Nangoro, the Ondonga king, was the protector of the Bushmen. The nearest Herero at this time were south of the Omatako Mountains (Hartmann cited in Köhler 1959:15). Under pressure from the incessant raids by Jonker Afrikaner, a well-armed bandit leader, some Herero tried to flee northwards with their cattle with the intention of joining Nangoro in Ovamboland, but on the way to Grootfontein they killed some Bushmen at the Waterberg (another traditional Bushman haunt, now the center of Hereroland). True to his role of "Protector of the Bushmen" (with a vested interest in ensuring their welfare, as we shall

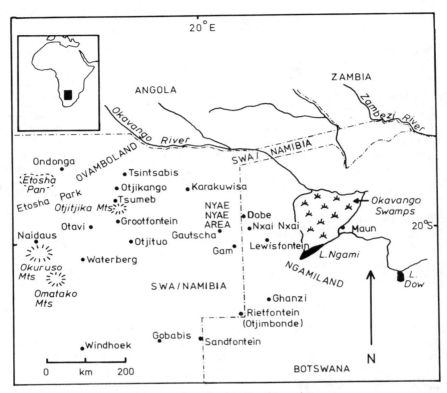

FIGURE 8.1   Bushmanland in Namibia and Botswana.

shortly see), Nangoro marched south and routed the Herero at Nuitsas and later again at Grootfontein so that they fled to beyond the Omatako Mountains. Due to the Khoi harrassment, a small group of Herero fled to Nangoro in abject poverty and succeeded in gaining succor. But that the Bushmen were more than just a horde of people incapable of taking decisive action is clear from Galton's description of how they set up game pits and fences near Otjikango:

> The whole breadth of the valley was staked and brushed across. . . . The strength and size of the timber that was used gave me a great idea of Bushman industry . . . and the scale of the undertaking would have excited astonishment in far more civilized nations. (Galton 1889:106; see also Serton 1954:57)

Galton and Andersson's visit to Ovamboland in the early 1850s inaugurated a new era during which white hunters trekked north in large numbers to hunt for ivory. Their favorite route and area was the Omuramba Omatako and especially its more northerly reaches. During this time, the Hereros "only came to the Bushman country as casual laborers to the Europeans during the hunting season" (Köhler 1959:16). A major base of these hunters for many years was Karakuwisa. A critical change occurred with the arrival of these mercantile hunters–traders, namely the introduction of modern firearms into the area, a variable that would dramatically affect the balance of power.

The next significant development was the establishment in 1884 of a small settlement of *"Trekboers,"* (or early European pastoralists) called the Republic of Upingtonia. It was instigated by a remarkable adventurer named Will Worthington Jordan (see de Klerk 1977) but collapsed a few years later in 1886. There were three basic reasons why this Republic was established where it was. First, the land was good for grazing and the development of a primitive method of cattle innoculation increased the likelihood of such an endeavor succeeding. Second, it was an area where there was no strong centralized authority to prevent settlement, insofar as it was seen by whites as a disputed territory between the Herero and the Ovambo. Third, the area obviously had valuable copper deposits. During all this time, the Herero presence was minimal (Köhler 1959), as is confirmed by Schinz (1891).

The advance of the Herero was checked by some singular resistance by a Heikom Bushman leader called Tsameb and his successor and son, Aribib. With the first appearance of Herero cattle on Bushman preserves, Tsameb organized raids. This led to the Herero indiscriminately killing any Bushman, male or female, they encountered. Tsameb then set about effectively organizing the various Bushmen clans to resist the Herero invasion. Because of the success of these strategies, he became known as a chief. Later, he obtained Khoi assistance and forced the Herero to retreat. Tsameb's group became known as the *Kai-ei-kwan* (or *Gaikokoin* in Grootfontein Bezirk 1913) and occupied "great places" ranging from Karuchas in Outjo District to what are now the farms Brandenburg and Wittenburg in the present Grootfontein District (Hahn to CNC 5/9/1940, A50/67[1]). Tsameb was succeeded by his son Aribib, who continued the proud and effective tradition of resistance to Herero encroachment (Hartmann cited in Köhler 1959; Hahn to CNC 5/9/1940, A50/67). Aribib concluded treaties with the Germans in 1895 and 1898 and was subsequently employed by the German government as a recruiter of Bushman labor and an apprehender of Bushmen miscreants wanted by the Germans. The Germans, however, hanged his younger brother, so he fled to Ovamboland where he was killed by either some Herero refugees for being in the employ of the Germans (Hahn to CNC 5/9/1940, A50/67), or on instruction from the Ondonga king, Nehale, while attacking some Herero refugees

[1]Unless otherwise indicated, such coded references refer to manuscripts of the Windhoek State Archives.

during the German–Herero war of 1904–1907. The latter version is probably more reliable. This led to the fragile unity of the Heikom clans being shattered, and subsequently they were hunted down by both the Herero and the Germans, who had by this time settled in the area, so that the Bushmen were driven from their great places such as Naidaus and Okoruso to the fringes of the Etosha Game Park (proclaimed in 1907) where they found temporary refuge.

The Impact on Trade of Merchant Capital

Perhaps the event that had the most disastrous implications for the Bushmen was the introduction of firearms, a consequence of merchant capital. Firearms had two major interrelated impacts: First, they upset the balance of power. Many writers of diverse backgrounds have suggested that the Khoi and the blacks did not really infringe on the traditional areas of the Bushmen in the northeast until after the introduction of firearms (see e.g., Swanepoel n.d.; Wilhelm 1954). This certainly appears to have been the case with the Herero and also along the Okavango River. Old German documents state for example that the Kwangari, who are now the most populous tribe in the Okavango area, were, even at the turn of the century, still largely north of the river because they feared the Bushmen (ZBU 1010(3)).

The second impact of firearms was seen in their ecological effect. Galton and Andersson were engaged in their journeys, they made some interesting discoveries that they did not record fully, namely that other representatives of merchant capital had been there before them. Andersson, for example, met some "Basters" from the Cape who had trekked with 47 wagons across the Kalahari to hunt. Galton met a Bushman at Rietfontein who was the proud owner of a three-legged iron pot. And both of them found that the game had retreated to beyond the 20°E line (Kienetz 1974). One of their near contemporaries, the artist Thomas Baines, found some Bushmen at Sandfontein who could speak Dutch (Baines 1864/1973:94).

In 1860, the renowned hunter Fredrick Green and a trader, Axel Erikssen, had established their hunting headquarters at Grootfontein (Vedder 1938:422–423). On Green's death, an American trader in South West Africa, Gerald McKiernan eulogized: "Fredrick Green was one of the most famous of African hunters, Gordon Cumming or no other could compete with him" (Quoted in Serton 1954:93). It was estimated that in his lifetime he killed between 750 and 1000 elephants (Serton 1954:93). The Omuramba Omatako and especially its upper reaches was a very popular and much frequented area for hunters, and there was a large hunting camp at Karakuwisa maintained largely by the "Griqua Bastard," Jac Kruger, and varying numbers of white companions such as John Hickey and Charles Sabatta. So intense was the hunting in this area that by 1865 Green was forced to move his hunting headquarters to Ondonga (Stals 1969).

Another famous hunter, Hendrik van Zyl of Ghanzi, visited the Gautscha area in 1874 (Tabler 1973). Van Zyl quickly discovered that the area north of Gobabis to the Okavango River was a "true hunter's paradise" (Burger 1978:42). He employed well over a hundred Bushmen (Trumpelmann 1948:16), many of whom served as "shootboys." Indeed, when van Zyl established the "world record" for killing over 103 elephants in one day, while killing over 400 elephants in 1877, most of them were accounted for by his Bushman shots. These deeds took place in the Gamveld, an area immediately south of the present-day Bushmanland and one traditionally held by Bushman. These kills yielded over 8000 lbs of ivory (Tabler 1973:116). It appears that many hunters and traders appreciated the qualities of Bushmen as hunters and trackers and, above all, as faithful servants, and thus they armed them and encouraged them to hunt for ivory and later for ostrich feathers. Travelers encountered Bushmen armed with rifles hunting in the Okavango region who, on a good day, produced 145 lbs of ivory (von Moltke n.d.). Indeed, some "great white hunters" were so afraid of elephants that they left all the hunting to Bushmen (Chapman n.d.). It was common for traders to trade ivory collected by Bushmen (Chapman 1868:157).

Schinz found them to be the most trustworthy and reliable of the various "natives." Their loyalty was such that they would work without pay. This conclusion was reached by other whites he spoke with (Schinz 1891:392). McKiernan found Bushmen always willing to perform even the most menial and boring services and satisfied with a ration of tobacco, beads, or a handkerchief as a reward (Serton 1954:77). Herbst described a situation in the southern Kalahari that certainly seems applicable to the northeast as well:

> When the Bushmen had learnt the use of the rifle from the Bastards (so-called "Coloreds") and Whites (in 1863), they were armed and had to do most of the hunting, while the Bastards remained at home. The skins and feathers were brought to them while the meat was eaten by the Bushmen. The rifle therefore played an important part in the taming of the Bushman for realizing the impotency of his own weapon as compared with that possessed by the Bastard, he naturally allied himself to the latter, at first, and when these became subject to the colonial laws, he went over to the Hottentots further north. (Cape Colony 1908:7)

It was customary for the traders and hunters—be they European, Cape Coloreds, Bastards, or Griquas—to arm the local populace in order to have them hunt on a commission basis. The Reverend Hahn gave evidence in 1882 that he had seen nearly 500 rifles south of Gobabis at trader Robert Duncan's outpost, which was "loaned out" to local people to use in hunting (Cape of Good Hope 1882:40). Other firms would send out wagons of up to 60 "natives" armed with rifles under the supervision of 1 or 2 Europeans. The wagons would return when they were loaded with about 4 tons of ivory, feathers, horns, and skins. One such firm alone had 60 wagons equipped like this (Frere 1881).

Palgrave provides some sense of the extent of this trade. He estimated the white population, which included missionaries and traders, to be 150 in South West Africa. In 1876, 34,500 lbs of ivory, 5800 lbs of ostrich feathers, and 3000 oxen were exported from Walvis Bay; the value of the ivory and ostrich feathers was estimated at £45,000 (Vedder 1938:446). Eriksen's trading firm was said to have had a turnover of £200,000 per year (Frere 1881; von Moltke n.d.).

By 1878 southern and central South West Africa had been virtually denuded of game, and the hunters were forced to move north into an area where cattle and horses suffered unless they were innoculated or "salted." The South African resident stationed at Walfish Bay reported that the Damaras (Herero) had dropped out of the hunting trade, preferring to develop their considerable herds of livestock than move farther afield in search of game:

> Today the Bushman is using the heavy elephant gun with a deadly effect as ever did Damara, Griqua, or Namaqua, and the Damara ponders over the thought of what the Bushman will do with his gun when the game is gone. He sees the trader pass by with the goods he once bought, to enrich tribes beyond over whom he feels he can lord it no longer. (Cape Colony 1879:136)

During this time, the major northern route of travelers, hunters, and traders was either via Karakuwisa or Tsintsabis. Cattle from Angola were often exported to the Rand mining area directly overland to avoid paying duties on shipments. They were driven to Eriksen's Putz, some 40 km from Otjituo, where they were massed, and then through the Kalahari to Lewisfontein, a route that took them through Bushman territory to Ngami and then to the Transvaal. By 1900 these routes had fallen into disuse, (Clarence-Smith 1979; Volkmann 1901) and, indeed, the ivory market had moved away from Walvis Bay to Mossamedes in Angola. As more and more traders made their way up to the northeast, trade changed so that a vicious circle developed, leading to the decimation of more and more game. For example, in the 1850s, Andersson reported a Ngamiland chief accepting three ordinary copper mugs for a large tusk and one musket for 1200 lbs of ivory (valued at that time at £240; Vedder 1938:304). Approximately 20 years later in Ovamboland, 40 lbs of ivory would be exchanged for an English rifle, while 300 lbs of ivory brought a better rifle or a small cannon (Stals 1969:248, 250). According to Andersson the problem was that Portuguese traders were coming down as far as 20° south latitude and giving 50 lbs of gunpowder and 100 lbs of lead for a single tusk, and the Boers were disposing of their ammunition in a liberal manner against their "coloured neighbours" (Andersson 1858:158).

Given such a situation it was not long before this northern area was denuded of game too. The last elephants were killed in the Etosha Pan area in 1881 (de la Bat 1982), and by 1886 elephants were declared "hunted out" in Ngami (Tabler 1973:65). Some contemporaries at that time raised their voices against the environmental pillage. Pieter Heinrich Brincker, a missionary, for example, wrote strongly about "the stupid, or rather inhuman, way in which ostriches have been hunted during the last few years, so that they have been almost exterminated," forcing traders and hunters to move farther into Ovamboland and the Okavango where "They still get . . . a fair quantity of ivory and feathers through trading and hunting themselves, in a way which many people would not care to undertake" (cited in Vedder 1938:447).

The death knell to this once flourishing trade came in 1892, when the Germans prohibited trade in arms and ammunition with blacks in their newly acquired colony (Stals 1969:290–291). This led, naturally enough, to large-scale smuggling operations between Angola and South West Africa in which Bushmen played a key role. In 1893 there was a minor revival because of the ostrich feather boom, and Bushmen were, at least in the southern Kalahari, major suppliers of the feathers and not above weighting the loads of feathers with a bit of iron or some rocks to obtain a better price (Jackson 1958).

Bushman were aware of what was happening. In 1920, the oldest Bushman at Tsintsabis police station complained to a visitor: "Elephants, lions, and game of all kinds abounded and have only disappeared since the white man came and shot them in large numbers" (H. J. K., 1920).

Generally, relations between Bushmen and white hunters were quite amicable. Each appreciated the other. Most hunters reported that the Bushmen were very helpful and would do anything for a small gift of tobacco (Chapman 1868; Nolte 1886). Indeed, the Bushmen's almost legendary weakness for tobacco was well established. Chapman noted that they would obtain tobacco by trading jackal skins to Chapa, a distance 240 km away. Other hunters, however, on occasion had to resort to taking Bushmen as hostages in order to force them to show them the way (Galton 1889), but they apparently treated them Bushmen well during these tribulations. Tales of Bushmen rescuing whites, including Boers, and blacks from thirst were common (Coetzee 1942; van der Walt 1926). Generally Bushmen guides were allowed to carry guns and served as messengers. Indeed, it is clear that they played a pivotal role in the communications network of the early white hunters and traders (Galton 1889; Green 1860). The prevailing advice to whites at this time was that the Bushmen were usually fine people unless they had been wronged (Serton 1954; Tabler 1973:49). Many whites and blacks were apparently killed for interfering with Bushmen women (Andersson 1856:359; Möller 1974:150; Wallis 1936:224), but retributive justice worked both ways. When van Zyl heard that a small child of one of the Thirstland Trekkers had wandered off and was killed by Bushmen, he let it be known that any amount of tobacco and brandy was available at his settlement. He invited Bushman to participate in this largesse at a specially constructed kraal, and after they were suitably inebriated, he ordered them tied up and taken near the place where the child had been killed, where he invited the Trekkers to shoot them. The Trekkers apparently declined his invitation, so he gave some rifles to the Bushmen attached to the Boers and ordered them to shoot after he had read the Biblical passage concerning an eye for an eye. Thirty-three Bushmen were murdered in this episode (de Klerk 1977:67). This event also signifies an important change: Relations started deteriorating with the immigration into the area of settlers and farmers. For instance, at the end of his life, Andersson would write: "I have come to the conclusion that Bushmen, as a race, deserve no pity" (1875:274). Earlier, he had already begun to become disillusioned with them, referring to them on occasion as "perfect devils" (1856:140).

A major incursion by whites occurred with the Thirstland Trek, a motley collection of whites from the Transvaal who decided, for a variety of reasons, but chiefly because of the "liberalism" of President Burger, to leave the South African Republic (Transvaal) and seek a new domicile. They crossed the Kalahari in a number of treks. The first trek arrived in what is now Rietfontein (in Hereroland), an area traditionally acknowledged to belong to the Bushmen, where they spent 2 years recuperating before moving north through present-day Bushmanland to the Okavango River. This trek consisted of 15 families, totaling 62 adults. They spent the winter of 1877 grazing their cattle at the Tebraveld. After many tribulations, they eventually made their way to southern Angola, where they managed to eke out a precarious existence. However, they were to make various return visits to the area inhabited by the Bushmen.

Their first return was under the guidance and encouragement of a remarkable man, William Worthington Jordan, an educated adventurer of "mixed blood" from the Cape who has become the subject of a powerful historical novel, *The Thirstland,* by the well-known Afrikaner author, W. A. de Klerk (1977). In 1885 he persuaded a group of Trekkers to return to the Grootfontein area to settle on farms which he allocated to them on most reasonable terms. Jordan had, as a result of negotiations with the Ondonga king, Kambonde, obtained a concession for some 957 mi^2 (25,000 km^2) of territory between Grootfontein, Otavi, Etosha Pan, and the Waterberg, on payment of some £300, 25 muzzle loaders, 1 salted horse, and a barrel of brandy (Rädel 1947). Jordan divided the territory into 3000-morgen (2570-ha) farms, of which he kept 5 for himself, as well as, and perhaps most important, all the mineral and trading rights in the area. In October 1885, the Trekboers announced the formation of the Republic of Upingtonia, named, on Jordan's insistence, after the prime minister of the Cape in an effort to ensure the

Cape's support for the precarious republic. Undoubtedly, this strategy was modeled on the pocket republic of Stellaland, which was established in 1882 and incorporated into British Bechuanaland in 1884. Forty-six Boers signed the agreement, establishing the republic, and within 16 months, 43 farms were allocated. Schinz estimated the Boer population at Grootfontein to be about 500 (Schinz 1891). However, because of the general uncertainty in the area arising from Bushman raids and robbery, they usually did not occupy their farms but concentrated together at a few places where they lived in *hartebeesthuises* (adobe-style dwellings) around which they planted small fields of wheat and *mielies* (corn). The republic collapsed after the murder of Jordan in June 1886, and the area was placed under German protection in May 1887, by which time most of the erstwhile settlers had already moved away to either Angola or the Transvaal.

The myth of the heroic, altruistic Jordan helping the Trekboers found the utopian republic that then collapses after his murder is only sustainable if one ignores the Bushman factor. A consideration of the role of Bushmen in this area leads to two important revisionist points: First, the Bushmen were responsible for the collapse of the Republic of Upingtonia, and, second, Jordan's motives in helping the Thirstland Trekkers might not have been so altruistic. In order to wrest the copper mines from Bushmen control, he needed a large number of whites in the vicinity to provide his investment with protection. The following evidence can be produced in support of these assertions. In one of his first letters to the German imperial official, Nels, President Prinsloo of the republic complained that "The Bushmen made up a commando and have shot Mr. James Todd and taken everything which he possessed. The Bushmen still wander among us. We do not know what they will do to us" (Quoted in Burger 1978:374, my translation).

Several sources (e.g., Burger 1978; Prinsloo and Gauche 1933:157ff.) show how the small Boer community had to cope almost daily with Bushman reprisals in which the Bushmen invariably had the upper hand since they were often well armed with rifles, a legacy of ivory hunting, and were more mobile than the Trekkers. Indeed, the Trekkers had considerable problems in mounting attacks because they lacked horses; they were forced to borrow them from Erikssen on one occasion. Judging by the few descriptions available, Bushmen counter-insurgency operations were well planned and successful, involving in one instance the confiscation of 500 cattle belonging to one Boer, Prinsloo, in one day (Prinsloo and Gauche 1933). As a long-time Grootfontein resident, the surveyor Hauptmann Volkmann wrote in the 1930s:

> As far as I can remember, the first Boers who came into this district in about 1880 had to leave very soon again, as there were too many Bushmen living here so that they

were unable to protect themselves against the continuous stealing of the Bushmen. (Volkmann letter, A50/67).

President Prinsloo of the republic explained the situation in his last letter to Reichskommisar Goring in June 1887:

> Due to our inability, we are obliged to move from here. It is due to our weakness and the rebelliousness of [local] nations that endanger the safety of our families that we are leaving, but should this land be taken into possession by some other possibility, we would like to retain our rights. (Quoted in Burger 1978:380, my translation)

Early traders and adventurers, such as McKiernan, visited the Bushman mining operations and were impressed by the richness of the lode. The only factor inhibiting McKiernan's attempt to take over the mines was the fact that they were too far away from the port of Walvis Bay to be economically viable; but this was only a small problem to a visionary such as Jordan, who dreamed of building a railway line from Walvis Bay to Zimbabwe (Wannenburgh n.d.:170)! The mineral wealth of the area was a prime factor in Jordan's and other whites' intentions, as is evident from the dispute that arose over the concession. Robert Lewis, a confidant of the Herero chief, Maherero, for example, also claimed the mineral rights over the area on the basis of a concession given to him by the Herero and did his utmost to have Jordan and his band of Trekkers removed from the vicinity; there is some suggestion by various authors that he might have played a role in the killing of Jordan.

After Jordan's death, his concession was acquired by an Anglo–German consortium, the South West Africa Company, which immediately set about organizing operations by sending out a mining engineer, Mathew Rogers, together with a large party of miners, who arrived in the area in December 1892 (Sohnge 1967). Rogers and his large party were followed shortly afterward by the establishment of a German police and military station, which prepared the way for the great land rush by white settlers after 1903.

Trade Items and Networks

Judging by the scanty historical material and especially the earliest ethnographic maps by Schinz (1891) and others, it would appear that the !Kung groups have lived in their respective territories for a long time. But it would be an error to see the !Kung as sticklers for remaining at home. In the early 1950s, The Commission for the Preservation of the Bushmen reported that

> Some of the so-called "wild" [Ju/Wasi] Bushmen in the Noma Omaramba, near Nyae-Nyae expressed concern at the fact that their relatives living on the outskirts of civilization were damaging the reputation of the tribe by killing European owned cattle but they explained that this was largely due to lack of official guidance. The people who perpetuated these misdeeds had left their home areas with the intention of enter-

ing . . . employment but on the very doorstep their hearts failed them and there was no one to help them to take the final plunge into an entirely foreign and . . . hostile world. So they hovered around on the outskirts in a totally unsuitable area where food was scarce and hard to come by and, eventually, hunger forced them to commit crimes. . . . Of their own accord, they mentioned that it would be a good idea if some of the Kung who had already settled on farms were to return to the tribe and each take out one or two others to work with them on farms. They did not want, however, to lose their relatives forever in this way and thought that the Government should see to it that the Kung returned to their tribal areas again as in the case with the Ovambos and Okavangos. (Schoeman n.d.b. para. 42)

Indeed, the whole area seems to have been crisscrossed with well-developed trading networks. Between August and September 1911, Hauptmann Muller led a reconaissance party to the Kaukauveld and found as trade items near Geitza the following: cowrie shells, glass beads, iron beads, copper rings, Ovambo knives, and Okavango wooden bowls. He found much evidence of Bechuanas trekking into the area via Lewisfontein for cattle grazing, hunting, and trading as well as selling ammunition to the Bushmen on a regular basis. They came with horses, wagons, and pack oxen, and went as far north as Kauara and Debra in the west. At Tsumkwe, Gautscha, Garu, and Nona, Muller found fresh traces of cattle kraals and dung. The *Ju/Wasi* would keep horns and hides in anticipation of these expeditions. Muller describes how:

Within a wind screen of the werft Kauara, I saw a bundle which was plaited like a weir basket. I caused it to be opened and found . . . ostrich feathers ready for dispatch! The people of Geitza keep the Ostrich feathers still more carefully. They cut a rod of the length of an ostrich feather from a shrub, grecia spec, which has a remarkable soft marrow. This marrow they push out and put the ostrich feather in its place. (Muller 1912)

J. H. Wilhelm, who farmed in the Grootfontein District from 1914 to 1919, presents a vivid description (1954:140–144) of similar parcels of ostrich feathers arranged by size and bound in bushels, while the choice feathers were protected in reed tubes that were taken by !Kung (and Ju/Wasi) to the Okavango River for trading purposes. Such expeditions would take place near the end of the winter period but before the onset of the rains. An expedition would consist of a number of men led by an elder who had been on such an expedition before. In provisioning such an expedition, hides would be removed from their storage place in the crowns of large trees, and ostrich-shell necklaces would be placed in collecting bags while ostrich feathers were arranged and snake skins and antelope horns were gathered. Once the expedition reached the Okavango werft where they wanted to trade, the leader went forward while the rest of the party waited. While they waited, they would ritualistically hide the articles that they thought would be most valued. The Okavango people anticipated these expeditions eagerly, because they needed the animal hides for cloaks and blankets and the ostrich-shell necklaces for their wives. In preparation they built up a good stock of clay pots, assegai points, knife blades, axes, knives, and metal rings.

After formal greetings and the smoking of a round of tobacco, the Bushmen would untie their packages and barter would proceed, with heavy haggling, item by item. The most valuable items, the objects hidden outside the kraal, were kept for last. Wilhelm (1954:140–144) provides some rates of exchange:

6 Duiker hides	=	1 cooking pot
1 Hartebeest hide	=	1 cooking pot
12 Springbok hides	=	1 axe and a few armrings
1 bundle ostrich feathers	=	1 musical pipe
1 python skin	=	1 wooden bowl
Jackal skins	=	tobacco
Ostrich shell necklaces (best price)	=	assegai points

There was much gaiety after trading; the Bushmen were given a gift of ground millet, which they cooked, and entertainment by the Okavango continued until late at night. The next morning, the Bushmen returned home, moving from water hole to water hole (Wilhelm 1954, see also H. J. K. 1921:119). These expeditions were still taking place after World War II, and, indeed, some !Kung complained to the Commission for the Preservation of the Bushmen that they were being molested and sometimes also robbed by Okavangos on their way to the river to trade (Schoeman n.d.a:par. 20).

Sometimes such expeditions would go to white-occupied farms, where horns and hides would be traded for tobacco, items of clothing, and knives. Farmers felt compelled to offer decent terms of exchange in such cases, for they feared that if they did not, they might lose some livestock. Needless to say, the government took a dim view of this type of trade since it was felt that it would encourage the Bushmen to decimate the game and, furthermore, would provide the farmers with an excuse for engaging in poaching. A typical expedition would bring in 20 antlers and 12 hides (Gobabis 15/9/1917, ADM 2241/6).

A different system of trading occurred when the traders, be they Bechuanas, whites, or, later, Herero, moved into the Bushman heartland to trade. In the 1850s, Galton found a Bushman cooking with a large iron pot at Tounobis (Rietfontein). "The Bushmen said that it was given to them by people from a wagon some distance to the east, and who had gone to the lake the previous season" (Galton 1889:16). The Bechuanas were especially keen to find tanned skins, which were renowned for their softness, throughout the country. Tobacco was the major traded commodity, and it was distributed according to three measures: one handful, two handfuls, and the hollow between the chest and the arms when folded (Wilhelm 1954). In addition, clothing, ironware, and cannabis were also regular items (Bleek 1928; Wilhelm 1954), while in the southern Kalahari, coffee was also apparently popular (16/4/1926, A50/27). Marshall describes the dynamics of the process:

> The odds are with the Bantu in the trading. Big, aggressive, and determined to have what they want, they easily intimidate the !Kung. Several . . . said that they tried hard not to trade with Herero if it was possible to avoid it because, although the Tawana were hard bargainers, the Herero were worse. /Qui . . . said he had been forced by a Herero . . . to trade [his] shirt and pants . . . for a small enamel pan and a little cup. /Tikay had more gumption. A Herero at the beginning of a negotiation with him brought out a good-sized pile of tobacco but took from it only a pinch when it was time to pay. /Tikay picked up the object he was trading and ran off . . . The Tawana values are a little better. A well-tanned gemsbok hide brings a pile of tobacco about 14 inches in diameter and about 4 inches high. The values vary. Some that were reported to us were three duiker or steenbok skins for a good-sized knife, five strings of ostrich-eggshell beads for an assegai. (1976:306).

The !Kung also traded among different groups. Thus, the Karakuwisa Bushmen were reported to go to Nurugas in order to trade pots obtained from the Bushmen at Blockfontein, while the Bushmen at Otjituo traded with the Auen. A shirt given by Vedder to a Bushman at Gaub went to the Auen via Otjituo, while beads emanating from Bechuanaland were traded in Grootfontein (Wilhelm 1954). Bleek, in her study of the Naron, also provides an indication of how far-reaching this trade network was: Ovambo knives and metal rings, which came from the north via the Auen, were found among Naron, who then traded them to the Koon (Bleek 1922/1928).

Exchange relations between Bushmen and Kavango migrant workers traveling on the route via Karakuwisa were atypical of that between strangers. Wust reported the experience of a church Brother who had allowed some Okavango migrant workers to accompany him on the journey to Grootfontein. The Brother watched incredulously as the Okavango workers systematically pillaged the Bushmen properties they came across. Meat, fruit, hides, and even items that they could hardly use were taken. The Bushmen responded by saying that they would seek retribution when the Okavangos came back and were not under the protection of a white man (Wust 1938:258). This illustrates two points: first, that such behavior was obviously intimately associated with Bushmen attacks on returning labor migrants, and, second, that the extension of white rule enabled blacks to exploit the Bushmen to a degree that was not previously possible.

After measures were taken to protect Okavango laborers from Bushmen attacks and the migrant labor recruiters, the Northern Labor Organization, started dotting the labor route with water pump stations, Bushmen settled near these stations and acted as wageless caretakers of these pumps. The Northern Labor Organization had no cause for complaint except that on occasion the Bushmen used too much water. These Bushman "settlers" were said to have given up part of their roaming life. Their settlements were surrounded by palisades (for protection against both animal and human predators), and they had small gardens that were cultivated with the assistance of hoes traded from the blacks. The crops they grew included maize, millet, and tobacco. The gardens were cleared in depressions in the ground, contained rich moist soil, and were surrounded with simple fences to protect the crops from game (Schönfelder Memorandum 1/2/1939, A50/26), all of which suggests a knowledge acquired through friendly interaction with the Okavango workers. Indeed, the Northern Labor Organization had reason to be pleased with these developments, because not only did they get free pump caretakers, but also the Bushmen would care for injured or ill labor recruits for weeks on end. These settlers also engaged in extensive trade, functioning often as middlemen for Bushmen relatives who lived in more remote areas and the labor recruits. The major items of trade were hides and ostrich-shell necklaces.

The situation of the !Kung living closer to the river was different in degree. As stated in one annual report:

> The natives are themselves too lazy to proceed outside the "inhabited" areas to gather fruit, and rely on the Bushmen to bring it in. In return for this service, the Bushmen are allowed to reside on the outskirts of the inhabited area during the reaping season, and greatly assist to finish off the meagre crop of grain. (U. G. 27/1934:45)

Of course, it might not be a matter of laziness as much as fear of possible Bushman attack, which occurred frequently at times. At this time, no Bushmen were reported actually living permanently in the so-called tribal areas of the Okavango Reserve. By 1945, the Bushmen were described as having "learnt to rely on Ovambo and Okavangos in times of shortage and have, in consequence, acquired the habit of eating cereal, which is obtained in exchange for ostrich eggshells, *veldkos* and honey" (Okavango Native Reserve 1945). Four years later the Okavango Reserve medical officer was able to discern a definite process:

> Seemingly more and more bushmen migrate to the banks of the Okavango every year, to assist the natives in the harvesting season in exchange for food, tobacco, beads, etc. The influence of the easier existence . . . (is) appreciated by the bushmen who will stay for longer and longer periods every year. (Regional Medical Officer 27/8/1949, A 50/67).

The !Kung apparently had a limited choice in this matter, since it was policy not to allow the Bushmen to engage in the only other alternative: contract labor to the police zone. " 'I have consistently refused their applications' wrote the Commissioner, 'on the grounds that I do not consider the Bushmen as sufficiently advanced to understand the obligations of an ordinary contract'" (N. C. Runtu, March, 1948, A50/67).

Details on the nature of these relations are scarce. What data we have must be seen in the context of the Okavango as a refuge area. Most of the so-called Okavango tribes only settled on the southern banks of the Okavango River after 1900, the area being regarded as the domain of Bushmen. The dominant economic political structure that emerged with black settlement of the southern banks of the Okavango was a form of slavery, or bondsmanship, as Bishop Gotthardt preferred to call it (Gotthardt, A403/1). It was estimated that as many as 50% of the adult population was involved in a slave relationship. As Gotthardt explained the system, each headman had a number of *wapika* (subjects) who in turn had their own *wapika*. Each subject was supposed to work and assist his or her master, and the master was supposed to provide his or her subject with fields for planting. Many Okavango chiefs and headmen had Bushmen hunters working full time for them and would entrust firearms to these hunters (Engelbrecht 1922; Wust 1938). Typically, Bushmen would reside about a mile away from their patrons' kraal, just outside what was defined as the inhabited area. They would also be employed as cattle herders. According to the native commissioner cattle theft was common because the Okavango did not attach as much value to their cattle as the Herero did; nor did they employ enough cattle herders.

Nevertheless, theft was brutally punished, as the count records show, but it should be borne in mind that many similar events occurred involving Okavango people at the receiving end. The conclusion reached in the 1945 annual report seems to have been the norm: Bushmen "are not molested or harrassed by the natives and are not interfered with by the Administration unless they commit the more serious crimes" (Okavango Native Reserve 1945; see also Eedes 19/1/1938, A 50/67).

While the !Kung lived to the northeast and southeast of Grootfontein, the Nama-speaking Heikom Bushmen were found to the northwest and east of Grootfontein. The Heikom are said to be easily distinguishable from the !Kung, not only on linguistic but also on physiological grounds. Groups said to be related to them include the Naron of the Gobabis District. Most of the areas in which the Heikom live have been expropriated by white ranchers and game reserves. According to "Cocky" Hahn, the well-experienced Ovambo native commissioner,

> The Heikom have perhaps suffered more than any other Bushman tribe. . . . Their various family clans or groups have become disintegrated and have been pushed further and further north . . . latterly by our own settlement schemes. Their hunting grounds and *veld kos* [plant foods] areas have either been completely taken from them or have shrunk to such an extent that in very many cases the wild or semi-wild Heikom

today finds it almost impossible to eke out an existence. . . . It is surprising that these
people do not indulge in more cattle and stock thieving. (Hahn, A 50/25 (1))

One Heikom oral history presents the following reconstruction of their
past:

> The first Heikom, Xameb [Tsameb?] came to the Namutoni area from Waterberg. At
> that time, Namutoni was the drinking place of innumerable elephants. The bushes
> were very thick and the trees were much higher than now. Thus, Xameb and his
> people moved further on in the direction of Ovamboland but they did not like the
> sandy soil of Obamboland and returned to Namutoni. They were great hunters and
> were left in peace. Only much later did the Hottentots [Khoi] and Damaras [Herero]
> arrive. The *Xaben* [Ovambo] were our first friends and we traded with them. The
> Herero were the first people with whom we made war. (Schoeman n.d.a.)

Trade, especially in copper, was one of the features that impressed many
early travelers. In 1850, Brochado entered Ovamboland from the north. He
found:

> On [Chief] Nangolo's periphery about 100 to 125 km away are *Kwankhala* [Heikom]
> who contrary to most other members of this race, are settled and possess large copper
> mines and have copper in abundance. Only the [o]Ndonga trade with them [trading
> copper for tobacco, beads and *pungo* (cannabis)]. However, the Ondonga do not
> precisely know where the mine is. Even the powerful Haimbili of Kuanyama is not
> allowed direct contact with them. (Quoted in Heintze 1971/1972:47)

Later travelers such as Galton (1889:136) and Andersson (1856:182) found
that the Bushmen brought ore to Ojtikoto to trade with the Ovambo. The very
notion of Bushmen being engaged in copper mining clashed with the standard stereotype of what Bushmen were supposed to do, as witnessed by the
Reverend Hahn in his first encounter with mining Bushmen: "We met two
Bushmen today who were taking copper ore from Otjorukaku to Ondonga
on their own account where they would sell it for corn, tobacco, and cal-
abashes. *This I never expected from Bushmen*" (Hahn Papers, A.2048 Cape
Archives, Cape Town, 18 July, 1857; my italics and translation). Details followed in his journey to Ovamboland, where he described how parties of
Ovambo (and Bushmen) would transport the ore in neatly woven baskets
made of palm leaves and provided with a sturdy handle. Filled, each basket
weighed 90 lbs and when food and water was added, this meant that each
porter would carry approximately 115 lbs! These porters would travel with
impressive military precision for 6–8 hours per day in parties of about 30.
Apparently one of the reasons why the Hahn party was attacked by the Ovambo king, Nangoro, on this expedition was precisely because the king wanted
their wagons to transport his copper.

Copper was melted in Ondonga and formed into decorative foot rings,
which the Ondonga then traded farther afield with their fellow Ovambo. On
his next journey in 1866, Hahn observed that the Bushmen were mining the

copper near Otavi and trading it to Ovambo who came down in large numbers. The Bushmen would still apparently refuse to allow outsiders to visit the actual site of mining. Hahn estimated that between 50 and 60 tons of copper per annum were exported to Ondonga. Other Bushmen apparently made salt from the salt pans of Etosha and fashioned these into a sugarloaf form. This salt trade was, according to Hahn, just as important to the Bushmen as the copper trade (Moritz 1980; Sohnge 1967; see also, Palgrave 1877:46).

Obviously, such mining activities were bound to attract the attention of mercantile adventurers, and McKiernan describes how in 1875 he managed to find the mine after much difficulty. He described it as being very rich: "Old smelting places were plentiful. Calcined stones, charcoal, and fragments of copper ore [were collected] in heaps." However, he felt that because the deposit was so far from the sea and there was a lack of water en route, the mine was impracticable (Serton 1954:53–54).

A few years later, Schinz (1891) confirmed the mining activities near the then Republic of Upingtonia. It is clear that Jordan, the trader and main instigator of this republic, was trying to take over this mining area, and thus, in retrospect, it is not surprising that the Bushmen waged such a bitter war against the Thirstland Trekkers. Schinz also confirmed that the Bushmen owed their allegiance to the Ondonga chief, Kambonde, but apparently by this time the Bushman monopoly on the salt trade had been broken, because the Ukuambi Ovambo and the Ongandjera Ovambo were also engaged in it (1891). A Bushman is credited with discovering the immensely profitable copper mines at Tsumeb (Lebzelter 1934:42).

In southern Angola, the Bushmen were apparently connected with the mining of iron. The major diggings were at Omupa, near Kuanyama, which was regarded as !Kung Bushman territory, and, according to Loeb, while Ovambo conducted expeditions to these diggings with the efficiency of a military expedition, "they always obtained Bushman consent" (Loeb 1962:192). Bushmen were also the owners of bellows and received a share of the iron in return for the use of these instruments (generally on mining, see Heintze 1971/1972).

These friendly relations even extended to the Bushmen living within the various Ovambo tribal areas. According to Galton, "The Bushmen appear to be naturalized and free to a distance very far north of Caconda" (1889:142). Apparently, it was not quite a free life, in that they had to pay tribute like all the subjects of Ovambo chiefs and kings. Payment to the Ondonga king was in ivory. Möller wrote that, like other citizens, the Bushmen living in southern Ovamboland paid a yearly tribute in salt, copper ore, or game. Game tribute payments had to be made with live animals because of the fear that the Bushmen might poison the king, and Möller describes some rather unusual methods involving the breaking of bones to achieve this result (1974:148, 152).

The Ovambo kings apparently appreciated the lesson that the Ottoman Turks had learned about the advantages of using outsiders for sensitive tasks. Bushmen were widely reported to have served as bodyguards, executioners, spies, special messengers, and professional hunters. So effective as spies were they that the missionaries complained that Nehale knew about events two weeks before they did (Lehmann 1955/1956). So trusting were relations that when Andersson went up to Ovamboland after Hahn and Green had been attacked, the Ovambo king took fright and fled to a Bushman werft for refuge (Vedder 1938). As befits their mercenary status, the Bushmen were "even more ornamented than the Ovambo themselves . . . [and were] a kind of standing army" (Galton 1889:142). The Ovambo kings would, on occasion, appoint some Bushmen as headmen or foremen of their bands. These Bushmen chiefs apparently wielded a lot of power. Their followers would, if ordered, kill men or women. One such Ovambo-appointed headman was Quben Qubu, who had his great place at Andoni but roamed from Ovamboland to the sandveld armed with two muzzle loaders and accompanied by his several wives. He was widely feared and respected by the Bushmen (see *Rex v. Qouigan and Habuson* 1919; *Rex v. Quben Qubu* 1920). There is also a case of a chief's wife appointing a Bushman as a foreman over Ovambo (Wulfhorst 1937).

Despite this clear association with the elite in Ovamboland, Bushman relations with the commoners were also extremely amiable. After detailed archival research, I failed to come across a single contrary report (see e.g., Ovamboland 1931, 1932, 1933). In times of drought, Bushmen would move in and live with Ovambo families, usually those with whom they had previously established trading ties in which they had obtained a little grain, tobacco, butter, or cannabis for skins, ostrich shells, and honey (Heintze 1971/1972; Ovamboland 1931). When old Bushmen could not fend for themselves, they too would attach themselves to an Ovambo household (Ovamboland 1939). After such a move, the men would generally assist the Ovambo in moving their livestock to outlying cattle posts during the winter months (Ovamboland 1933). Stock theft by Bushmen was unknown, and, indeed, they would return stray cattle (Schoeman n.d.a, b). As Schoeman noted, a surprising number of Bushmen had settled in Ovambo-style houses and had fields and cattle.

Perhaps the best social indicator of discrimination involves sex. Intermarriage appears to have been quite common with the Heikom Bushmen but not so common with the !Kung. It was not only a case of Ovambo men marrying Bushmen women, but also the other way around, and there was no stigma attached to the offspring of such unions. Wulfhorst, for example, relates the story of a young Kuanyama, whose father was a Bushman. He went south on a labor contract, and later, on his way back to Ovamboland, met some of his father's relatives and decided to stay with them. He eventually married a Bushman woman, but when she died in childbirth, he returned to Kuanyama (Wulfhorst 1937:37).

It was not just the commoners who intermarried. The veteran native commissioner and author, "Cocky" Hahn, pointed out that the father of Chief Martin of the Ondonga, Kathikua, and the father of the former Ngandjera chief, Tshanika, were half-blooded Heikoms (Ovamboland 1939). Another useful material indicator of intergroup relations is the terms of trade in exchanges, and certainly by this count, exchanges are the most equitable in South West Africa: Six ostrich eggs would apparently fetch one Ovambo cow (Lebzelter 1934). This is also indicative, of course, of the relatively lower value that Ovambo attach to cattle, which, as is discussed later in this chapter, is a chief cause of friction with the pastoralists.

Whereas Bushman relations with the agricultural Ovambo were generally friendly and those with the Kavango people, who practised a mixed subsistence of cattle and horticulture and were recent invaders, were variegated, those with people who practiced pastoralism were generally of a negative nature. Such a statement would appear to be globally applicable (see e.g., Leacock and Lee 1982; Schott 1955). This is not to deny that elements of exploitation can and are present in all three types of relations. Work by Kalahari researchers has, however, challenged this view. Nurse and Jenkins, for example, have suggested that Bushmen–pastoralist (in this case Herero) relations are voluntary or habitual, lacking in coercion and mutually beneficial to both parties (1977:77). Wilmsen has gone farther in arguing that there is a long tradition of "co-existence" between Bushmen and Hereros in the Ngami area, stretching back at least a thousand years. Ignoring the reality of exploitation, he argues the proposition that "compatible forms of interaction" operated in this area. For example, he finds the fact that Tounabis, is also known as Otjimbonde (Herero) and Rietfontein (Afrikaans) as well as being generally acknowledged to be the permanent home of Bushmen is an excellent example of "overlapping claims," but he fails to address the obvious issue of the legitimacy or justification of such claims (Wilmsen 1980).

In South West Africa, the situation is apparently different from that in Botswana as reported by Wilmsen (1980). And this can probably be attributed to the fact that the Herero in Botswana are very much a minority group. Vedder, in evidence to the South West African Constitutional Commission (SWACC) in 1936, pointed out that the Herero had in precolonial and German colonial time occupied the Okahandja, Omaruru, Otjimbingue, and part of the Waterberg area. A few families had "travelled up to the north but they knew very well it was Bushmanland" (SWACC 1936:1234). Old maps confirm this. For example, a map illustrating the Herero war of 1904 shows the northernmost point of Herero settlement to be on the southern point of the

Waterberg, while the nearest Herero settlement to what later became the Epukiro Reserve was some 150 km away. Various written sources confirm this. The annual reports from the Grootfontein District point out that before the World War I, Otjituo was a major Bushman settlement, while Bleek in her pioneering research at Sandfontein, east of Gobabis, found that all her old informants claimed that the Herero and Tswana only came into their area when they were middle-aged. Perhaps the most interesting evidence for the recency of Herero contact with Bushmen is to be found in the diary that Reverend Hahn kept on his journey of exploration from Otjimbingue to Ovamboland in the north. He found that his Herero servants referred to the Bushmen as "Ozombushmana," a term clearly derived, as he recognized, from Dutch (Moritz, 1980:21).

Of course, there were Herero claims to land of the Bushmen, but changing the name of the place does not establish title to it. Many of these claims were quite specious. Maharero, as we have seen, claimed the Otavi area and the copper mines in it on the grounds that the Herero had mined the copper first and that Grootfontein had previously been occupied by Hereros. However, as Schinz pointed out, the Herero word for copper was *otjikoporo,* a word clearly of English origin, and, moreover, the Bushmen in the area recognized the hegemony of Kambonde, the Ondonga king, but not that of Maherero (Schinz 1891).

Pastoralism is detrimental to hunting, not so much because stock compete with browsing and grazing game, but rather because pastoralists have fire-arms that denude the area of game. The situation was further aggravated by white ranchers displacing the Herero from their prime ranch land in the central highlands and forcing them into the more marginal areas in the Kalahari, land that just happened to belong to the Bushmen. The Herero have always valued their cattle highly and been swift in their retribution of any harm done to their herds. Farming in marginal areas raised the relative worth of their cattle and made retribution even more severe, especially in the absence or minimal presence of any overarching statial checks. The Bushmen have long been afraid that the Herero would penetrate farther into their hunting grounds and take possession of the land (Köhler 1957:49). Indeed, in 1926 a Bushman headman is reported to have crossed the border from Botswana into the Epukiro Reserve and given warning that the Bushmen would not tolerate any further encroachment either by man or beast (Gobabis 26/5/1926, A50/26).

Encroachment did not occur only from the west however. In 1917, the Tawana from Ngami were given permission to use the Nyae Nyae area for winter grazing on the condition that they maintained good relations with the Bushmen and did not engage in hunting. The Tawana sent their herds out under the care of Herero. Some Bushmen lost their lives resisting this incursion, which resulted in various police patrols being sent to the area both from Grootfontein and from Maun in Botswana. One patrol, headed by Sgt. Harold Brooks in the winter of 1935, found 138 Hereros at Gautscha and Gora with over 800 head of cattle, 9 horses, 98 donkeys, and 400 sheep and goats, all of which belonged to Muruwera, the owner of Mahupa. They claimed to have been making this winterly trek for the past 30 years. Brooks threatened to shoot the cattle if they did not immediately remove them. In 1937 a beacon marking the border was put up (A50/101), but it is obvious that it was difficult and indeed rare for either the South West African or Botswana police to patrol this area.

Most historical sources concur that relations between Bushmen and Herero were bitter. Even Andersson, who was no admirer of the Bushmen and certainly on a friendly footing with the Herero, noted in 1856 that "Some Bushmen surprised and killed eight Damara [Herero] women. This was not to be wondered at, for the Damaras themselves are always waging an exterminating war on the Bushmen. Indeed, they hunt them down, wherever met with, like wild beasts" (Andersson 1856:210–211). A few years later Thomas Baines wrote in his journal:

> Another even less welcome piece of intelligence is the confirmation of a report that Chapman's Damaras during his absence had borrowed guns of his servant John, an old soldier of the 74th Highlanders, and instead of hunting as they had promised, had attacked the Bushmen in the hills, killing some, and returning loaded with their almost worthless plunder. This outrage, the result of some ancient feud, is likely to set the Bushmen at enmity with us. (Baines 1864/1973:91).

In 1877 the wife of hunter Fredrick Green witnessed an incident in which a Herero and 20 of his men first stunned a captive Bushman with knobkieries and then beat him raw with sjamboks before finally burning him alive (Tabler 1973:48). Möller observed how, even during the German colonial era, the Bushmen residing in Hottentot and Herero areas, in contrast to those residing in Ovamboland, "live as oppressed pariahs who are unscrupulously exterminated wherever they are found" (1974:147).

Vedder observed that the Bergdamaras and Bushmen "were regarded by the Hereros as having no right there at all and they were looked upon as pests. They were killed wherever they were encountered. Women and children were carried off and put to work at domestic tasks and as herdboys" (1938:143). In view of the preceding evidence, this account seems eminently plausible. This pattern of antagonistic relations between Bushmen and Herero is still to be found.

Today (1984), the general pattern of Bushman–Herero interaction consists, at least initially, of the Bushmen moving to the Herero settlements during the dry season, where in return for doing various domestic chores such as collecting firewood and water, herding, and milking they are given a variable amount of tobacco and food (especially milk) depending on the availability of the supplies. Such ties are usually established with Hereros with whom there is some preexisting relationship, generally in terms of past relationships with relatives or because of trade. Bushmen still bring hides and skins to Herero for trade. Sometimes these sojourns are extended beyond the onset of the rains, when the Bushmen are expected to leave for the bush and subsequently return the next season to the same family. Where these relationships developed into ones of year-long permanence and the year had been good, the Bushmen servants might be rewarded with a goat or a calf at the end of the year. Today too, cans and bottles of beer have also made an appearance as rewards. In essence, this process of sedentarization is a logical extension of hunting and gathering strategies.

However, relations did vary at times. Perhaps the most significant such case was the Waterberg massacre, which resulted in 24 Herero being found guilty of cold-bloodedly massacring 13 Bushmen: 2 males, 4 females, and 7 children (*Rex* v. *Majarero and 23 others* 1947): In those years, there was clearly little peace between Herero and Bushmen. A Herero was killed by a Bushman arrow while on a 15-man mounted commando trying to recover some cattle allegedly stolen by 2 Bushmen. The next day, a commando of between 26 and 45 Herero mounted on horses and donkeys set out to exact retribution. They managed to surround the band of fleeing Bushmen, and while those on horseback patrolled the periphery to prevent any escape, those who had ridden there on donkeys went in for the kill on foot. Using clubs and assegais, they ripped open stomachs and severed hands. In this well-planned and cold-blooded atrocity, not a single Herero was wounded. Three Bushmen males managed to escape and told other Bushmen, who eventually informed the police and visited the site of the massacre. The three men who escaped were also later apparently murdered, but the state did not have enough evidence to charge people for these murders. In passing sentence, the judge again commented on the unsatisfactory nature of the evidence given by the Hereros, and, indeed, two of the accused were later convicted of perjury. The Herero were outraged that the accused were sentenced to 7 years imprisonment and promptly appealed the sentence only to have the chief justice of the South African Appeal Court confirm the sentence. A year later, that great champion of African liberation, Chief Hosea Kutako, led a deputation asking for the release of the incarcerated Hereros on the grounds that they had suffered enough already for their misdeed!

It is probable that similar events are still occurring. In 1981, the Botswana government applied for the extradition of two Tswanas, Messrs. Ditsabue and Mothebi, sometime residents of Aminuis Reserve, on the charge of having murdered two Bushmen in Botswana. The Gobabis magistrate granted the extradition request, but the Tswanas' lawyer appealed and was successful on a technicality, which meant that the Botswana government had to reapply.

While all this wrangling was going on, the accused were released on bail of R.1000 each in June 1981. In May 1982, they jumped bail, but also wrote a litter to the Gobabis police detailing why they did so. Their explanation was that they were tired of waiting and that there were others involved in the deed and proceeded to mention names, including that of a prominent Tswana councillor. They also claimed that there were three rifles used in perpetrating the deed and that the third rifle belonged to the Tswana chief, Kgoswang. The court declared the bail forfeit in March 1983.

The version I gathered during field enquiries in the Gobabis District provides further background. Apparently the Tswanas in Aminuis were becoming quite upset at all their cattle losses, which were alleged to be committed by Bushmen marauders from across the Botswana border, so they worked out a plan with Herero connivance to solve the problem. Their solution involved chasing the Bushmen on horseback and armed with firearms. At least five Bushmen were said to have been killed both in the area between Aminuis and the border and in Botswana. When the culprits realized that the long arm of the law was being extended toward them, they arranged for Ditsabue and Mothebi to take the blame and thus exculpate the others. At the same time, they arranged for bail and the services of one of the best and most expensive lawyers in Windhoek. Certain elements suggested that this cover-up was made possible with the aid of government money because, as these people pointed out, the Tswana and Herero were prominent supporters of the government and known to be benefiting from the fashionable pork-barrel politics. Officials in the attorney general's office in Windhoek agreed that events as sketched in the preceding were quite probably valid but pointed out that there was nothing they could do because the two main parties had vanished and the events were said to have taken place in Botswana.

That tensions between Herero and Bushmen still exist is evidenced by the statement of the leader of the Heikom, who complained that white-occupied farms were being taken over by Hereros in the north of the country and that the Heikom refused to work for the Herero (*Die Republikein,* 3/12/1980).

Conclusion

It is not that Lee is wrong in his representation of reality. Indeed he has shown himself to be quite flexible on the issue of contact and interaction (see e.g., Solway and Lee 1981). The problem lies in how others interpret Lee's statements (see Lee 1976:182). For example, in a review article, Richards observed that some of the most prominent and influential Africanist historians (e.g., Curtin *et al.* 1978)

> believe that "it is a remarkable comment on the unchanging character of late Stone Age life" that a twentieth century San was able to recognize a range of vegetable

remains and tools excavated from a 4,000 year old camp site. . . . It seems especially important not to confuse technical and social categories in this respect. The ability to call a spade a spade even after several millennia must not be taken to imply continuities of social and political life. (1983:38–39).

Part of the problem with the isolationist stance is that it places too much uncritical reliance on oral history, as indeed it in a sense had to do, since few researchers have managed to use the Namibian archival material or Afrikaans language publications. But another part of the problem lies in the fact that oral history was the vogue in the early 1960s, whereas since the 1970s more and more researchers are starting to ask critical questions about the validity of oral history as a resource (see e.g., Clarence-Smith 1977). This source is important in any study, but it must be used with caution because in the final analysis, as many of my Melanesianist colleagues have discovered, it tells us more about the self-perceptions of the people studied than about the actual events.

Long-term contact between Bushmen and other people was complex, but it generally supports Denbow's argument for a long history (this volume). But whereas archaeologists generally have to use that much-neutered term *interaction,* or *interdigitation,* a historical study enables us to flesh out the social, economic, and cultural milieu of such exchanges. Exchanges on such a frontier (defined as a zone in which different modes of production articulate) go through different phases, and this can be related to changes within the world system and the local systems. But in all this, the role of terror, that is, the arbitrary use of violence, must be stressed as a means of controlling the !Kung. When all is said and done, Wilmsen's statement that "It is more than merely possible that the San are classless today precisely because they are the underclass in an inclusive class structure" (1983) takes on a new emphasis.

To conclude with a comment on ethics, anthropologists and archaeologists should be aware of the consequences of their work on the people with whom or region in which they work. One of the major justifications for South African Army recruitment of Bushmen has been precisely the myth that the Bushmen are supposed to be such good hunters and trackers and hence ideally equipped to fight a guerilla war. On the other hand, archaeologists should be aware that their work showing the historical interaction between Bantu and Bushmen will be used by the emergent petit bourgeoisie in Botswana to justify their expansion into land historically regarded as belonging to the Bushmen.

Acknowledgments

Funding for this research was provided by the University of Vermont and a Walshe-Price Fellowship, courtesy of the Maryknoll Missioners. My special thanks go to Carmel Schrire for encouraging me to write up this work for the present volume.

References

Andersson, Charles J.
  1856 *Lake Ngami.* Hurst, London
  1858 Travel and adventure in Ovamboland. *Cape Monthly Magazine* 4(21):156–163
  1875 *Notes of travel in South Africa.* Hurst, London
Baines, Thomas
  1973 *Explorations in South West Africa.* Pioneer Head, Salisbury. (Original work published 1864.)
Bleek, Dorothea F.
  1928 *The Naron.* Cambridge University Press, Cambridge. (Original work titled Report on anthropological research among the Bushmen in the SWA Protectorate, mimeograph on file, Windhoek State Archives, Windhoek, 1922.)
Burger, N. A.
  1978 *Die Dorslandtrek: 'n Histories-geografiese studie.* Ph.D. thesis, Department of History, University of the Orange Free State
Cape Colony
  1879 *Cape Colony blue book on native affairs.* Government Printer, Cape Town.
  1908 *Report on Rietfontein area by J. Herbst.* Government Printer, Cape Town.
Cape of Good Hope
  1882 *Report of select committee on gunpowder trade.* Government Printer, Cape Town.
Chapman, James
  1868 *Travels in the interior of South Africa* (2 vols.). Bell & Daldy, London.
Chapman, William J. B.
  n.d. Unpublished reminiscences of William J. B. Chapman, South West Africa and Angola manuscript. On file, Windhoek State Archives, Windhoek.
Clarence-Smith W. G.
  1977 For Braudel: a note on the "Ecole des Annales" and the historiography of Africa. *History in Africa* 4:275–282
  1979 *Slaves, peasants and capitalists in Southern Angola 1840–1926.* Cambridge University Press, New York.
Coetzee, J. A.
  1942 *Dorsland-Avontuur.* Voortrekkerpers, Johannesburg.
De Klerk, Willem A.
  1977 *The thirstland.* Penquin, Harmondsworth.
De la Bat, Bernabe
  1982 Etosha 75 years. SWA Annual 1982:11–22.
Engelbrecht, L.
  1922 Wagposte aan die Oekavango. *Brandwag* (Pta) 13(9):263–268.
Frere, Bartle
  1881 On temperate South Africa. *Proceedings of the Royal Geographical Society* 3:1–19.
Galton, Francis
  1889 *Narrative of an explorer in tropical South Africa.* Ward, Lock, London.
Gordon, Robert J.
  1984 The myth of the Bushmen: an excursion into the underside of Namibian history. Manuscript on file, Department of Anthropology, University of Vermont.
Green, Francis
  1860 Narrative of a journey to Ovamboland. *Cape Monthly Magazine* 7(41):302–307; 353–362.
Grootfontein Bezirk
  1913 *Annual Report Grootfontein Bezirk.* Windhoek State Archives, Windhoek.

H. J. K.
  1920   A trip to the Okavanga. *Nonggai* December:626–628.
  1921   A trip to the Okavanga. *Nonggai* March:115–120.
Hahn, Theophilus
  1870   Die Buschmanner. *Globus* 16:65–68; 81–85; 102–105; 120–123; 140–143; 153–155.
Heintze, Beatrix
  1971– Buschmanner unter Ambo—Aspekte ihrer gegenseitigen Beziehungen. *Journal of*
  1972   *the South-West Africa Scientific Society* 26:45–56.
Jackson, A.
  1958   *Trader on the veld.* Balkema, Cape Town.
Kienetz, Arthur
  1974   *Nineteenth century SWA as a German settlement colony (Parts 1 and 2).* Un-
         published Ph.D. dissertation, Department of History, University of Minnesota,
         Milwaukee.
Köhler, Oswin
  1957   Dokumente zur Entstehung des Buschmann-problemes in Sudwestafrika. *Af-*
         *rikanische Heimatkalender:*54–62.
  1959   *A Study of Grootfontein District.* Government Printer, Pretoria.
Leacock, Eleanor, and Richard B. Lee (editors)
  1982   *Politics and history in band society.* Cambridge University Press, New York.
Lebzelter, Viktor
  1934   Die Buschmanner Sudwestafrikas. *Africa* 7:70–81.
Lee, Richard B.
  1976   The !Kung's new culture. In *Science Year,* pp. 180–195. World Book Encyclopedia,
         Chicago.
  1979   *The !Kung San: men, women and work in a foraging society.* Cambridge University
         Press, New York.
Lehmann, F. R.
  1955– Die verhouding van die Duitse Beskermingsadministrasie in SWA tot die Ambovolke.
  1956   *Journal of the South-West Africa Scientific Society* 11:5–32.
Loeb, Edwin Meyer
  1962   *In feudal Africa.* Indiana University, Bloomington.
Makin, W. J.
  1929   *Across the Kalahari Desert.* Arrowsmith, London
Marshall, Lorna
  1960   !Kung Bushman bands. *Africa* 30:325–355.
  1976   *The !Kung of Nyae Nyae.* Harvard University Press, Cambridge
Möller, P.
  1974   *Journey through Angola, Ovampoland and Darmaraland 1895–1896.* Struik, Cape
         Town.
Moritz, Walter (editor)
  1980   *Erkundungsreise ins Ovamboland 1857 Tagebuch Carl Hugo Hahn.* Lempp,
         Schwabisch.
Muller Hauptmann
  1912   Die Buschleute im Kaukauveld. *Deutsche-Sudwest-Afrika Zeitung* 65 and 66.
Nienaber, G. S.
  1952   Die Woord 'Boesman'. *Theoria* 4:36–40
Nolte, K.
  1886   Die westliche Kalahariwuste und die angrenzenden distrikte. *Deutsche Kolonialzeit-*
         ung 380–385

Nurse, George, and Trefor Jenkins
1977 *Health and the hunter–gatherer.* S. Kargen, Basel.
Okavango Native Reserve
1934– Annual reports. Windhoek State Archives, Windhoek.
1947
Ovamboland
1931– Annual reports. Windhoek State Archives, Windhoek.
1940
Palgrave, William Coates
1877 *Report of W. Coates Palgrave, Esq., Special Commissioner to the tribe of the Orange River, of his mission to Damaraland and Great Namaqualand in 1876.* Government Printer, Cape Town.
Prinsloo, J. G., and J. G. Gauche
1933 *In die woeste Weste.* Voortrekkerpers, Pretoria.
Rädel, F. R.
1947 *Die Wirtschaft und die arbeiterfrage Sudwestafrika.* Doctor of Commerce dissertation, Department of Economics, University of Stellenbosch.
Rex v. Majarero and 23 Others
1947 32 SCW. Proceeding on file, Windhoek State Archives, Windhoek.
Rex v. Qouigan and Habuson
1919 SCC. Proceedings on file, Windhoek State Archives, Windhoek.
Rex v. Quben Qubu
1920 SCC. Proceedings on file, Windhoek State Archives, Windhoek.
Richards, Paul
1983 Ecological change and the politics of African land use. *African Studies Review* 26(2):1–72
Schinz, Hans
1891 *Deutsch-Sudwest-Afrika.* Schulzesche Hof-Buchhandlung, Leipzig.
Schoeman, P. J.
n.d.a *Voorlopige verslag van die Kommissie vir die behoud van die Boesmanbevolking in Suidwes-Afrika 1950* (interim report). Mimeograph on file, Windhoek State Archives, Windhoek.
n.d.a *Report of the Commission for the preservation of Bushmen in South West Africa* (final report). Mimeograph on file, Windhoek State Archives, Windhoek.
Schott, Rudiger
1955 Die Buschmanner in Sudafrika. Eine studie uber die schwierigkeited der akkulturation. *Sociologus* n.s. 5:132–149.
Serton, Petrus (editor)
1954 *The narrative and journal of Gerald McKiernan in South West Africa 1874–79.* The Van Riebeeck Society, 35 Cape Town.
Sohnge, W.
1967 *Tsumeb, a historical sketch.* South-West Africa Scientific Society, Windhoek.
Solway, Jacqueline S., and Richard B. Lee
1981 *The Kalahari fur trade: San articulation with the world system.* Paper presented at the American Anthropological Association meeting, Los Angeles.
South West African Constitutional Commission (SWACC)
1936 *Minutes of evidence.* SACC. Proceedings on file, Windhoek State Archives, Windhoek.
Stals, Ernst L.
1969 Die Aanraking tussen Blankes en Ovambos in South West Africa 1850–1915. *Archives Yearbook* 2. Government Printer, Pretoria.

Swanepoel, P. G.
    n.d.   *Polisie-avonture in Suidwes-Afrika.* Perskor, Johannesburg.
Tabler, E. C.
    1973   *Pioneers of South West Africa & Ngamiland 1738–1880.* Balkema, Cape Town.
Trumpelmann, G. P. J.
    1948   Die Boer in Sudwes-Afrika. *Archives Yearbook* (II). Government Printer, Pretoria.
Van der Walt, A. J.
    1926   *Nordwaarts.* Nasionale Pers, Cape Town.
Vedder, Heinrich
    1938   *South West Africa in early times.* Oxford University Press, London.
Volkmann, Hauptmann
    1901   Reise von Grootfontein nach den Okavango. *Deutsche Kolonialblatt* 12:866–868, 908–909
Wallis, J. P. R.
    1936   *Fortune my foe.* Jonathan Cape, London.
Wannenburgh, Alf
    n.d.   *Forgotten frontiersmen.* Howard Timmins, Cape Town.
Wilhelm, J. H.
    1954   Die !Kung-Buschleute. *Jahrbuch des Museums für Volkerkunde zu Leipzig* 12.
Wilmsen, Edwin N.
    1980   *Exchange, interaction, and settlement in northwestern Botswana: past and present perspectives.* Working Paper 39, African Studies Center, Boston.
    1983   The ecology of illusion: anthropological foraging in the Kalahari. *Reviews in Anthropology* 10(1):9–20.
Wulfhorst, Rev. A.
    1937   Bushleute im Norden von SWA. *Berichte Rheinische Missions* 94(2):36–40.
Wust, Pater J.
    1938   Ein sterbendes volk. *Monatsblatt des Oblaten* 45(10):254–259, (11):292–297, (12):325–329

9

Ideological Continuities in Prehistoric Southern Africa: The Evidence of Rock Art

J. DAVID LEWIS-WILLIAMS

Introduction

Since the late 1960s southern African archaeologists have given considerable attention to prehistoric subsistence strategies and seasonal mobility
(Carter 1970; Deacon 1969, 1976; Parkington 1972), but the ideological aspects of these strategies have not been considered. Although researchers
sometimes refer to rock art as a possible though obscure source of ideological data, they do not seem to believe it possible to reconstruct prehistoric
ideology with any confidence.

Contrary to this general belief, bridging the gap between the historic and the
prehistoric past is a viable enterprise, principally because there are two distinct
bodies of ethnography on which we can draw: one from the nineteenth
century and another from the twentieth century. The nineteenth-century
ethnography is contemporary with the last artists. Of this older ethnography,
the most important is the voluminous verbatim material collected by the Bleek
family in the 1870s from southern informants (Lewis-Williams 1981a:25–31).
Another highly significant but smaller collection of myths and comments on
rock paintings was obtained in 1873 by J. M. Orpen (1874) from a San guide in
the southeastern mountains. Neither Orpen's nor any of the Bleeks' informants
were themselves artists, but they recognized the art as the work of their own
people, and Orpen's informant actually guided him to some sites and ex-

225

plained the paintings found at these locations (Lewis-Williams 1980). The southern San groups from which these informants came are now extinct.

The second major ethnographic source, the San living today in the Kalahari Desert (e.g., Lee 1979; Marshall 1976; Silberbauer 1981; Tobias 1978), clarifies much that is obscure in the nineteenth-century collections. Despite wide separation in both space and time and the facts that the Kalahari people speak different languages from the extinct southern groups and do not paint, it has become increasingly clear that they all shared a great many beliefs and rituals, albeit with minor local variations. When explaining the southern paintings, it is therefore legitimate to draw cautiously on the northern material in areas where specific and detailed parallels between it and the nineteenth-century southern ethnography can be demonstrated (Lewis-Williams 1981a:25–27; Lewis-Williams and Biesele 1978; Vinnicombe 1972a).

Rock Art and Trance Performance

Analysis of San ethnography suggests that many parietal paintings were closely associated with medicine men, or shamans (Lewis-Williams 1980, 1981a, 1981b, 1982, 1983; Vinnicombe 1976:323–345). Among present-day San groups about half the men and a third of the women become medicine people. There is nothing esoteric about their work, and they talk freely about their experiences and understandings of the spirit world they enter while in trance. Trance usually occurs at a curing or medicine dance, but sometimes special circumstances may warrant a man entering trance outside the context of a full dance. At a dance, the women sit in a tight circle around a fire to clap and sing songs believed to contain a potency or energy that also resides in medicine men themselves. The songs are named after such diverse but potent things as eland, giraffe, gemsbok, honey, and the sun. The combination of the songs and the rhythmic exertions of the men, as they dance one behind the other around the women, induces trance in those who have mastered the technique; hallucinogens are very rarely used. Such dances are held a couple of times a week if there is a sufficiently large gathering of people, and all present are treated by the trance dancers who, by laying on hands, are believed to draw sickness from their patients before casting it back at the evil, constantly threatening spirits. The nineteenth-century southern groups recognized four overlapping classes of medicine people: first, those who, as in the Kalahari today, cured sickness; second, those who controlled the rain; third, those who controlled the movements of antelope herds; and, finally, although somewhat vaguely identified, those who maliciously shot "arrows of sickness" into their enemies. The modern northern groups do not seem to make these distinctions, though their beliefs and rituals of trance are essentially the same as those of the southern people (for detailed accounts of northern San trance rituals see Biesele 1975; Katz 1982; Lee 1968; Marshall 1969).

Numerous rock paintings are apparently realistic representations of trance dances in which men are shown dancing in distinctive postures while women, often but not always seated, clap the rhythm of the potent songs (Figure 9.1). Other paintings show animals that were symbols of potency, while still others depict hallucinations of trance. These last include geometric forms (phosphenes), therianthropic conflations of men with the animal power they harnessed, potency entering a man, his spirit leaving the top of his head on out-of-body travel, and rain in the form of a fantastic animal (Figure 9.2). The detailed depiction of hallucinations, together with other factors, suggests that the paintings were often done by the medicine men themselves.

The geographic relevance of this explanation for San rock art has been debated because styles and the numerical emphasis on animal species vary from region to region (e.g., Cooke 1983; Willcox 1983). The objection is, however, not valid. It is true that the paintings of such widely separated areas as the southwestern Cape and the Natal Drakensberg are generally distinguishable, but style should not be confused with meaning. The conceptual unity of the art, from the Cape (Maggs and Sealy 1983) to Zimbabwe (Huffman 1983), is suggested by the depiction and combination in all areas of such significant details as distinctive dancing postures, nasal hemorrhaging, erect hair, dying postures, eared serpents, so-called infibulation, phosphenes, and so forth (I explain some of these features in the following). An even

FIGURE 9.1   Dance scene. Bending-forward dancers support their weight on two sticks. The dancers wear caps with two animal ears attached; these were sometimes worn by medicine men of the game in the belief that the wearer could influence the movements of game (Bleek 1935:45, 1936:144). Standing and seated women clap rhythm of dance. Color, red. Orange Springs, eastern Orange Free State.

FIGURE 9.2 Hallucinatory forms in San rock art: (A) therianthrope with hoofs and eland head. Color, red. Burley I, northeastern Cape Province; (For complete panel see Lewis-Williams 1981a: Figure 23). (B) elephant surrounded by sinuous line. Color, red. Heksriver, southwestern Cape Province. (C) phosphene. Color, red with upper margin outlined in white. Brakfontein southwestern Cape Province; (After Maggs and Sealy 1983:Figure 7). (D) human figure running on line of potency with lines from top of head, probably representing departing spirit, and superimposed white figure with red lines on its face. Colors, red and white. Cullen's Wood, northeastern Cape; (For more of this panel see Lewis-Williams 1981b:Figure 1, 1983:Figure 16.)

greater spatial relevance of the trance hypothesis has been suggested by the publication of Tanzanian rock paintings (Leakey 1983), which show the same dancing postures, phosphenes, nasal hemorrhage, attenuation of the human figures, animals surrounded by hallucinations, and therianthropes. The similarities in content between the Tanzanian and the southern African art are so detailed that, despite obvious stylistic differences, it is legitimate to hypothesize that the northern art was also associated with hunter gatherer trance performance. More research is required to test this hypothesis.

It is details such as those I have listed that suggest conceptual unity, not the depiction of certain species. To insist that depiction of different species implies different concepts is to confuse principles with content. In the southeastern mountains and in the southwestern Cape the eland is the most frequently painted animal. Elsewhere, as one may expect, other animals are emphasized (Vinnicombe 1972a, 1972b), but the key metaphors and diagnostic details recur, and these show we are dealing with the same fundamental beliefs. Once the principles are recognized, the differences in animal subject matter between regions assume less importance. Unfortunately, rock art researchers have failed to notice the metaphors that are depicted by a variety of easily overlooked animal and human postures and other details.

The extensive spatial distribution of San ideology, for at least the area south of the Zambezi and Cunene rivers, was suggested by McCall (1970), who wrote of a "pan-San" cognitive system. Since then the suggestion has received considerable support from ethnography and rock art (Lewis-Williams 1981a; Lewis-Williams and Biesele 1978; Vinnicombe 1972a) and can now be accepted with confidence. Such extensive uniformity in space may be thought to imply considerable time depth, but, for many, confidence in the relevance of the ethnography and the explanation based on it diminishes as we go back in time to consider older and older paintings. Some argue, rightly, that we cannot simply assume that San beliefs were the same 2000 years ago as they were in the nineteenth century. The direct historical approach, which employs ethnography to explain demonstrably related archaeological situations, grades into the general comparative approach as, over the millennia, the postulated relation grows more tenuous. One way out of this difficulty is to declare that interpretations pertain to more recent paintings only (Lewis-Williams 1981a:24), leaving the meaning of older paintings unessayed.

This position is unsatisfactory for a number of reasons. For one thing, we are unable to distinguish older from more recent paintings, except in a very rudimentary way by superposition and degree of preservation. Although certain styles may be discerned, no clear temporal disjunctions are apparent. Moreover, we do not know the actual age of the oldest paintings presently preserved on the walls of rockshelters. Subject matter sometimes shows some to be only a century old, although others have been estimated to date back a few thousand years. All attempts at dating parietal art by radiometric or chemical means have so far proved inconclusive (Rudner 1983:16).

Reliable dates have, however, been obtained for a number of portable painted and engraved stones (Thackeray 1983). This *art mobilier* may be divided into two groups. The first and more numerous one (A) comprises painted and engraved stones dated to the past 10,000 years, though most examples come from the past 4000 years; the second group (B) comprises only the painted stones from Apollo 11, Namibia. These remarkable finds have been dated to as much as 26,000 years b.p. (26,300 ± 400 [Pta-1040]; 26,700 ± 650 [KN-I·813]; 28,400 ± 450 [KN-2056]; Wendt 1974, 1976) and are therefore contemporary with some of the Upper Paleolithic art of western Europe. Some difficulties with the stratigraphy have caused some researchers to suggest that the stones may be more securely dated to the base of the stratum immediately above them, that is, 19,000 b.p. (Butzer *et al.* 1979:1203), but others, such as Thackeray (1983:25), believe 26,000 b.p. to be acceptable. It is not yet entirely clear if the gap between these two groups represents a break in tradition or if it is caused by a sampling problem. Thackeray believes the tradition to have been unbroken because the presence of engraved ostrich eggshell at 15,000 b.p. (Deacon 1976:190, Figure 27) shows that some art forms were practiced during the intervening period.

My argument for the same conclusion proceeds in two stages. The first part, which is largely theoretical, defines ideology more rigorously and considers the type of archaeologically detectable changes that may have accompanied changes in ideology; in this discussion I am greatly indebted to Friedman (1974), Godelier (1975, 1977, 1978), and others. In the second part, the hypothesis derived from these theoretical considerations is tested against dated *art mobilier.*

Ideology and Prehistoric Change

Ideology may be defined as the set of ideas that legitimizes the form and functioning of any society. Closely associated with ideology are religious symbols and rituals, such as San trance performance. The regulation of the economy and its relation with nature exists within the framework of social and natural relationships and is expressed in systems of representation. The exact relation between a specific set of religious symbols and rituals and ideology must be empirically determined; accordingly, I show briefly how the concept of symbolic work integrates religious belief and ritual with the ideology of the later Stone Age San social formation (for a fuller, though not exhaustive, discussion see Lewis-Williams 1982).

We cannot predict the kind of ideas that will function as ideology because ideology is always specific; it is associated with a particular articulation among three things: (1) the social relationships (be they kinship, religious, or political) into which people enter to produce the necessities of life (relations of production), (2) the material and intellectual means used by a society to extract the means of existence from nature (forces of production); and (3) the particular ecological context in which this process takes place. None of these three factors is in itself determinant, and it is simplistic to postulate straightforward cause and effect relations. We speak rather of constraint and permission: Certain social and ideological forms are excluded by specific articulations, and a given articulation obviously requires a compatible ideology.

Kinship lies at the heart of the social and economic interactions of modern San (Lee 1979), dominating interpersonal relationships and economic activities. Nineteenth-century San ethnography suggests that kinship (together with a possible fictive extension in name relations; Marshall 1957) provided the ideology that legitimized relations of production at earlier periods. We may distinguish three functions of the relations of production.

The first is access to resources. For example, waterholes are "owned" by related individuals who form the core of a camp, and access to the resources in any area is said to be by kinship (consanguineal, affinal, or fictive), though in practice it is highly improbable that a stranger would be refused water. These rights of access underpin and facilitate the reproduction of the San social formation in a fundamental way. Camps are potentially ephemeral because the unpredictability of southern African rainfall means that waterholes can dry up, plant foods fail, and antelope move to distant parts. In such hazardous circumstances a camp can survive only by splitting up, the members moving to better-endowed areas where they are able to activate kinship ties (Keenan 1977; Lewis-Williams 1982).

Part of the medicine men's symbolic work concerns these "invisible" intercamp relations. Trance dances are usually held when visitors arrive from distant camps, and San recognize that the dance facilitates integration on such occasions; all relationships, even the most tenuous, are caught up and dramatized in the dance. After the dance, medicine men tell the people what they experienced in trance. Prominent among these accounts are reports of out-of-body travel to distant camps. One nineteenth-century medicine man said he assumed the form of a jackal to accompany people returning to a distant camp. They had to spend a night on the way and, when they heard him barking, they called out that they were well. After observing their safe arrival, he returned to his own people, resumed his human form and assured them that all was well with their friends (Bleek 1935:15–18). On another occasion, a medicine man found that the people he was visiting on extracorporeal travel were not at home. His alarm was assuaged when he discovered they had killed game and were packing up the meat prior to bringing it back to their camp (Bleek 1935:25). He knew then that the distant hunters were successful and his people could, if necessary, claim a share of the resources. Such reports recalled kinship ties with people in distant camps and reflected on the ideological level access to resources in far-off and better-endowed areas. Medicine men reminded people of the wider, invisible nexus of which they were part; they could well imagine the distant people and places of which the medicine man spoke because, through the changing membership of camps, they themselves had actually been there. Trance is therefore a ritual practice that dramatizes the kinship ideology of the San.

Unfortunately, the role of trance as a symbolic practice associated with kinship ideology has been obscured, partly because kin groups are not visibly distinguished during the dance, and also because reports of trance experience are seldom couched in explicit kinship terminology. However, the kinship ties that medicine men dramatize are tacit; they lie behind all social contact and do not require explicit enumeration. The social contacts and economic relations of which medicine men speak are literally unthinkable without kinship.

The second function of relations of production is to regulate and allocate the labor force. Traditional San labor essentially involves hunting and gathering, tasks that are largely performed by men and women, respectively. This dichotomy is reflected in the trance dance, in which women clap and sing potent medicine songs while dancing men encircle them. In the same way that men and women perform their allotted tasks in the daily process of labor, so in the ritual context the distinctive contribution of each (singing and dancing) is essential for the symbolic work to be effective. Thus, the cooperative enterprise of symbolic work parallels the cooperation of daily labor.

A third function of the relations of production is to determine the social form of distribution. In San society, women retain the vegetable foods they collect for their own families, but kinship provides the organizing principle for the distribution of meat. Sharing is done carefully so that every family and individual receives an equitable portion (Marshall 1961, 1976). Hunting is a chancy enterprise, and a man may go for long periods without success. The kinship-based rules of distribution counterbalance the unpredictability of supply by ensuring that no one has a monopoly and that all receive a share of the product. Nevertheless, tensions do arise over the distribution of meat and tempers flare if a man considers he has received a niggardly portion. The trance dance is recognized by the San themselves as an effective means for reducing these (and other) tensions. They sometimes contrive to have men between whom there is animosity dance one behind the other because rhythmic unity is thought to reestablish amity (M. Biesele, personal communication, 1975). Similarly, after a large kill, when visitors, activating their kinship links, come to claim a share of the meat, it is customary to hold a trance dance to maintain the social relationships that underlie networks of distribution.

Among modern San people, relations of production therefore assume three principal functions. First, they determine the social form of access to resources as well as controlling these resources and their exploitation, secondly, they allocate the labor force, and, finally, they determine the social forms of distribution. These elements are crucial in accounts of modern San behavior, and if we were to argue that changes had occurred in San ideology in the past, we should have to demonstrate concomitant shifts in prehistoric relations of production. The mere passage of time is insufficient in itself to argue for radical changes in ideology, and the great antiquity of some southern African *art mobilier* is not in itself sufficient reason for believing the ancient paintings expressed a radically different ideology from more recent art.

Conversely, we must not a priori suppose the millennia of southern African prehistory to have constituted a single, unchanging belief system. We must rather examine the archaeological data to see whether other aspects of forager life have changed radically and then use modern parallels to hypothesize possible concomitant ideological shifts. At present we have interesting and provocative indications of changes through time in places like the southwestern Cape where almost two decades of archaeological research have allowed workers to infer

> alteration(s) in group size, changes in territorial ranges, a shift from game-oriented to plant-oriented movement strategies, a move toward overall greater dependence upon plant foods and shellfish as staples, innovations in hunting and gathering techniques and major redistributions of populations as changing climates rendered regions more or less attractive. (Manhire *et al.* 1983:29; see also Parkington, this volume)

Likewise Denbow (this volume) argues convincingly for prolonged interaction between foragers and pastoralists in the Kalahari. What is particularly interesting here is that the ideological system of the descendants of these foragers, the present !Kung San, has remained strikingly similar to that recorded for now-extinct southern San people, who apparently lived beyond the range of Iron Age pastoralists throughout their prehistory.

Instead of simply assuming that circumstances such as those in the southwestern Cape and the Kalahari triggered ideological change, we must assess the probable impact of the changes noted in the archaeological record on the social relations of production and ideology. One way to start is to ask whether environmental variations necessarily affect ideology. Distributional studies of rock art, read in conjunction with nineteenth-century ethnography, suggest that the belief system of the San living in the well-watered southeastern mountains was essentially similar to that of the modern San living in the more arid Kalahari Desert (Lewis-Williams 1981a). Arguments that ecological changes through time must necessarily have changed ideology are therefore groundless; San ideology is compatible with diverse environments.

Similarly, although archaeological analyses reveal profound changes in land–sea relations with the onset of the Holocene, changes that transformed an open grassland on the southern coast to a more closed, evergreen forest (Klein 1972, 1975, 1977), there is no evidence to suggest that this was accompanied by any major shifts in the hunting and gathering relations of production other than a possible increased emphasis on snaring (Klein 1972:139). Again, unless changes in the relations of production can be demonstrated, we have no reason to suppose changes in ideology.

Historical records provide considerable illumination on this point. For example, in the Kalahari, along the Nata River, where permanent water and relatively rich resources occur, we find comparatively sedentary villages with territorial claims to resources and storage of wild plant foods and agricultural products. However, even these villages move, on average, every third year. There has also been an ideological shift from bilateral to more heavily patrilineal inheritance. Under these conditions medicine men have grown more important in group affairs and trance dances have become "large communal affairs" (Hitchcock 1982:253; see also Barnard 1979; Guenther 1975–1976). Nevertheless, "Middle and Late Stone Age archaeological remains found in the area do not indicate that local hunter–gatherer groups were sedentary" (Hitchcock 1982:247–248). Indeed, it seems neither large-scale storage, nor class-based monopolies, nor sedentism were feasible at any period of the southern African Stone Age, given the ecological conditions of southern Africa and the hunter gatherer level of the productive forces. Archaeologists have sometimes erred in assuming that the changes they observe in stone tools and hunting strategies were associated with fundamental social and ideological changes. Stone Age archaeologists usually deal with the forces of production or parts thereof, and changes in the forces of production are not in themselves sufficient to trigger complete systemic change.

In summary, the archaeological record provides no evidence for sedentism, storage, or social stratification at any point during the later Stone Age; I therefore suggest that there is no reason to believe that kinship did not inform prehistoric relations of production and ideology as it does in the ethnographic present. I must emphasize that I refer only to the form, not to the content, of kinship ideology, for I do not wish to imply that hunter gatherer society is timeless and necessarily frozen. I argue only that consanguineal, affinal, and fictive relationships probably performed the three functions I have described, but I do not specify the exact nature of those relationships or any given balance among them; such details might well have changed during the millennia without altering the structure of kinship ideology. Similarly, the proposed continuity does not imply that specific myths or the details of rituals, such as the choreography of the trance dance, remained unchanged. It is not the events or narratives of myth that are important, but its structure and the symbols and metaphors that it incorporates.

Certainly the various San groups of the Kalahari do not share all myths today, and none of the southern San myths recorded in the nineteenth century has so far been found among the northern groups.

This conclusion allows us to test with more confidence on the *art mobilier* the hypothesis that trance and its concomitants were long lasting. If the trance hypothesis makes sense of specific depictions in southern African *art mobilier* as it does for the parietal art, it will be reasonable to conclude that trance together with its system of representation was practiced during the periods from which the art comes and that a similar ideology obtained. The mere practice of art in remote periods is not enough to suggest continuities between the ethnographic and the prehistoric past; specific, unequivocally diagnostic depictions must be identified.

Art Mobilier

Many painted stones from the past 10,000 years (Group A) are so poorly preserved that it is difficult to decipher the depictions; others have simple, nondiagnostic paintings of human beings or animals about which little can at present be said that is relevant to the meaning of San *art mobilier*. Furthermore, many stones were unfortunately excavated long before the development of absolute dating and modern excavating techniques, so that in most cases we have no idea of their age or context. Nevertheless, some have been reliably dated and do bear depictions that are relevant to this enquiry.

Perhaps the most important of these comes from Cave 5 at Klasies River Mouth (Singer and Wymer 1969, 1982). Shells directly associated with this stone (Figure 9.3) have been radiocarbon dated to 2285 ± 105 b.p. (GX-1397; Singer and Wymer 1982:137). The paintings, which are somewhat indistinct, are of at least one man and four fish or, more probably, dolphins. As with some other painted stones, the correct orientation is uncertain, and there has therefore been some doubt about the posture of the man. In their original publication, Singer and Wymer (1969:509) suggested two interpretations but favored the first: that the man is swimming or that he is in a sitting position, possibly holding a stick. Their illustration is, in any event, an imaginative reconstruction of the painting as it might have appeared when first executed rather than a facsimile of it in its present condition. Later, in their definitive publication on the Klasies River excavations, they observe that the position of the man's arms is indistinct and that the stick or fishing rod (they note evidence for later Stone Age fishing) is "very faint and may be no more than a misleading stain on the stone" (Singer and Wymer 1982:138). Since what is a stick in one interpretation is an arm extended in the action of swimming in the other, both must be regarded as conjectural. The conjecture is, moreover,

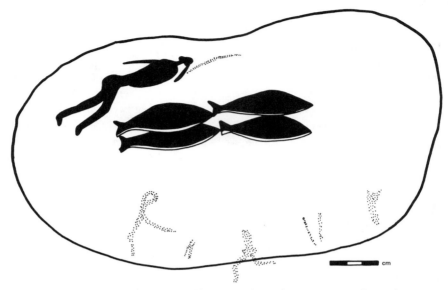

FIGURE 9.3   Painted stone. Colors, black and white. Klasies River Mouth, southern Cape coast; South African Museum number KRM 29350; (Drawn from stone and from copy in Rudner, 1971:Figure 3; see also Singer and Wymer, 1982:Plate 48.)

based on the assumption that southern African rock art comprises literal depictions of secular daily life, and the writers therefore interpret the figure in terms of familiar activities and postures.

Figure 9.3 is based on examination of the actual stone as well as Rudner's (1971:Figure 3) drawing. The very faint rod or arm does seem to be an extraneous stain, but it is nevertheless shown in the figure. The awkwardness and unfamiliarity of the man have led the excavators to suggest a posture that seems to them "natural," but he is more probably in a complex dancing posture still observable in the Kalahari and frequently depicted in the parietal art (e.g., Lewis-Williams 1981a:Figures 20, 26, 31, 33, 1983:Figures 8, 20, 21, 24, 62). The most distinctive feature of this dancing posture is that the arms are held behind the back. A modern San trance dancer explained that medicine men dance like this when they are "asking God to put potency into their bodies." The man is also bending forward slightly, a stance often more exaggerated than it is here. Modern medicine men bend forward as the intensity of their experience increases (Marshall 1969). They say their stomach muscles contract into a tight, painful knot, and this makes them adopt the characteristic posture (Katz 1982:98). My view that this figure represents a trance dancer is supported by a third feature that is unexplained by the fishing and swimming interpretations. The clear line falling from the man's head probably represents nasal blood. As southern medicine men entered trance they often bled from the nose (Bleek 1935:14, 20, 34; Orpen 1874:10), and the curing dance became known as the "Dance of Blood" (Arbousset 1846:246–247). The curers then smeared their blood on the sick in the belief that its odor would keep evil influences at bay (Bleek 1935:20, 34). Epistaxis is, indeed, one of the principal and most frequently painted diagnostic features of trancing medicine men in the parietal art, and its depiction in combination with the arms-back, bending-forward posture suggests strongly that the figure on the Klasies River Mouth stone is a trance dancer.

The same highly significant posture is more clearly and unequivocally depicted on two stones found in 1917 at Robberg. One of these (Figure 9.4) was discovered, together with four large limpet shells, apparently placed over a skeleton. Although it was excavated in 1917 (Rudner and Rudner 1973:94), it

FIGURE 9.4   Painted stone; with two of the figures continuing around the edge of the stone. Color, black. Robberg, southern Cape coast; South African Museum number SAM 2616.

has since been possible to obtain a radiocarbon date for the associated limpet shells of 1925 ± 33 b.p. (Pta-014; Rudner 1971:55). So long delayed a determination and, moreover, one using shell is not entirely satisfactory, but the depiction and the date accord well with the stone from the modern excavation at Klasies River Mouth. On the Robberg stone is a confused medley of 10 human figures, some of which appear to be simply walking and are therefore not unequivocally trance dancers. However, the central figure at the top is very clearly in the arms-back posture, though its head has not been preserved. The same posture also appears toward the left of the second, undated, stone (Figure 9.5). The posture was therefore undoubtedly of significance to the artists of 2000 years ago.

Other figures on these Robberg stones may also be explained by trance performance. The man in the upper right of Figure 9.4, who by the orientation of the stone in the illustration would be supine, is dancing in a more pronounced bending-forward posture than the man in Figure 9.3. Poor preservation unfortunately makes it impossible to be sure if his arms are in a characteristic hanging position or whether (more probably) he is holding two dancing sticks in a manner frequently shown in the parietal art (cf. Figure 9.1). A bending-forward, arms-hanging figure is also found in the center of the stone in Figure 9.5.

After men have been dancing in such postures for some time, they enter trance and often fall to the ground. The problem of orientation makes it impossible to say if the lowermost man in Figure 9.4 is prostrate, though the position of his head suggests he is. We may more confidently identify a

FIGURE 9.5 Painted stone. Color, black. Robberg, southern Cape coast; South African Museum number SAM 2825/6/8.

FIGURE 9.6 Painted stone, the painted surface of which has been slightly used as lower grindstone. Color, black. Coldstream, southern Cape coast; South African Museum number SAM 8387; (From early photograph in Peringuey, 1911:Plate XXVII, Figure 199.)

characteristic kneeling posture at the extreme right of Figure 9.5. Trancers often sink to this position, and it is frequently represented in the parietal art.

The postures I have so far identified in the *art mobilier* are adopted by male trance dancers. I turn now to those postures more characteristic of women. The first is on a stone from Coldstream. The paintings are very poorly preserved, but an old photograph (South African Museum collection) shows that there are three standing women and a seated figure that may also be female (Figure 9.6). The central standing woman is clearly clapping, and the other two may be dancing. The clapping posture is highly significant because it suggests the singing of medicine songs; many paintings throughout southern Africa depict medicine dances with women clapping (cf. Figure 9.1). Similar depictions are on a stone discovered in 1872 in a shelter at Knysna. Peringuey (1911:Plate XXVII) published a photograph of it on which Figure 9.7 is based; today only one of the figures can be distinguished, the others having almost completely disappeared. Peringuey (1911:162–163) thought it "permissable to consider the scene as not men dancing, but men inhumed or going to be inhumed." He based his interpretation on the flexed position of many southern Cape later Stone Age burials, but if it is viewed as in Figure 9.7, it suggests not obsequies but a trance dance similar to those often found

FIGURE 9.7   Painted stone, the painted surface of which has been rubbed or painted with red ochre and possibly used for grinding ochre, although there is no groove. Color, black. Eastern Head Cave, Knysna, southern Cape coast; South African Museum number SAM 8386; (From early photograph in Peringuey 1911:Plate XXVII, Figure 200.)

in the parietal art. The lower right figure is dancing in the bending-forward posture, while the two figures to the left are sitting with their arms in a distinctive clapping position. The upper right figure is rather ambivalent; it may be seated or it may be dancing. Another, more distinctive, sitting posture is depicted on the Coldstream stone (Figure 9.6). The smallest of the figures is in the posture of the so-called mother goddesses of Zimbabwean rock art that are associated with trance performance (Huffman 1983:51–52). Comparable figures in the southeastern mountains are also related to trance (Lewis-Williams 1983:Figure 19).

The heads of the women on the Coldstream stone (Figure 9.6) are depicted in a conventionalized form characteristic of male figures as well and frequently seen in the parietal art. The form is more distinct on another stone from Coldstream, which is by far the best preserved and most detailed of all the stones; it has therefore frequently been illustrated (Haughton 1926; Lee and Woodhouse 1970:Figures 4, 144; Lewis-Williams 1983:Figure 44; Rudner and Rudner 1970:Plate 45; Woodhouse 1968, 1979:Figure 55). It depicts three human figures. The central one carries a hunting bag containing a bow and arrows slung over its shoulder and holds in its hand what is thought to represent a feather and a palette. It has accordingly been identified as the portrait of an artist (Woodhouse 1968). The most interesting feature for our purposes is the manner in which the heads of all three figures have been painted. They are of the 'hooked' type with a white face (see also Figure 9.6). Across each face are four horizontal, very finely drawn red lines. One of these lines on the face of the central figure is only partially preserved and has given a false impression of a mouth painted with red lips. Such red lines across white faces are a widespread feature of San rock art from the western Cape to the Drakensberg. Although they have long been thought to represent scarifications or facial paint (Peringuey, 1911; Woodhouse 1970), it seems more probable that they are often stylized depictions of nasal hemorrhage. Some paintings show blood falling from the nose in the manner I have described and also radiating in lines from the nose. Whether this specific interpretation is correct or not, the lines are clearly not facial markings because they also appear on the faces of animals, especially eland, and therianthropes, but rather are related in some way to trance performance (Lewis-Williams 1984).

Unfortunately, a caveat must be entered at this point. The extraordinarily good preservation of the paintings on this stone, coming as it does from a rather damp cave deposit, has led some workers to question its authenticity. Two possibilities exist: Either the stone is a complete forgery, or it has been considerably touched up. The second of these possibilities may be correct because it seems unlikely a forger in 1911, when the stone was found, would have known about some of the details in the painting and because, if it has been touched up, the workers of that time may not have considered it necessary to record their restoration. Chemical tests performed on samples of paint from the stone have shown only that the ochres are of a kind that could have been used by the artists (W. van Rijssen, personal communication, 1984); we must therefore reluctantly reserve judgment on this remarkable object.

The paintings I have discussed so far are all literal depictions of distinctive postures or features of people in trance dances: bending forward, arms back, arms hanging, using dancing sticks, clapping, sitting, and nasally hemorrhaging. These depictions are persuasive evidence that trance performance was practiced at least two millennia ago and enable us to turn to other paintings of Group A to show that the trance hypothesis explains a wider range of depictions and associations.

One such association is on the Klasies River Mouth stone (Figure 9.3). The juxtaposition of the trance dancer with the fish or dolphins is better explained by a trance metaphor than a literal view such as swimming. The southern San discerned an analogy between trance and being underwater (Lewis-Williams 1981a:112). Both experiences are characterized by sounds in the ears, distorted vision, inhibited breathing, a sense of weightlessness and of being in another world, and, finally, unconsciousness. In parietal art, this metaphor is sometimes depicted by associating medicine men with fish, and the rain animal, which was believed to live underwater and which could be captured only in trance, is often shown surrounded by fish (e.g., Lewis-Williams 1983:Figure 18). My interpretation of the human figure as a trancing medicine man is therefore consonant with the fish or dolphins, and the composition on this stone is part of the San painting tradition as it is known from parietal art. The four fish metaphorically express the trance dancer's altered state of consciousness.

In addition to these marine creatures, terrestrial animals are also depicted on the stones. The trance hypothesis enables us to suggest that these otherwise enigmatic paintings of animals are, like those of the parietal art, probably symbols of the potency harnessed by medicine men. Indeed, the proportion of animals to human figures in *art mobilier* is very similar to that of parietal art (Lewis-Williams 1972:50), and this suggests the *art mobilier* is not a radically different artistic expression. This symbolic interpretation of the animals is supported by a posture in which the animal's head is lowered (Figure 9.8). Animals in this position often appear in parietal art in which other painted details sometimes suggest proximity to death. These features include erect hair, a stumbling gait, and blood or foam falling from the nose or mouth. Some paintings in rockshelters juxtapose dying antelope with medicine men who were, and in the Kalahari still are, said to die when they enter trance. The relation implied by such paintings seems to be twofold. The San observed an analogy between dying antelope and "dying" medicine men: both tremble,

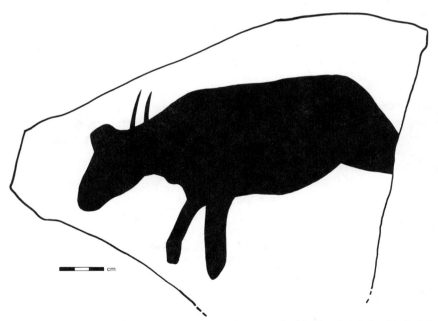

FIGURE 9.8 Painted stone, with a depiction of an animal on both sides. Color, black. Robberg, southern Cape coast; South African Museum number SAM 2822.

stagger, lower their heads, bleed from the nose, and, finally, collapse uncon-
scious; hair was furthermore believed to grow on the back of a trancing man
(Bleek 1935:2, 23), and dying antelope are sometimes shown with exaggerated erect hair (Lewis-Williams 1981a:91–93). The second significance of
dying animals is that the supernatural power that some large antelope are
believed to possess is thought to be released at death. !Kung medicine men
consider a dance performed next to a recently killed eland to be particularly
efficacious (Lewis-Williams and Biesele 1978). Thus, if the head-down animals
on the painted stones are seen in the context of other clearer suggestions of
trance performance, both on the stones themselves and in the rockshelters, it
seems at least possible that they too are painted metaphors of trance experience and power.

Animals are, however, also depicted in standing or walking postures that
cannot be said to be diagnostic. One rather indistinct animal from the
Boomplaas excavation has been dated to 6400 ± 75 b.p. (UW-306; Deacon *et
al.* 1976). Two others, also from Boomplaas, are a red indeterminate antelope
and a bichrome eland that have been dated to 1955 ± 65 b.p. (UW-336;
Deacon *et al.* 1976). Without any diachronic control, we may wonder if the
rich symbolic associations we know the eland to have had for the nineteenth-
century San and for modern Kalahari San were attached to this antelope in
more remote periods. This problem is partly answered by the other material I
have described. It may be impossible to claim with any certainty that the
eland was associated with girls' puberty rituals (Lewis-Williams 1981a:41–53)
2000 years ago, but we may more confidently suggest that its very intimate
association with the power exploited by medicine men was a factor influencing its depiction by the artists of long ago, as it was in more recent centuries,
because the eland was part of the whole interrelated complex of trance rituals
and beliefs, and, as I have shown, the complex has considerable time depth.

So far I have dealt with realistic representations of human beings and
animals; I now turn to an altogether different category of depiction, the so-
called geometric forms. The oldest example, from the Wonderwerk excavation (Figure 9.9), has been dated to 5180 ± 70 (Pta-2544; Thackeray *et al.*
1981:66). It has a complex grid engraved on both sides. Slightly less complex
engraved grids and a ladder-like design from the same site have been dated
to 4890 ± 70 (Pta-2797) and 4240 ± 60 (Pta-2541; Thackeray 1983:25). A
painted example, with a grid on both sides (Figure 9.10) comes from the
Klasies River Mouth excavation and, though it was separated vertically by a
meter of shell accumulation from the one showing the man and the dolphins,
the excavators believe it to be approximately the same age (i.e., 2285 ± 105;
GX-1397; Singer and Wymer 1982:137).

Thackeray *et al.* (1981) have interpreted the engraved examples as depicting trance hallucinations. According to cross-cultural studies, neurologically

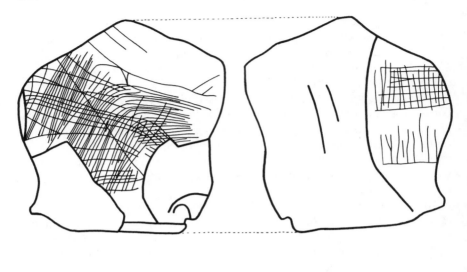

FIGURE 9.9   Engraved stone; Wonderwerk Cave, northern Cape Province; S28/4bI; (After Thackeray *et al.,* 1981:Figure 3.)

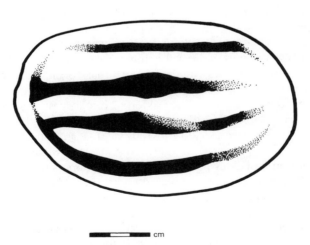

FIGURE 9.10   Painted stone with grid painted on both sides. Color, red. Klasies River Mouth, southern Cape coast; South African Museum number KRM 29477; (Drawn from stone and Singer and Wymer, 1982:Plate 49.)

controlled geometric forms are experienced in an early stage of trance and in migraine attacks (Siegel and Jarvik 1975). Among these forms are grid patterns such as those on the Klasies River Mouth and Wonderwerk stones and also zigzag, herringbone, and chevron patterns (Figure 9.2C). In parietal art, the zigzag and chevron patterns are sometimes associated with rain animals (e.g., Willcox, 1963:Figure 10; Woodhouse 1979:Figure 124) and have been mistaken for purely literal depictions of clouds, rain, or rainbows. I suggest that the tracing artist saw the fantasy or hallucinatory rain animal, a feature of a later and culturally controlled stage of hallucination, projected onto a neurological pattern that may or may not have been interpreted as clouds. In the western Cape, elephants and therianthropic figures with elephant heads are sometimes associated with similar encircling zigzag or denticulate lines formerly thought to depict traps or marshland (Figure 9.2B; Maggs and Sealy 1983). This evidence suggests that the grid patterns on the stones from Klasies River Mouth and Wonderwerk are also part of the beliefs, experience, and expression of trance performance. The Klasies River Mouth one is, in a sense, complementary to the larger stone from the same site: one shows a medicine man in a typically dancing posture, while the other preserves the sort of hallucination he may have seen.

All the stones I have discussed so far belong to what I have called Group A *art mobilier,* and are all of Holocene age. There is a very large time gap between them and the Pleistocene-dated Group B stones, which are as old as 26,000 years.

All six Group B stones come from Apollo 11 in southern Namibia. Among the depictions are a black rhinoceros, the body of an antelope covered by a red line, two white animals with black stripes that may be zebras, and a therianthrope. The therianthrope (Figure 9.11) appears to have a feline body with human hind legs that may have been added after the original legs had faded somewhat (Wendt 1974:27). If these Apollo 11 stones are also associated with trance performance, this feline therianthrope may be readily explained. As I have shown, San medicine men were, and still are, believed to go on extracorporeal journeys in feline form while in trance. Some believe that they adopt their feline persona so throughly that they can mix with a pride of lions (Heinz 1975:29). A nineteenth-century medicine man who was fatally wounded by the owner of an ox he had killed claimed he had been on such a feline magical journey (Bleek 1936:132). Another expression of the association between medicine men and lions was the belief that, if a man on out-of-body travel were not cared for by having antelope fat rubbed on him, lion's hair would come out on his back (Bleek 1935:2, 23). This belief seems to have been a metaphor for the violent behavior of a man in the throes of trance (Lewis-Williams 1981a:97). If such beliefs did indeed have very great

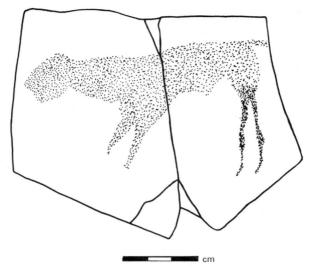

FIGURE 9.11   Painted stone broken into two parts. Color, black; Apollo 11, southern Namibia; (After Wendt 1974:Figure 12.)

antiquity, the feline therianthrope from Apollo 11 may be seen as an extraordinarily remote extension of the painting tradition that, in recent times, was closely associated with the activities of medicine men. Among the more recent parietal paintings, numerous felines are associated with trance performance (e.g., Lewis-Williams 1981a:Figure 31, 1982:Figure 4), and there is at least one leonine therianthrope from whose head a long white line rises to a small human figure (Woodhouse 1979:135); the line and its attached figure probably represent the feline medicine man's spirit leaving on an out-of-body journey.

Hallucination includes conflation of emotionally charged elements (Siegel and Jarvik 1975), and the feline therianthrope from Apollo 11 shows that people of that time did indeed conflate human and animal forms. If, as I have argued, there is nothing to suggest changes in the structure of ideology during the southern African later Stone Age and the ability to hallucinate existed as long ago as 26,000 b.p., it seems reasonable to suggest an ideological continuity that would explain the Apollo 11 painted stones in the same way as more recent art.

The numerous and diverse images of trance performance on both Group A and Group B stones enable us to reconsider in a new light the context and possible function of San *art mobilier*.

For a number of years all painted stones have been loosely referred to as burial stones because many excavated near the beginning of the century were said to come from burials. For example, Peringuey (1911:156) quotes a report by the excavator of the Coldstream cave: "In every case flat stones were found to cover the skeletons. These stones appear to have been placed directly upon the body, as shown by the evidence of the bones in some cases adhering to the stones, and other indications produced by decomposition of the flesh." Peringuey (1911:163) himself adds that the painted stones from Coldstream were found on skeletons and the funerary position of the best-preserved one was noted by Haughton (1926). Some of the stones from Robberg were also said to have been associated with burials. These and other reports (Hewitt 1922; Louw 1960) all suggest that painted stones were sometimes an item of grave furniture, a view supposedly confirmed by Peringuey's interpretation of some figures as corpses prepared for burial (Figure 9.7). On the other hand, most of the stones from more recent excavations were not associated with burials. At Boomplaas, for instance, the painted stones were apparently used, along with many more unpainted ones, to cap storage pits. Because there are only four painted stones for more than 60 pits, the excavators believe it is unlikely that they were markers of ownership or directly associated with the pits in a similar way (Deacon *et al.* 1976:145).

If we bear in mind the careless excavation techniques of early workers and the indisputable fact that at least some painted stones were definitely not associated with burials, we must conclude that the popular practice of referring to all painted stones as burial stones is tendentious. Painted stones may, on occasion, have been placed in graves, but this was clearly not always the case. Little more can at present be said of those examples that were not placed in graves. The association of the Boomplaas stones with storage pits seems to be fortuitous, and we can only conclude that the meaning of San *art mobilier* did not differ in any significant way from the parietal art: Like depictions on the walls of shelters, painted stones presented images of the most important San ritual.

However, a tentative and frankly speculative explanation for the presence of at least some painted stones in graves can be formulated within the framework of the trance hypothesis. These stones may have reflected the belief that medicine men visit the world of the spirits on their extracorporeal journeys as part of their attempts to cure the sick. When they are unsuccessful in their attempts, they believe the spirits or God himself has taken their patient away to the spirit world (Marshall 1969). Medicine men themselves die when they visit that world, but they are enabled by their powers to return to the living. It might, then, have been deemed appropriate to place in graves symbols of the ritual that links this world with the beyond and so with the dead themselves.

Conclusion

In the San social formation kinship is intimately associated with economics. It is hardly possible to study the economic strategies implied by seasonal mobility without attending to the role played by kinship and its rituals. Similarly, to study Stone Age economics is to study also the ideological framework for economic activity. Ideology and associated systems of representation are not epiphenomena, but were at the very heart of the logical functioning and reproduction of southern African later Stone Age society. The instruments of production, which archaeologists dig up, point not merely to the technical process of daily labor (hunting, preparation of skins, and so on), but also to the social conditions and ideology within which that labor was performed. It is therefore not possible to divorce purely economic activities, such as the scheduling of resource exploitation, from sets of ideas and beliefs. In southern Africa specifically, it is impossible to contrast economy and kinship as if they were two different institutions as they are in modern Western society.

Perception of the environment (social and natural) and man's place in it is the grand theme of systems of representation. San rock art, as I have shown, is no exception. The art's close association with medicine men and their symbolic work is demonstrated by symbols, metaphors, hallucinations, and more literal depictions of trance performance. This association is clear in the abundant parietal art of southern Africa. Southern African *art mobilier,* with its own very specific representations of trance performance, enables us to project later Stone Age ideology at least two millennia and possibly as much as 26,000 years into the past. It seems highly probable that, throughout the Holocene at least, seasonal strategies and concomitant aggregations and dispersals inferred by archaeologists were underwritten by kinship and trance performance and medicine men were agents of social reproduction and integration. The *art mobilier* thus begins to fill the lacuna in archaeological accounts of southern African prehistory by suggesting the ideological component of ancient social formations.

Acknowledgments

I am greatly indebted to Jalmar Rudner, who most generously allowed me to use his notes on and copies of San *art mobilier.* The Director of the South African Museum, Cape Town, permitted examination of the stones in the museum collection. The redrawings were done by Bruce Fordyce. Numerous colleagues kindly read and made useful comments on drafts of this chapter: Mike Evers, David Hammond-Tooke, Tom Huffman, Tony Humphreys, Jan Loubser, Carmel Schrire, Mike Taylor, and Lyn Wadley. Denise Gelling typed successive versions of the chapter.

References

Arbousset, Thomas
  1846 *Narrative of an exploratory tour of the north-east of the Cape of Good Hope.* Robertson, Cape Town.
Barnard, Alan
  1979 Nharo Bushman medicine and medicine men. *Africa* 49:68–79.
Biesele, Megan
  1975 *Folklore and ritual of !Kung hunter–gatherers.* Unpublished Ph.D. dissertation, Department of Anthropology, Harvard University.
Bleek, Dorothea, F.
  1935 Beliefs and customs of the /Xam Bushmen: VII Sorcerors. *Bantu Studies* 9:1–47.
  1936 Beliefs and customs of the /Xam Bushmen: VIII. More about Sorcerors and Charms. *Bantu Studies* 10:131–163.
Butzer, Karl W., G. J. Fock, L. Scott, and R. Stuckenrath
  1979 Dating and context of rock engravings in southern Africa. *Science* 203:1201–1214.
Carter, Patrick L.
  1970 Late Stone Age exploitation patterns in southern Natal. *South African Archaeological Bulletin* 25:55–58.
Cooke, Cranmer K.
  1983 Comment on J. D. Lewis-Williams, The Social and Economic Context of Southern San Rock Art. *Current Anthropology* 24:538.
Deacon, Hilary J.
  1969 Melkhoutboom Cave, Alexandria District, Cape Province: a report on the 1967 investigation. *Annals Cape Provincial Museum (Natural History)* 6:141–169.
  1976 Where hunters gathered: a study of Holocene Stone Age people in the Eastern Cape. *South African Archaeological Society Monograph Series* 1.
Deacon, Hilary J., Janette Deacon, and Mary Brooker
  1976 Four painted stones from Boomplaas Cave, Oudtshoorn district. *South African Archaeological Bulletin* 31:141–145.
Friedman, Jonathan
  1974 Marxism, structuralism and vulgar materialism. *Man* 9:444–469.
Godelier, Maurice
  1975 Modes of production, kinship, and demographic structures. In *Marxist analyses and social anthropology,* edited by Maurice Bloch, pp. 3–27. Malaby Press, London.
  1977 *Perspectives in Marxist anthropology.* Cambridge University Press, Cambridge.
  1978 Infrastructures, societies, and history. *Current Anthropology* 19:763–771.
Guenther, Mathias G.
  1975– The San trance dance: ritual and revitalization among the farm Bushmen of the
  1976 Ghanzi District, Republic of Botswana. *Journal of South West Africa Scientific Society* 30:45–53.
Haughton, Sidney H.
  1926 Note on a burial stone. *Transactions of the Royal Society of South Africa* 13:105–106.
Heinz, Hans-Joachim J.
  1975 Elements of !Ko Bushman Religious beliefs. *Anthropos* 70:17–41.
Hewitt, John
  1922 On several implements and ornaments from Strandloper sites in the Eastern Province. *South African Journal Science* 18:454–467.

Hitchcock, Robert K.
  1982   Patterns of sedentism among the Basarwa of eastern Botswana. In *Politics and history in band societies,* edited by Eleanor Leacock and Richard B. Lee, pp. 223–267. Cambridge University Press, Cambridge.
Huffman, Thomas N.
  1983   The trance hypothesis and the rock art of Zimbabwe. *South African Archaeological Society Goodwin Series* 4:49–53.
Katz, Richard
  1982   *Boiling energy: community healing among the Kalahari !Kung.* Harvard University Press, Cambridge.
Keenan, Jeremy
  1977   The concept of the mode of production in hunter–gatherer societies. *African Studies* 36:57–69.
Klein, Richard G.
  1972   The late Quaternary mammalian fauna of Nelson Bay Cave (Cape Province, South Africa): its implications for mega faunal extinctions and for environmental and cultural change. *Quaternary Research* 2:135–142.
  1975   Ecology of Stone Age men at the southern tip of Africa. *Archaeology* 38:239–247.
  1977   The ecology of early man in southern Africa. *Science* 197:115–125.
Leakey, Mary D.
  1983   *Africa's Vanishing Art: The Rock Paintings of Tanzania.* Hamilton, London.
Lee, D. Neil, and Herbert C. Woodhouse
  1970   *Art on the rocks of southern Africa.* Purnell, Cape Town.
Lee, Richard B.
  1968   The sociology of !Kung Bushman trance performance. *Trance and possessive states,* edited by R. Prince, pp. 35–54. R. M. Bucke Memorial Society, Montreal.
  1979   *The !Kung San: men, women and work in a foraging society.* Cambridge University Press, Cambridge.
Lewis-Williams, J. David
  1972   The syntax and function of the Giant's Castle rock paintings. *South African Archaeological Bulletin* 27:49–65.
  1980   Ethnography and iconography: aspects of southern San thought and art. *Man* 15:467–482.
  1981a *Believing and Seeing: symbolic meanings in southern San rock paintings.* Academic Press, London.
  1981b The thin red line: southern San notions and rock paintings of supernatural potency. *South African Archaeological Bulletin* 36:5–13.
  1982   The social and economic context of southern San rock art. *Current Anthropology* 23:429–449.
  1983   *The rock art of southern Africa.* Cambridge University Press, Cambridge.
  1984   The empiricist impasse in southern African rock art studies. *South African Archaeological Bulletin,* 39:58–66.
Lewis-Williams, J. David, and Megan Biesele
  1978   Eland hunting rituals among northern and southern San groups: striking similarities. *Africa* 48:117–134.
Louw, Johannes T.
  1960   Prehistory of the Matjes River rock shelter. *National Museum Bloemfontein Memoir* 1:1–143.

McCall, Daniel F.
  1970   Wolf courts girl: the equivalence of hunting and mating in Bushman thought. *Ohio University Papers in International Studies Africa Series* 7.
Maggs, Timothy M. O. C., and Judith Sealy
  1983   Elephants in boxes. *South African Archaeological Society Goodwin Series* 4:44–48.
Manhire, Anthony, John E. Parkington, and William van Rijssen
  1983   A distributional approach to the interpretation of rock art in the south-western Cape. *South African Archaeological Society Goodwin Series* 4:29–33.
Marshall, Lorna
  1957   The kin terminology system of the !Kung Bushmen. *Africa* 27:1–25.
  1961   Sharing, talking, and giving: relief of social tensions among !Kung Bushmen. *Africa* 31:231–249.
  1969   The medicine dance of the !Kung Bushmen. *Africa* 39:347–381.
  1976   *The !Kung of Nyae Nyae.* Harvard University Press, Cambridge.
Orpen, Joseph M.
  1874   A glimpse into the mythology of the Maluti Bushmen. *Cape Monthly Magazine* (n.s.) 9(49):1–13.
Parkington, John E.
  1972   Seasonal mobility in the Late Stone Age. *African Studies* 31:223–243.
Peringuey, Louis
  1911   The Stone Ages of South Africa. *Annals of the South African Museum* 8:1–218.
Rudner, Ione
  1983   Paints of the Khoisan rock artists. *South African Archaeological Society Goodwin Series* 4:14–20.
Rudner, Jalmar
  1971   Painted burial stones from the Cape. *Rock paintings of southern Africa,* edited by Murray Schoonraad, pp. 54–61. South African Association for Advancement of Science, Johannesburg.
Rudner, Jalmar, and Ione Rudner
  1970   *The hunter and his art.* Struik, Cape Town.
  1973   A note on early excavations at Robberg. *South African Archaeological Bulletin,* 28:94–96.
Siegel, Ronald K., and M. E. Jarvik
  1975   Drug-induced hallucinations in animals and man. *Hallucinations: behaviour, experience, and theory,* edited by Ronald K. Siegel and L. J. West, pp. 81–862. John Wiley and Sons, New York.
Silberbauer, George B.
  1981   *Hunter and habitat in the central Kalahari Desert.* Cambridge University Press, Cambridge.
Singer, Ronald, and John Wymer
  1969   Radiocarbon date for two painted stones from a coastal cave in South Africa. *Nature* 224:508–510.
  1982   *The Middle Stone Age at Klasies River Mouth in South Africa.* University of Chicago Press, Chicago.
Thackeray, Anne I.
  1983   Dating the rock art of southern Africa. *South African Archaeological Society Goodwin Series* 4:21–26.
Thackeray, Anne I., J. Francis Thackeray, Peter B. Beaumont, and Johannes C. Vogel
  1981   Dated rock engravings from Wonderwerk Cave, South Africa. *Science* 214:64–67.

Tobias, Phillip V. (editor)
  1978   *The Bushmen*. Human and Rousseau, Cape Town.
Vinnicombe, Patricia
  1972a   Myth, motive, and selection in southern African rock art. *Africa* 42:192–204.
  1972b   Motivation in African rock art. *Antiquity* 46:124–133.
  1976   *People of the Eland*. Natal University Press, Pietermaritzburg.
Wendt, W. Eric
  1974   'Art mobilier' aus der Apollo 11-Grotte in Südwest-Afrika. *Acta Praehistorica et Archaeologica* 5:1–42.
  1976   'Art mobilier' from the Apollo 11 Cave, South West Africa: Africa's oldest dated works of art. *South African Archaeological Bulletin* 31:5–11.
Willcox, Alexander R.
  1963   *The rock art of South Africa*. Nelson, London.
  1983   Comment on J. D. Lewis-Williams, The social and economic context of southern San rock art. *Current Anthropology* 24:538–540.
Woodhouse, Herbert C.
  1968   The Coldstream burial stone: a painting of a prehistoric painter. *South African Journal of Science* 64:341–344.
  1970   Three widely distributed features depicted in rock paintings of people in southern Africa. *South African Journal of Science* 66:51–55.
  1979   *The Bushman art of southern Africa*. Purnell, Cape Town.

10

To Find Ourselves: Art and Social Geography of Prehistoric Hunter Gatherers

MARGARET W. CONKEY

Introduction

Paleolithic art is an inclusive term that is applied to a wide range of visual images and material culture made by humans during the Upper Paleolithic period of 35,000–10,000 years ago: Media categories include engraved and carved bone, antler, and ivory, animal and human figurines, painted imagery on cave walls, bas-reliefs, and clay modeling. The makers and users of these images appear to have been fully modern humans, *Homo sapiens sapiens.* Although there is important evidence for both rock art and engravings on bone or other objects and surfaces from other parts of the world at ca. 20,000 years ago (e.g., Wendt 1976) and from even earlier archaeological sites in southwestern Europe (e.g., the "incised" bone from Pech de l'Azé; see Bordes 1969), the bulk of this ancient artistic activity has left its mark in archaeological contexts of southwestern Europe and, more sporadically, across southern Germany, central Europe, and the Russian plain.

The term *Paleolithic art* has promoted the notions that this is a holistic, self-contained subsystem of a continuous Upper Paleolithic life, that this is a persistent artistic tradition, and that we might be able to explain and interpret it as a unitary phenomenon. Maps that display the distribution of painted caves and engraved objects literally collapse as many as 20,000 years of artistic activity into a unidimensional framework. Yet, as is often pointed out (e.g., Conkey 1983; Lorblanchet 1977; Ucko and Rosenfeld 1967), there is more diversity than homogeneity in media, subject matter, techniques, visual conventions, and spatiotemporal distributions. The famous cave paintings are only part of a much wider repertoire of visual imagery, and even they appear to have been limited or restricted in their spatiotemporal distributions within the greater region of Paleolithic art. Since the full acceptance of the ice age antiquity of Paleolithic art in 1902, explanations for it as a unitary phenomenon have been sought in the lifeways of known hunter gatherers. As views on hunter gatherers have changed, so have the interpretations of Paleolithic art.

Because of Paleolithic art, the people of the European Upper Paleolithic are characterized as a particularly successful and elaborate variant of hunter gatherers as compared to contemporary hunter gatherer groups that have been observed. This is to be expected because the interpretation of Paleolithic art is directly derived from the interpretive frameworks of ethnographic hunter gatherer research in general. This chapter first discusses two major premises of hunter gatherer research, then how these have structured interpretations of Paleolithic art, and finally, how we might restructure our future inquiry. Particular reference is made to understanding the art in its sociospatial context. Although it may be intellectually traditional to discuss what Paleolithic art means, the relevance of Paleolithic art studies for prehistory, for hunter gatherer archaeology, and for understanding human symbolic behavior has more dimensions than reading for the meaning of Paleolithic art. There are some lessons to be learned from the historical development of Paleolithic art studies; these are stressed here.

Two particular features of hunter gatherer research have structured interpretations of the Upper Paleolithic and, by implication, Paleolithic art. First, because of the emphasis on hunter gatherers as the baseline for understanding what it is to be human, interpreters of the Upper Paleolithic have followed a "presentist," rather than a "historicist," perspective: The past is studied for the sake of the present; past phenomena are viewed in abstract relation to analogs in the present (Stocking 1968:3–4). Second, it is increasingly recognized that the study of social phenomena in hunter gatherer life has been relatively underdeveloped. Concomitant with this has been an overemphasis on ecological determinants. These two general features of hunter gatherer research are summarized here. From these, a particular corollary follows: The lifeways of prehistoric hunter gatherers—especially the art-making and art-using peoples of the European Upper Paleolithic—have been homogenized and cast in utopian imagery. Discussion of this corollary, its genesis, its implications, and its necessary replacement are organized into three parts:

1. A historical review of the concepts and interpretations of Upper Paleolithic art illustrates how monolithic and inclusive interpretations of

the art have contributed to a homogenized, utopian view of these pre-historic hunter gatherers, so that they are seen as a prehistoric extension of the ethnographic present.

2. Although some interpretations of Paleolithic art have focused on so-cioecological phenomena as clues to the adaptive context of the art, these have merely coupled the homogenized and presentist perspectives to an adaptationist or functionalist program. Despite the inadequacies of functional theories that have considered the art as part of the Upper Paleolithic social geography, a theory of hunter gatherer social geography is central to reinterpreting the archaeological record of the Upper Paleolithic.

3. A more expanded theory of hunter gatherer social geography needs to be developed, including a set of assumptions about art and visual imagery in general and Upper Paleolithic visual systems in particular. Such theoretical expansion is attempted here.

Some Questionable Premises

Paleolithic art studies are used here to augment questions that have been raised about some central premises of hunter gatherer research. The effects of these premises have been profound on the archaeology of hunter gatherers and on the relatively few attempts to study symbolic and cognitive phenomena in prehistory. First there is the suite of assumptions or premises that have promoted an overemphasis on both the role and the investigation of biological, environmental and ecological parameters, if not determinants, in hunter gatherer behavior. Anthropologists have held two inclusive generalizations about hunter gatherer life, and both perspectives have engendered a preoccupation with ecological variables. The early version was that hunter gatherers were savages and therefore closer to nature; thus, they were to be understood in terms of nature. The revised version (Lee and DeVore 1968) views foragers as adaptable, flexible, if not often affluent, fully cultured variants of ourselves. However, this is a version of a wiser people, in equilibrium with and below the carrying capacity of their environments, ecologically sensitive, knowledgable, and to be understood in terms of their ecology. Since the revised version appeared in the mid-1960s, hunter gatherer social organization has continued to be characterized as fluid and flexible (Leacock and Lee 1982:3). Thus, this amorphous socal form seems to elude analysis in terms of the more traditional (and specified) social structural categories in the anthropologist's analytical repertoire. As a result, forager behavior is usually viewed as more determined by biological (e.g., viable mating networks) and ecological (e.g., resource procurement strategies) parameters than by socially constructed frameworks (Collier and Rosaldo 1982:277).

Certainly there are exceptions. There is at least the recognition that "only *part* of the behavior of hunter gatherers can be accounted for by even the most fine-grained ecological analysis" (Lee 1978 cited in Wiessner 1982:61). More substantively, there have been attempts to deconstruct social structural categories or to introduce modified or new ones (e.g., Collier and Rosaldo 1982; Hamilton 1982). The concept of *flexibility*, for example, has been reconsidered. Rather than an inherent feature of hunter gatherers, flexibility may be part of particular, historical trajectories (see Schrire 1980). Furthermore, flexibility may be only apparent and "not true flexibility in itself but the product of a structured system of social relations operating according to certain principles" (Wiessner 1982:61).

The general notion is that hunter gatherers are somehow at least more influenced by nature and natural laws then agrarian and urban peoples. The methods of analysis that follow from this have been particularly appealing to archaeologists. Archaeologists are still struggling with a Comtian intellectual heritage that ranks prehistoric economy and ecology as more accessible, if not also more deterministic, than social or ideological phenomena (see Hawkes 1954 for a classic view). Many American archaeologists are still caught on the epistemological horns of an empiricist dilemma (Wylie 1981) that has strong positivist linkages and emphasis on confirmation and validation. This has further enhanced the attraction to the priority of ecological phenomena in the study of hunter gatherer life.

Of particular appeal to archaeologists has been the application of ecological optimization approaches to the study of hunter gatherer subsistence and foraging. At the very same time that some hunter gatherer ethnographers are questioning the general ecologically based paradigm and are reformulating the social constructs used to characterize hunter gatherers, the study of foraging has become the example par excellence of the application of an evolutionary ecological paradigm to human behavior (e.g., Winterhalder 1981; Winterhalder and Smith 1981). It is not surprising that optimal foraging models have had particular appeal to archaeologists (e.g., Keene 1981; O'Connell and Hawkes n. d.) despite the fact that several attributes of these models are incompatible with the nature of archaeological data and the antinormative goals of contemporary archaeological inquiry (see Keene 1983). These models emphasize individuals as units, and are normative in that they specify how organisms should behave under specified conditions. In applying models with such characteristics, optimal foraging studies exemplify how far one can go in avoiding the existence of social phenomena (but see Moore 1981).

Fortunately, the sociobiological-optimization interpretations of Paleolithic art have been few and are not widely known or well received. The most notable is Eaton's idea (Eaton 1978a,b) that the art serves as a display of trophies of the successful male hunter. Natural selection would have favored those "individuals who kept and displayed trophies because this would demonstrate their suitability as mates and even status in male groups" (Eaton 1978b:6).

Although the revised general version of hunter gatherers of the mid-1960s altered how we thought about their social forms and evolutionary status, the ecological preoccupation remains and has even been elaborated in the form of optimal foraging studies. At the same time that the revised version stressed the fluidity and flexibility of hunter gatherers (e.g., in Damas 1969), the concept of culture was redefined by American archaeologists as the human means of adaptation (Binford 1965; after White 1949). Thus, in the archaeological study of foragers, social phenomena were viewed within the adaptive framework. Ritual, art, or symbolic behaviors were assigned a low research priority because of their association with the normative concept of culture that was being replaced (see Fritz 1978). If any of these domains were included in archaeological injury, they, too, were viewed within the adaptive framework. But even the social components of this adaptive framework have remained vague and unspecified for prehistoric people. Those social forms that are discussed, such as a family group, are only indirectly derived from the types of archaeological sites (e.g., base camps or hunters' blinds). Or these social forms may be derived from very general dichotomies of subsistence and settlement patterns that are primarily ecological in genesis: for example, focal/diffuse (Cleland 1966), aggregation/dispersion (Conkey 1980b), or forager/collector (Binford 1980).

Thus, hunter gatherer research in ethnography and archaeology has been more concerned with the ecological and less successful at elucidating the social. A predominant concern in hunter gatherer research has been "discovering how and why hunting [and gathering] peoples are, or are not, like ourselves" (Collier and Rosaldo 1982:277). There is slight concern for other central features of forager behavior, such as social constructions or the organization of meaning, yet these features are certainly central if one is dealing with art, ritual, or symbolic behavior. The production of meaning is also central if one is starting from an expanded concept of culture as more than just the human means of adaptation (Conkey 1978a:63); that is, if human culture is conceptualized as a framework of meaning in terms of which humans exist, cope, and adapt.

We are all familiar with the textbook justifications for the study of both prehistoric and contemporary hunter gatherers. They are the baseline for understanding what it means to be human, they span 99% of human culture history, and ever since the appearance of fully *sapiens* populations—they have been heralded as a "slice of ethnography" (Isaac 1976). We are all familiar with the nineteenth-century reactions to the discovery of both living and prehistoric hunter gatherers: They were viewed as examples of an early

(and savage) stage of human cultural evolution. Studies of that era emphasized the ways in which they were not like us. Paleolithic cave art was the
product of magic—prereligious, prescientific thought. More recently, the
emphasis has been on demonstrating that Upper Paleolithic art-making peoples did have cognitive systems and cultural behaviors and products just like
ours (e.g., Marshack 1972a, b).

In other words, whatever perspective one takes, most research is clearly
presentist. This term is used by Stocking (1968) in an argument on the
interpretation of history developed by Butterfield (1963): The past (or the
"other") is studied for the sake of the present "to produce a story which is the
ratification if not the glorification of the present" (Butterfield 1963:v). For the
sake of polemic convenience, Stocking contrasts presentism with *historicism,*
which he views as "the commitment to the understanding of the past for its
own sake" (1968:4). The resultant attributes of a presentist interpretation
include a judgmental mode (rather than an understanding), a focus on agents
or agencies that direct change (rather than a concern with the complex
processes by which change emerges), and a decontextualization of phenomena (from their contemporary context) in order to view them in ab-
stracted relation to analogs in the present (Stocking 1968:3–4).

The points to be drawn from the presentist–historicist distinction include
(1) the recognition of this interpretive mode as prevalent in hunter gatherer
research, particularly in prehistoric aspects and (2) the implications and
results of the presentist method for general theory building. As currently
practiced, the presentism of Paleolithic hunter gatherer archaeology includes
a drive to discover the links—the decontextualized analogs—between us and
them. Furthermore, when coupled with an amorphous and indeterminant
notion of hunter gatherer social organization, presentism has generated a
homogenized and utopian view of Upper Paleolithic life.

Art and Homogenization of the Upper Paleolithic

There are two major approaches in the study of Paleolithic visual imagery.
These have contributed in different and yet convergent ways to the homoge-
nization of Upper Paleolithic hunter gatherers. First there are those who take
the art forms as a given; Paleolithic art appeared about 35,000 years ago full
blown. The aim of this approach is to elucidate what the art, as an entity
means. Included are the two prevalent interpretations in the history of Paleolithic art studies: art as hunting magic (e.g. Breuil 1952), and its replacment,
art as mythogram (e.g. Leroi-Gourhan 1965, 1972, 1982). There has been
much discussion on the shortcomings of the sympathetic-hunting-magic hypothesis (e.g., Ucko and Rosenfeld 1967:174ff.), whether applied to Paleolithic art or to the rock art of ethnographically known hunter gatherers

(Lewis-Williams 1982:430). The source for this hypothesis came from late nineteenth-century notions on the mentality of primitive peoples; these are notions that we now dismiss as "vague and misguided" (Lewis-Williams 1982:430).

The art-as-hunting-magic notion is a simple functionalist explanation; studies have been made that undermine most of the original empirical justifications. But it is important to note that in the first and most persistent interpretations, Paleolithic art had been linked to generalizations about hunter gatherer ritual and spiritual life. This life was ultimately rooted in the dynamics and intensity of hunting and the ecological challenges of hunting as a resource base (Breuil 1952).

By 1965 there was an apparent revolution in Paleolithic art studies. The art-as-hunting-magic notion was replaced by what has come to be called the art-as-mythogram hypothesis. This replacement was effected by a reanalysis of the imagery, assuming now some very modern thinking on the part of the artists. Instead of random placement on sacred cave walls of those images desired to be captured, it was assumed that there would be order and patterning derived from cosmological principles. Instead of the simple functionalist concern with what the art might do for its makers, the art-as-mythogram approach asks what the art might say, or what generative principles are behind the message. Based on topographic and associational studies of the images of cave art in particular, Leroi-Gourhan concluded that there is an underlying structure or set of principles that generated the art.

Originally, Leroi-Gourhan (1965) linked the covarying classes of animals, signs, and cave locales with male and female valences. He has since moved away from assignment of meaning, but still retains the notion that the making and placing of specific images (e.g., bison, horse, mammoth) derive from underlying cultural premises, or a mythogram. This structuralist approach is congruent with certain contemporary intellectual trends in the analysis of symbolic and cognitive aspects of human life, and this particular study has been acclaimed by proponents of symbolic and cognitive archaeology (Hodder 1982; Leone 1982).

However, the art-as-mythogram approach is still—as was the art-as-hunting-magic—a monolithic interpretation to account for thousands of diverse images and media that are differentially distributed over Eurasia and from temporal contexts that may span 20,000 years. Both interpretations lack linkages to particular features or contexts of Upper Paleolithic life and to the makers or users of the imagery. There is little, if any, concern for the origins of the visual forms or for the differential patternings except as variations within a master pattern of art making. In both approaches, the art is treated as decontextualized analogs. Art as hunting magic was analogous to the inferred magical behaviors of the Australian hunter gatherers reported by Spencer and

Gillen (1899). Art as mythogram assumes fully modern cognitive capacities and strategies and a persistent tradition of art making. This persistent tradition implies a continuity and homogeneity of the social groups producing the art, particularly since the generative principles of the art are assumed to be part of the cultural cosmological schema (Leroi-Gourhan 1965:32; Sieveking 1979:20).

Leroi-Gourhan's approach is compelling in that he has shown how there could be at least one standardized system of visual representation among the imagery that we call Paleolithic art. Most of his system applies to the painted cave art, and it may well be that he has derived a set of generative principles for its production. Certainly he had shown that many images are not randomly placed and that there are tendencies for groupings or associations. To a certain extent, this analysis has begun the task of dissecting the phenomenon we call Paleolithic art. But it has not been unquestionably accepted that these generative principles underlie all depictions or are based on valid analytical techniques (e.g. Parkington 1969; Ucko and Rosenfeld 1967:179ff.).

If we want to know—as I believe we do—how and why standardized systems of Paleolithic visual imagery constituted the meaningful frameworks for human action that we assume at least some of the art to be, then we must first identify the system, the patterns, and their contexts. The latter aspect is missing in the Leroi-Gourhan analysis; the images—once generated—are "there." They are decontextualized from human viewers, from use, and from economic, social, or even ideological contexts. One might propose that the art-as-mythogram interpretation is primarily a more sophisticated, structuralist version of the old *l'art pour l'art* hypothesis, one of the earliest notions called on to account for rock and cave art. Lewis-Williams has appropriately criticized *l'art pour l'art* as innatist: "ecology, economics, social structure, and demography . . . are eschewed in favor of supposed individual states of mind" (1982:429). This critique is easily rewritten to address the weakness of the structuralist version in which ecology, economics, social structure, and demography are eschewed in favor of supposed cultural states of mind.

Upper Paleolithic society and life are homogenized in both all-inclusive interpretations that have dominated Paleolithic art studies. The art-as-hunting-magic interpretation derived from early global generalizations about how hunter gatherers think and relate to nature, how they are different from us, and how the food quest played a central role in their spiritual lives. There was potential in the hypothesis to seek linkages between the economic domain (hunting) and the art and its ideological system. An interest in the fit between ecology and ideology, however, would have been intellectually precocious in the early 1900s. The art-as-mythogram hypothesis is structuralist; it begins with universal aspects of human behavior and is thus ahistorical. The art-as-mythogram hypothesis, which implies social continuity and equilibrium of the makers of the imagery, promotes a view of Upper Paleolithic society that is utopian.

In their studies of contemporary utopian societies, sociologists have identified specific characteristic attributes (e.g., Dahrendorf 1958). Several of these attributes are clearly invoked by the inclusive interpretations of Paleolithic art. Several of these are attributes that emerge if one takes a presentist approach in the study of past societies. Thus, in dissecting the intellectual baggage that lies behind Upper Paleolithic hunter gatherer research, conceptual links between the utopianization of the Upper Paleolithic and the presentist framework are made apparent. The following is a list of some of these connections:

Some attributes of presentism in (pre)historical analysis (after Stocking 1968)	Some attributes of Utopian societies (after Dahrendorf 1958)
judgment (informed by normative commitment) rather than understanding	universal consensus on values and institutional arrangements
	social harmony explains stability
sequence rather than process	social processes follow (recurrent) patterns that are part of a design
agency of change rather than process of emergence	
analogs rather than context	society is isolated, disconnected from historical developmental process

Context and Diversity in Paleolithic Art

There is a second major set of perspectives on Paleolithic art that have had only a minor impact on the field. They are also occasionally found in texts that primarily emphasize the grand schemes or the current consensus view. These perspectives have emerged in the 1970s and for the most part are products of the Anglo-American intellectual climate. Most are processual, systemic, and adaptive. They exemplify another feature of the presentist framework, which is an emphasis on the origins of Paleolithic art. Unlike the Leroi-Gourhan 1965 approach, which assumes the art to be "there" to be interpreted, many of these studies begin with a simple diachronic dichotomy: the absence of art followed by the presence of art. The focus has been on what happened at the interface, at the transition that presumably coincides with the Middle–Upper Paleolithic transition, and with the archaic–modern *sapiens* transition.

These studies (e.g., Conkey 1978a; Gamble 1982; Pfeiffer 1982) view hunter gatherer art in relation to what it means to be human. They present the Upper Paleolithic as a variant of the ethnographic record and are concerned with the origins of the ethnographic present. Although we have been consistently seduced in archaeology to seek out origins—a central feature of a presentist

perspective—there are many reasons why the energies expended on Paleolithic art as the origins of human art are misguided. First, we may never
know if this is—or if some of it is—the "first art." We may never know if
dozens or thousands of years of artwork on perishable media preceded the
engravings and carvings of Upper Paleolithic art either in Europe or elsewhere. What Paleolithic art does appear to be is the first extensive and systematic system of visual representation in permanent archaeologically visible
media. Thus, the question is not what are the origins, but rather—given what
we do have for the European Aurignacian, or from the Apollo 11 cave in
southern Africa at ca. 20,000 years (Wendt 1976), or from any other period or
site—why visual images, why in those media, and what are the contexts, uses,
and meanings?

The relevance of Paleolithic art for inquiry into the symbolic and ritual
behavior of prehistoric hunter gatherers derives from the fact that it is an
excellent example of the differential production and reproduction of symbolic repertoires. It is very unlikely that Paleolithic art is a unitary phenomenon, reducible to a single set of generative principles that derive from a
homogeneous, continuous, harmonious hunter gatherer society. The media,
the systems of visual imagery, are differentially distributed across space and
throughout the ca. 20,000 years of the Upper Paleolithic. For example, most
female figurines are temporally restricted to the early Upper Paleolithic, but
cave painting appears to have begun later; 80% of the decorated or incised
artifacts are middle to late Magdalenian, and cave painting is not isomorphic
in general geographic distribution with portable art (see Conkey 1983 for
some elaboration and references).

The available archaeological record does not support a continuous trajectory of subsistence and settlement patterns (e.g., Binford 1972; Freeman 1973;
Straus 1978; White 1980). Furthermore, very little has been convincingly said
about the social dynamics beyond notions of aggregation/dispersion (e.g.,
Conkey 1980b) or simulations of the extent of mating networks (Wobst 1974;
but see Moore 1981; Oleksiak 1982 for critiques). There is some irony in the
reconstruction of Upper Paleolithic hunter gatherers, particularly if we are
trying to use them as an example for a general understanding about art in
prehistoric life. Many reconstructions (e.g., Mellars 1985) imply a level of
sociocultural complexity that compares better with ethnographically known
hunter gatherers of the U.S. Northwest Coast or California, which are usually
listed as exceptions to the ethnographically observed patterns of forager life
(e.g., Leacock and Lee 1982:7).

Despite the relatively loose resolution of Upper Paleolithic archaeology,
this second set of interpretations of Paleolithic art have been concerned with
context, if only because they are essentially adaptationist and are concerned
with how art fits into the adaptive framework of Upper Paleolithic hunter

gatherers. Rather than conceptualizing the imagery as art for art's sake, or for magicoreligious purposes, most of these studies seem to hold what one might call a hydraulic theory of art. That is, in Upper Paleolithic life there were socioecological pressures or needs that were exerted on societies, including the need for greater amounts of information to be stored and transmitted (Pfeiffer 1982), for maintaining more extensive mating networks (Gamble 1982); the need for meditation of increasingly more defined social boundaries, due to increasingly more complex social geography (Conkey 1978a; White 1982), to integrate a new kind of cooperative hunting group (Hammond 1974); and the need to deal with periodic migrations of people into the cave art-making region during climatic deteriorations (Jochim 1982).

As a result of these pressures, art arises, or emerges, in response to the socioecological challenges of Upper Paleolithic hunter gatherer life. All of these views seek the origins and existence of Paleolithic art in terms of a general notion of social geography, that is, in the way in which people are distributed and the way in which they arrange and maintain their groupings and interrelationships within a region. The appearance of art is adaptive information to solve sociospatial needs. On the one hand, such a perspective is theoretically attractive to contemporary British and American archaeologists. It is congruent with trends from the 1970s on that incorporate art and ideological phenomena into the ecological perspectives (e.g., Anderson 1979:25–51; Rappaport 1979). These views show how art (in ethnographically known societies) works as an agent of social control, or as a means of storage for core cultural messages, or as a statement on sociopolitical hierarchy. When Paleolithic art is also shown to be adaptive information, it is not surprising that the Upper Paleolithic appears as a "slice of ethnography."

However, these sociospatial perspectives on Paleolithic art contribute to, as well as derive from, the homogenized, presentist view of the Upper Paleolithic and the global, unspecified concept of prehistoric hunter gatherer life. Several questions may be raised on both methodological and theoretical grounds. First, there are the problems of an adaptationist, neofunctionalist framework. In most studies, the assumption is that if the art came into existence, it must, somehow, have been adaptive (e.g., Conkey 1978a). As Lewis-Williams has summarized in a review of theories accounting for southern African rock art: "The adaptationist and hence . . . functionalist argument is . . . inadequate rather than necessarily illogical. . . . [It is part of] a degenerating programme which no longer throws much light on the problems of rock art: all roads lead to social solidarity" (Lewis-Williams 1982:430, 431).

Moreover, there is the problem of invoking broad sociocultural phenomena (even if phrased systematically and ecologically) that lack the specificity for adequate testing with the available archaeological data. There is too great a methodological gap between the sociocultural phenomena to be demonstrated and the data that is both being explained by and used to support the phenomena. In one of the better adaptive studies of Paleolithic art, in which art is not viewed as a unitary phenomenon and a specific temporal and geographic context is used, Gamble (1982) has suggested that a necessary extension of early Upper Paleolithic alliance networks is reflected in the appearance of female figurines and other material items (e.g., ornaments) of public display. But even if one had good reason to believe that such alliance extensions were, first, necessary and, second, taking place, the linkage between these particular material objects and these particular social processes is not made. There is not yet adequate support for the inferred claims that Paleolithic art was meaningful and was therefore produced and differentially reproduced for the kinds of sociocultural contexts and situations proposed.

Theoretically then, these art-as-adaptive studies have accomplished little more than to bring the presentist perspective up to date, that is, into the vocabulary and framework of the post–World War II era of cybernetics and information theory and of "stress" as a core cultural and explanatory agent. A more subtle and sophisticated functionalist view has been formulated. With few exceptions the relatively homogeneous reconstruction of Upper Paleolithic life has been retained (but cf. Bahn 1977 for the proposal that art making occurred in just a few "outbursts"). We must be careful, however, not to turn social geographic contexts or a concern with information as a resource into babies to be thrown out with a neofunctionalist bathwater. Rather, it is perhaps the case that most of the art-as-adaptive studies have been arguing with an impoverished or underdeveloped theory of art, ritual behavior, and social geography, as well as with an impoverished repertoire of models for hunter gatherer life.

On Theoretical Expansion

My first attempt at a theoretical framework for studying Paleolithic art was from an adaptationist perspective (Conkey 1978a). In conjunction with Binford's (1972:291) characterization of the Upper Paleolithic as a time of increasingly complex social geography, I suggested that the appearance and elaboration of Paleolithic art could be understood as new and increasing symbolic patterning to resolve adaptational stress that was concomitant with the definition, mediation, and maintenance of social boundaries. In order to test these grand hypotheses, I advocated, and partially attempted, systematic investigation of the nature of variability in some Upper Paleolithic material culture, particularly the engraved bone and antlers that are abundant during the Magdalenian (Conkey 1978b). To a great extent, I assigned research priority to the analysis of the structure of the material culture (Conkey

1980a). However, this structural and materialist emphasis turned out to be at the expense of the social geographic or more contextual perspectives. The definition of bounded Upper Paleolithic groups, or what amounts to a complex social geography, remains to be defined. However, given that humans are both materialists and symbolists simultaneously, there are compelling reasons why a social geographic framework is central to analysis of Paleolithic art.

The current problem is to develop the concept of social geography and to make a case for retaining a sociospatial perspective. Paleolithic visual imagery was differentially produced and reproduced. These art forms can be viewed simultaneously as formal material structures and in the context of social geography. The issue is why does Paleolithic visual imagery, when viewed this way, have more potential not only in our study of the Upper Paleolithic, but also in its contribution to a general theory of hunter gatherers.

There is more to the notion of social geography than the spatial description of social phenomena, such as the maps of Upper Paleolithic style zones (e.g., Smith 1966:389 for the Solutrean) or art occurrences (e.g., Sieveking 1979:16). At the most general, vulgar level, the notion of social geography refers to the deployment or mapping of social units and their members onto the landscapes. No member of a social species lives in a homogeneous field of social interaction, but, rather, there are lattices of interpersonal cohesions among individuals and the varying social units of which they are a part (Lancaster 1975:44ff.; Preziosi 1979:25). This pattern is called social geometry. Thus, at the most fundamental level, we can define human social geography as the deployment of humans and social groupings of humans and as the resultant lattices within space.

However, there is a second level of human social geography that is concerned with the fact that the participants in human social life have to have knowledge of deployments and lattices. Although this knowledge is differentially held and incomplete, even to the actors in the social system, it is a crucial resource (see Moore 1981). Obviously our potential to reconstruct prehistoric knowledge of social geography is severely limited, particularily when we think of this knowledge only in the form of ideas or spoken language. In the past, this knowledge most certainly could be manifest and constituted by an entire range of what is now, to us, archaeological data: occupation sites, art forms, artifacts, clothing, structures or architecture, and features such as hearths or pits. It is theoretically possible to define direct linkages between the differential patternings of such data and the prehistoric social geographic knowledge or information that they constituted. Thus, material forms structure and constitute social geographic knowledge and social geometries for those participants in the sociospatial world.

A third level of social geography is a metatheoretical level, which is mentioned here because it augments the foregoing premise that social geography does not just exist out there, but must be constituted and depends on knowledge for its perpetuation. Hillier *et al.* (1978:343) have identified this level as that of a "morphic language"; spatial organization is a member of a family of morphic languages. "In general morphic languages are used to constitute rather than represent the social through their syntax (that is the systematic production of pattern)" (Hillier *et al.* 1978:343). All three levels of the concept of social geography are depicted in Figure 10.1. The recursive arrows suggest that social geography is an active phenomenon, dynamic and not static, involving not only the patterned distributions of humans in their social space and landscapes, but also their knowledge of these patterns and the potential for this knowledge to not only have a material form but also to constitute social geometries.

The sociospatial dimension is not just a backdrop or setting for human cultural life but an active element; the sociospatial is simultaneously the setting and a character. "Social structures are only practised within spatial structures, and vice-versa" (Tilley 1982:33 in reference to Gregory 1978:121). It is the practice of the social structure within spatial structures and vice versa that is accessible archaeologically. One way to discuss this practice is in terms of "environmental structuration" (Preziosi 1979).

Humans have become masters at environmental structuration: "a transformed environment is a good alternative to a bigger brain" (Wagner 1972:xi). Not only do humans structure their environment, but these structuring acts structure humans, from object manipulation to the architecture that obviously

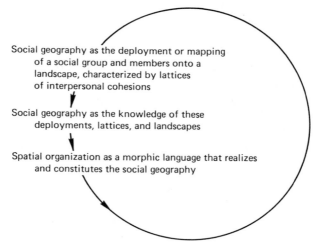

FIGURE 10.1   Conceptual levels of the notion of social geography.

constitutes a built environment. Environmental structuration is sociospatial in its genesis and in its perpetuation.

We do not often think of hunter gatherers as major contributors to the built environment partly because a narrow definition equates the built environment with architecture and relatively permanent structures. However, hunter gatherers certainly generate a structured environment, if only by means of the differential deployment of personnel through the landscape and of the locations that they settle and use. Hunter gatherers are mobile, but they utilize differential patterns of mobility and differential production and reproduction of these patternings. Because of this, their social geography may be a much more powerful structural principle than we have realized. Particularly as the more monolithic concepts, such as fluidity and flexibility, are deconstructed and as the underlying and varying principles that must exist are elucidated, the concept of social geography in the study of hunter gatherers may become more important and productive.

For example, environmental structuration is, in part, the patterning of movement and use of the landscape by humans. But it is also the material use of the landscape. Materials can generate certain actions. Materials also can regulate social actions by stipulating the forms that actions should take. Studies of materials as environmental structuration in particular hunter gatherer contexts are rare. Collier and Rosaldo (1982) have advanced some general suggestions about the circulation of objects in forager societies, which they consider as brideservice societies: "it is because things in brideservice societies are unlike women in having no longterm consequences for social inequality that they can move so easily between people and thus serve so effectively to mark relations of cooperation" (Collier and Rosaldo 1982:299). One particular example of this general observation is Wiessner's interpretation (1982) of the !Kung exchange networks (*hxaro*) as instrumental in the articulation of economically necessary social relations. Her study is also one of the few that looks explicitly at the social geographic contexts of material culture among hunter gatherers (see also Wiessner 1983).

With some expanded notions on social geography and a concept of environmental structuration, one can then look for the ways in which materials are generated, are used through social and spatial lattices, and contribute to the practice of the social within the spatial. Thus, it is not a contradiction to advocate a structural, formal materials analysis of Paleolithic imagery on the one hand and a sociospatial, social geographic analysis on the other hand. They are simultaneous aspects of the differential production and reproduction of the formations we call Paleolithic art. Figure 10.2 depicts the simultaneous analytic paths of a materials approach and a sociospatial one, as well as the way in which each path is linked and defined in terms of each other. It

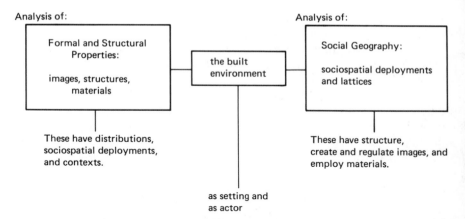

Analysis of:

Formal and Structural
Properties:

images, structures,
materials

the built
environment

Analysis of:

Social Geography:

sociospatial deployments
and lattices

These have distributions,
sociospatial deployments,
and contexts.

These have structure,
create and regulate images, and
employ materials.

as setting and
as actor

FIGURE 10.2   Simultaneous analytic paths toward interpretation of Paleolithic art.

is not likely that an interpretation of Paleolithic art forms will be approached without this simultaneous perspective.

We can now turn to Paleolithic art and some suggestions for its analysis and interpretation. There have been other attempts to expand the theoretical framework for the analysis of hunter gatherer rock art (e.g., Lewis-Williams 1982). However, Paleolithic art is more than rock art. It is the diversity of Paleolithic art that is also its potential strength. On the one hand, the media, materials, and images are as varied as one might imagine: Almost every known artistic technique was used, from clay modeling, to bas-relief, to the more widely known carving, engraving, and painting. There appear to be many techniques of painting, and the visual conventions for all the art are equally diverse and wide ranging (Lorblanchet 1977). At the same time that there is potential for the formal structural analysis of materials and images (e.g., Conkey 1980a, 1982), there is potential for the distributional analysis of these as well.

Paleolithic art comprises formations and transformations of materials and of the less observable meanings. These forms were produced differentially and reproduced differentially in temporal and spatial contexts. The differential making and using of these art forms are part of the practice of social structures in spatiotemporal structures. A short discussion of the variability in formations should show why a study of the differentials might lead to understanding the fuller concept of social geography rather than just citing the sociospatial aspect as the cause of Paleolithic art. The classic division of media into cave art and portable art, for example, has not been fully expanded. The cave art is clearly unmovable; the audience must come to it. It has the immediate potential of signifying and marking place. The imagery on cave walls becomes another dimension to the built environment of Upper Paleolithic peoples, who we know structured some of their living contexts with stone pavements (e.g., Gaussen 1980) or with their use of naturally occurring stone blocks in their sites (e.g., Rigaud 1978).

Where the cave art is—and where it is not—does give us some fixed geographical and, by implication, social nodes. The differential occurrence of cave art over the Eurasian Upper Paleolithic world is a provocative but relatively unstudied phenomenon. In an exceptional consideration of this differential distribution, Jochim (1982) seeks the causes in ecological factors that promoted larger populations in the cave art–making regions. Although ecology is still the structuring variable, there is the potential to link ecological and the social variables given the hypothesized population shifts and the sociospatial implications. Jochim points out that cave walls are blank in southwestern Germany, even though occupants were making and using portable art. He suggests that the paintings of caves in southwestern France and Spain may be related to demographic shifts into the region from the north at times of more harsh climates. Even within the classic painted cave region of the Dordogne of southwestern France, there is a notable difference in number and density of known cave art sites between the two adjacent valleys of the Vézère and Dordogne rivers, with a much denser distribution along the Vézère.

In addition, there is the portable art that has the potential not just to move around, but also to move around several orders removed from the original makers and users. There are many different kinds of portable art including figurines, engraved implements, and sculpted plaques. There are those objects considered to be ornamentation, such as pendants or necklaces. Many of these are perforated shells that can be identified as having origins in the Mediterranean or the Atlantic Ocean, and the distributions of these shells throughout the regions of southwest Europe attests to some networks of interaction or movement of goods. To date, only linking arrows have been drawn on regional, large-scale maps (Bahn 1982). In a mode that is different from the painting of fixed-locale caves, objects of ornamentation have more obvious potential to be linked with individuals and to mark persons more than places because of the fact that are worn by only one person at a time.

As a distinct media, portable art is so diverse that it is not surprising that the different forms are not distributed evenly across the spatiotemporal span of the European Upper Paleolithic. At least 80% of the portable art from the Magdalenian in the Périgord derives from just 4 major sites. There are the same notable differential densities in Cantabrian (Spain) Magdalenian sites and those in the French Pyrenees (Bahn 1982). We assume that these differential densities derive primarily from the fact that people visited these sites more often, or in greater numbers, or on occasions that led to the deposition of such materials. These sources of dense deposits are basic issues of social geography and the use of place because they raise the question: why these forms, in these densities, in these locales, at this time? All too often, these issues are dismissed as being due to differential recovery or curation of portable art (e.g., G. A. Clark in Conkey 1980b). However, the patterns are repetitive from region to region, and this, together with the association of dense deposits of portable art in the Magdalenian with other archaeological phenomena, such as large site size or specific kinds of topographic locations (see Bahn 1982; White 1980), suggest that there are contextual factors of site use that may help explain the presence and abundance of portable art as well as how the art forms structured the social uses of the sites and the region. In other words these differential densities are the starting point for a social geographic analysis.

The past century of interpretations of Paleolithic art have drawn on generalized models of hunter gatherers. They have depended on various ethnographic versions of hunter gatherer life, and they have attempted to make direct comparisons between the ethnographic present and the Upper Paleolithic past. This has been epitomized in the studies that have sought the origins of Paleolithic art as the first art. The result, as I have suggested in the preceding, has been a homogenized, utopian picture of the Upper Paleolithic as a time when art and symbolism flourished. We have found ourselves in this past by depicting the Upper Paleolithic as a decontextualized analog of ethnographic hunter gatherers who are viewed as being ecologically structured, socially amorphous, and well adapted.

We now need a different interpretive framework. First, we have the materials and structures of the art forms themselves that have not been fully exploited. The classificatory systems that brought the varying art forms into existence have not been fully explored (but cf. Leroi-Gourhan 1965, 1972). The active attributes of the art forms have not been investigated in order to ask how certain raw materials, shapes, implement types, designs, or animal depictions defined certain social and cultural actions.

At the next level of analysis, these materials and structures have distributions and differential patterns through time and space. A handful of studies have explored the existence of these differential trajectories (e.g., Hahn 1972, 1981), but few have linked the patterns to possible and specific social or ecological contexts (e.g., Bahn 1977; Gamble 1982; Jochim 1982). We need more systematic linkage of the formal and structural attributes to specific sociospatial deployments and lattices.

At the same time, there must be more inquiry into these factors of sociospatial patternings. It has not yet been possible to describe even the first level of Upper Paleolithic social geography with high degrees of confidence, although there have been serious and important attempts (e.g., Bahn 1977, 1982; Straus 1978; White 1980). None of these descriptions view the social geographic pattern as active and self-structuring; nor is there particular regard given to how particular sites, specific settlement patterns, and particular assemblages of material culture together generate a particular historical built environment.

This reorientation of our interpretive framework must aim at and use the archaeology of the Upper Paleolithic. The focus of study must be on this particular trajectory of hunter gatherer art and symbolism. A methodology of modeling as advocated by Wylie (1981) might be appropriate here. In this method, certain constraints or attributes, such as the spatial dimensions of cave painting, are specified. These are then used to construct and test paramorphic models, which are built on the basis of highly specified (not generalized) ethnographic or historical contexts. They must represent past cultural contexts, or, more accurately, the generative processes that led to the material or other output of these contexts. Thus, the data of the particular archaeological record that one is investigating acquire significance as evidence only in relation to the models of context that the framework has set up (Wylie 1981). For example, the painted cave walls acquire significance as evidence for sociospatial dynamics only in relation to the social geographic framework that is constructed as the model of context.

"Because perception and action take place in continuous dependence upon the environment, they cannot be understood without an understanding of that environment itself" (Niesser 1976:183). Grasping the particular historical contextual environments of Upper Paleolithic hunter gatherers demands that we expand our perceptions of social geography and of these groups' social dynamics and social action. We must also deconstruct the epistemologies and analytical frameworks that we have used to study one of their most spectacular products, their art. Evidence of this art has promoted a linkage between past and present. This linkage and the corresponding aesthetic bonds are perhaps necessary but also challenging if we are to understand rather than judge the past.

Acknowledgments

I gratefully acknowledge the support of the Werner Reimers Stiftung for travel and attendance at the conference for which an original version of this chapter was prepared in June 1983. In particular, thanks go to Carmel Schrire and Edwin Wilmsen for including me as a participant and to Carmel, in particular, for helpful editorial suggestions and patience. If any one person's influence is behind this chapter, it is that of Sarah Williams, who constantly challenges and demands answers. Without the advice and encouragement of Lester Rowntree, the typing and help of Peggy Roe and the SUNY, Binghamton Manuscript Center, there would be no material form of the thoughts discussed here.

References

Anderson, Robert L.
  1979 *Art in primitive societies.* Prentice Hall, Englewood Cliffs, N.J.
Bahn, Paul
  1977 Seasonal migration in southwest France during the late glacial period. *Journal of Archaeological Science* 4:245–257.
  1982 Inter-site and inter-regional links during the Upper Paleolithic: the Pyrenean evidence. *Oxford Journal of Archaeology* 3:247–268.
Binford, Lewis R.
  1965 Archaeological systematics and the study of culture process. *American Antiquity.* 31:203–210.
  1972 *An archaeological perspective.* Academic Press, New York.
  1980 Willow-smoke and dog's tails: hunter–gatherer settlement systems and archaeological site formation. *American Antiquity.* 45:1–17.
Bordes, François
  1969 Os percé mousterien et os gravé acheuleen du Pech de l'Azé II. *Quaternaria* 11:1–6.
Butterfield, H.
  1963 *The Whig interpretation of history.* Norton, New York.
Breuil, Henri
  1952 *Four hundred centuries of cave art.* Centre d'études et de documentation préhistorique, Montignac, France.
Cleland, Charles
  1966 The focal-diffuse model: an evolutionary perspective on the prehistoric cultural adaptations of the eastern United States. *Midcontinental Journal of Archeology* 1:59–76.
Collier, Jane F., and Michelle Z. Rosaldo
  1982 Politics and gender in simple societies. In *Sexual meanings: the cultural construction of gender and sexuality,* edited by Sherry Ortner and Harriet Whitehead, pp. 275–329. Cambridge University Press, Cambridge.
Conkey, Margaret W.
  1978a Style and information in cultural evolution: Toward a predictive model for the Paleolithic. In *Social Archeology,* edited by Charles Redman *et al.,* pp. 61–85. Academic Press, New York.
  1978b *An analysis of design structure: variability among Magdalenian engraved bones from northcoastal Spain.* Unpublished Ph.D. dissertation, Department of Anthropology, University of Chicago.
  1980a Context, structure, and efficacy in Paleolithic art and design. In *Symbol as sense,* edited by Mary L. Foster and Stanley Brandes, pp. 225–248. Academic Press, New York.
  1980b The identification of prehistoric hunter–gatherer aggregation sites: the case of Altamira. *Current Anthropology* 21:609–630.
  1982 Boundedness in art and society. In *Symbolic and structural archaeology,* edited by I. Hodder, pp. 115–128. Cambridge University Press, Cambridge.
  1983 On the origins of Paleolithic art: a review and some critical thoughts. In *The Mousterian legacy: human biocultural change in the Upper Pleistocene,* edited by Erik Trinkhaus. *British Archaeological Reports, International Series* 164:201–227.
Dahrendorf, R.
  1958 Out of Utopia: toward a reorientation of sociological analysis. *American Journal of Sociology* 2:115–127.

Damas, David (editor)
1969 Band societies. *National Museums of Canada Bulletin* 229.
Eaton, Randall
1978a The evolution of trophy hunting. *Carnivore* 1(1):110–121.
1978b Meditations on the origins of art as trophyism. Manuscript on file, Quaternary Research Center, University of Washington, Seattle.
Freeman, Leslie G., Jr.
1973 The significance of mammalian faunas from Paleolithic occupations in Cantabrian Spain. *American Antiquity,* 38(1):3–44.
Fritz, John M.
1978 Paleopsychology today: ideational systems and human adaptation in prehistory. In *Social archaeology,* edited by Charles L. Redman *et al.,* pp. 37–60. Academic Press, New York.
Gamble, Clive
1982 Interaction and alliance in Paleolithic society. *Man* 17:92–107.
Gaussen, Jacques
1980 Le Paleolithique superieur de plein air en Périgord. *XIVe supplément à Gallia Préhistoire.* Editions du Centre national de la recherche scientifique, Paris.
Gregory, David
1978 *Ideology, science and human geography.* Hutchinson, London.
Hahn, Joachim
1972 Aurignacian signs, pendants and art objects in central and eastern Europe. *World Archaeology* 3(2):252–260.
1981 Recherches sur l'art paleolithique depuis 1960. In Aurignacièn et Gravettian en Europe. *Actes des rèunion de la 10eme commission de l'U.I.S.P.P. Etudes et recherches archeologiques de l'Universitè de Liege* 3:79–82.
Hamilton, Annette
1982 Descended from father, belonging to country: rights to land in the Australian western desert. In *Politics and history in band societies,* edited by Eleanor Leacock and Richard B. Lee, pp. 85–108. Cambridge University Press, Cambridge.
Hammond, Norman
1974 Paleolithic mammalian faunas and parietal art in Cantabria: a comment on Freeman. *American Antiquity* 39:618–619.
Hawkes, Christopher
1954 Archeological theory and method: some suggestions from the Old World. *American Anthropologist* (n.s.) 56:155–168.
Hillier, B., A. Leaman, P. Stansall, and M. Bedford
1978 Space syntax. In Social organization and settlement, edited by David Green *et al. British Archaeological Reports, International Series* (suppl.) 47(11):343–381.
Hodder, Ian
1982 Theoretical archaeology: a reactionary view. In *Symbolic and structural archaeology,* edited by Ian Hodder, pp. 1–16. Cambridge University Press, Cambridge.
Isaac, Glynn L.
1976 Stages of cultural elaboration in the Pleistocene: possible archaeological indicators of the development of language capabilities. In *Origins and evolution of language and speech,* edited by S. Harnard, Horst Steklis, and Jane B. Lancaster, pp. 275–279. New York Academy of Sciences, New York.
Jochim, Michael
1982 Paleolithic cave art in ecological perspective. In *Hunter–gatherer economy in prehistory,* pp. 212–219. Cambridge University Press, Cambridge.

Keene, Arthur S.
   1981   Optimal foraging in a nonmarginal environment: a model of prehistoric subsistence
          strategies in Michigan. In *Hunter–gatherer foraging strategies,* edited by Bruce Win-
          terhalder and Eric Alden Smith, pp. 171–193. University of Chicago Press, Chicago.
   1983   Biology, behavior, and borrowing: a critical examination of optimal foraging theory
          in archeology. In *Archeological hammers and theories,* edited by James Moore and
          Arthur Keene. pp. 137–155. Academic Press, New York.
Lancaster, Jane B.
   1975   *Primate behavior and the emergence of human culture.* Holt, Rinehart, and Winston,
          New York.
Leacock, Eleanor, and Richard B. Lee
   1982   Introduction. In *Politics and history in band societies,* edited by Eleanor Leacock and
          Richard B. Lee. *Editions de la Maison des Sciences de l'Homme,* Cambridge and Paris.
          Cambridge University Press, Cambridge.
Lee, Richard B.
   1978   *Issues in the study of hunter–gatherers, 1968–1978.* Paper presented at the Interna-
          tional Conference on Hunter–Gatherers, Paris (June 1978).
Lee, Richard B., and Irven DeVore (editors)
   1968   *Man the hunter.* Aldine, Chicago.
Leone, Mark P.
   1982   Some opinions about recovering mind. *American Antiquity* 47(4):742–760.
Leroi-Gourhan, André
   1965   *Treasures of Paleolithic art.* Abrams, New York.
   1972   Considerations sur l'organisation spatiale des figures animales dans l'art parietal
          paleolithique. In *Santander Symposium Actas del Symposium Internacional del Arte
          Préhistórico.* Santander, Spain.
   1982   *The dawn of European art.* Cambridge University Press, Cambridge.
Lewis-Williams, J. David
   1982   The economic and social context of southern San rock art. *Current Anthropology*
          23(4):429–449.
Lorblanchet, Michel
   1977   From naturalism to abstraction in European prehistoric rock art. In *Form in indi-
          geneous art,* edited by Peter J. Ucko, pp. 44–56. Australian Institute of Aboriginal
          Studies, Canberra.
Marshack, Alexander
   1972a *The roots of civilization.* McGraw-Hill, New York.
   1972b Cognitive aspects of Upper Paleolithic engraving. *Current Anthropology* 13:445–477.
Mellars, Paul A.
   1985   The ecological basis of social complexity in the Upper Paleolithic of southwest
          France. In *Prehistoric hunter–gatherers: the emergence of social and cultural com-
          plexity,* edited by T. Douglas Price and James A. Brown, Academic Press, New York.
Moore, James A.
   1981   The effects of information networks in hunter–gatherer societies. In *Hunter–
          gatherer foraging strategies,* edited by Bruce Winterhalder and Eric Alden Smith, pp.
          194–217. University of Chicago Press, Chicago.
Niesser, Ulric
   1976   *Cognition and reality.* Appleton, New York.
O'Connell, James F., and Kristen Hawkes
   n.d.   Can optimal foraging models explain hunter–gatherer subsistence patterns? *Ameri-
          can Anthropologist*

Olesiak, Deborah
    1982   A critique of Wobst's simulation of Paleolithic population structure, or when is a
            maximum band not a mating network. Manuscript on file, Department of An-
            thropology, State University of New York, Binghamton.
Parkington, John
    1969   Symbolism in Palaeolithic cave art. *South African Archaeological Bulletin* 24:
            3–13.
Pfeiffer, John
    1982   *The creative explosion*. Harper and Row, New York.
Preziosi, Donald
    1979   Architecture, language, and meaning: the origins of the built world and its semiotic
            organization. *Approaches to Semiotics* 40. Mouton, The Hague.
Rappaport, Roy
    1979   *Ecology, meaning, and religion*. North Atlantic Press, Oakland, California.
Rigaud, Jean-Philippe
    1978   The significance of variability among lithic artifacts: a specific case from southwestern
            France. *Journal of Anthropological Research* 34:299–310.
Schrire, Carmel
    1980   An inquiry into the evolutionary status and apparent identity of San hunter–
            gatherers. *Human Ecology* 8(1):9–31.
Sieveking, Ann
    1979   *The cave artists*. Thames and Hudson, London.
Smith, Philip E.
    1966   *Le Solutréen en France*. Imprimeries Delmas, Bordeaux.
Spencer, W. Baldwin, and Frank J. Gillen
    1899   *The native tribes of central Australia*. Macmillan, London.
Stocking, George
    1968   On the limits of "presentism" and "historicism." In *Race, evolution and culture,*
            edited by George Stocking, pp. 1–12. University of Chicago Press, Chicago.
Straus, Lawrence G.
    1978   Of deerslayers and mountainmen: Paleolithic faunal exploitation in Cantabrian Spain.
            In *Toward theory building in archeology,* edited by Lewis R. Binford, pp. 41–76.
            Academic Press, New York.
Tilley, Christopher
    1982   Social formation, social structures, and social change. In *Symbolic and Structural
            archaeology,* edited by Ian Hodder, pp. 26–38. Cambridge University Press,
            Cambridge.
Ucko, Peter J., and Andrée Rosenfield
    1967   *Paleolithic cave art*. McGraw-Hill, New York.
Wagner, Phillip
    1972   *Peoples and environments*. Prentice Hall, Englewood Cliffs, N.J.
Wendt, W. Eric .
    1976   Art mobilier from the Apollo 11 Cave, Southwest Africa: Africa's oldest dates works of
            art. *South African Archeological Bulletin* 31:5–11.
White, Leslie
    1949   *The evolution of culture*. McGraw-Hill, New York.
White, Randall
    1980   *The Upper Paleolithic occupation of the Périgord: a topographic approach to subsis-
            tence and settlement*. Unpublished Ph.D. dissertation, Department of Anthropology,
            University of Toronto.

1982   Rethinking the Middle–Upper Paleolithic transition. *Current Anthropology* 23(2):169–192.

Wiessner, Polly

1982   Risk, reciprocity, and social influences on !Kung San economics. In *Politics and history in band societies,* edited by Eleanor Leacock and Richard B. Lee, pp. 61–84. Cambridge University Press, Cambridge.

1983   Style and social information in Kalahari San projectile points. *American Antiquity* 48(2):253–276.

Winterhalder, Bruce

1981   Optimal foraging strategies and hunter–gatherer research in anthropology: theory and models. In *Hunter–gatherer foraging strategies,* edited by Bruce Winterhalder and Eric Alden Smith, pp. 13–35. University of Chicago Press, Chicago.

Winterhalder, Bruce, and Eric Alden Smith (editors)

1981   *Hunter-gatherer foraging strategies: ethnographic and archeological analyses.* University of Chicago Press, Chicago.

Wobst, H. Martin

1974   Boundary conditions for Paleolithic social systems: a simulation approach. *American Antiquity* 39:147–148.

Wylie, M. Allison

1981   *Positivism and the new archeology.* Unpublished Ph.D. dissertation, Department of Philosophy, State University of New York, Binghamton.

Author Index

Numbers in italics represent pages on which complete references can be found.

Subject Index